Personality, Character, and Leadership in the White House

Other Titles of Interest from Brassey's, Inc.

The Kennedy Presidency
by Deborah Hart Strober and Gerald S. Strober

Nerve Center: Inside the White House Situation Room
by Michael K. Bohn

The Fate of America: An Inquiry into National Character
by Michael Gellert

Personality, Character, and Leadership in the White House

PSYCHOLOGISTS ASSESS THE PRESIDENTS

Steven J. Rubenzer, Ph.D.,
and
Thomas R. Faschingbauer, Ph.D.

Brassey's, Inc.
Washington, D.C.

Library of Congress Cataloging-in-Publication Data

Rubenzer, Steven J., 1957–
   Personality, character, and leadership in the White House : psychologists assess the presidents / Steven J. Rubenzer and Thomas R. Faschingbauer.—1st ed.
      p.   cm.
   Includes bibliographical references and index.
   ISBN 1-57488-815-3 (alk. paper)
   1. Presidents—United States—Psychology.   I. Faschingbauer, Thomas R.   II. Title.
E176.1.R89   2004
973'.09'9—dc22   2004008632

ISBN 1-57488-815-3

(alk. paper)

Printed in the United States of America on acid-free paper that meets the American National Standards Institute Z39-48 Standard.

Brassey's, Inc.
22841 Quicksilver Drive
Dulles, Virginia 20166

First Edition

10   9   8   7   6   5   4   3   2   1

CONTENTS

ACKNOWLEDGMENTS

THIS BOOK could not have been completed without the dedication of the biographers, journalists, and scholars upon whose knowledge and hard work we based our analyses. Each contributed nearly three hours to completing our questionnaires. Some provided data on as many as five presidents. Quite a few went beyond their initial commitment, serving as reviewers for drafts of the manuscript and fitting our deadlines into their schedule. All did it out of interest and dedication to their field—none were paid. In particular we would like to thank the following: K. Aldrich, W. Allen, H. Ammon, D. Anderson, J. Anderson, L. Banning, J. Barber, R. Barileaux, P. Bergeron, W. Best, F. Binder, T. Blessing, H. Booraem, P. Bourne, J. Brazier, J. Broadwater, J. Bruning, J. Capps, J. Choate, J. Clark, K. Clements, J. Codling, D. Cole, P. Coletta, M. Collins, D. Conrad, J. Cooke, D. Cottrill, E. Craddock, H. Cunningham, W. Cutler, B. Daynes, J. Davies, E. Dumas, W. Edel, J. Ehrlichman, L. Falkof, R. Ferrell, M. Fox, J. Gable, R. Gilbert, S. Godbold, R. Goldhurst, R. Gunderson, L. Haapanen, D. Hahn, M. Hargreaves, M. Hecht, K. Hendrickson, C. Hines, J. Hoff, S. Hoff, F. Holden, J. Hogan, K. Holland, H. Holzer, A. Hoogenboom, A. Jarvis, P. Johnson, J. Kaminski, R. Ketcham, L. Koenig, D. Kucharsky, P. Lampe, R. Larsen, J. Lee, C. Lloyd, D. Long, A. Mapp, E. Matthews, D. McCoy, R. McElroy, B. McEwan, K. McFarland, C. Meister, D. Merrill, F. Mevers, R. Miller, E. Morris, J. Mushkat, P. Nagel, W. Niven, G. Nordham, M. Nowak, W. Pederson, W. Pemberton, B. Perry, M. Peterson, J. Phipps, W. Pippert, D. Preston, R. Quackenbush, T. Reeves, M. Riccards, W. Ridings, N. Risjord, M. Rogin, D. Rose, H. Rosenbaum, P. Rulon, R. Saulnier, S. Savage, P. Schwab, J. Shneidman, T. Silver, D. Simonton, H. Sirgo, D. Skaggs, E. Smith, G. Smith, J. Smith, A. Spetter, W. Spragens, R. Strong, M. Swain, D. Tays, N. Topalian, L. Tyler, L. Ultran, M. Urofsky, F. Van der Linden, R. Whelan, L. Wikander, A. Williams, F. Williams, D. Wilson, and T. Wolf. Psychologists Stewart McCann, Paul Costa, and Dean Simonton reviewed and offered guidance on an earlier version of the manuscript, and Aubrey Immelman provided personality ratings for G. W. Bush. Our thanks, too, to the librarians at the University of Houston, the Houston Public Library, and Rice University Library for their support in locating our experts, and at the Harris County Public

Library for obtaining many requested materials. Most important, we would like to thank our families for putting up with us over the years that this work required. Lastly, Steve Rubenzer would like to thank his ex-brothers-in-law, Son and Anthony Nguyen. Son provided support to manage frequent computer problems, often with little compensation, and Anthony volunteered his assistance and skill in retouching the final "morphs" that appear in this book.

PREFACE

THIS BOOK is the first of its kind. It is based on the participation of more than 120 experts on the presidents, most of whom contributed at least two hours of their time, and some much more. After they completed our questionnaires, we looked at their ratings through the eyes of the recent research in the psychology of personality, using spreadsheets and statistical programs to sift through a mountain of numbers. The results, expressed in everyday language, are in the pages that follow.

In the course of presenting our work to people of different backgrounds, including our spouses, we've found that some people just do not get it. Others seem immediately fascinated by the project and any findings we have at hand. This may be a difference in personality between our fans and the disinterested. Some people delight in objectifying and quantifying things that most people think of as intangibles, like love or inspiration. Most social scientists are of this persuasion. However, we recognize that appreciating the significance of our work will not come naturally to everyone. In this section, we try to explain our approach and why we think it matters. Appendix A also addresses this and other technical issues in a more formal manner.

Many of the scores and portraits we present throughout the book will strike the reader as intuitively accurate. Some may even dismiss them as "obvious." They are not. As a demonstration, try matching the presidents in the first column with the description of that president in the second column:

1. Washington	_____ indecisive, wishy-washy
2. Jefferson	_____ slow to grasp new ideas
3. Lincoln	_____ thin-skinned, sensitive to slights
4. Theodore Roosevelt	_____ wise
5. Nixon	_____ effeminate
6. Reagan	_____ overcomplicates matters
7. Clinton	_____ shallow, unintellectual, unreflective

These presidents all are well known and have highly visible personalities. So it may come as some surprise that the *answers are already in the right order!*

Washington was described as indecisive by one of our experts, Jefferson as slow to grasp new ideas by another, et cetera. Each of these descriptions represents the opinion of a respected author or scholar who may have written a biography or spoken at length on the respective president at professional conferences. As it turns out, their colleagues do not share their opinions.

It is easy to dismiss one such opinion when presented like we did above. However, this is precisely what a best-selling biography is based on—*one person's interpretation* of a life. Though a biographer typically culls information from many sources, looking at personal letters, talking to coworkers and family members, maybe even reviewing school transcripts or medical records, what is examined or pursued is the researcher's judgment of what is important, the interpretation of what is turned up, and how these conclusions are then presented. Are they brought up in passing or made a central theme of the book? Are they embraced, rationalized, or disputed with other material? These decisions are subjective and may be influenced by factors completely unrelated to the subject's personality. The treatment a subject receives in a book is likely to be influenced by concern for the organization and thematic unity of the work, as well as marketing concerns.

When a biographer supports an interpretation with compelling anecdotes, it is easy to assume that any reasonable person would agree with the author's interpretation. However, the anecdotes the author presents, and the manner in which they are conveyed, are chosen by idiosyncratic standards. Another expert may offer different interpretations or be able to cite twice as many stories that "prove" the opposite. Another may not even address the issue or the trait that is supposedly being portrayed, considering it insignificant. Biography is a highly subjective enterprise, and the fact that such works are often well written and contain rich anecdotes can be highly misleading. Such factors are irrelevant to the accuracy of the portrayal, but they create a sense of intimacy and validation. An artful, emotionally appealing, but wholly contrived personality portrait may be far more convincing than one that is accurate but sparsely rendered.

There are several means we employed in our study to increase objectivity. Most importantly, we obtained more than one expert for each president wherever possible. For nearly every president we discuss in this book, we obtained three experts; for many presidents, we have more than a half dozen. Second, we asked the same questions, the same way, of all our experts. If we had not ensured that each expert consider the same personal qualities in his or her respective president, we would be doing something akin to asking three blind physicians—a dermatologist, an ear, nose, and throat specialist, and a proctologist—to examine an elephant. Each would likely focus on different attributes and apply the standards of their own profession and experience. Something very similar happens when people make personality judgments. Military professionals tend to value courage and leadership. Therapists value capacity for intimacy and ability to reflect on one's own behavior. Employers want workers who are reliable and diligent. Left on their own, each group will focus on different qualities and overlook many that are not central to their concerns.

Through our 592-item questionnaire, we led each expert around the whole "elephant." By requiring all of the ratings to be made on a five-point or nine-point rating scale, we also gave them something of a standard ruler, so that they were taking their measures with the same unit of measurement. After they completed their examination, we found that they still had some differences of opinion. We have no reason to believe one is more accurate than the others are, so we took the average of their figures.

Even when two people focus on the same trait, and the same person, there is still plenty of room for disagreement. Unless they are together all the time, people witness their subject from different perspectives and in different contexts. One may see the person with family and at baseball games, the other at work and at parties. They may interpret the same events differently and have different ways of making their judgments. One person may describe others as "friendly" if they are friendlier than herself. Another may use a friend who she considers friendly as a comparison. One rater may call almost all people friendly—another only those who are friendlier than three of four people—or one out of ten. These factors all contribute to differences among raters when they describe someone they both know. We cannot eliminate these problems, but at least we can reduce them. In our portraits, we do not use a description unless the raters assign a score on the item (i.e., friendly) that is in the upper or lower 15 percent relative to other presidents. We also limited the type of raters we used. Though a few recent presidents have family members who might have provided their insights and ratings, the vast majority of presidents are not survived by any personal acquaintances. To include such a different class of raters for just a few presidents would potentially spoil our ability to make comparisons to those who were rated only by biographers and scholars.

Another way to conceptualize our results is as the difference between a well-built home and a Hollywood façade. It is not hard for a good writer, with even a modest knowledge of his subject, to paint a convincing personality portrait. In fact, any good fortune-teller should be able to do this with hardly any information. Superficially, a charlatan's personality portrait, like the façade of a house, may be every bit as convincing as the real thing. But a real house is expected to stand up to storms and to meet the needs of the people that live in it. It is built on the science and technology of hundreds of years of experience with weather conditions, building materials, construction techniques, geography, and marketing factors.

Our analysis is based on decades of research on the organization of personality traits, methods of measuring them, and statistical techniques. The scientific goal of our portraits is to be objective, accurate, and reasonably complete. We also think they are terribly interesting. We anticipate that results we present in this book will prove useful to a variety of potential readers, including historians and political scientists.

Most importantly, we offer information to intelligently and responsibly make one of the most important decisions required of people in a free society: choosing who will govern. We believe this should be done not just on political issues, but also on the personal qualities of each candidate.

NOTE ABOUT ILLUSTRATIONS

THE ILLUSTRATIONS in this book were created by morphing images of two or more presidents representative of the type, usually one or more of those profiled. The program Morpheus was used, and some retouching was done using Adobe Photoshop. Although the morphs represent the common or averaged features of the people who contribute to the image, they should be viewed as artistic illustrations rather as a part of our analysis. There has been little scientific research that relates personality characteristics to facial features. However, in one of the great coincidences of this project, one of the three studies located dealt with presidents' faces and their rated greatness.

PART I

Personality and the Presidency

CHAPTER I

Personality and Character

ANDREW JACKSON had just been shot in a duel. Though the bullet lay next to his heart, Jackson took careful aim, fired, and killed the man who he felt had slandered his wife. He walked from the field, his boots sloshing with his own blood, and he carried the bullet in his body the rest of his life. Besides killing several men in duels, as a young man Jackson had a penchant for gambling, fighting, and drinking. He was not a man of high moral character and restraint, like Washington was. Yet, both are considered among the greatest presidents.

This book attempts to sort out this and other paradoxes of personality and performance in the Oval Office. As psychologists who specialize in assessing personality, we found the debate about presidential character during the Clinton years fascinating. But no data had ever been collected to show whether character really matters in a president.

Biographers and pundits have speculated and described politicians' personalities since the days of Washington. Some of them have done a very good job, producing lush personality portraits and good stories. Our work has a different set of goals and produces results of a different nature. Science requires that measurements be as precise as possible and follow specific procedures that other experimenters can use to get comparable results.

As scientific psychologists, we attempt here to measure the personality characteristics of the presidents. Personality can be measured, though not with the precision that we take for granted with a typical thermometer or bathroom scale. Still, personality tests are effective instruments that help us do a difficult job.

In this chapter, we begin with an overview of the project, introduce the "Big Five" approach to understanding personality, and report which presidents scored especially high or low on each of these qualities. In the rest of the book, we focus on the personalities of the presidents as never before, using the best instruments available, multiple experts for each president, and findings from current personality research to interpret the results. Personality measurement and other technical issues are presented in more depth in Appendix A.

THE PERSONALITY AND THE PRESIDENCY PROJECT

Ours is the first project to have biographers, journalists, and scholars complete a normed personality test about the presidents they have studied. This has never been done on any president before now. We collected data on our first forty-three chief executives. Three or more experts, whom we will refer to as "specialists" throughout this book, rated most presidents. Specialists are either authors of book-length biographies or were nominated by other experts as especially knowledgeable about a particular president. One hundred and seventeen specialists completed our questionnaire, some on as many as five presidents. Based on our data, we conclude:

- ✔ On the average, men who become presidents have traits that set them apart from other Americans.
- ✔ Nonetheless, they differ substantially among themselves. Based on our data, there appear to be eight distinguishable types of presidents.
- ✔ A president's character has no relation to how good a president's historians judge him to be.
- ✔ A number of personality traits and qualities do predict presidential success.
- ✔ The ability to lie and deceive is an important quality for success in the White House, and presidents who are less straightforward typically make better presidents.
- ✔ Despite his recent popularity and reputation for integrity, John Adams's personality closely resembled Richard Nixon's.
- ✔ Presidents are much more Extraverted today than in the past and less intellectually curious than in the past. They may also be lower in character.
- ✔ Jimmy Carter is the only modern president that much resembles Founding Fathers Jefferson and Madison and the greatest president of the nineteenth century, Abe Lincoln. Eisenhower is the only modern president much like Washington.
- ✔ Franklin Roosevelt seems to be the template for modern presidents, with recent presidents showing high (Kennedy, Clinton) or moderate (LBJ) similarity to him. Reagan resembled his as well.

✔ George W. Bush appears to most resemble Andrew Jackson and Ronald Reagan.

✔ Modern Democratic presidents tend to be very Extraverted, achievement-oriented, ebullient, and sympathetic to the poor, but are willing to deceive and relatively unprincipled.

✔ Modern Republican presidents tend to be less sympathetic to the less fortunate and much more inclined to rely on traditional sources of moral authority than on average Americans.

OUR QUESTIONNAIRE

The questionnaire we sent out contained three major instruments designed to assess the full scope of personality. One, the *Revised NEO Personality Inventory* (NEO), is one of the newest and most respected personality tests. The version we used is designed to be completed by a family member, friend, acquaintance—or anyone who knows the person well. The rater does not need to have personal contact with the person rated, just have an adequate information base about the person's behavior and characteristics. The NEO explicitly attempts to measure the full range of personality traits. Its items, such as "He is a worrier," measure five broad traits of personality and thirty narrower "facet" traits. The Big Five traits (Neuroticism, Extraversion, Openness to Experience, Agreeableness, and Conscientiousness) are described later in this chapter.

Typically, personality and ability items are grouped together into scales consisting of anywhere from a few to dozens of individual items. Scores on personality scales are more reliable than answers to individual items, since people sometimes misread an item, put the mark in the wrong place, or focus too much on the last time the person made a fool of himself. If you rely on answers to a single item, you may be seriously misled by such an error. If you add up the answers to twenty items, on a personality scale, such mistakes are less catastrophic; answers to other items mitigate the effect of an error on one item.

Personality scales provide another crucial advantage: They help define terms such as "character" or "assertiveness." One expert we spoke with believed Franklin Delano Roosevelt (FDR) had character because of the courage and persistence he showed confronting polio. That interpretation may be legitimate, assuming he showed courage and persistence in other circumstances as well. But most people regard character as encompassing quite a few other traits, including impeccable honesty and marital fidelity—qualities that FDR did not exemplify. If different people use the word character differently, the term has no stable meaning. A personality scale helps ensure that different people are making their judgments on the same basis.

In addition to the NEO, our questionnaire included two other respected personality instruments, both designed to cover the full range of personality differences. We also estimated intellectual abilities. Though we could not directly measure IQ through our questionnaire, we could ask about the qualities that most people, including psychologists, associate with intelligence. Things like "learns many different things quickly," or "can do several things at once." These items correspond to general intelligence. We also included items to gauge math and science ability, vocabulary and speaking skill, musical talent, social skills, and physical strength and grace.

Terms like "talented" and "special" help assess these qualities, presumably related to intelligence and leadership, and also help detect bias in the rater. Adjectives like "evil" and "depraved" obviously reflect a negative opinion, but may also describe real personality traits. Some researchers believe that extreme terms (referred to as Positive and Negative Valence) are legitimate and necessary parts of a complete description of personality. Others disagree. We included them to make sure our questionnaire was comprehensive. Lastly, forty-nine items referred to the behavior and perceptions of the president while in office (e.g., "rarely allows opponents to outflank him," "regarded as a world leader"). Results from these items are reported when we discuss the presidency of each man profiled.

OTHER EXPERTS

In addition to our primary raters, we enlisted a second group of experts. These were either authors of general reference books on the presidents as a group or board members of the Center for the Study of the Presidency. These "generalists" are highly knowledgeable about the presidents as a whole, but do not necessarily know individual presidents in depth. They were asked to complete a much shorter (sixty-item) questionnaire on the forty-one presidents up until that time (data collected in 1995–1996). This gave us a second set of ratings to compare to our findings from specialists.

Another source of data came from Dean Simonton, a psychologist at Berkeley, who conducted a pioneering study some fifteen years ago. He compiled descriptions of the presidents from respected media sources. Seven graduate students studied each dossier and then rated each man on 110 adjectives such as "friendly" or "kind." The adjectives were combined into scales, so that Simonton was able to score each president on fourteen personality scales. Prior to our work, this was by far the most comprehensive, objective assessment of presidential personality. Later, he obtained ratings of each president's behavior while in office. We will cite his findings along with our own throughout this book. Appendix C lists Simonton's personality and presidential behavior scales and their items.

THE "BIG FIVE" PERSONALITY TRAITS

There are many ways of looking at personality. Psychoanalysis focuses on unconscious conflicts. The Myers-Briggs Type Indicator, a popular test used in business and counseling centers, measures a person's preferences in directing his or her attention and processing information. The trait approach we use is based on a fifty-plus year program of research on people in real-life settings. Though based on completely familiar terms, like "friendly" and "generous," it is grounded in science. Unlike many other approaches, the "Big Five" model of personality is not based on theory, but on research on how people actually describe themselves.

Every language includes many words for differences among people. After all, people make judgments about who to do business with, who to befriend, or who to marry, in all societies. The language of a culture reflects the meanings and distinctions its people make and consider important. For example, consider the words *intelligent, smart, gifted, brilliant, astute,* and *talented.* Obviously, our culture values intellectual ability enough to devote many slots in the dictionary to it. This is true for many important personality traits. Psychologists looked for ways to organize the many hundreds of different traits and adjectives and understand their relationship to one another. Since the 1940s, teams of researchers have been mining the English language, searching for the fundamental dimensions of personality. Using a statistical technique called factor analysis, it has been found that a great many personality characteristics can be expressed in terms of one or more of five dimensions.[1] These *Big Five* personality factors are described below:

Neuroticism (versus Emotional Stability): High scorers are moody, tense, self-conscious, prone to feeling downhearted and discouraged, and have difficulty resisting their impulses.[2] High scorers among presidents include Nixon, who took prescription medication to control anxiety, and Lyndon Baines Johnson (LBJ), who suffered from ulcers and self-doubt. Low scorers are calm, relaxed, secure, well balanced, and able to see to the heart of problems. They are at ease with themselves and accept their limitations without self-blame. Presidents Reagan, FDR, and Ford all score low on Neuroticism. Each suffered per-

STATISTICS FOR PEOPLE WHO HATE NUMBERS

Norms

Like measures of IQ, scores on personality scales are meaningful only if you know how other people score. To calculate norms, you must know the average score and how much the scores differ for a group of people who have taken the test. A test is normed on a particular set of people, whether they are applicants for a job, presidents of the United States, or a representative sample of Americans. In our work, we use two sets of norms: "Average" Americans and the forty-three presidents. We cite most of our findings in terms of the norms from the NEO, which are based on a sample of about 2,000 current American adults.

Test Scores

Most of our results are reported in percentile scores. A score of 50 is average—as many people score above average as below average. A score at the 98th percentile means the person scored above 98 out of 100 people; a score at the 2nd percentile means two out of one hundred people scored lower, the rest higher. A score of 99.97, as TR (Theodore Roosevelt) earned on Extraversion, indicates that he scored higher than would 9,997 out of 10,000 people. Although percentiles are useful for communicating results to a general audience, they can't be used to average scores from different raters or to perform other mathematical operations. Therefore, our analyses were based on standard scores (like those used on the SAT) and the results converted to percentile scores, which are easier to understand.

Correlation

Correlation is a way of expressing how much two things are related. Correlations can range from −1.00 to +1.00. A positive correlation between height and weight, for example, means that most who are taller are also heavier. If two variables are negatively correlated (e.g., −.50), one score would fall as the other rises and vice versa. The absolute value of the correlation is as important as its direction: −.80

denotes just as strong a relationship as +.80, and is just as useful. A correlation cannot be used to argue that one variable causes the other—just that there is some relationship between them. An advertising campaign a few years back reported that people who eat more strawberries are smarter. Strawberries probably do not make us smarter, but smart people may eat more fruit of any kind, for financial or health reasons.

sonal or political attacks without apparent defensiveness or loss of confidence. On the NEO, six facet scales assess Neuroticism, each measuring a specific component. These scales are Anxiety, Angry Hostility, Depression, Self-Consciousness, Impulsiveness, and Vulnerability. These scales are defined in Table 1.1, with examples of presidents who score high and low. Throughout this section, we cite only presidents who were rated by three or more raters.

Extraversion: Those scoring high in Extraversion are sociable, enthusiastic, energetic, adventurous, talkative, assertive, and outspoken. They demonstrate a fast personal tempo and enjoy parties and small talk. They are uninhibited and may be bold, brash, friendly, and warm. Theodore Roosevelt (TR), Clinton, and Harding all scored very high. TR went big-game hunting, tracked down outlaws, and was a real-life cowboy. Clinton is known for his boyish charm, tendency to talk too much, and his interest in women. Harding loved just ambling along and talking to whomever he met. Introverts like Coolidge and Hoover are low key, retiring, reserved, and sober, and may be shy or overcontrolled. Extraversion includes the facets of Warmth, Gregariousness, Assertiveness, Activity, Excitement Seeking, and (a tendency to experience) Positive Emotions.

Openness to Experience: This dimension contrasts poets, philosophers, and artists with farmers, machinists, and "down-to-earth" people who have little interest in theories, aesthetics, or fanciful possibilities. High scorers like Jefferson and Lincoln are original, creative, and idealistic. They have wide interests, are philosophical, and value intellectual matters. Jefferson exemplified these qualities, being an accomplished musician, architect, scientist, and inventor, as well as a political philosopher and the author of the Declaration of Independence. Low scorers are described as conservative, commonplace, simple, and conforming. Jackson and Truman are prominent examples. Openness facets on the NEO include Openness to Fantasy, Aesthetics, Feelings, Actions, Ideas, and Values.

TABLE 1.1
Facets of Neuroticism

Facet Scale	Description of High Scorers	High-Scoring Presidents	Low-Scoring Presidents
Anxiety	Anxious, tense, fearful, prone to worry; not confident*	J. Q. Adams, Nixon, Adams	Reagan, Grant, T. Roosevelt**
Angry Hostility	Tendency to experience anger, irritation, impatience, and disgust; anxious	Jackson, Nixon, LBJ	Ford, Madison, Van Buren
Depression	Prone to feelings of sadness, discouragement, guilt, and loneliness	J. Q. Adams, Lincoln, Adams	Reagan, FDR, TR
Self-Consciousness	Prone to shame, embarrassment, sensitive to teasing; shy	Nixon, Adams, Coolidge	Reagan, TR, Harding
Impulsiveness	Unable to control urges and cravings; moody	Clinton, LBJ, TR	Wilson, Madison, Carter
Vulnerability	Feel unable to cope, respond to stress by seeking help, panicking, or giving up; not clear-thinking or self-confident	Harding, Adams, J. Q. Adams	Eisenhower, TR, Washington

*Definitions and adjectives that define the core of the concept are given before the semicolon (;), while those coming after merely are correlated (related) to the scale.
**Henceforth, TR.

Those scoring high on Openness to Values question tradition; low scorers look to the church and elders for moral guidance.

Openness is the only personality dimension related to IQ, with more open people tending to score higher in intelligence. Some of the ratings of general mental ability we collected in this study were so highly correlated with Openness that they seem to be measuring the same thing in our select group (presidents), even though few Openness items make mention of being good at anything. We will report findings for Openness and intelligence ratings separately in various parts of the book, but this fact should be remembered.

Agreeableness: High scorers are sympathetic, kind, forgiving, appreciative, trusting, softhearted, modest, and considerate. They like other people and are usually liked by them. Few presidents score high on this scale, but Lincoln and

TABLE 1.2
Facets of Extraversion

Facet Scale	Description of High Scorers	High-Scoring Presidents	Low-Scoring Presidents
Warmth	Affectionate, friendly, like people and easily form attachments	Harding, TR Clinton,	Hoover, Nixon, Coolidge
Gregariousness	Prefer being around people; sociable and outgoing	Harding, Ford Clinton,	Hoover, Wilson, Coolidge
Assertiveness	Speak up without hesitation, socially ascendant, dominant, forceful; aggressive	TR, LBJ, Jackson	Taft, Harding, Coolidge*
Activity	Rapid tempo, vigorous movement, need to keep busy, energetic	TR, LBJ, Carter	Coolidge, Taft, Grant
Excitement Seeking	Crave excitement, thrills, "action" and stimulation; pleasure seeking and daring	Kennedy, TR Clinton,	Coolidge, Fillmore, J. Q. Adams
Positive Emotions	Prone to joy, happiness, love, and excitement; enthusiastic, humorous	TR, FDR, Clinton	J. Q. Adams, Nixon, Hoover

*Almost all presidents are well above average on this scale. The men listed here were the lowest scoring presidents, though only Taft scored lower than average Americans.

Harding topped the list. Both were folksy and enjoyed talking with common people. As president, Lincoln set aside four hours a day to meet with ordinary citizens. During the Civil War, he often granted pardons to deserters, a quality that did not endear him to his generals who needed to maintain discipline. Disagreeable people are stubborn, ruthless, critical, skeptical, unkind, demanding, and uncooperative. If they are also extraverted, they are likely to be bold, assertive, and domineering. Nixon, Lyndon Johnson, and Jackson all score quite low on Agreeableness. Nixon was deeply distrustful and vindictive; LBJ bullied his wife and staff; Jackson was renowned for his hatred of his political enemies. Facets of Agreeableness are Trust, Straightforwardness, Altruism, Compliance, Modesty, and Tender-Mindedness.

Conscientiousness: High scorers like Wilson, Washington, and Carter are organized, thorough, hardworking, principled, deliberate, precise, and dependable. Wilson's devotion to principle led to his dramatic League of Nations defeat, where he seemed incapable of sensible compromise. Washington's accuracy and

TABLE 1.3
Facets of Openness to Experience

Facet Scale	Description of High Scorers	High-Scoring Presidents	Low-Scoring Presidents
Openness to Fantasy	Vivid imagination and rich fantasy life; dreamy	Reagan, Kennedy, Harding	Taft, Truman, Hoover
Openness to Aesthetics	Deep appreciation of art, music, poetry, beauty; artistic, original	J. Q. Adams, Jefferson, Carter	Grant, LBJ, Jackson
Openness to Feelings	Receptivity to own inner feelings and emotions. Experience emotions fully and value them; excitable, spontaneous	TR, Wilson, Lincoln	Madison, Coolidge, Hoover
Openness to Actions	Willing to try new activities, go new places, do things differently; wide interests, adventurous	Jefferson, Clinton, Kennedy	Coolidge, Truman, Taft
Openness to Ideas	Intellectual curiosity, willingness to consider new ideas; idealistic, inventive	Jefferson, J.Q. Adams, Madison	Jackson, Grant, Truman
Openness to Values	Readiness to reexamine (or reject) social, political and religious values; unconventional	Clinton, Kennedy, Jefferson	Reagan, Hoover, Harding

reliability was such that the maps he prepared as a surveyor are still considered definitive today. Customers who bought nails made at his estate did not bother to check the count, as was customary for other vendors. Low scorers are lazy, careless, distractible, inefficient, frivolous, and irresponsible. They see sexual possibilities with people and in situations others might not. Harding, Clinton, and Kennedy score low on this factor; all had mistresses or affairs while in the White House. Clinton's early weeks in office were chaotic, with important posts going unfilled for months. In the days of Camelot, secretaries swam naked in the White House pool. The facet scales of Conscientiousness are Competence, Order, Dutifulness, Achievement Striving, Self-Discipline, and Deliberation.

While much of personality is understandable in terms of the five factors, they cannot provide a rich or detailed portrait of a flesh and blood person. The five factors are very broad, and a person who scores high or low on one of these traits will probably not show all of the features we described above. Consider Ronald Reagan. He was a very conservative man, and scored quite low on most aspects of

TABLE 1.4
Facets of Agreeableness

Facet Scale	Description of High Scorers	High-Scoring Presidents	Low-Scoring Presidents
Trust	Believe others are honest and well-intentioned; forgiving	Harding, Grant, Lincoln	Nixon, Adams, LBJ
Straight-forwardness	Frank, sincere, ingenuous; not complicated or demanding	Fillmore, Grant*	LBJ, FDR, Nixon
Altruism	Generous, considerate, willing to *personally* help others in need	Ford, Taft, Harding	LBJ, Nixon, Adams
Compliance	Meek and mild, defer to others, inhibit anger, aggression; not stubborn or demanding	Harding, Fillmore, Madison	Jackson, Nixon, LBJ
Modesty	Humble, self-effacing; not show-offs or seen as clever	Fillmore, Grant, Madison	LBJ, TR, Adams
Tender-Mindedness	Friendly and warm; sympathy and concern for others, especially less fortunate	Clinton, Carter, Kennedy	Nixon, Taft, Reagan

*Almost all presidents are average or below on this scale compared to average Americans.

Openness to Experience—except for Openness to Fantasy. On this scale, which measures daydreaming, imagination, and a rich inner life, he scored highest of all presidents. If we described him solely based on his overall score on Openness to Experience, we would have missed this aspect of his personality—one that was quite important in understanding him.

Throughout this book, we present our personality findings at three levels: (1) the Big Five factors and Character; (2) the Facet Scales; and (3) responses to individual items. Each contributes important information not available from the others. The five factors are both traits and a coordinate system. They supply points of reference to guide us in understanding the many facets of a person—as the periodic table does in chemistry. They allow us to present a summary of a president's personality on a simple graph that captures a great deal about the man. The Facet Scales from the NEO allow us to be more specific than the Big Five factors and still make direct comparisons to average Americans. Like the factor scales, norms are available for average people, not just presidents. Lastly, there are the items themselves—the statements that the raters actually responded to in

TABLE 1.5
Facets of Conscientiousness

Facet Scale	Descriptions of High Scorers	High-Scoring Presidents	Low-Scoring Presidents
Competence	Sense that they are capable, sensible, & effective; well-prepared to deal with life; efficient	Van Buren, Eisenhower, Washington	Harding, Grant, Jackson
Order	Neat, tidy, well-organized; thorough	Hoover, Wilson, Carter	Lincoln, Clinton, J. Q. Adams
Dutifulness	Adhere strictly to principles, fulfill obligations; not defensive, distractible	Washington, Wilson, Eisenhower	Kennedy, Clinton, FDR
Achievement Striving	High aspirations, ambitious goals, & work hard to achieve, purposeful; thorough, ambitious	TR, Carter, J. Q. Adams	Grant, Harding, Reagan*
Self-Discipline	Start and complete tasks despite boredom, setbacks, distractions, fatigue; organized, not lazy	Eisenhower, Washington, TR	Clinton, Taft, Kennedy
Deliberation	Think before acting, cautious, deliberate	Van Buren, Coolidge, Washington	Jackson, Truman, Kennedy

* Only Grant was below the average of typical Americans.

the questionnaire. Though items have been paraphrased to protect the security of the tests used in our study, they retain the flavor of the original questions. If raters agreed with a statement like "He is a warm and friendly person," our portrait will state something like "he was friendly and warm." Like the example for Reagan given above, the items on a scale may reflect qualities distinct from the interpretation given to the scale. Lincoln, for example, scored low on the Straightforwardness scale, but was still rated as honest on individual items. Paraphrasing items allows the reader to appreciate what the raters read and responded to, rather than having to accept an amalgamation of their opinions from scale scores.

Character: The word "character" is used in at least two ways. Sometimes it is a synonym for personality, or at least the parts that are stable and enduring over time. In political discussions, character also refers to the subset of personality traits that have moral connotations. Where does it fit in the Big Five? Research on Integrity tests, which businesses use to hire honest employees, indicates that character is two parts Conscientiousness and Agreeableness and one part low Neuroticism.[3] However, there are facets of Conscientiousness, such as Order, that have little relation to measures of character or integrity.

Because the question of character was so salient in the Clinton years, we created more than a dozen scales to measure it for our study. One scale was composed of items like "lies, cheats, and steals," or "had many sexual affairs"—the sort of behaviors that make for scandals when discovered. A second index contained adjectives and descriptions that seem clearly related to character or the lack of it, for example "dependable, reliable, responsible" or (conversely) "cruel, ruthless, vindictive." A third scale contained more subtle indications, such as "direct, frank, straightforward" versus "cynical, distrustful, skeptical, suspicious." Yet another index simply asked the rater whether, in his or her opinion, the president rated was "of good moral character." This approach allowed the rater to make an assessment on his or her definition of what character is. Since the different indexes generally agreed with each other, and there was no clear reason to prefer one index more than another, we averaged them to create a composite measure of character.

The NEO Facet Scales most related to the composite measure of character are Dutifulness, Impulsivity, and Deliberation. Others that correlate highly with character are shown in Table 1.6. These twelve scales were combined to create the index of character that we use most often in the rest of the book. Because it

TABLE 1.6
NEO Facet Scales Most Correlated with Character

Facet Scale	Correlation (r) with Character
Dutifulness	.67
Impulsivity	− .60
Deliberation	.59
Altruism	.57
Straightforwardness	.57
Self-Discipline	.57
Competence	.55
Angry Hostility	− .52
Modesty	.50
Compliance	.49
Trust	.49
Vulnerability	− .45

is based on the NEO (which has good norms), we can compare presidents' scores on this character index to those of average Americans. We do this and much more in the next chapter.

Some Facet Scales that might have been expected to contribute to Character did not make the cut. Concern for the less fortunate seems to be an inherent part of character, but the NEO Tender-Mindedness scale did not meet our criterion. This may be because the items on this scale ask about *concern* or *sympathy* for the poor, elderly, or less fortunate, but not about actually *doing* anything charitable. The Altruism scale, which refers to generous and polite behavior, did make it into the character index.

In the next chapter, we show how presidents as a group score on the Big Five personality factors and on Character compared to Americans today and to each other. We also look at how presidents have changed since the time of Washington and illustrate how Democrats are different from Republicans in more than just politics. Finally, we identify the major changes in personality from one administration to another.

CHAPTER 2

Who Are These Guys?
Personality Traits of Presidents,
Founding Fathers, Democrats,
and Republicans

THE VOICES behind the door were muffled but excited. The president and his young assistant were in the bathroom adjacent to the Oval Office. After some minutes, the door flew open. The president looked a bit rumpled but relieved, the secretary a bit worse for wear. Lyndon Johnson was giving dictation from the toilet again.[1]

Every president to date has been a white male of Western European ancestry. Most were successful, professional politicians. Many of the rest were military men or lawyers. How well do they reflect the range of people whom they represent? Are they made of special stuff not found in the rest of us?

Presidents do differ among themselves. Some came from wealthy families; others were very poor. The most startling contrast is level of education. Some (e.g., Jackson and Lincoln) had virtually no formal schooling. Others, such as Jefferson and J. Q. Adams, were among the most learned men of their time; Wilson held a Ph.D.

Despite their range of education, it is almost certain that, as a group, presidents were brighter than the average Americans of their time. Leaders, almost by definition, must be able to comprehend problems and articulate or resolve them better than their followers. Research confirms that they typically score at the 90th percentile of the group they lead in intelligence.[2] Most modern presidents, such as Richard Nixon, Jimmy Carter, and Clinton, have been very smart men. Even those with more modest intellectual reputations (e.g., Reagan and Ford), were college graduates, and Ford graduated in the top third of his law school. A president doesn't have to be the smartest person in the land, but he ought to be above average. When there is a question about this, as with Harding, the results are unhappy.

There were no IQ tests in Washington's time, but there were other ways that intelligence could be estimated. Nearly a hundred years ago, a team of researchers attempted to gauge the intelligence of 301 eminent people by systematic analysis of their writings, both as children and adults.[3] They studied a variety of professions, including scientists, artists, and political figures. Included in their group were a number of early presidents. John Quincy Adams, the only child prodigy among the presidents, was estimated to have the highest IQ at 170, which is above the 99.99th percentile. Grant was lowest, with an IQ estimate of 115—about the 84th percentile. It should be noted that these estimates, based on written works, might underestimate ability in areas such as spatial relations. This would put generals, such as Washington and Grant, at a disadvantage relative to scholars. Incidentally, Washington's estimated IQ was 130; John Adams's, 140; Jefferson's, 145.

Since intelligence tests are now widely used in schools, businesses, and medical settings, it's increasingly possible to get actual IQ scores on presidents and candidates. Nixon was widely reported to have an IQ of 132, which is approximately at the 98th percentile of Americans. As part of his evaluation for Alzheimer's disease, Reagan almost certainly took an IQ test, though his score could be significantly lower than it would have been before the disease. As we will see in the next chapter, intelligence is one of the best predictors of performance for all jobs, particularly complex ones.

PERSONALITY OF THE AVERAGE PRESIDENT

The "average president" is the average score of all presidents, presented here on the Character scale and each of the Big Five factors. The measure of character is the combination of twelve facet scales from the NEO we identified in the last chapter. This index has the advantage (over other indexes of character) of being directly comparable to typical Americans, just as other scales from the NEO are.

We use charts of personality scores throughout this book as a way to visually present some of our findings. Some readers may be chart-phobic. For that reason, all of the important information in the charts is discussed fully in the text as well. Still, we encourage you to study the graphs.

Chart 2.1 shows how presidents score compared to average Americans. Scores

CHART 2.1
Scores of Presidents Compared to Average Americans

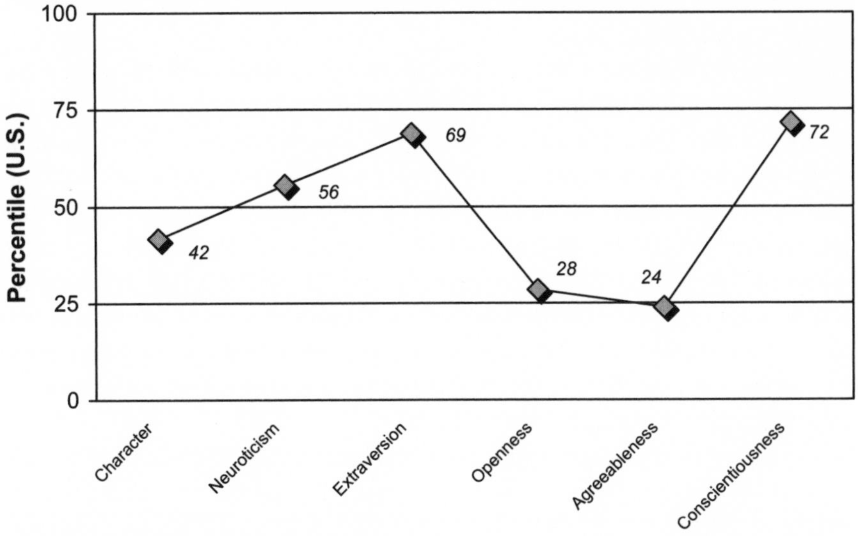

NB: On this and most charts, "Average Americans" score at the 50th percentile line on all scales.

are expressed in percentiles, with 50 being average. The average president scores a bit below most Americans on Character (42nd percentile), slightly above average on Neuroticism (56th), and considerably higher on Extraversion (69th) and Conscientiousness (72nd). He scores quite a bit below non-presidents on Openness to Experience (32nd) and Agreeableness (24th). For most of these dimensions, there are presidents scoring all over the place—some high, some low. There is one big exception. No president scored above the 82nd percentile of everyday Americans on Agreeableness.

Next, we look at presidents' scores on the NEO Facet Scales. Men who become president score high on Assertiveness and Achievement Striving, and to a lesser extent, on Self-Discipline and Openness to Feelings. They score low on Straightforwardness, Openness to Actions, and Openness to Values. Most of these findings make sense. Presidents are expected to lead (high Assertiveness), to have ambitious goals, and to work hard to accomplish them (Achievement Striving). They should be good at handling people and getting programs past opposition (low Straightforwardness). The low scores on the two Openness facets are less easily explained. They indicate the presidents, as a group, have accepted traditional values and moral authority (the Bible, church) much more than today's Americans. They do not seek novelty or readily change their habits or routines (low Openness to Actions), but value their emotions and the way they feel about things (Openness to Feelings).

Chart 2.2 shows the average scores of all the presidents on the thirty NEO Facet Scales (in percentiles), beginning with those for Neuroticism (Anxiety, Angry Hostility, etc.), and running through Conscientiousness. There is one trait where the chief executives are not much different from average people, although we would expect them to be. Given that presidents are more intelligent than average and are selected to lead from literally millions of potential candidates, it's surprising to find that they are barely more Competent (capable, showing sound judgment) than the average person. The average score of presidents is about the 61st percentile. Although high Competence contributes to successful performance as president, at least two important presidents, Andrew Jackson and Ronald Reagan, scored quite low on it.

We have shown that, as a group, men who become presidents have some traits that set them apart. But, they also vary greatly among themselves. In fact, on twenty-six of the thirty NEO Facet Scales, they differ *more* among themselves

CHART 2.2
Average Scores of Presidents on the NEO Facet Scales

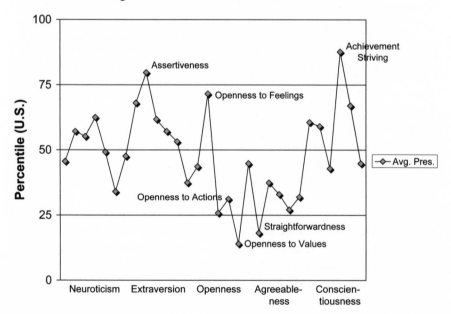

than does a sample of the general population.[4] Most of these differences are small and can be explained by several factors. But the main point is that presidents differ among themselves about as much as a random sample of forty-three people would.

We can also use the individual items on our questionnaire to get a sharper picture of the average president. We cannot use U.S. norms this time, since we do not have them for the items. But we can look at which items received the highest (i.e., 8.5 out of 9) or lowest (i.e., 1.3) average ratings across the forty-two presidents up to Bush. As a group, presidents take seriously such civic responsibilities as voting. They are not "depraved" or "perverted" and they do not steal. In line with their high scores on Achievement Striving, they work hard to achieve their goals, which are often set very high, and they are productive. They are also described as quite competent, of good moral character, dependable, and responsible. Most behave consistently with their own personal values and emerge as the leaders of groups they belong to in many walks of life.

Interestingly, the descriptions from the scale scores (e.g., low Straightforwardness and high Achievement) appear to match well with our conceptions of modern politicians, while the *items* seem more congruent with our image of the Founding Fathers. We will return to this issue later in this chapter.

SCORES OF INDIVIDUAL PRESIDENTS

Now that we know overall trends and scores, we can look at individual presidents. In the next few pages, we list presidents in order of their scores on the major dimensions of personality. We do not consider this list a ranking for two reasons. First, this would imply a level of measurement precision that does not exist. The scores we report are *estimates* of each president's true score obtained from our data. If different raters were used, the scores could be somewhat different.

Second, we list only presidents who were rated by three or more experts. Those not meeting this criterion were Monroe, William Harrison, Tyler, Taylor, Andrew Johnson, Arthur, Cleveland, McKinley, George H. W. Bush and George W. Bush. Rankings would be misleading based on less than the full group. The scores are percentiles relative to typical Americans today, based on the NEO norms. The ordering would not change if the scores were based on norms for the presidents rather than for average Americans.

Table 2.1 shows the scores of presidents on the index of character we created from the NEO. Millard Fillmore, despite being a rather obscure president, scored highest of all on this index of character (95th percentile); he was followed by Eisenhower, Madison, and Lincoln. As will be apparent later in this chapter, a

TABLE 2.1
Scores of Presidents on Character (NEO)

President	Percentile
Fillmore	95
Eisenhower	89
Madison	87
Lincoln	85
Washington	85
Ford	85
Carter	82
B. Harrison	76
Van Buren	64
Grant	64
Pierce	58
Jefferson	56
Coolidge	56
Wilson	54
Buchanan	46
Truman	46
Reagan	42
Hoover	39
Harding	26
Roosevelt, T.	24
Roosevelt, F.	19
Polk	10
Adams, J.Q.	9
Kennedy	5
Clinton	2
Adams	2
Nixon	0.9
Jackson	0.4
Johnson, L.	0.10

different character index shows Lincoln as highest. This is not surprising. Different indexes can be expected to give somewhat different results. However, all indexes of character are highly correlated, and those that score high on one generally score high on the others. But there are some notable exceptions. John Adams scores quite low on the NEO index, but average or high on others. Truman's middling score on the NEO is an underestimate of his ratings on other character indexes.

Low scorers on Character include Lyndon Johnson, Nixon, Jackson, John Adams, and Clinton. Johnson's score was *really* low—lower than 999 of 1,000 typical Americans. It should be noted that Clinton's ratings were obtained in 1995, before the scandal that resulted in his impeachment trial; his score might be lower if assessed today.

John Quincy Adams got the highest Neuroticism score (99.6th percentile, see Table 2.2), followed by his father, John Adams. Two recent chief executives, Lyndon Johnson and Nixon, obtained high scores and were well known for their high-strung qualities. Reagan clearly had the lowest score (4th percentile), followed by FDR and Ford.

Extraversion is one of the most visible of personality traits. People notice

TABLE 2.2
Scores of Presidents on Neuroticism

President	Percentile
Adams, J. Q.	99.6
Adams	98
Nixon	97
Johnson, L.	95
Coolidge	86
Lincoln	82
Hoover	81
Polk	79
Carter	76
Pierce	76
Wilson	75
Truman	75
Harrison, B.	71
Taft	65
Jefferson	59
Clinton	58
Jackson	56
Buchanan	53
Harding	46
Madison	46
Washington	40
Roosevelt, T.	32
Eisenhower	30
Kennedy	27
Fillmore	26
Van Buren	23
Grant	21
Ford	15
Roosevelt, F.	14
Reagan	4

energy, enthusiasm, and talkativeness. Theodore Roosevelt embodies this description. Bill Clinton is a close runner-up, scoring higher than 999 of 1,000 people. Closely following him were Harding, FDR, Kennedy, LBJ, Jackson, and Reagan.

There were also some extreme Introverts among the presidents, the most notable being "silent" Calvin Coolidge. His Extraversion score is lower than 996 of 1,000 average Americans. There are dozens of anecdotes of his taciturnity and dry wit. Once, reporters repeatedly questioned him to no avail. "Have you any statement on the campaign?" "No." "Can you tell us something about the world situation?" "No." "Any information about Prohibition?" "No." As he left the press conference, Coolidge turned back to them, "Now, remember—don't quote me." Other clearly introverted chief executives were John Quincy Adams and Herbert Hoover, who both score below the 3rd percentile.

Renaissance man Thomas Jefferson was most Open to Experience, scoring above the 99th percentile. The intense scholar John Q. Adams scored nearly as high, followed by the less-educated but sensitive and freethinking Abe Lincoln. Low scores are more common than high ones on this dimension. Lowest of the group is Andrew Jackson, who was rated as less Open than 995 of 1,000 typical Americans; he was followed by Taft and Truman. Truman's low score on Openness may explain the frequent perception of him as a plain, ordinary man. Though Jackson also scored low, as a highly impulsive, temperamental war hero, he was in little danger of being seen as commonplace.

Millard Fillmore, winner of the Character race, also finished highest on Agreeableness (Table 2.5), and even he scored at the 82nd percentile—much lower than the top scores on other scales. Abe Lincoln was second highest at the 76th percentile. His low score on Straightforwardness brought down his overall score here (see Chapter 11). Low scorers are easy to find. Four presidents—nearly 10 percent of the group—score below 99 of 100 typical Americans on this trait. Nixon is the lowest, scoring lower than 9,998 of 10,000 Americans. LBJ and Jackson both scored lower than 999 of 1,000 Americans.

Plenty of presidents scored high on Conscientiousness. Wilson led the group, scoring just above the 99th percentile. Not only was he conscientious, he was in some ways a classic Obsessive-Compulsive (Chapter 6). Closely following him were Washington, Carter, Hoover, Nixon, and Eisenhower. Four of the five lowest scorers are twentieth-century presidents. Harding is lowest, scoring lower than 96 of 100 people, followed closely by Clinton and Kennedy at the 5th percentile. Ronald Reagan also scored low, as did Grant.

TABLE 2.3
Scores of Presidents on Extraversion

President	Percentile
Roosevelt, T.	99.97
Clinton	99.90
Harding	99.87
Roosevelt, F.	99.8
Kennedy	99.6
Johnson, L.	99.4
Jackson	99.0
Reagan	98.3
Truman	95
Ford	91
Taft	81
Van Buren	78
Pierce	75
Lincoln	75
Eisenhower	71
Grant	69
Carter	58
Fillmore	39
Wilson	37
Washington	28
Harrison, B.	27
Jefferson	23
Polk	22
Buchanan	12
Adams	9
Nixon	7
Madison	6
Hoover	2.4
Adams, J. Q.	1.0
Coolidge	0.4

DEMOCRATS VS. REPUBLICANS

Franklin Roosevelt can be said to be the first modern Democrat, as well as the prototype for those that followed. He was an ebullient, charming, sometimes manipulative man. LBJ, Kennedy, and Clinton all have personalities similar to Franklin Roosevelt's. Truman varies from the type in some ways, and Carter is a true outsider. Republicans seem to be cut from a different mold, with no central figure dominating.

TABLE 2.4
Scores of Presidents on Openness to Experience

President	Percentile
Jefferson	99.1
Adams, J. Q.	98
Lincoln	95
Kennedy	82
Clinton	82
Carter	77
Wilson	64
Madison	62
Adams	61
Roosevelt, T.	56
Fillmore	46
Roosevelt, F.	45
Pierce	37
Van Buren	31
Harrison, B.	30
Eisenhower	29
Polk	21
Coolidge	17
Washington	14
Nixon	14
Reagan	10
Harding	10
Hoover	8
Ford	8
Johnson, L.	7
Buchanan	5
Grant	2.3
Truman	1.7
Taft	1.0
Jackson	0.5

On the average, recent Democrats do differ from recent Republicans (Ike, Nixon, Ford, Reagan, and G. H. W. Bush) in a number of ways—sometimes dramatically so.[5] We do not intend to imply that either Democrats or Republicans are a homogeneous group. If that were true, there would be no reason for Chapter 4, and little reason for this book. The descriptions we provide are based on groups and may not apply to all members of the group. In fact, much of what we say about Democrats as a group does *not* apply to Carter.

Democrats generally score low on Character (average of 10th percentile). Their average, on our charts, would be much lower if it weren't for Carter's

TABLE 2.5
Scores of Presidents on Agreeableness

President	Percentile
Fillmore	82
Lincoln	76
Harding	66
Madison	62
Carter	56
Grant	54
Pierce	54
Ford	53
Taft	51
Jefferson	51
Harrison, B.	39
Truman	33
Eisenhower	33
Reagan	26
Clinton	24
Coolidge	18
Van Buren	16
Washington	16
Wilson	13
Buchanan	13
Adams, J. Q.	11
Kennedy	11
Roosevelt, F.	10
Polk	10
Hoover	6
Roosevelt, T.	2
Adams	1
Jackson	0.1
Johnson, L.	0.1
Nixon	0.02

score. Republicans score right at the American average, with their average pulled way down by Nixon. Neuroticism scores of Democrats (60th percentile) are substantially higher than Republicans (41st percentile) on average. Democrats are very Extraverted, averaging about the 98th percentile, while Republicans typically score higher than 81 of 100 typical Americans. Members of the GOP receive low ratings (8th percentile) on Openness, while Democrats are a little below average (42nd; see Chart 2.3). Presidents from both parties score about the 13th percentile on Agreeableness. Lastly, Republicans are more Conscientious (57th versus 50th percentile).

TABLE 2.6
Scores of Presidents on Conscientiousness

President	Percentile
Wilson	99.2
Washington	98.6
Carter	98.5
Hoover	98.3
Nixon	98
Eisenhower	98
Coolidge	97
Harrison, B.	96
Buchanan	96
Adams, J. Q.	94
Madison	90
Truman	90
Roosevelt, T.	89
Adams	87
Fillmore	86
Van Buren	82
Jefferson	78
Lincoln	75
Johnson, L.	72
Ford	69
Pierce	67
Taft	59
Polk	51
Jackson	31
Roosevelt, F.	27
Grant	9
Reagan	9
Kennedy	5
Clinton	5
Harding	4

Recent Democrats show a distinct pattern of scores on the NEO Facet Scales. Often, they score quire high on one facet of a given Big Five factor but low on another (see Table 2.7). In parentheses, we show the first letter of the Big Five Factor the scale belongs to (Neuroticism, Extraversion, Openness, Agreeableness, or Conscientiousness), and if the scale contributes to the Character scale.

Let's start with Agreeableness. As a group, Democrats scored very low (1st percentile) on Straightforwardness. Consistent with this score, raters indicated the typical Democrat "does not have a hard time deceiving others."[6] They scored lower than nearly 90 percent of typical Americans on Modesty. However, they

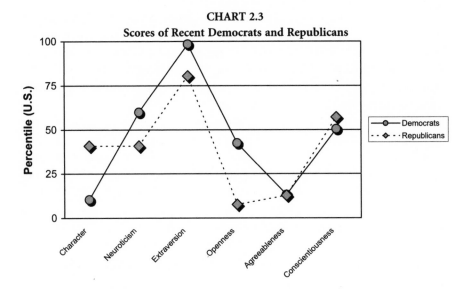

CHART 2.3

Scores of Recent Democrats and Republicans

felt that we can never do too much for the poor and elderly, are sympathetic to the less fortunate, and scored high on Tender-Mindedness (92nd percentile). All three of these qualities are facets of Agreeableness. Relative to Republicans, Democrats would rather be known as "merciful" than as "just."

Achievement Striving is an aspect of Conscientiousness, and Democrats score quite high (95th percentile). But, more than most presidents, they fail to keep promises and finish projects. They aren't "dependable, reliable, responsible" or "prompt, punctual" and often fail to live up to their principles. They scored at the 11th percentile on Dutifulness and Deliberation. As a rule, they act extemporaneously and are not dignified, formal, or mannerly.

TABLE 2.7

Characteristics of Recent Democratic Presidents

High	Percentile	Low	Percentile
Achievement Striving (C)	95	Straightforwardness (A, Character)	1.3
Activity (E)	93	Deliberation (C, Character)	11
Tender-Mindedness (A)	92	Dutifulness (C, Character)	11
Positive Emotions (E)	90	Modesty (A)	13
Openness to Feelings	90		
Assertiveness (E)	89		
Gregariousness (E)	87		

In contrast to the mixed pattern of Conscientiousness and Agreeableness traits, Democrats are a group of unadulterated Extraverts. They move quickly, have a fast-paced lifestyle, and scored at the 92nd percentile on Activity (level). They experience high levels of Positive Emotions (90th percentile), are Assertive (89th percentile), and Gregarious (87th percentile). As presidents, they initiated much new legislation and many programs.

Democrats are high on Openness to Feelings (90th percentile), indicating that they attend to and value their emotions as an important part of life. They are not high or low on any other NEO Openness facets compared to average Americans. Democrats are definitely not conservative in values or "conventional, traditional." They value open-mindedness over ideals and principles. They believe social policies should change with the times and, relative to the presidents as a group, do not support freedom for business. Taken together, they have had extramarital affairs and are not devoted family men—though this was clearly not true of Truman or Carter. Most swore frequently and were prone to indulge their impulses.

Modern Republicans are less distinct; they got fewer extreme scores and showed a very different pattern. Like Democrats, they are low on Straightforwardness, but to a lesser degree. They score very low relative to average Americans—at the 3rd percentile—on Tender-Mindedness. Much less than most presidents over the past two hundred years, they do not believe that human needs outweigh economic ones or that society can never do too much for the poor and elderly. They score low on Openness to (Liberal) Values—they rarely question traditional moral beliefs—and Openness to Ideas, indicating a disinterest in philosophy and intellectual puzzles.

One personality description is not tied to any of the NEO scales and is surprising. Republican presidents were described as "forgetful, absentminded." This was true, in varying degrees, of all of them except George H. W. Bush. (G. W. Bush is not included in this and other analyses in this section.) Ronald Reagan scored

TABLE 2.8
Characteristics of Recent Republican Presidents

High	Percentile	Low	Percentile
NONE		Tender-Mindedness (A)	3
		Openness to Values	3
		Openness to Ideas	10
		Straightforwardness (A, Character)	12

high, which is not surprising since he may have suffered occasional effects of Alzheimer's disease. But Ford scored higher still.

As presidents, Republicans are generally cautious and conservative in action. They rely on a staff system, deciding among options formulated by advisers, more so than most presidents.

Next, we explore how the two parties differ from each other most. The largest difference—and it's a very large one—is on the item "feels we can never do too much for the poor and elderly." Republicans are also much more likely to be conservative in values, but much more likely to keep their promises. Democrats are more perceptive and observant, but uncomfortable around their superiors (before becoming president). Democratic presidents empathize with people more readily and are more likely to become completely absorbed listening to music.

As we will show in the next chapter, some of the personality differences between the parties have implications for being a successful president.

FROM CHARACTER TO PERSONALITY? THE EIGHTEENTH TO THE TWENTY-FIRST CENTURY

The Founding Fathers are remembered as brave, honorable, farsighted men. Current politicians have a very different reputation. Did our leaders really change so much? Fortunately, we can easily look at how presidents have changed over time by plotting their scores on the NEO, starting with Washington and ending with Clinton.

Presidents in the early days of the Republic differed from contemporary presidents in a number of ways.[7] Three separate measures, comprising three different methodologies, indicate that modern presidents score higher on Need for Power: They want to have impact and prestige, to be in charge, and they want people to know it. (The line ends at 1992 because data for Bush was not available on these indexes and measures are taken at the beginning of a president's term.) Though we fear power-hungry people, power motivation is associated with better performance in the White House.[8] Modern presidents also value and show greater need for close relationships (Need for Affiliation). Chart 2.4 shows the trends for these traits, each based on the average of three measures.[9]

Both Need for Power and Need for Affiliation correlate with the Big Five Factor of Extraversion. Two of our four measures of Extraversion increased significantly from 1789 to 2002. So did the Extraversion facet scales of Positive Emotions and Excitement Seeking, and the increase in Activity scores nearly

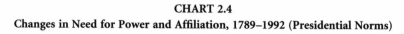

CHART 2.4

Changes in Need for Power and Affiliation, 1789–1992 (Presidential Norms)

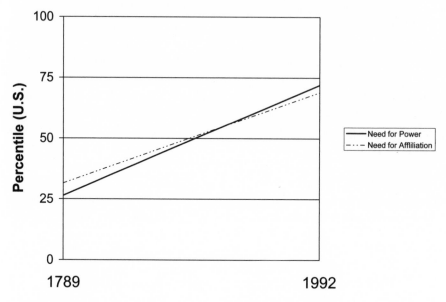

reached statistical significance. Chart 2.5 shows the trends for these traits. In Washington's time, we would expect an average president to score around the 31st percentile on Extraversion. Now, that score would be about the 93rd percentile. That's a very big change.

Chart 2.6 shows presidents' scores on the NEO Extraversion scale over time, along with a trend line. Unlike other graphs we present, this one reflects plots of the underlying standard scores, so the percentile labels on the graph are no longer evenly spaced. This is necessary to show the actual magnitude of some very high scores, and because extreme scores strongly affect the trend. As can be seen, *all* the early presidents were on the introverted side. The first Extravert, Andrew Jackson, was not a subtle change. He scored at the 99th percentile.

Not only did scores increase over time, so did the range of scores.[10] Very few presidents before 1900 had extreme Extraversion scores; Jackson was by far the highest and J. Q. Adams the lowest. Then came TR, posting an all-time presidential high at the 99.97th percentile, followed soon after by Coolidge, posting the lowest score yet seen (0.4th percentile). Seven presidents in the past one hundred years scored above 99 out of 100 typical Americans on Extraversion, and another (Reagan) scored at the 98th percentile. Yet, three twentieth-century chief executives were more introverted than 92 out of 100 of their compatriots (Coolidge, Hoover, and Nixon).

CHART 2.5
Changes in NEO Extraversion and Extraversion Facets, 1789–2004

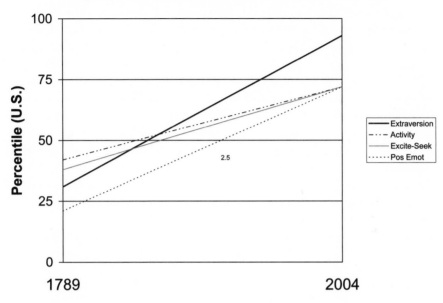

CHART 2.6
NEO Extraversion Scores over Time

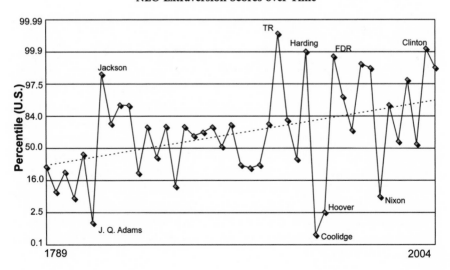

What about character? Certainly Washington, Adams, and Jefferson were not of the same mold as LBJ, Nixon, and Clinton. Though that is true, it is also misleading. Adams scored quite *low* on some measures of character. Jefferson's reputation has been sullied a bit by allegations that he fathered a child with a slave girl. And what about upstanding modern presidents like Carter, Ford, and Eisenhower?

Three of our thirteen character scales did show a statistically significant decrease in modern times (from Washington through Clinton). Other character scales also decreased, but the changes were sometimes quite small. One of two measures of Negative Valence (evil, depraved) increased. In Chart 2.7, we show scores on a character index. As an average of several character scales, it reflects many dimensions of character. It shows a modest decrease over time but not a significant one. Only presidents rated by three or more experts are labeled.

The trend line in Chart 2.7 shows that in Washington's time, the average president would score at about the 68th percentile on Character. As of 1992, that score would be at about the 33rd percentile. One other observation stands out.

CHART 2.7
Presidents' Character Scores, 1789–2004

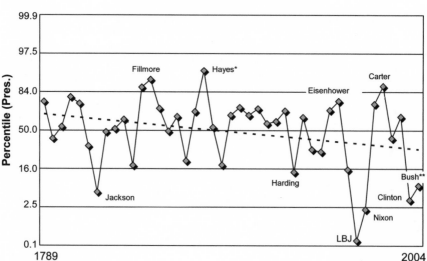

*Hayes had only one rater.
**Only the two authors and Dr. Immelman rated G. W. Bush.

The late 1960s and early 1970s were a time of turmoil and questioning of authority. It was also the period in which the two presidents who scored lowest in character were in office, back-to-back. Was this a factor? Or were Nixon and LBJ merely a product of their times? Correlational studies like ours cannot answer this question. We can conclude, though, that character is not merely a Republican or a Democratic issue.

One more change is notable. Modern presidents score well below average Americans on Openness to Experience—unlike the Founding Fathers. The Facet Scale of Openness to Ideas shows the largest change, declining from the 50th percentile to about the 20th percentile now. (Clinton was a notable exception.)

We can also look at changes in the ratings given to individual items on our questionnaire over time. Though there is much more stability than change, a number of items were rated as considerably more true of modern presidents (Teddy Roosevelt through Clinton) than of the whole group. They had less difficulty being deceptive and were less "ethical, honest, moral, principled, sincere, truthful." They lived a faster-paced lifestyle, often appeared to be rushing or short of time, and had a greater taste for excitement than earlier chief executives. They were more willing to bully or flatter people to get their way and were more optimistic, cheerful, high-spirited, and happy but had less interest in philosophy and the nature of the universe. More recent presidents have "done very foolish things in (his) life" and have had affairs.

CHANGES IN PERSONALITY FROM ONE ADMINISTRATION TO ANOTHER

There have been several transitions in American politics where the shift in personality has been as dramatic as that in policy. When FDR took over from Hoover, he brought not just a new vision of government. Even before the Great Depression sucked the joy from his life, Hoover was a sober, serious, but very competent man who enjoyed solitary pursuits. FDR was ebullient, loved an audience, and was endlessly optimistic. His personality provided hope to the America of the 1930s and 1940s.

Another change came in 1974, this time unaccompanied by a major shift in policy. Nixon became the first president to resign from office. A bright, hard-working, self-made man, he was also unscrupulous, suspicious, and aggressive. These qualities, combined with his willingness to act upon them, eventually led to his resignation. Gerald Ford, "Mr. Nice Guy," replaced him, and the nation cautiously began to trust the Oval Office once more.

We can measure how similar two personalities are by calculating a correlation between their average ratings on our 592 questionnaire items. A positive correlation indicates they were alike, and a negative correlation indicates a personality difference between presidents. In Chart 2.8, we graph the degree of personality change from one president to the next. The first data point at 1797 shows the similarity (correlation) between Washington and Adams, the second, that between Adams and Jefferson, et cetera. High points on the graph indicate greater personality change between consecutive presidents.

The three largest personality changes, from one president to another, were when FDR succeeded Hoover, when Harding succeeded Wilson, and when Taft replaced TR. Woodrow Wilson was a serious, aloof, intellectual, imaginative, idealistic man and president. Warren Harding was nearly the opposite. Wilson was moralistic and attempted to civilize the world; Harding promised little but a good time. The country seemed ready for a vacation and got it with Harding. TR was a zealous, energetic reformer; Taft was a gentle, sluggish, conservative man. The numerous reform efforts begun under TR withered under Taft's administration.

CHART 2.8

Changes in Personality from One Administration to the Next, 1789–2004

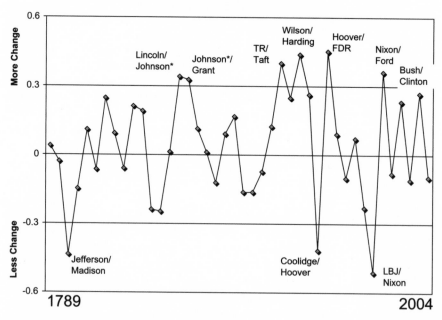

NB: Numbers on the Y (More Change/Less Change) axis are correlations.

Several successions stand out as offering much *less* change than usual. Jefferson and Madison were both self-disciplined intellectuals who were high in Conscientiousness. Hoover was nearly as introverted than Coolidge; both also were high on Conscientiousness and low on Openness. LBJ and Nixon were highly similar on Character and all of the Big Five factors except for Extraversion.

SUMMARY

Presidents are different from average Americans in some ways, but they also vary greatly among themselves. Modern Democrats and Republicans show, on average, markedly different personalities. In some respects, Republicans are more like the Founding Fathers—less extraverted and high in character. However, all of the Founding Fathers except Washington were well above the average president on Openness, while Republicans score quite low. On average, today's chief executives are livelier, more extraverted, and quite variable in Conscientiousness and Character. Lastly, changes in administration can bring not only major changes in policy, but in personality as well. Which is more important has not yet been studied, but may vary with the needs of the country at different times.

CHAPTER 3

Predicting Presidential Success

WITH DENIZ S. ONES*

CANDIDATE BRAD JOHNSON does not manipulate or bully people and is perfectly happy to compromise. He inspires trust—what you see is what you get. He is easygoing both with his family and his coworkers. He does not monopolize meetings and is a team player. He is not afraid to ask for directions, and often does. He does not effuse emotions or hug people; he talks calmly and quietly about his vision for America. He believes in personal responsibility and that people get out of life what they put into it. He is not a workaholic: While other men around him neglected their families for their careers, Brad took his children to the beach and to Disneyland. Brad is a nice guy. He is also fictional. He was created as an illustration of a particularly *poor* personality match for the job of being president.[1]

Which personality traits are associated with superior presidential performance? Harry Truman said, "Being dumb is just about the worst thing there is in a high office." Was he right? In this part of the study, we use personality tests and statistics to answer this question. But in order to predict presidential success well, we have to define "success" and be able to measure it.

MEASURING PRESIDENTIAL SUCCESS

When companies want to measure job performance of employees in regular jobs, they often rely on ratings by supervisors. To date, presidential job performance,

---

*Deniz S. Ones, the primary author of this chapter, holds the Hellervik Distinguished Chair in Industrial/Organizational Psychology at the University of Minnesota. She is edi-

despite intense public scrutiny of the job and its incumbents, has not been studied using detailed job-performance ratings. For most other jobs in the economy, scientifically sound rating forms have been developed that give examples of good and bad performance on the job. A good secretary, for example, should type quickly with accuracy, be friendly and courteous to coworkers and clients, and order new supplies before old ones run out. A bad secretary comes in late, talks on the phone to her boyfriend during working hours, and, in one infamous case caught on video, urinates on her boss's chair. This last item probably would not make it onto any questionnaire, because—hopefully—the behavior is so unusual that it would rarely be reported. But aside from this, we could create an overall rating of a secretary's value as an employee by summing up ratings on "good" items ("types accurately") and subtracting the ratings on "bad" items ("pees on my chair").

For our study, we developed a job-performance rating form based on legal requirements for the presidency, historical relevance, a job analysis of the presidency, and the scientific job-performance literature. The resultant form has forty-one items measuring specific and general job-performance aspects of the presidency (see Table 3.1). Each item reflects a different part of the president's work or behavior in the White House.

Ten of our *generalist* experts (scholars knowledgeable about the presidents as a group) rated each president on the forty-one job-performance items. The ratings were collected mostly in 1995. The total score for each president was our measure of overall job performance. The most highly rated presidents were FDR, Lincoln, and Washington. The lowest were Harding, Pierce, and Grant.

It is very hard to tease apart different aspects of an employee's performance on the job. Bosses tend to give high marks in all categories to workers they like, and low marks across the board to those they do not. Sometimes called the halo effect, it operates just as strongly when historians rate presidents on different categories of performance. William Ridings and Stuart McIver conducted one such poll, which we cite throughout this book. Though historians were asked to rate each president on five categories of performance (Leadership Qualities, Accomplishments and Crisis Management, Political Skill, Appointments, Character and Integrity), the scores clustered together tightly. For example, Lincoln's rankings in the five categories ranged only from first to third, Harding's, from thirty-eighth to forty-first. From the standpoint of statistics, these five measures are primarily measuring only one thing—overall performance as president.

tor of the *Handbook of Industrial/Organizational Psychology* as well as the *International Journal of Selection and Assessment*. She is one of the world's leading experts in the relationship of personality to job performance.

TABLE 3.1

Aspects of Presidential Job Performance

- Role as Chief of State
- Role as Chief Executive
- Role as Chief of Foreign Relations
- Role as Legislative Leader
- Role as Commander in Chief
- Role as Party Leader
- Role as Guardian of Prosperity
- Role as Molder of Public Opinion
- Role as International Leader
- Role as Chief Law Enforcement Officer
- Planning, development & implementation of policies
- Establishment of responsibilities & procedures
- Coordinating functions & operations of executive agencies
- Reviewing activity & reports to determine progress, revising objectives as appropriate
- Development & implementation of public relations policy
- Supervision of subordinates
- Concern for the country
- Addressing the country's problems
- Transcending party politics for the good of the nation
- Providing emotional leadership
- Providing moral leadership
- Avoiding exploitation of other nations or groups of people
- Written & oral communication
- Expending extra effort to meet challenges
- Self discipline: avoiding vices at work
- Facilitating team performance
- Leadership
- Interpersonal skills displayed on the job
- Productivity
- Quality of work performed
- Job-related knowledge
- Problem solving
- Compliance with the constitution & the laws
- Compliance with rules & procedures
- Avoiding unethical behavior
- Enhancing the office & prestige of the presidency
- Commitment to the job
- Initiative
- Cooperation with others
- Overall job performance

When we analyzed the ratings from our questionnaire, we got similar results—if a president was rated highly overall, he was rated high on most of the items. We refer to this total score as *Overall Job Performance*. However, we did find a smaller, second dimension, which included the items:

✔ Self-discipline: Avoiding vices at work
✔ Compliance with the constitution and the laws
✔ Compliance with rules and procedures
✔ Avoiding exploitation of other nations or groups of people
✔ Avoiding unethical behavior

We refer to this factor as *Ethics on the Job*. Low scorers on this scale would seem to be prone to scandal and, thus, distraction from their duties. The highest-scoring presidents on this scale were Washington, Truman, and Eisenhower. The lowest were Nixon, Harding, and Grant. Although Ethics on the Job is correlated with Overall Job Performance, it is distinct enough that those personality traits that predict one dimension may not predict the other.

As our last measure of presidential success, we used the results from a previously conducted poll of historians by Robert Murray and Tim Blessing published in 1982. More than a dozen polls of presidential greatness have been conducted. Of these, Murray and Blessing's study stands out as the largest and most comprehensive. They sent a nineteen-page questionnaire to all members of the American Historical Association who hold Ph.D.s. Eight hundred and forty-six respondents returned completed questionnaires. However, the bulk of the questionnaire was devoted to the background and possible biases of the raters. The actual rating of the presidents' performance was a single item answered on a 1 to 5 scale.

Historians believe that a president cannot be fairly assessed until he has been out of office for about thirty years. This is partly due to the need for the perspective of hindsight. But new information also becomes available about what really happened during those years. Memoirs will be written, the president and his closest aides will likely pass away, and their personal letters and journals will be released to scholars. This can reveal some real surprises. In the case of Eisenhower, it showed him much more involved and knowledgeable than previously thought. With Truman, the shift was more of perspective than of new information. People forgave him for his lack of charismatic leadership and recalled that he dealt competently with an extraordinary series of crises.

Returning to the issue of measurement, the correlation between historical greatness ratings and our Overall Job Performance measure was very high. This indicates that our questionnaire and the historian polls of greatness are largely measuring the same thing, despite considerable differences in approach. Therefore, we will use the term "Presidential Success" from here on to refer to both Overall Job Performance and historians' ratings of greatness.

In sum, there appear to be two different questions we ought to ask when describing and attempting to predict presidential success: (1) Which personality traits predict Presidential Success? and (2) Which traits predict Ethics on the Job?

ELECTING THE RIGHT PRESIDENT

One role of industrial (work) psychologists is choosing the right people for the job. Personnel selection as scientific practice has existed for over a hundred years, but employers have had to decide whom to hire for thousands of years. For any job, those who hire must identify the skills, knowledge, abilities, and personality traits of successful performers.

In the past, employers and psychologists used their intuition and experience to identify "success factors." This is no longer good enough. Today, if you want to hire people with a certain trait or quality, you should show that the traits you require are truly relevant to the job. People who score high must actually perform better on the job, on the average, than those who score low. For example, we might expect good secretaries to score high on Conscientiousness and Agreeableness. These traits must be measured, usually by a personality test. Next, indicators of good performance (supervisory ratings, number of typing errors, etc.) are obtained. Finally, these two sets of data, personal qualities and measures of job success, are analyzed. If there is a sizable correlation (either positive or negative) between the trait and the measure of success on the job, then the trait can help select successful employees. In the secretary example, we might find Conscientiousness correlated .28 with performance ratings, Agreeableness, .08. Conscientiousness appears to be a useful predictor, while the role of Agreeableness is much weaker. Based on information like this, employers can hire those with the traits and qualities they need to do the job. In essence, this is a method of forecasting on-the-job performance before someone is hired.

There is already clear evidence that at least one personality trait is related to being *elected* president. Psychologist Martin Seligman found that the more optimistic candidate, as reflected by his speeches, was elected over his opponent in nineteen of twenty-three presidential elections from 1900 to 1988. Moreover, the difference in optimism between the candidates was highly correlated with the margin of victory: Highly optimistic candidates not only won, they won big. But being elected and being successful once in office are two different things.

Below, we identify which personality characteristics are related to being a better-than-average president and, as a related question, what traits relate to undesirable, immoral behavior on the job. We begin with the value of Character for predicting Presidential Success and Ethics on the Job, then move on to the Big Five dimensions along with their facet scales.

QUALITIES OF A SUCCESSFUL PRESIDENT

Previous research has shown there are some personal qualities that predict good performance in almost any job. The first of these is IQ. Smart people, other things being equal, tend to do better in almost any job that involves more than sweeping or digging. This is true of receptionists and NFL quarterbacks—and it is especially true of more complicated jobs. Although we do not have presidential IQ scores, we do have ratings of their abilities in a number of different areas.

Integrity (or character[2]) is also a reliable and strong predictor of success in most jobs. Integrity tests help identify those unlikely to miss work, steal, or abuse drugs. Integrity tests primarily measure Conscientiousness and secondarily measure Agreeableness and emotional stability (low Neuroticism). Aside from moral arguments, findings from work psychology suggest that good character should be related to performance as president. But is it?

CHARACTER AND PERSONALITY AS PREDICTORS OF PRESIDENTIAL PERFORMANCE

Character

Table 3.2 shows the correlations of Character and the Big Five personality factors with measures of performance in the Oval Office. Only correlations that are large enough to be important are shown here.[3] Character shows a moderately strong relation to Ethics on the Job ($r = .41$). It has *no* relationship to Presidential Success ($r = -.05$ with Overall Job Performance and $r = -.01$. with historians' ratings of greatness).[4] Conscientiousness shows a similar pattern. Though presidents scoring high on Character and Conscientiousness avoided illegal and unethical behavior during their presidency, there is virtually no relationship between these qualities and Presidential Success.

But were not two of our greatest presidents, Washington and Lincoln, both

TABLE 3.2
Correlations (r) of Character and the Big Five to Measures of
Success and Ethics on the Job as President

Personality Characteristic	Presidential Success	Ethics on the Job
Character		.41
Neuroticism		
Extraversion	.17	−.18
Openness to Experience	.32	.31
Agreeableness		.18
Conscientiousness		.38

NB: Near-zero ($| r | < .15$) correlations that are not shown; those over .40 are considered large; those over .20, moderate. Negative (inverse) correlations indicate that as scores on a personality facet increase, performance ratings decline, and vice versa.

high in character? Some facets of character, such as Competence and low Vulnerability, are related to success as president (Table 3.3). However, Straightforwardness is central to character, and straightforward people, on the average, make *poor* chief executives. To a lesser degree the same is true of Compliance. There are advantages and disadvantages to character that balance each other out when the issue is presidential job performance (as the low correlations cited above show).

Neuroticism

People high on Neuroticism tend to cope poorly with stress. They blame themselves or others, withdraw or give up, and often try to cope in ways that make things worse rather than better. Well-adjusted people *seem* to be a better match to this very stressful job. But Neuroticism is not related to Presidential Success or Ethics on the Job. Being anxious, depressed, angry and hostile, or self-conscious does not result in poor presidential performance—or even immoral behavior. Good presidents can be well adjusted or neurotic. In fact, as we will show below, good presidents tend to be a bit touchy. So why does the media try so hard to get a candidate to show his anger on camera?

One aspect of Neuroticism does matter a bit. Presidents who feel unnerved by stress, who feel unable to cope with problems on their own (score high on Vulnerability), are likely to be given low marks by historians. Emotionally hardy presidents, like Washington and TR, tend to do better; more Vulnerable chief executives, like Harding, do worse. They also have lower Ethics on the Job rat-

TABLE 3.3
Personality and Ability Scales that Predict Presidential Success

Scale	Correlation (r) with Presidential Success	Correlation (r) with Ethics on the Job
Assertiveness (E)	.37	
Tender-Mindedness (A)	.34	.34
Achievement Striving (C)	.32	.44
Straightforwardness (A)	−.30	.16
Activity (E)	.30	
Intellectual Brilliance*	.30	.33
Positive Emotions (E)	.29	
Openness to Values	.29	
Competence (C)	.26	.48
Openness to Feelings	.26	
Openness to Actions	.25	
Openness to Fantasy	.25	
Openness to Aesthetics	.25	.40
Spatial Ability	.23	
Excitement Seeking (E)	.21	−.20
Order (C)	−.21	
Compliance (A)	−.20	
Vulnerability (N)	−.18	−.25

*Other scales related to general intelligence were also predictive but to a lower level. They are not shown for brevity.

ings, perhaps because their dependence on others interferes with setting and enforcing ethical standards. Not surprisingly, high scores on Impulsiveness (inability to resist impulses and cravings) also lead to low Ethics on the Job. Two cases where this seemed to be the case are Kennedy and Clinton.

Extraversion

In this century, we have come to expect our presidents to have energy and charisma. This is not an entirely superficial taste. Extraversion predicts Presidential Success to a modest degree (r = .17). Unfortunately, Extraverts also receive lower scores on Ethics on the Job (r = −.18).

The most important Extraversion facet for a president is Assertiveness. In fact, it is the single best predictor of Presidential Success examined in our study (r = .37); it can be thought of as a general capacity for leadership. Those who score high on this scale have emerged as a leader at many times in their lives and naturally take charge. They also may be forceful and dominant, but are not necessarily so. Highly assertive, successful presidents include Jackson and TR; Harding and Coolidge scored low on Assertiveness and were less effective chief executives.

Assertiveness is also positively related to Ethics on the Job. Though less valuable than Assertiveness, being active (Activity), enthusiastic and optimistic (high Positive Emotions), and Excitement Seeking also contribute to success in the highest office. But high scores on Excitement Seeking entail a risk for lower Ethics on the Job—Bill Clinton being a classic case. Gregariousness is another Ethics on the Job risk factor, unrelated to Presidential Success. Clinton again scored high; a man who can easily seduce the public may do the same with interns.

Openness to Experience (and Intelligence)

This is the most important Big Five trait for predicting Presidential Success, and unlike Extraversion, it is positively related to Ethics on the Job. Openness to Experience correlated .32 with Presidential Success, and .31 with Ethics on the Job. Highly Open presidents are both effective and principled.

Successful presidents tend to be receptive to art and beauty (Openness to Aesthetics), attentive to their emotions (high Openness to Feelings), and willing to question traditional mores (Openness to Values). Though all facets of Openness anticipated success in historian polls, Openness to Ideas was the weakest predictor. Higher Ethics on the Job is foretold by greater Openness to Aesthetics and Openness to Ideas. Successful, open presidents include Jefferson and Lincoln. Those scoring low (e.g., Grant and Taft) did less well.

When interpreting the findings above, we need to remember that Openness is correlated with IQ. The ratings of intellectual abilities we collected are even more correlated to Openness scores than are scores from an IQ test. Moreover, if we first consider the ability ratings of each president, Openness does not improve our ability to predict Presidential Success. There are two other very good reasons for preferring the ability ratings. Measures of ability are well established as valid predictors of job performance in almost all jobs; Openness is not. Secondly, Openness to Values is clearly related to political positions. We aim to identify personality traits related to Presidential Success without regard to issues and politics. Therefore, we used the ability measures, not Openness, in the analyses below.

Agreeableness

Agreeableness is a highly desirable trait in a boss, neighbor, or spouse. Who does not prefer dealing with people who are caring, polite, cooperative, and honest?

But scores on Agreeableness are of little value in predicting Presidential Success. In fact, *Disagreeable* presidents do somewhat better. High scores on Agreeableness are generally not good in a president but are associated with ethical behavior in office ($r = .18$).

Although the overall Agreeableness score was of little value, several facets of this trait proved useful. Tender-Mindedness (concern for the less fortunate) was helpful in predicting both Presidential Success and Ethics on the Job. FDR and Lincoln scored high on this trait, while Buchanan and Nixon scored low. Straightforwardness and Compliance were both *inversely* related to good performance in the Oval Office—good presidents typically score *low* on these scales. Presidents who are not straightforward use a variety of tactics to persuade people and achieve their ends—LBJ and FDR being prime examples. Very low scorers are willing to trick, cajole, flatter, bully, or mislead to get their way. They are true politicians, playing the right tune to each crowd. Lastly, successful presidents are not cooperative and easily led (low Compliance). Harding was, and it was his downfall. Better-than-average chief executives tend to be stubborn, hardheaded, and ready to fight back if picked on—like TR or Wilson.

Conscientiousness

Though Conscientiousness is not a good predictor of Presidential Success, some of its facets are. Achievement Striving is one of the strongest correlates of overall success in the presidency, and Competence is also a solid predictor. Presidents who succeed set ambitious goals for themselves and move heaven and earth to meet them. TR was such a man; Grant and Harding were not. Highly rated presidents tend to have good judgment and are broadly capable—like Washington and Eisenhower. These same qualities also are highly related to Ethics on the Job—they are an unqualified asset in a president. Several other Conscientiousness facets (Self-Discipline, Dutifulness, and Deliberation) are also useful in forecasting Ethics on the Job, but not Presidential Success.

Lastly, presidents who are highly organized are generally less effective. This surprising result was also found in a previous study by psychologist Stewart McCann (1992), using Simonton's (1986) data. Tidiness (methodical, organized, thrifty versus courageous) was found characteristic of poor presidents rather than good ones. Buchanan and Coolidge, two relatively unsuccessful presidents, were very organized. Lincoln and Jackson, two great chief executives, were not. (Tables 3.3 and 3.4 summarize these results.)

TABLE 3.4

Personality and Ability Scales that Predict Ethics on the Job

Scale	Correlation (r) with Ethics on the Job
Competence (C)	.48
Science & Math Ability	.44
Achievement Striving (C)	.44
Openness to Aesthetics	.40
Tender-Mindedness (A)	.34
Intellectual Brilliance*	.33
Dutifulness (C)	.32
Self-Discipline (C)	.31
Openness to Ideas	.29
Gregariousness (E)	−.26
Vulnerability (N)	−.25
Impulsiveness (N)	−.20
Excitement Seeking (E)	−.20
Modesty (A)	.19
Music & Kinesthetic Ability	.17
Straightforwardness (A)	.16

Other scales related to general intelligence were also predictive but to a lower level. They are not shown here for brevity.

The Right Stuff

We have identified which traits are related to being a good president. However, it is one thing to say that higher Openness, for example, is related to Presidential Success. It is quite another to say that successful presidents score high on Openness relative to average Americans. They do not. As we will show below, even presidents who score above their peers on Openness still score below the U.S. average.

In this section, we show the profile of a typical successful president, showing how high or low he scores on each of the NEO traits. For this discussion, good presidents are those who scored in the upper third on our two measures of Presidential Success. They include Washington, Adams, Jefferson, Jackson, Lincoln, TR, Wilson, FDR, Truman, Eisenhower, Kennedy, and LBJ. The profile discussed next is an average of their scores. As shown in Chart 3.1, good presidents score *lower* on Character than both the average chief executive and other Americans. If this is true, why does low character not predict *good* performance in the White House? Because poor presidents also score low—about the 35th percentile (not shown). Average presidents, those who are rated in the middle third, do score

CHART 3.1

Scores of Good Presidents Compared to Scores for the Average of Presidents

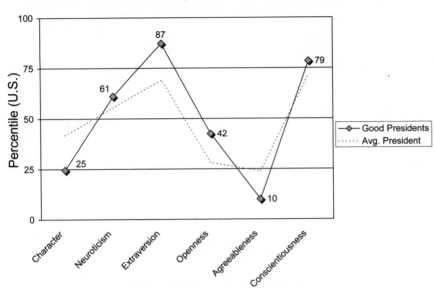

higher. A similar pattern occurs for Agreeableness. Successful presidents score higher than both average presidents and poor presidents on Extraversion and Openness to Experience.

On the Facet Scales (see Chart 3.2), a trend apparent on Chart 3.1 is reinforced: Successful presidents differ from their peers on the same traits that typical presidents differ from average Americans. Successful presidents scored above the 90th percentile of typical Americans on Assertiveness, Achievement Striving, and Openness to Feelings. They have a high Activity level (85th percentile), are sometimes irritable (Angry Hostility, 77th percentile), and act before thinking (low Deliberation, 25th percentile). Still, they are more Self-Disciplined than 75 percent of the population. Better presidents are high on Excitement Seeking and Positive Emotions—both at about the 72nd percentile (the two data points after Activity on Chart 3.2).

They are at the 6th percentile, on average, on Straightforwardness, and are not Modest (12th percentile) or Compliant (15th percentile). Lastly, one average score is important. Successful presidents are right at the average of U.S. citizens on Tender-Mindedness; poor presidents score quite low.

Many of the traits that we report as predictive of good presidential leadership

CHART 3.2
Facet Scores of Good Presidents

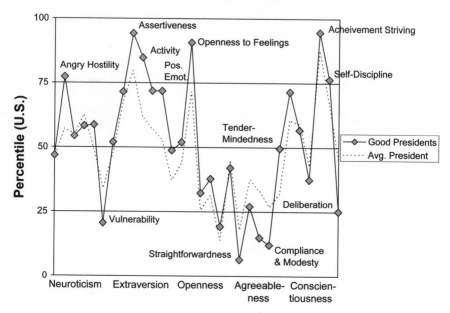

are not generally desirable. This is evidence that our raters did not indiscriminately give great presidents generally positive ratings and vice versa for poor chief executives. As you will see in coming chapters, the profiles of the three most highly rated presidents (Washington, Lincoln, and FDR) are quite different.

THE DONALD FOR PRESIDENT? THE CEO METAPHOR

Our research leads us to conclude that the most successful presidents have been ambitious, intelligent, assertive, and competent—but not necessarily straightforward or brimming with integrity. Do our top business leaders fit the same profile? Would a stellar CEO be likely to be a winning U.S. president? What about the opposite? Could a leader like Clinton slide easily into a CEO's role?

Another reason for turning to business leaders is to address basic issues concerning the validity of our conclusions. Although we asked raters to assess presidents on the five-year period of their lives before assuming office, it is possible that their knowledge of the outcome (how good of a president he turned out to be) influenced their assessment of personality. Armed with knowledge of their presidency, a rater might give higher ratings on Assertiveness and other qualities intuitively related to leadership. If so, our analysis would be circular. Lastly, the relatively small sample of forty-one individuals (George W. Bush was not included in this analysis) means that our conclusions can be made with less statistical certainty than is desirable.

Fortunately, we can compare these leadership traits to those found in a meta-analytic study[5] of successful business executives completed by Ones, Hough, and Viswesvaran. Two major differences from our study make this a powerful test of our conclusions. First, the traits were measured by self-report: Managers and CEOs completed the personality tests themselves. Secondly, most took the tests *before* they were promoted or hired. This prevents any confounding of their assessment of their personalities with how well they later performed in their jobs. This study found that successful business executives scored high in:

Assertiveness—degree of impact and influence one displays

Energy Level—degree of enthusiasm and energy

Achievement Orientation—tendency to strive for competence in one's activities.

This study was not based on the NEO, so the definitions of the variables differ a bit from those we have used throughout this book. Both Assertiveness and Achievement Orientation include elements that are not part of the NEO scales with similar names.

Though successful presidents and business leaders share some qualities, they differ in at least one way: Openness to Experience was a factor in the success of presidents. It was not a factor in determining successful business leaders.

Other differences may be more a function of roles and social space than personality. The sphere of influence is smaller and more intimate for a business leader. Not many of us meet the president of the United States, but business leaders are usually more accessible. The power base of the business leader is more likely to rest on essential individual alliances and bottom line results in a way that a U.S. president cannot afford to consider. This creates an immediate accountability that puts greater pressure on business executives to watch the integrity—not just the popularity meter. President Clinton enjoyed his highest ratings during his most troubling trials with integrity and character. For a president to have job satisfaction ratings of 60 percent is great news. For the CEO of a company, it would be a death knell.

CREATING AN INDEX TO PREDICT PRESIDENTIAL SUCCESS

Because personality traits are related to performance as president, we can quantify each president's degree of match with qualities advantageous to the job. Taking the results from above, we first eliminated traits that are redundant, taking note of those traits that have not been found useful in similar studies. Based on our findings and the scientific literature on job performance, the formula in Table 3.5 will predict Presidential Success.

Those who score high on the index[6] in Table 3.5 have the personality qualities that enable a president to be effective. Using it, we can estimate future historical greatness without waiting thirty years—or even until a president is elected. This formula is able to account for about 25 percent of the differences in performance among presidents.

How much does this help us to choose a better president? In Chart 3.3, we show the predicted Presidential Success score and the Greatness ratings for twentieth-century presidents. We use data from the Ridings and McIver historian poll because it rates all presidents up through Clinton.[7] The line for Greatness becomes dotted at LBJ to indicate that, when the surveys were conducted, thirty years had not yet passed since his presidency. Greatness ratings for him and more recent presidents are less reliable than for TR through Kennedy.

There is an extraordinarily close match between the lines from 1900 until 1970, the year beginning the time for which historical opinion is not yet settled (repre-

TABLE 3.5
Personality Predictors of Presidential Success

	Positive Indicators	Negative Indicators
Presidential Success =	Intellectually Brilliant & Smart* + Assertiveness + Achievement Striving + Competence + Activity + Positive Emotions + Tender-Mindedness	− Straightforwardness − Vulnerability

*This is a combination of two separate scales. Intellectual Brilliance was identified by Simonton. It includes statements like "interests wide," "artistic," and "inventive." We created a similar scale in our questionnaire that was completed by specialists. Smart is based on three items: "bright, intelligent, smart," "dull, ignorant, unintelligent" (reversed scored), and "seems to have a high level of intellectual capacity."

CHART 3.3
Predicted and Actual Presidential Greatness Ratings

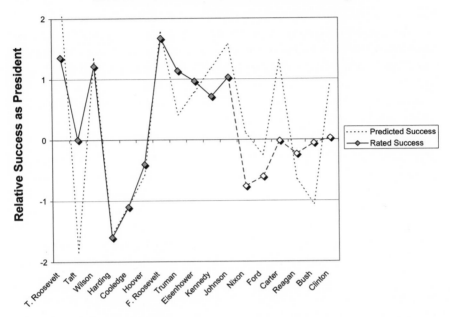

sented by a dashed line). Only Taft shows much of a gap between predicted and actual historian ratings. Matches for Wilson through FDR are truly remarkable, and the correspondence between the two lines continues to be good through Ford. After that, the ratings get mushy and float around the average—but our predictions do not. Carter and Clinton are better than average fits for the job, while Reagan and G. H. W. Bush appear less suited than the average president.

If our results hold up over the next few decades, the historical rankings of Carter and Clinton should improve, while the rankings of Reagan and especially of G. H. W. Bush should decline. However, our predictions may prove wrong. Though Carter's overall score is good, he was weak in two crucial leadership areas: Assertiveness and willingness to stretch the truth and handle people to his advantage (low Straightforwardness). Clinton's impeachment could permanently mar his reputation, despite his other assets for the job. Reagan and Bush may prove exceptions to the rule.

Correspondence between predicted and actual greatness ratings for all the presidents rated in the Ridings and McIver poll is not as impressive as shown in Chart 3.3. Few of our specialists rated many nineteenth-century presidents, so the personality ratings, and the predictions derived from them, may be less accurate. In addition, personality may have become a more potent factor in presidential performance in recent years (see below).

Table 3.6 shows the ranking of presidents in terms of personality fit for the presidency. TR stands far above the rest—he is the prototypical successful president. While in the Oval Office, he lamented that the relatively tranquil era in

TABLE 3.6
Personality Fit for Office and Actual Greatness Ranking by Historians

	Index of Personality Match	President	Actual Rank
Well-Suited	2.5	T. Roosevelt	5
	1.8	F. Roosevelt	2
	1.6	L. Johnson	12
	1.3	Wilson	6
	1.3	Carter	19
	1.2	Kennedy	15
	1.0	Van Buren	21
	0.9	Clinton	23
	0.8	Eisenhower	9
	0.7	Lincoln	1
Average	0.4	Truman	7
	0.3	Washington	3
	0.1	Jefferson	10
	0.1	Nixon	32
	−0.1	Madison	10
	−0.2	Fillmore	36
	−0.2	Jackson	8
	−0.3	Ford	27
	−0.4	J. Q. Adams	18
Poorly Suited	−0.6	Hoover	24
	−0.6	Pierce	37
	−0.7	Reagan	26
	−0.9	J. Adams	14
	−1.0	Polk	11
	−1.1	Coolidge	33
	−1.6	Harding	41
	−1.8	Taft	20
	−1.9	Grant	38

Rankings given are based on the Ridings and McIver poll. Only presidents rated by three or more raters are presented. The Index of Personality Match is reported in z-scores relative to other presidents.

which he served would relegate him to the second tier of great presidents. Lincoln, TR thought, would never be remembered had it not been for the Civil War. Our data suggest he was right on both counts.

Are good presidents one in a million? Can anybody make a good president? Because our index is based on the NEO, with norms for the U.S. population, we can estimate how rare the combination of traits in the index is. People with the personality to be an *average* president (or lower) are not rare: About one person out of three will do. However, only 4 percent of people have the combination of qualities found in better than average presidents such as Washington, Lincoln, FDR, and Truman.[8]

We do not need all nine personality traits to predict presidential performance: The following equation works almost as well as the full index:

$$\text{Presidential Success}^9 = .136(\text{Assertiveness}) + .315(\text{Achievement Striving}) - .214(\text{Straightforwardness})$$

The three traits in this equation are those on which presidents differ the most from ordinary Americans (Chapter 2). To use it, multiply the trait score by the number preceding it. Scores must be standard scores, not percentiles. Although fairly accurate overall, this index does produce some anomalous results: Nixon is now predicted to be second only to LBJ in greatness.

We are not the first to conclude personal qualities are important to the performance of a president. McCann (1992) advocated for the following equation based on Simonton's personality and physical data on the presidents:

$$\text{Presidential Success} = .42(\text{Intellectual Brilliance}) + .15(\text{Height}) - .24(\text{Attractiveness}) - .33(\text{Tidiness}) + .32(\text{Achievement Drive})$$

Height was included because it is associated with leadership. This equation suggests that successful presidents should be smart, tall, unattractive, a little messy, and achievement-oriented. Lincoln, usually rated the most successful president, fits this description perfectly.

Next, we turn to predicting Ethics on the Job. As for Presidential Success, we can create an index based on personality characteristics (see Table 3.7). The index contains all of the Facet Scales for Conscientiousness except Order. This is not too surprising; conscientious people are work-oriented, not play-oriented, and more prone to follow rules. More surprising is the contribution by scales related to intellectual and artistic interests—Openness to Aesthetics and Ideas. We do not see any compelling explanation for this finding.

TABLE 3.7

Personality Characteristics that Predict Ethics on the Job

	Positive Indicators	Negative Indicators
Ethics on the Job =	Competence + Achievement Striving + Openness to Aesthetics + Tender-Mindedness + Dutifulness + Self-Discipline + Deliberation + Openness to Ideas	− Gregariousness − Excitement Seeking − Impulsiveness − Vulnerability

WOULD GEORGE WASHINGTON MAKE IT TODAY?

The presidency as a job has evolved over the years and is now quite different than it was two hundred years ago. Historians refer to the "modern presidency," meaning those presidents from TR onward. Certainly, the Executive Branch has grown tremendously in size. Before 1857, presidents paid for their own personal secretaries. Now, the Executive Office of the President employs 1,600 people directly, and tens of thousands more indirectly. Mass media make it possible for the president to speak directly to billions of people at once. Given the many changes in the office and the country since 1789, we wondered if the same personality traits are related to success for twentieth-century presidents as for the whole group.

For the most part, they are, but three traits are especially important for modern presidents: (1) Extraversion; (2) lack of Vulnerability; and (3) Competence. As we showed in the last chapter, modern presidents are more Extraverted, perhaps due to the changing nature of politics and communications since the eighteenth century. Back then, it was considered unseemly to seek the office, and candidates were expected to sit back and let others sing their virtues. Now, candidates make an exhausting number of appearances, seeking to connect with a wide variety of people. The office is also much "bigger" now, with greater responsibility and demands. Surrounded by increasing numbers of persuasive and able people, some of whom have neither the president's nor the country's best interests at heart, the job increasingly requires a self-possessed, emotionally hardy person with sound judgment.

So, how would Washington do as president today? Our analysis suggests he would perform adequately, but not with distinction. His competence, ability to tolerate stress, and willingness to sacrifice in pursuit of his goals are even more relevant today than in 1789. But his relative lack of optimism and cheerfulness would probably limit his effectiveness and might prevent him from getting elected in the first place.

HOW SUCCESSFUL PRESIDENTS ACT

Forty-nine of the items in our questionnaire asked specifically about a president's personality and behavior while in office apart from how well he performed particular tasks. We correlated these items with historians' ratings of presidential greatness. Based on these analyses, a successful president tends to:

✔ be innovative in his role as an executive
✔ be characterized by others as a world figure
✔ initiate new legislation and programs

An unsuccessful president tends to:

✔ be a middle-of-the-roader
✔ support constitutional government
✔ be cautious, conservative in action

There were a couple of surprises here. Eminent historian and biographer Robert Dallek proposed half a dozen qualities that he argued were related to presidential success. Among them was "recognizes need to build a consensus." Our data suggest he got this wrong—successful presidents get out in front on an issue. They rated low on Dallek's factor.

Similarly, "supports constitutional government"[10] would *seem* to be an asset. The reason it is not is clear when we look at the other descriptions: Successful presidents either bend the rules or claim new prerogatives. They assume power not clearly designated to them and enlarge the office in the process. TR once asked if there was any law to keep him from declaring a tract of land as a federal bird sanctuary. Told there was not, he stated, "I so declare it." Unsuccessful presidents seem bound by tradition or other's expectations.

These trends are even stronger for modern presidents; being "cautious and conservative in action" now is virtually synonymous with a failed presidency. This item correlated − .70 with historian ratings for TR through Clinton, and − .92 when we omitted presidents of the past thirty years, whose historical ratings are not yet set. Does this mean a good president should be rash? A number of good ones, including Jackson and TR, were. But, it seems that an *absence* of unnecessary caution or inhibition is important in a modern leader, not rash behavior, per se.

Other qualities also came into play in recent administrations. Successful modern presidents "show artistry in manipulation." FDR is a prime example, while

Coolidge and Carter provide examples where this quality was lacking. "Tricky Dick" and "Slick Willie" may lack standing as moral leaders, but their tactics seem part of a successful presidency.

Do these findings mean that anyone, regardless of their true personality, would be successful in the White House if they only acted Machiavellian? Probably not. It is hard to act out of character for long—Al Gore's attempts to seem less stiff were hardly more successful than Nixon's. Someone who suddenly begins to act boldly, after a lifetime of caution, is not likely to be very good at it.

BUT WAIT . . .

We have examined the relation of personality traits and abilities to historians' assessments of greatness. But what if the historians are, as a group, systematically biased? Some have claimed that they tend to be liberal in orientation, which could result in more favorable assessments of like-minded presidents and harsh appraisals of conservatives. There is some indirect evidence of this: Democrats tend to be rated higher than Republicans. There is also some data from our study: Two NEO Facets Scales, Tender-Mindedness and Openness to Values, clearly reflect liberal versus conservative issues. Both had substantial correlations with historian ratings of greatness, and neither have been found related to job performance in other studies of executives or managers. Openness to Values is not included in our prediction index (ratings of IQ make it and other Openness scales redundant), but Tender-Mindedness is. Whether it should be is a matter for future research. Despite the issues raised, it should be noted that Murray and Blessing, who conducted one of the major polls of presidential performance, concluded that conservative and liberal historians show considerable agreement in their ratings.

CONCLUSION

Elections already are influenced by the personality of candidates. Those perceived as optimistic are more likely to be elected. But Optimism is only one of the traits needed to be a good leader, and not one of the most important. Our study indicates the most important personal qualities are Assertiveness, Achievement Striving, and low Straightforwardness. There is some evidence that Extraversion, resilience to stress (low Vulnerability), and Competence are increasingly important for modern presidents.

Clinton's former adviser, Dick Morris, argued that voters elect a president to accomplish a set of goals and that character has become irrelevant. Our conclusion is that regardless of a candidate's agenda, certain personality traits make it more or less likely he will be successful in seeing goals through to completion. Few things happen easily in government. A president who lacks leadership, salesmanship, and the ability to wholeheartedly pursue goals will likely accomplish little. Though one can perform contrary to his or her personality for a while, an introvert will likely continue to find it very hard to make cold sales calls day after day. Successful presidents, not surprisingly, have shown a pattern of leadership, achievement, and flexible persuasive tactics over the course of their lives.

CHAPTER 4

Types of Presidents

I
N THIS CHAPTER, we group the presidents according to similarities in their personalities. Personality typologies for presidents are not new; over thirty years ago, Barber proposed one that is still widely used. He argued in *The Presidential Character* that presidents might be grouped according to two psychological dimensions: activity versus passivity and positive versus negative emotional tone. According to Barber, a president who is active and enjoys his work (positive emotional tone) would be most successful and least prone to emotional disturbance in office—FDR would be the modern exemplar. This approach is simple and intuitive and does not change with new presidents, but it does have some limitations. Barber did not formally measure the traits used to assign presidents to a type; he relied solely on his own judgment. Even more limiting, he used only two personality dimensions to compare presidents.

Our approach was very different. Instead of beginning with theoretical dimensions and fitting presidents into preset categories, we allowed the presidents to define the categories. Our rationale for grouping was simple: We calculated the scores for each president (up to 1997) on 592 personality and ability items,[1] averaging across all the raters for that president. We then correlated the results with the scores of all the other presidents on the same items. Those two presidents who were most similar (i.e., correlated highest over all items) formed the kernel of each type. Other presidents were added to the type if they were more similar to presidents in that type than to presidents not in it. This process was repeated to identify other types, starting with another kernel of two presidents not in the first type who correlated highly with each other. (Appendix A offers more detail.)

This kind of typology depends on the individuals in the sample and some clear procedural rules, rather than the insights or whims of some judge. It can be replicated by others and can be expected to change as new presidents are added. For this reason, as well as because some presidents were assessed by only one rater, we present our findings as a work in progress, with full knowledge that modifications may be required in the future.

When we group multifaceted people together, it is wise to remember the adage, "All generalities are false, including this one." All typologies are false, including this one, but they still can be useful. The men we profile in each of our eight types share many features; they may differ on nearly as many. Yet, the typology itself may be (as Picasso said of art) "the lie that tells us the truth." By providing a set of landmarks to guide our understanding of the presidents included, it can have lasting value even as we acknowledge that it is, by itself, a changing shadow of reality.

THE DOMINATORS

The first group of presidents clusters around two of the most similar men in our analysis, Richard Nixon and Lyndon Johnson. Other presidents were added to the group in order of their similarity to the first two. The Dominators include, after LBJ and Nixon, Andrew Johnson, Jackson, Polk, TR, and Arthur. Van Buren is a possible addition, but not a member of the core group.

Most of these men had the reputation of being someone to be reckoned with. As Andrew Jackson approached death, it is said someone asked one of his slaves if the master would make it into heaven. "If General Jackson takes it into his head to git to heaven," he responded, "who's gwine to keep him out?" TR was known as "a steam engine in trousers." Nixon used the IRS and FBI to intimidate political enemies. LBJ kept Mac Wallace, a convicted murderer, on his payroll and was rumored to have had his enemies killed.[2]

The average profile of a Dominator president is presented in Chart 4.1.[3] Compared to most Americans, as well as most presidents (gray, dashed line), he was very Disagreeable (0.7th percentile), low on Character (2nd), and not Open to Experience (13th). Every single Dominator was low on Agreeableness and Character, while they demonstrated a very wide range on Extraversion. Still, they averaged at the 85th percentile on Extraversion, 84th on Neuroticism, and 74th on Conscientiousness.

On the fine-grain NEO Facet Scales, the average Dominator scored as shown below. All of these scores are significantly different from those of average Americans. Moreover, *every* president in this group scored in the direction indicated (high or low).

Compared to average Americans, Dominators were very dominant and assert-

CHART 4.1

Average Scores of Dominators on Character and the Big Five Traits

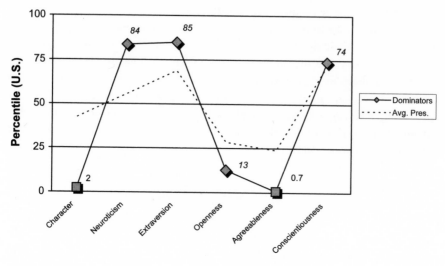

High	Percentile	Low	Percentile
Assertiveness (E)	96	Straightforwardness (A, Ch)	1.0
Angry Hostility (N, -Ch)	95	Compliance (A, Ch)	3
Achievement Striving (C)	94	Modesty (A, Ch)	3
		Openness to Values (O)	6
		Altruism (E, Ch)	7

ive (high Assertiveness), temperamental (high Angry Hostility), and willing to use indirect or forceful tactics to influence others (very low Straightforwardness). They did not cooperate with others (low Compliance) and were not modest or humble (low Modesty). They worked hard to achieve their goals (Achievement Striving), were traditional in their values (low Openness to Values), and were not generous or selfless (low Altruism). On all the scales in the table that contribute to character (Angry Hostility, Straightforwardness, Compliance, Modesty, Altruism), they scored in the direction of low character.

Compared to other presidents, Dominators also scored low on indicators of religious devotion and conservatism. On the individual items of our questionnaire, they were described as prone to bully others and to disregard the feelings and rights of those not on their side.[4] They were bossy, demanding, and domineering; they flattered or manipulated people to get their way. They bent or broke rules, and as presidents, stretched the constraints of constitutional government. They were not religious or spiritual, and tended to be prejudiced. They preferred being praised to complimenting others and were seen as self-centered and egotistical. They were not considerate, sympathetic, or even-tempered, and not prone to forgive and forget. They were impatient in conferences, and easily got disgusted with people.

As a group, historians rate Dominators as average presidents, but the spread is wide. Jackson, LBJ, TR, and Polk are all regarded as clearly successful presidents, while Andrew Johnson and Nixon received low marks. Most of the qualities that distinguish Dominators (bossiness, low Straightforwardness), even though undesirable, are related to positive performance as president. The exception is their low score on Openness to Values.

In Chapter 5, we profile Jackson, LBJ, and Nixon in depth. TR, another prominent Dominator, is profiled in Chapter 12 as an Extravert, where he fits slightly better.

THE INTROVERTS

The Introvert presidents are John Adams and his son, John Quincy Adams, Nixon, Hoover, Coolidge, Buchanan, Wilson, and Benjamin Harrison (in order of inclusion). Evidence of social withdrawal or aloofness is not hard to find in the anecdotes, quotes, and details of their lives. John Quincy Adams described himself as "a man of reserved, cold, austere, forbidding manners." "Silent Cal" Coolidge was aptly named. Alice Roosevelt, TR's irrepressible daughter, observed that Coolidge looked like he had been weaned on a pickle. It was said that Benjamin Harrison's handshake felt like a wilted petunia and that he could make an enemy in granting a favor, while McKinley could make a friend in denying one.

But reserve sometimes went with more desirable traits. With Coolidge, it was his wry wit. A society woman once approached him and introduced herself by saying that she had bet that she could get more than two words out of him. "You lose," he replied. With Hoover, the gift was for modesty. When political backers wanted to publicize his rescue of a child in China, he tore up the article and told them, "You can't make a Teddy Roosevelt out of me."[5]

Their choice of leisure activities also reflected Introversion. John Adams regretted in old age that he did not have time to learn Chinese and Sanskrit so he could read ancient texts in their original language. Nixon's latter years were spent writing scholarly analyses of foreign affairs. With Hoover and Coolidge, it was trout fishing; Hoover even had part of the Rapidan River rebuilt and restricted for his solitary use while president. Others had no interests outside politics. Each seemed to enjoy silence, solitude, and his own company more than that of others.

Introverts are clearly distinct as a group from other presidents by their low score (7th percentile) on Extraversion. Compared to average Americans they stood out even more by their high scores on Conscientiousness (96th). They also scored high on Neuroticism (87th) and low on Agreeableness (12th). Every single Introvert was very high on Conscientiousness, yet their average score on Character was only 34th—in part because of the very low score of Nixon.

On the NEO Facet Scales, Introverts received the following average scores compared to current-day Americans, and *all* scored in the direction (high or low) shown below.

Introverts were distinguished most from other presidents by their low scores

High	*Percentile*	*Low*	*Percentile*
Achievement Striving (C)	97	Warmth (E)	3
Angry Hostility (N, -Ch)	90	Openness to Values (O)	3
		Altruism (A, Ch)	10

CHART 4.2

Average Scores of Introverts on Character and the Big Five Traits

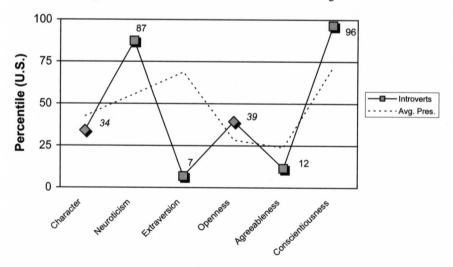

on Warmth, Gregariousness, Positive Emotions, and Agreeableness and by their high scores on Neuroticism, Conscientiousness, and Simonton's Moderation scale.

The items show that these presidents were psychologically minded, complex, deep men. They were not regarded as warm and friendly, and had difficulty controlling social situations. They preferred to work alone and avoided close relationships. Often jittery or tense, they were not happy or high-spirited; they tended to overreact and to feel irritable and overwhelmed by stress. They were inhibited and restrained and were often self-conscious; most people did not like them.[6]

On average Introverts made below average presidents. Their performance was hampered by their lack of enthusiasm (Positive Emotions), restraint, moral conservatism (Low Openness to Values), and vulnerability to stress. In Chapter 6 we profile the Introverts John Adams and Woodrow Wilson.

THE GOOD GUYS

The Good Guys include Hayes, Taylor, Eisenhower, Tyler, Fillmore, Cleveland, Ford, and Washington (in order of inclusion). Ford was known as "Mr. Nice Guy." Eisenhower's campaign slogan ("I like Ike") was perhaps the only one in U.S. history to trumpet the candidate's affability. Fillmore was heartily liked by the citizens of his native Buffalo. The saying, "If Millard Fillmore says it's true, it must be," became a local homily. Cleveland's attitude toward office was summarized in his campaign slogan: "A public office is a public trust." He was so trustworthy that he was described as "ugly honest." He nonetheless spent much of his free time, before becoming president, drinking beer and singing songs in pubs. When accused of fathering an illegitimate child in a potentially devastating scandal, he quietly paid child support and instructed his staff: "Above all, tell the truth."

As can be seen in Chart 4.3, Good Guys as a group are high on Character (87th percentile) and Conscientiousness (86th), low on Neuroticism (22nd) and Openness (31st), and higher than most presidents on Agreeableness (53rd). Every single Good Guy president was both low on Neuroticism and high on Conscientiousness.

On the NEO Facet Scales, Good Guys received average scores as indicated below. They were distinguished from other presidents by their high score on Conscientiousness and measures of character, and by their low scores on Neuroticism and its facets, particularly Depression, Vulnerability, and Anxiety. They

CHART 4.3
Average Scores of Good Guys on Character and the Big Five Traits

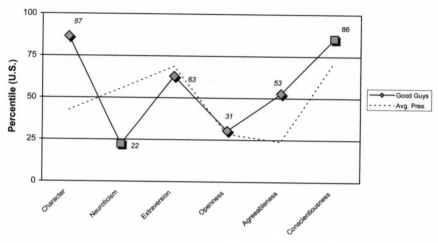

scored considerably higher than most presidents on Straightforwardness. They almost never felt themselves to be worthless, were rarely jittery or tense, and did not feel overwhelmed by stress. They made good decisions even under adversity. They had a hard time lying, were not crafty or sly, and did not trick, bully, or flatter people to get their way. They did not spend much time fantasizing and daydreaming, nor did they deny unpleasant thoughts, perceptions, or feelings by pretending they did not exist. They were able to visualize alternatives and weigh the long-term consequences of their choices.

High	Percentile	Low	Percentile
Achievement Striving (C)	89	Anxiety (N)	8
Self-Discipline (C, Ch)	89	Depression (N)	14
		Vulnerability (N, -Ch)	14

Good Guys made, on average, average presidents. They selected their advisers for their competence and encouraged independent judgment by their aides. They generally were distinguished for the quality (not quantity) of their work. Two, Washington and Eisenhower, were highly rated. The rest are mostly footnotes in history. They were the highest-scoring group on most measures of character, and they were less prone than most to scandal in office. Their strengths included resilience to stress and high Achievement Striving, but their high score on Straightforwardness can be a liability as president.

In Chapter 7 we profile two prominent Good Guys, Eisenhower and Ford. Washington is presented as a special case in Chapter 13 because of his prominence and marginal status as a Good Guy.

THE INNOCENTS

This group contains two of the lowest-rated presidents in most polls, Harding and Grant, though Taft is the central member. Each man was somewhat overwhelmed in office by the forces or people around him. Grant's administration was the most corrupt until that time, although Grant himself was honest. Harding was picked by business interests to avoid another activist administration like TR's or Wilson's. Though not intellectually limited, Taft was clearly not the man to be following in the footsteps of TR, an indomitable crusader for reform. Like Harding, he was a modest and generous man who disliked conflict and had no strong agenda of his own. When TR returned from a safari and denounced his successor, Taft tearfully responded, "I don't know how I could've done any better."

Innocents were distinguished by high scores on Extraversion (93rd percentile), although this was driven by Harding and not shared by Grant and Taft. They scored low scores on Openness (3rd) and Conscientiousness (17th) on Chart 4.4. They were more Agreeable (58th) than most presidents, though only slightly more so than average Americans. They were about average on Character (46th) and Neuroticism (44th).

On the NEO Facet Scales, there are only two scales where the Innocents are notably different from Americans today. Innocents scored low on measures of creativity, achievement drive, assertiveness, and wit. They were submissive, accepted domination easily, and were "gullible, naive, suggestible." Not autonomous, independent or individualistic, they sometimes did not assert themselves when they should have.

Compared to other presidents (who were an industrious lot), they had trouble getting motivated and down to work, and were lethargic, sluggish, lazy, and slothful. Innocents did not work hard to achieve their goals, gave up when things went wrong, and were relatively unambitious and aimless. They were not curious or inquisitive, were not "impressive, remarkable," and were perceived as "aver-

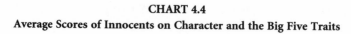

CHART 4.4

Average Scores of Innocents on Character and the Big Five Traits

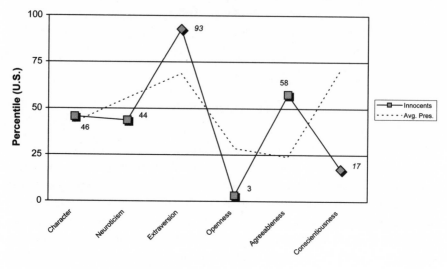

High	Percentile	Low	Percentile
None		Openness to Ideas	4
		Tender-Mindedness (A)	4

age" men. They did not set high standards for themselves or their work, sometimes felt totally worthless, and had difficulty resisting temptation.

As presidents, Innocents did not keep themselves well informed by reading briefings or background reports. They were not innovative executives, lacked a vision of what they wanted to accomplish, and did not view the presidency as their own. They were middle-of-the-road politically, allowed cabinet members much independence, and lacked energy and determination.

Innocents were the least successful type of president, with two clear failures (Grant and Harding) and one middling performer (Taft). Almost all that distinguished them from other presidents, or from average Americans, was a weakness for high office. Although Taft is the best example of this type, we profile Grant because he was one of the few presidents from the late nineteenth century for whom we have sufficient data and because he was also a great Civil War general. Warren Harding is profiled elsewhere as an Actor, where he is a core member.

THE ACTORS

The Actors group includes Reagan, Harding, William Henry Harrison, Clinton, and Pierce (in order). Reagan, of course, was the only professional performer, but each warrants the label Actor for one reason or another. Harding, the key president in this group, never wanted the job and reported it was beyond him; still, he looked the part. Harrison was the first president around whom a modern campaign was organized: Bands, campaign songs, and log cabins celebrated his supposed humble, backwoods origins. In fact, he grew up in a mansion.

All Actors scored high on Extraversion (98th percentile), and all but Pierce were low on Conscientiousness (16th). Actors also scored below most Americans on Character (26th), Neuroticism (39th), Openness (31st), and Agreeableness (40th). Their average profile is shown in Chart 4.5. On the NEO facets, Actors averaged as shown in the table on page 70.

Compared to other presidents, the Actors scored low on Conscientiousness and Achievement Striving, but high on Extraversion, Agreeableness, Warmth, and Gregariousness. Even on the Facet Scales, it is difficult to tell Actors and Extraverts apart, though the latter scored lower on Vulnerability. But the items, presented below, tell a different story.

CHART 4.5
Average Scores of Actors on Character and the Big Five Traits

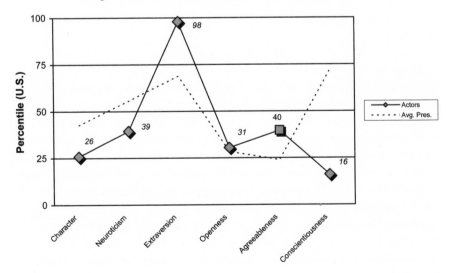

High	Percentile	Low	Percentile
Gregariousness (E)	96	Dutifulness (C, Ch)	11
Excitement Seeking (E)	86	Deliberation (C, Ch)	15
Openness to Feelings (O)	84	Straightforwardness (A, Ch)	15

Actors were gullible, naive, suggestible, warm, and self-disclosing; they allowed their feelings to show on their faces and in their posture. They were not meticulous, perfectionistic, or precise; they tended to waste time before getting to work and to tolerate unethical behavior in colleagues. Actors were enthusiastic, spirited, vivacious, zestful, charismatic, and charming. They were described as handsome, outgoing, and friendly toward strangers; they had poise and presence and were at ease around people. Extraverted, optimistic, gregarious, and sociable, they were trusting of others and enjoyed big parties. They were rarely bored at social functions. Aside from sociability, they were distinguished by the enjoyment they take in developing elaborate daydreams and fantasies. They did not resist temptation easily and were uninhibited and unrestrained.

As a group, they were the second least successful type of president. Their low score on Achievement Striving, relative to other presidents, was their primary liability. They were high on two other traits with implications for their job performance. Excitement Seeking is a positive trait for overall presidential success, but both it and Gregariousness lead to more ethical problems on the job. In Chapter 9 we profile two of the Actors with quite different reputations: Harding and Reagan.

THE MAINTAINERS

The Maintainers include McKinley, George H. W. Bush, Ford, and Truman (in order). Three of these men followed a more prominent president, and McKinley preceded one. As can be seen in Chart 4.6, their distinguishing feature is a very low score on Openness (5th percentile) and fairly high scores on Extraversion (83rd), Conscientiousness (70th), and Character (68th).

Relative to other presidents, Maintainers scored lower on Openness to Experience, Fantasy, Actions, and Ideas. Maintainers also scored high on the Interpersonal (egalitarian, interactive) style of leadership and below average on Intellectual Brilliance. On the NEO facets, they had average scores as shown in the table on page 71.

As regards items, Maintainers stayed focused on the job, worked slowly but

CHART 4.6
Average Scores of Maintainers on Character and the Big Five Traits

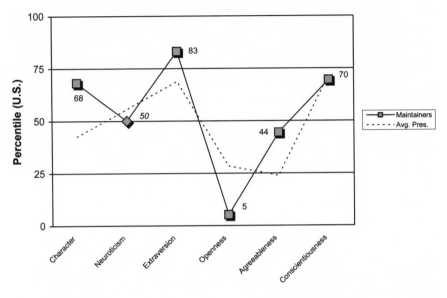

High	Percentile	Low	Percentile
Achievement Striving (C)	89	Openness to Ideas	6
		Openness to Values	10
		Openness to Fantasy	11

steadily, and were "industrious, persistent, tenacious, thorough." They were "uncreative, unimaginative," and did not indulge in elaborate daydreams and fantasies. They were conforming and conventional, not rebellious. Few people considered them cold or calculating, self-centered or egotistical.

None have been complex or deep or have liked to ponder abstract ideas or puzzles. They think in conventional ways and do not have many interests. They have difficulty grasping new ideas and problems and do not express their thoughts well. When traveling to a familiar place, they usually take the same route, and do not like to try foreign foods. They did not steal and were dependable, reliable, and responsible. They did not perceive sexual opportunities in situations, practice restraint, and were less likely than most presidents to have extramarital affairs. They trusted religious authority on moral issues.

Maintainers did not become disgusted with people around them and were not frustrated by minor problems. They worried less than other presidents, and rarely felt deeply guilty, sinful, or dejected; they rarely compared themselves to others. As presidents, they emphasized teamwork; deciding among options formulated by advisers. They were appreciated by their staffs for their consideration and courtesy and for their willingness to give credit to others.

Maintainers, as a group, made moderately successful presidents. Though overly conservative and not philosophical, they were hardworking (Achievement Striving) and more versatile in their persuasion (low Straightforwardness) than the Good Guys, who they closely resembled. They were more Extraverted than the average president, which is also a positive factor. In Chapter 10, we profile two Maintainers, Truman and George H. W. Bush.

THE PHILOSOPHES

The term *Philosophe* (fill-a-sawf') originally referred to any of the leading political, philosophical, and social writers of the eighteenth-century French Enlightenment. This movement emphasized the use of reason to scrutinize previously accepted doctrines and traditions. This led to many advances of benefit to mankind, including government "of the people, by the people, and for the people," to quote Lincoln, one of the Philosophe presidents. The Philosophe presidents are Garfield, Lincoln, Jefferson, Madison, Carter, and Hayes (in order of inclusion).

Jefferson and Madison were two of the best-educated men of their time and became the intellectual fathers of their country. Lincoln had little formal education, but he read and had a clever and creative mind as well as a profound wisdom. When Ohio congressman James Garfield, following Lincoln's assassination, intercepted an angry crowd headed toward the anti-Lincoln *New York World*, he addressed them: "Fellow citizens! God reigns, and the government at Washington still lives!" His words transfixed the crowd and were described as more potent than Napoléon's guns at Paris. Carter was known to be bright and intellectual, in an engineer's sort of way, but he also has a broad appreciation of art and music, and of course, spiritual issues.

The profile of the average Philosophe president is presented in Chart 4.7. They were distinguished by their high scores on Openness to Experience (87th percentile) and Character (85th), where every Philosophe scored above average. Their average score on Conscientiousness was also high (86th), although there was

CHART 4.7

Average Scores of Philosophes on Character and the Big Five Traits

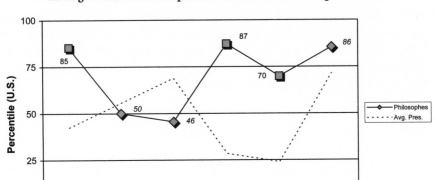

considerable variability among them. Their score on Agreeableness (70th) was the highest of all the types.

Only a few NEO Facet Scores distinguish the Philosophes from modern Americans:

High	Percentile	Low	Percentile
Achievement Striving	92	Impulsiveness	14
Openness to Ideas	84		

Compared to other presidents, Philosophes were curious and inquisitive, interested in science, and fascinated by patterns in nature and art. They were concerned with philosophical issues (e.g., religion, the meaning of life), had many interests, and enjoyed solving brain-twister puzzles. They saw themselves as broad-minded and believed that students should be exposed to new ideas and controversial speakers. Despite being analytical, logical, and good at math, they valued art and beauty and were attentive to the moods of different settings. They were also "nice" people: They believed that everyone is deserving of respect and preferred complimenting others to being praised themselves. They were not hardheaded or tough-minded and did not have emotional outbursts.

Philosophes were the most successful type of president, with the average scoring at the 68th percentile. Their strengths were in intelligence and most facets of Openness. Their high scores on Character also suggest that they were less prone to scandal while in office. In Chapter 11, we profile three of the Philosophes, Lincoln, Jefferson, and Carter. The first two are among the most revered of presidents, while Carter is probably the most respected ex-president, despite the less successful reputation of his administration.

THE EXTRAVERTS

The Extravert cluster includes nearly all the colorful personalities among the chief executives, even some that are also classified in other clusters. FDR and Kennedy form the kernel of this cluster, and are followed by Clinton, TR, Reagan, William Henry Harrison, Harding, Jackson, and LBJ (in order of inclusion). FDR was renowned for the optimism and ebullience he brought to the job as well as for his resonant and confident voice. Kennedy partied with stars and prostitutes, while Clinton stands out for his love of crowds and his seeming desire to sample all life has to offer—from Renaissance Weekends with intellectuals to family and fatherhood to an occasional young intern. Harding's favorite pastime was "bloviating"—hanging around people and talking. Jackson was distinguished as a young man by the amount of trouble and mischief he got into. LBJ and TR were exceptional in their dominance, energy, and excesses. TR once climbed a mountain all day and then stayed up all night talking about it. LBJ would routinely work until late into the night and forced his staff to do so too.

Extraverts, obviously, were distinguished by their extremely high score on Extraversion (99.6th percentile). They also scored moderately low on Character (17th), Neuroticism (40th), Agreeableness (9th), and Conscientiousness (24th). They were very similar to Actors, differing only on Agreeableness; the Actors scored near the U.S. average and the Extraverts well below it. Compared to current-day Americans, Extraverts were distinguished by scores on the NEO Facet Scales following on page 75.

Compared to other presidents, Extraverts scored low on Conscientiousness, measures of Character, and Deliberation, but high on Friendliness (outgoing, cheerful, charming), Extraversion, and Gregariousness. Extraverted presidents were enthusiastic, spirited, vivacious, and zestful; they called attention to themselves. They were "impetuous, uninhibited, unrestrained" and "demonstrative, exhibitionistic, flamboyant." They were not consistent, predictable, or steady, or "careful, cautious." They indulged their impulses and showed their feelings

CHART 4.8

Average Scores of Extraverted Presidents on Character and the Big Five Traits

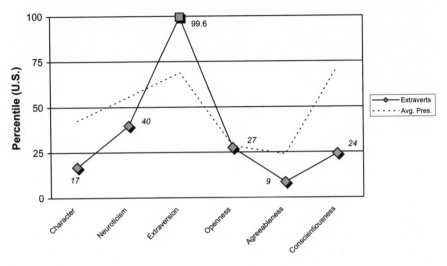

High	Percentile	Low	Percentile
Gregariousness (E)	94	Straightforwardness (A, Ch)	2
Excitement Seeking (E)	93	Deliberation (C, Ch)	6
Openness to Feelings	92	Modesty (A, Ch)	6
Impulsivity (N, -Ch)	91		
Activity (E)	89		

through their faces and body language. They did things extemporaneously and had a flair for the dramatic, but were not dependable and responsible. They did not take pride in being rational or objective, did not plan carefully before taking a trip, made decisions prematurely, and acted without thinking.

Extraverts were the second most successful type of president. Their Extraversion, Activity level, and low Straightforwardness were their prime assets. Low scores on Character, Conscientiousness, and Deliberateness, and high scores on Impulsiveness and Excitement Seeking, predisposed them to Ethics on the Job problems.

In Chapter 12, Theodore and Franklin Roosevelt are profiled, as is JFK. Clinton is presented in Chapter 13 as a special case.

Personality Portraits of U.S. Presidents

I N THIS SECTION, we present descriptions of individual presidents based on our data. The following chapters profile presidents for each of the eight personality types, one to three presidents in each type. Biography, anecdotes, observations, and quotations drawn from other sources illustrate and give context to our findings. They are not part of our data.

Each chapter begins with a summary noting similarities of the men featured, based on our data and Simonton's. Each presidential personality portrait starts with a brief biography emphasizing the man's personality and development, created from standard sources such as respected biographies. Next, we present our findings. First, we profile the scores of the featured president on Character and the Big Five personality factors, comparing these scores to the presidents' average. This provides a concise overview to the man's personality. Charts accompanying this personality data indicate a wide range of opinion with a diamond and a value shown in italics; scores where higher levels of agreement were present are denoted with a square and a data label in normal font. Next, a table details which specific traits from the NEO were most descriptive of that president. Scores are given in terms of percentiles relative to Americans today. In these tables, those scale names and scores in italics indicate significant differences among raters. Then, we identify traits where that president scored very high or low compared to other presidents on our scales or Simonton's. These are expressed as rankings, which are subject to change over time. Unlike Chapter 2, they are based on all presidents (except George W. Bush), even those rated by less than three raters.

A narrative personality portrait, based on the exact items/descriptions (e.g., "He is warm and friendly to strangers.") that our experts endorsed, follows the rankings. The items are paraphrased to maintain the security of the tests and to avoid repetition. Because raters assigned a rating to each item (1 = "very untrue"; 9 = "very true"), each item has a score just as if it were a personality scale. In our personality portrait, we use only items where the president scored in the upper or lower 15 percent of presidents and on which the raters generally agreed among themselves. If only three specialists rated the president being pro-filed, a final, stringent criterion was invoked: In addition to meeting the other conditions, *all* three raters had to have agreed that the president was clearly high or low (in the upper or lower third of all presidents) on that item. These inter-pretive rules are more formally described in Appendix B.

Unlike the personality scores we reported earlier, the standard of comparison for the narrative is other presidents—not typical Americans. This is because we know how each of the presidents scored on the items but do not have similar data on a representative group of average Americans. As we saw in Chapter 2, presidents do score higher on Achievement Striving and Assertiveness and lower on Straightforwardness, but most of their other scores are not very different from average Americans. Still, it is likely the personality portraits would contain more descriptions about being ambitious, dominant, and willing to bend the truth if norms for typical Americans were available.

We start each personality portrait with the item/description that received the highest or lowest rating compared to other presidents. A long item ("enjoys focusing on his daydreams, letting each one develop in its own way") may form its own sentence, but more often descriptions from several items will be com-bined to form a compound sentence. Once a personality trait is described, we list items describing similar traits (e.g., "is imaginative and dreamy") before moving on to another theme. Items with the most extreme scores are presented first: This ordering holds true for the overall description, paragraphs, and indi-vidual sentences. In other words, the items that were judged most distinct and accurate are presented first.

We indicate how extreme the rating score is by use of modifiers such as "exceedingly," "exceptionally," "clearly," listed in descending order of magni-tude: Extreme descriptors indicate an extreme score. We also had to deal with items that are phrased in the negative, such as "he is not warm and friendly." If this phrase is used in our description, it means that he was rated in the *lower* 15 percent of presidents on this item—not merely that he was not rated highly. We could reverse the wording of such items, but this might be misleading, since an-tonyms are not always psychological opposites. We indicate the relative magnitude of the "not" ("didn't," "wasn't," etc.) by adding emphasis through *italics*, capitalizing ("NOT"), or a modifier (e.g., "decidedly" not). For truly low scores, combinations ("clearly NOT," "certainly *wasn't*") or more extreme modifiers (e.g., "not at all") are used. Table II.1 specifies these rules in detail.

In some cases, we simply amplified the word in the original statement rather than adding a modifier. For example, we might change "liked" to "loved," or "good" to "great."

Lastly, we emphasize that our personality portraits are not facts and they are *not* our interpretations as psychologists. When psychologists conduct evaluations in a clinical context, with few exceptions they must interview the person. That was not possible for the majority of our subjects and our goal is not a clinical assessment but a research project involving public, historical figures. The portraits reflect the opinions of our raters, relative to the opinions of raters of other presidents. For example, relative to most presidents, Andrew Jackson was rated high on the item "Steals." Based on our limited study of his life, we cannot cite one single thing he ever stole. Presumably, our experts could. The point is our evidence is different than that typically relied on by historians, biographers, or journalists, but very similar to polls of presidential greatness. Further, we do not presume that family members, or the subject himself, would necessarily agree

TABLE II.1
Modifiers Used to Show Level of Item Scores

High Scores	*Low Scores*
>99.9th percentile	<0.1th percentile
exceedingly, extraordinarily, *extreme*	*not at all, definitely not, clearly not*
99th to 99.9th percentile	0.1th to 1st percentile
exceptionally, remarkably, extremely, was exceptional, exceptionally able, to a remarkable degree, much more than most people, much more than most presidents, very much	not at all, by no means, definitely NOT/*didn't*, decidedly NOT/*didn't*, NOT, clearly *not/didn't*, etc.
95th to 99th percentile	1st to 5th percentile
every, markedly, highly, decidedly, particularly, clearly, unmistakably unusually, plainly, deservedly, particularly prone to, highly prone, to a marked degree, was clearly, much given, undeniably	NOT, *not, didn't*, decidedly *not*, clearly unable, *un*able, clearly didn't, certainly didn't, clearly not, certainly did not

with the descriptions provided. Richard Nixon, for example, might have been a very different person as a father than he was as a politician. Our profiles reflect the opinions of biographers when asked to rate the person, with little direction about what area of his life to count most. We did not have benefit of the president's self-appraisal nor input from family members and close friends, except as reflected in the materials reviewed by our raters.

After the presentation of our data-based portraits, we include a section on *Miscellaneous Observations* which includes material deemed interesting that did not seem to fit elsewhere. This includes personality quirks and habits, reported from various sources. Finally, we cite quotations, by the presidents and others, pertaining to their personalities. Typically, we use only material that is consistent with our profiles and exclude those that are merely the vitriol of political opponents.

Quotations and anecdotes can be colorful and limitless in variety and add freshness and warmth to the portraits. But they have many limitations when the goal is scientific description, and they should not be regarded as part of our findings. Nonetheless, we also attempted to enlist our raters as reviewers of the portraits to ensure that the biographies are correct and that the quotations and anecdotes are accurately represented. For virtually every president profiled, we were able to obtain two such reviews.

Next, we provide a very brief summary of each president's administration, citing his greatness ranking by historians. Drawing on our findings from Chapter 3, we graph his personal assets and liabilities for the Oval Office, and discuss how well he would be expected to perform based solely on those personal qualities. We then cite items that our raters indicated were particularly descriptive of his actions and behavior in office.

Finally, we identify the presidents who appear to be the most similar and dissimilar to the subjects of their biographies. Similarity is reported in the form of a correlation and ranges from -1.0 to 1.0 (see section in Chapter 1). This figure is based on overall similarity of ratings on the 592 items of our questionnaire, averaged across raters for each president. Although we include all presidents in this analysis, readers should remember ratings by less than three experts, such as those for Andrew Johnson, are likely to be somewhat unreliable and subject to change as more data is collected. Lastly, we reflect on how the president's personality affected his reputation and place in history.

WHAT'S IN THE PICTURE?

This book describes the personalities of U.S. presidents, focusing on traits and behaviors. We do not attempt to uncover every possible nuance of their personalities, glimpse the recesses of their souls, or explain how their personalities came to be. Though these explorations have a place in the intensive study of *individual* personalities, our goal is an overview—to be able to examine the presidents individually, and as a group, from the same perspective. We focus on the normal personality features that different observers can agree on and that are useful in predicting performance on the job in real-life business settings.

Readers may assume that such personality *description,* as opposed to depth *analysis,* is easy. Cannot everyone agree that Nixon was suspicious, or that TR was an Extravert? In some extreme cases, yes. But research has shown that people typically do not agree when asked to describe someone they know. Not surprisingly then, biographers of the same president often view him differently. For example, was Washington an Extravert or an Introvert? The answer you get depends largely on which authority you ask. Our ten experts produced scores that ranged from the 5th to the 96th percentile on the Extraversion scale.

Does such a range of opinion mean that we have failed to measure Washington well? Not necessarily. With ten raters, we can have some confidence in the average, even when there is a wide range of opinion (see Appendix A). With three raters, though, we might need to look for corroboration if they do not agree among themselves. Ratings from generalists and from Simonton's studies, for example, can help in these cases. When they do not agree with our findings, we say so. Nonetheless, the reader should understand that although seemingly precise scores are reported, these are simply best estimates. In many cases, opinions of different experts differed widely, and the score reported is a compromise.

We do not attempt to explain how personalities formed or developed because that would be speculative. Researchers have found that genetics accounts for about 50 percent of the differences among people for most traits. The second major factor is family environment—variables like birth order and family roles—which account for about 15 percent of individual variation. Differences between families, including social class, account for only 5 percent. The remaining 30 percent is largely unexplained. Since genetics and family dynamics are not emphasized in biographies, we will not presume to explain the personality of most presidents we portray in terms of life events.

Lastly, we do not attempt to relate personality findings to individual actions in office. Personality is only one cause of behavior. Presidents are subject to an enormous variety of pressures and influences. Advisers give advice, constituents must be appeased, and enemies confronted or outwitted, and the judgment of history is always looking over their shoulders. Without a detailed knowledge of the entire situation, any attempt by us to attribute individual actions to traits would be intellectually reckless.

Now that we've explained our approach, let's look at some personalities.

CHAPTER 5

Three Dominators—Andrew Jackson, Lyndon Johnson, and Richard Nixon

Morphed image of Lyndon Johnson and Richard Nixon.
National Archives

THE THREE MEN we profile in this chapter all cut a broad swath through their times. Their personalities were as strong as their impact on the political scene. All three were very Disagreeable and low on Openness and Character. They were exceptionally "bossy, demanding, domineering, manipulative;" none was even-tempered. All acted assertively, were self-centered and egotistical, stubborn and hardheaded, and thought highly of themselves. Table 5.1 shows the traits on which all three Dominators scored at the 85th percentile or above compared to average Americans, or below the 15th percentile.[1]

Now, we profile each one of these colorful men in detail.

TABLE 5.1
Traits Shared by Jackson, LBJ, and Nixon

All High	All Low
Angry Hostility, Assertiveness	Straightforwardness, Modesty, Trust, Compliance, Altruism, Openness to Aesthetics, *Religiousness*, Dutifulness

ANDREW JACKSON

Brief Biography

Andrew Jackson was the only member of his immediate family born in America. His parents and two older brothers came from Northern Ireland to settle along the North Carolina/South Carolina border in 1765. Two years later, Andrew Sr. died from unknown causes; he may have worked himself to death trying to provide for his family on the infertile, red soil. Elizabeth, pregnant with the future president, took her two sons to live with her sister in South Carolina. Andrew Jackson Jr. was born there on March 15, 1767.

The youngest of three boys, he endured a terrible childhood marked by shortages, stress, and the brutality of war. His mother had hoped he would become a minister; he grew instead into a hot-tempered, foul-mouthed young man. But his mother did not help develop restraint with advice like "Never sue for assault or slander; settle them cases for yourself." She also counseled him "not to lie, steal or quarrel as long as his manhood was not in jeopardy." At age fourteen, he was left an orphan when she died of cholera. Jackson lived with uncles and at fifteen received a modest inheritance from his grandfather. Invested wisely in business, land, or education, this might have given him a solid start in life. Instead, he gambled and, by some accounts, chased women in Charleston until his money was gone.

Though he later wrote and spoke with great power, even quoting Shakespeare, he had little formal education. Instead, he found himself caught up in the American Revolution at an early age. At thirteen, he fought his first battle at Hanging Rock under Colonel William Richardson Davie, on whom he modeled his personal style. Throughout his life, Jackson impressed and associated with important men who helped his career.

The Americans narrowly lost the Battle of Hanging Rock, and about a year later the British took Jackson and his older brother prisoner after a minor skirmish. When Jackson refused to polish an officer's boots, the man swung at his head with his sword. Deflecting the blow with his arm, Jackson received serious gashes to his head and fingers. He and his brother were jailed with about 250 other prisoners of war without bandages or medicines for their wounds. They were separated from each other, robbed, and contracted smallpox, from which his brother died. Though seriously ill, Jackson walked forty-five miles home. He was without a coat, barefoot, and it was raining, but his strong will kept him going. And so it would many times as he later led troops in combat against his country's enemies.

The sole survivor of his family at age fourteen, he gained a reputation for being wild and fun-loving as well as self-willed, overbearing, and a "fighting cock." He enjoyed dancing and playing games and pranks, and he enjoyed women. He joined a dance school in Salisbury, North Carolina, where he was reading law at age seventeen. Placed in charge of the school's annual ball, he invited the town's two whores, who showed up in their finery and were summarily evicted. Called on the carpet for the prank, he claimed that he never expected them to show up. Years later, when he was running for president, one Salisbury resident asked, "What! Jackson for President? *Jackson*? *Andrew* Jackson? The Jacksons that used to live in Salisbury? Well, if Andrew Jackson can be President, anybody can!" He was remembered by another as "the most roaring, rollicking, game-cocking, horseracing, card-playing, mischievous fellow that ever lived."

But then, he was only seventeen. As he matured and educated himself, his intellect tempered his risk taking, though he did get himself arrested once for the vague civil complaint of "trespass on the case." He was admitted to the Bar in 1787 and practiced law for six months in central North Carolina. Not long after, a friend offered him an appointment as public prosecutor for the Western District of the state. Later, the two were instrumental in forming the state of Tennessee.

Before Jackson got to Nashville, he had fought his first recorded duel—both parties fired into the air. He also saved his traveling companions from an Indian ambush by noticing there were far too many "animal" calls in the night.

Throughout his life, Jackson's legendary temper helped him to get his way. Later in life, he may have consciously used it as a tactic, exaggerating it for effect. Jackson was six feet tall, but never weighed over 145 pounds and often was cadaverously thin. He had sandy hair that seemed to want to stand straight up, as if, like his own posture, it was at attention.

Although he was hardly the figure of a bully, people spoke of his intense blue eyes that could not hide his rage and seemed to look right through you. Once, while a judge in Tennessee, a huge man being tried for cutting the ears off his infant son in a drunken rampage cursed Jackson and the court and walked out of his trial. When the sheriff was unable to subdue him, Jackson approached the man with a pistol in each hand. The man immediately surrendered meekly. Later he said, "I looked him in the eye, and I saw 'shoot' . . . so I says to myself, says I, 'Hoss, it's about time to sing small,' and so I did."

In Nashville Jackson met his future wife, Rachel, who was then married to another man. While she and Jackson immediately clicked, her husband and Jackson immediately clashed. Once, Jackson heard that Rachel's husband had commented on his paying too much attention to her, and he threatened to cut the husband's ears off if he ever mentioned Jackson's name again. Later, when she had left her husband, Jackson helped Rachel. They ended up living together for three years without a valid U.S. marriage being performed. They claimed to have gotten word that Rachel had been divorced and said they were married. But no record of their marriage could ever be found, and Rachel's divorce had never been completed. When the illegitimacy of her relationship with Jackson was exposed, Rachel was so humiliated that she spent the rest of her life in apparent atonement as a near-fanatical, evangelical Christian. Jackson later killed a man in a duel for mentioning the matter in public.

Jackson also clashed with John Sevier, governor of Tennessee, in 1803. Meeting on the street, Jackson made some mention of his services to the country. Sevier sneered: "Services? I know of no services you have rendered the country, except taking a trip to Natchez with another man's wife." "Great God!" exclaimed Jackson, "Do you mention her sacred name?!" Shooting followed. Senator Thomas Benton enjoyed telling people, "General Jackson was a very great man. I shot him, sir." He had, in 1813, but went on to become a warm Jackson supporter.

In 1796, Jackson was elected to Congress as Tennessee's first and only representative. The following year he was elected to the U.S. Senate. Thomas Jefferson, then vice president, recalled his arrival: "His passions are terrible. When I was President of the Senate, he could never speak on account of the rashness of his feelings. I have seen him attempt it repeatedly, and as often choke with rage." In fact, he did little as a senator and soon resigned without explanation or apology. Apparently, he realized he had made a fool of himself.

On his return to Nashville, he was elected judge, a position in which he performed well. In 1812 Governor Blount, a close friend and political crony of his, chose him to lead fifteen hundred men in the defense of New Orleans. Jackson took great pride in his men and put their comfort and health above his own. On January 8, 1815, he overwhelmingly defeated a much larger British force at New Orleans. The British later admitted 2,037 casualties, compared to 52 or fewer killed or wounded Americans. It was the greatest military victory in the history of the country and virtually the only American success of the war (which had officially ended two weeks before, though neither side knew that). Jackson was a hero from one end of the United States to the other. He remained so for the rest of his life.

Prior to and after the Battle of New Orleans, he was a successful Indian fighter. Believing he was acting on coded instructions from President Monroe, he entered Spanish Florida in 1818, occupied a Spanish fort, took down its flag, burned three hundred homes, and executed two British subjects who had been instigating Indian raids into bordering American communities. He then proclaimed himself provisional governor of all of Florida. Biographer Robert Remini described this as an act of colossal arrogance that invited declarations of war from both Spain and England. The world was stunned by Jackson's coup. President Monroe fled Washington to avoid reckoning with ambassadors from the offended countries, but Secretary of State John Quincy Adams backed him before the Spanish ambassador. Jackson's legend grew.

Complementing his bold actions was his pattern of resigning for reasons of health. He carried with him many wounds from his adventurous life, including bullet fragments so close to his heart they could not be removed. He would repeatedly come close to death, dangerously lose weight, and need weeks of bed rest to save his life.

By 1823, he was back in the Senate with his emotions held in check. In 1824, he ran for president and received a plurality in the first popular election. Though he polled a third more popular votes than John Quincy Adams, the runner-up, two other candidates split the Electoral College vote, leaving no one with a majority. One of these candidates, Henry Clay, met with Adams and swung his supporters to the Adams camp. The House of Representatives chose Adams as president and he promptly appointed Clay secretary of state.

Kentucky clinched the win for Adams in the House, though he had polled not a single vote in that state. The opposition was outraged at this supposed skull-duggery. Immediately, Jackson's supporters began to boost him as their candidate in 1828. During the campaign, Whigs circulated a catalog of Jackson's "youthful indiscretions," which included accounts of fourteen incidents in which he had "killed, slashed and clawed various American citizens." Jackson defeated Adams again in 1828 and became president.

He and Rachel had no biological children, although they adopted an Indian boy and cared for him and two other children as their own. Jackson was reportedly a strong and loving father. Just before he left for Washington, his beloved wife Rachel died suddenly. He never forgave his political opponents, who made her and their marriage a scandal in the campaign. He never remarried; his daughter-in-law served as First Lady. For his inaugural, he opened the White House to the public. They nearly demolished it, and Jackson barely escaped suffocation as they crowded around him in adulation. By the time he became president, decades of hard living and numerous gunshot wounds had seriously sapped his vitality.

Personality

Jackson received extreme scores on four of the six broad personality scales (Chart 5.1). He scored very high on Extraversion (99th percentile) and very low on Agreeableness (0.10th), Openness (0.5th), and Character (0.4th). Seven experts rated him. Though they agreed well on his overall pattern of personality, there was a significant range of opinion on four of the six scales: Character, Neuroticism, Openness, and Conscientiousness. In addition to the disagreement among specialists, as a group they rated Jackson much higher on Negative Valence and lower on Intellectual Brilliance and Openness to Experience than did generalists.

On the NEO Facet Scales, he received scores on 15 scales (out of 30) that were

CHART 5.1
Jackson's Scores on Character and the Big Five Traits

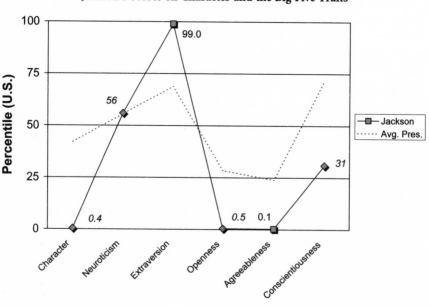

in the top or bottom 10 percent of Americans. This can be taken as a measure of how "strong" a given personality is—the number of ways it stands out from the average. On the average, a person would be expected to have about six scales listed in this table. Jackson scored as follows:

High	Percentile	Low	Percentile
Angry Hostility (N, −Ch)	99.7	Openness to Ideas	0.10
Assertiveness (E)	99.3	Compliance (A, Ch)	0.2
Activity (E)	94	*Deliberation* (C, Ch)	0.2
Excitement Seeking (E)	94	Modesty (A, Ch)	3
Openness to Feelings	91	*Openness to Aesthetics*	3
		Straightforwardness (A, Ch)	3
		Tender-Mindedness (A)	3
		Trust (A, Ch)	3
		Openness to Values	4
		Dutifulness (C, Ch)	9

NB: Scale names shown in italics showed considerable range of opinion among raters.

These NEO scores indicate an explosive (Angry Hostility), forceful (Assertiveness) man of action (low Openness to Ideas) who chose his own path (low Compliance)—often without thinking about it (low Deliberation). His score on Angry Hostility was highest of all presidents; his scores on Openness to Ideas, Compliance, and two measures of character were the lowest. He was rated second lowest on Openness to Aesthetics, one measure of IQ, and Science and Math Ability.

We now report the data from individual questionnaire items to flesh out a description of his personality. Jackson decidedly *lacked* an exceptional vocabulary; he often spelled a word several different ways on the same page. He was *not* intellectually curious and clearly had little interest in science, the nature of the universe, or the human condition. He was probably the only president who believed the world was flat. Surprisingly, for a man who worked in so many professions, he had few interests. He quickly lost interest in theoretical discussions, did not enjoy contemplating philosophy or ideas, and found art and beauty unimportant. He favored ideals and principles over open-mindedness, had a "black and white" moral code,[2] and did not indulge in daydreams and fantasies. He was not good with numbers.

He was exceptionally "explosive, tempestuous, volatile," quick to fight if picked on, and known as touchy and temperamental. Unmistakably excitable, strong emotions clearly gave his life meaning, and he experienced intense happiness as well as anger. He often became disgusted with people he dealt with, and if he did not like you, you knew it! He expressed hostility directly and without hesitation. Much more prone to compete with others than to cooperate with them, Old Hickory was bullheaded, obstinate, and stubborn.

Jackson was unmistakably impetuous, uninhibited, unrestrained, and "demonstrative, exhibitionistic, flamboyant." Assertive, dominant, and forceful, he valued his independence and autonomy. Definitely not "orderly, organized, systematic," he liked to keep his options open, but he was not indecisive. He wanted "action" and did things just for excitement. He acted vigorously and was active, energetic, and dynamic. Held up at gunpoint on a lonely road and ordered to dance, Jackson claimed that he could not oblige without his slippers, which were in his trunk. Allowed to open the trunk, he removed two pistols instead. "Now you infernal villains, you shall dance for me. Dance . . . DANCE!"

Greatly admired by his followers, who held him in awe, he had personal magnetism. He rarely felt guilty and he had fewer fears than most people. He did not feel inferior to others.

Miscellaneous Observations

Though Jackson was explosive, he was also courteous, diplomatic, polite, and tactful to his many close friends. He went out of his way to do favors for them, and above all, was fiercely loyal. He was both a man's man and a ladies' man, and he was well loved by many people. During his long and colorful career as a frontiersman, teacher, lawyer, storekeeper, judge, and finally a planter with hundreds of acres and dozens of slaves, he gradually gained affluence and culture. Although he retained some frontier habits, his manners were close to aristocratic. He modeled himself on the gentlemen of Virginia and Charleston, particularly Thomas Jefferson.

Jackson appeared to have a talent for compartmentalizing beliefs and actions that did not fit together. Once, he was telling a dinner guest a war story with great enthusiasm and a healthy dose of expletives when his wife asked him to say the blessing. He did, and then resumed his story in the same manner as before. A famous hell-raiser as a young man, he took a strong stand toward law and order once in authority. A strong believer in equality, he nevertheless helped perpetuate slavery and the harsh treatment of Indians.

Though known for his partisanship and temper, Jackson could also be principled and restrained. While commanding during the Battle of New Orleans, he was attacked in print by the editor of the local newspaper. After he won, Jackson jailed the editor, who appealed to a federal judge. When the magistrate issued a writ freeing the newspaperman, Jackson had the judge jailed too. After martial law was lifted, the judge charged Jackson with contempt of court and fined him one thousand dollars. Leaving the courthouse, Jackson found a throng of supporters ready to avenge him. He stood up in his carriage and said, "I have during the invasion exerted every one of my faculties for the defense and preservation of the Constitution and the laws. . . . Considering obedience to the laws, even when we think them unjustly applied, is the first duty of the citizen, I did not hesitate to comply with the sentence you have heard, and I entreat you to remember the example."

But Jackson also was known for his expansion of the spoils system ("to the winner go the spoils"). When a man asked him for a postmaster position for a friend who had lost a leg in battle, he confided that his friend had voted against him. "If he lost a leg fighting for his country, that is vote enough for me," Jackson replied.

Jackson Quoted

"I know what I am fit for. I can command a body of men in a rough way; but I am not fit to be President."

Jackson Described

"He could hate with a Biblical fury and would resort to petty and vindictive acts to nurture his hatred and keep it bright and strong and ferocious."—Robert V. Remini

"The way a thing should be done struck him plainly."—Supreme Court Justice John Catron

"His passions are, no doubt, cooler now; he has been much tried since I knew him, but he is a dangerous man."—Thomas Jefferson

"A barbarian who could not write a sentence of grammar and could hardly spell his own name."—John Quincy Adams

"No man knew better than Andrew Jackson when to get into a passion and when not."—a friend of Andrew Jackson

President Jackson

Jackson is rated as one of the near-great presidents in every major poll of historians—the only president whose name symbolizes his era ("The Age of Jackson"). The Ridings and McIver poll of historians ranked him the eighth best president overall, just behind Truman and ahead of Eisenhower. His highest ranking was in Leadership Qualities (fifth), his two lowest in Character and Integrity (eighteenth) and Appointments (nineteenth).

Chart 5.2 profiles his scores on the scales comprising our Presidential Success prediction index. The profile indicates strengths—scores substantially above the 50th percentile—and weaknesses—scores below 50th. For two scales, Vulnerability and Straightforwardness, low scores are desirable for presidential success. To keep the chart easy to read, scores were plotted as "Not Vulnerable" and "Not Straightforward," so high points still indicate positive qualities for performance as president. The scales are grouped according to three categories: Achievement Potential, Leadership and Influence, and Miscellaneous Assets. Two qualities, Intelligence (Intell. & Smart) and Not Vulnerable, are assets for both Achievement Potential and Leadership, so they are placed in the boundary between the two.

Jackson performed as president better than predicted by our equations, which would have placed him about average. His strengths were his willingness to stretch the truth (low Straightforwardness), his commanding personality (high Assertiveness), and Activity level. However, he was rated as less intelligent than other presidents and is the only successful president to receive such a low rating.

CHART 5.2
Personality Assets and Liabilities of Jackson as President

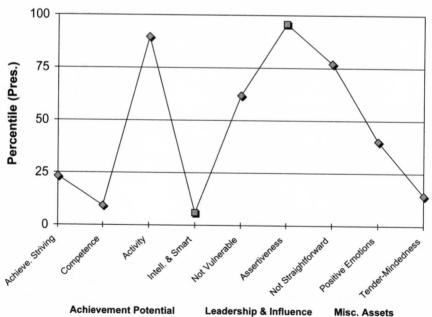

Achievement Potential   **Leadership & Influence**   **Misc. Assets**

He was also occasionally lacking in judgment (low Competence; another rarity among better presidents) and was unsympathetic to people in need (low Tender-Mindedness).

Jackson is remembered for standing up for the common man. He was the first chief executive to proclaim that he represented all Americans, not just the landed and well-to-do. He feared that wealthy Easterners were scheming to control the government. By closing the Bank of the United States, he hoped to thwart such plans. If America is thought of as a country of successive revolutions in the spread of liberty, we have Jackson to thank. At a time when immigration, the move west, and the rapid growth of cities called for a far greater enfranchisement of the uneducated, both tenant farmers and tenement dwellers, Jackson took the reins. Yet he defended slavery and opposed the participation of women in politics.

Jackson greatly expanded our borders and our markets abroad, reformed American politics, stopped the first attempt of the South to depart from the Union (Nullification in 1832), and greatly broadened the definition of liberty. Robert Remini argues that he laid the groundwork for America as we know it today. Of course, this included the removal of Native Americans from their lands and their eventual conquest.

Behavior as President (our data)

Jackson received the highest score of all presidents on Simonton's ratings of Creative leadership, and the lowest on our ratings of Deliberative presidential style. He did *not* keep thoroughly informed by reading briefings or background reports and was not at all cautious or conservative in his actions. He was charismatic and conveyed a clear-cut, highly visible personality. He was abrupt in conferences and emphatic in expressing his opinions. He was often a "one-man show" and did not credit his advisers' contributions. After Jackson sent Congress his first annual message, he asked a friend how it was received. "They say it is first rate, but nobody believes that you wrote it." "Well," Jackson responded, "don't I deserve just as much credit for picking out the man who could write it?" Though often an advocate of the common man, he believed he knew what was best for people. He rarely allowed his opponents to outflank him and had the ability to maintain his popularity both at home and abroad. Lastly, he showed less personality change after assuming the office than most presidents.

Jackson in Perspective

Jackson was most similar to LBJ (r = .56), G. W. Bush (r = .52), and Andrew Johnson (r = .40).[3] He was least similar to Madison (r = −.64), Fillmore, (r = −.46), and Carter (r = −.41). He was a blast of fresh air in the White House: The first extravert, the first "common man," the first (former) brawler and gambler, the first war hero since Washington. All of the previous presidents were dignified gentlemen, most of considerable learning. Jackson was none of these, and it worked to his advantage. Even overseas, he was a celebrity, sort of an American Napoléon. Once a major American folk hero, his luster has faded—his handling of Native Americans is now regarded as shameful.

LYNDON JOHNSON

Brief Biography

Lyndon Baines Johnson was born on August 27, 1908, near the Pedernales River in Texas. His father, Sam Ealy Johnson, was a Texas legislator, a natural politician, and according to one, "the best man I ever met." As a state representative, the elder Johnson distinguished himself by his honesty and extraordinary efforts to obtain government benefits for deserving constituents, sometimes personally driving them hundreds of miles to the appropriate office. Booze, beefsteak, and blondes were common perks for legislators. Sam Johnson did not abstain, but unlike most, he paid his own way. Both of Johnson's parents valued the arts and learning but settled in a place where those qualities were liabilities.

The Texas Hill Country appeared lush to its early settlers, covered in dense prairie grass. But the root system of the grass was the only thing keeping the soil in place. Once tilled for farming, the rains washed it away. Johnson's father invested everything in his farm, going deeply into debt to his neighbors—many of whom he had helped obtain government benefits. Unable to pay them back, he went from being a liked and respected pillar of the community to an embittered, broken man unable to look people in the eye.

Johnson initially idolized his father and accompanied him in his government dealings. As a teen, he distanced himself, apparently regarding his father as a failure. In a *College Star* editorial, he wrote about fathers with shortcomings with great understanding and maturity for a nineteen-year-old. Still, years later, admiring references to Sam Johnson bothered him.

His mother was the college-educated daughter of a minister and the most refined lady in the county. She provided lessons in reading and music to neighbor children that sometimes changed their lives forever. By some accounts, she was less successful as a housewife, never really mastering the art of frugality despite the family's financial problems. Nonetheless, the marriage was mostly a happy one, and the elder Johnson idolized his wife. However, one source indicated that LBJ was "the object of conflict between his father and mother [which] made much of his life miserable."

As a young child, Johnson's mother dressed him in sailor suits and other "cute" outfits that were outlandish for the Hill Country. Johnson did not mind—he liked standing out in a crowd. By the age of twelve, he would hold court in the local barbershop, reading the newspaper out loud to the adult patrons and offering his insights on the news. If someone disagreed with him, he would not stop arguing until his point carried. If he had a ball, you had to play his game or he would leave. Despite his contrary ways, Johnson was something of a sissy according to biographer Robert Caro: As a boy he "threw like a girl" and "wailed if anyone laid a hand on him."

His parents wanted him to go to college, but he would not go. He ran away to California and worked in a lawyer's office for a time, but the attorney drank and allowed the practice to fail. Johnson returned home and worked at manual labor jobs. Finally, seeing a limited future without an education, he took his parents' advice.

When he first came to Southwest Texas State Teachers College, he lived and ate at a boardinghouse run by a motherly woman named Mrs. Gates. He later moved to a room above the college president's garage for which he paid no rent. He shared the room with another student named Johnson, with whom he became good friends. They had no shower in the room and had to trek across the street to the women's gym after it was closed to bathe.

It was at college that Johnson first displayed his remarkable political talents. Within weeks of arriving, he had charmed the dean of the school, an aloof, prickly man, and won a job as assistant secretary to the university president. On the face of it, the job was menial; but Johnson stationed his desk outside his boss's office and became his gatekeeper. He acquired the power to award and disperse student aid, an all-important benefit for nearly all of the students. Soon, he was a well-known but controversial figure on campus.

He also became politically active, entering one of the campus's secret societies. The Black Stars were athletes who got special privileges and won elections on campus. As a nonathlete Johnson had no hope of joining them and never tried. He and several others formed the White Stars as a rival fraternity. Johnson managed to create a powerful political system and to dominate it, but his opponents reviled him. His campus nickname was "Bull"—short for "Bullshit." In the school's yearbook, he was portrayed with the sketch of a jackass and the caption, "How we see you on campus." When he later ran for public office, the college collected all the yearbooks they could locate and excised these negative portrayals.

In college Johnson demonstrated another trait that some saw as instrumental in his career. He was respectful, some said obsequious, to teachers and those in authority. According to Caro, he would sit at the feet of lecturers, gazing up to them in admiration, and would change his opinions from one class to the next to match his instructors'. "He was a real ass-kisser, just sickening," recalled one classmate. As editor of the school paper, Johnson wrote articles about Registration Day and other mundane events, and penned editorials about the virtues of patriotism, courtesy, sincerity, and good character. In one, he described teaching as "the greatest of vocations."

Following college he took a job as a teacher and acting principal in Cotulla, Texas, a largely Mexican community. He completely revitalized the school and was genuinely admired by parents, staff, and most students for his dedication and enthusiasm. At a subsequent job in Houston, he propelled the debate team to runner-up in the state championship, making them campus heroes and the subjects of pep rallies.

When dating, he seemingly gravitated toward the daughters of wealthy men. He was engaged to one such girl, but her father objected. Claudia "Lady Bird" Taylor, his wife-to-be, was also the daughter of a rich man, but unassuming and shy. Johnson proposed to her the first day they met and rushed her to the altar. His previously solicitous behavior changed almost at once. He would order her around in a way that shocked some. "Bird, get me a drink! Now!" She inherited money when her father died, and she and Johnson invested in a radio station in Austin that eventually grew into an empire worth millions.

Johnson's political career began as the office administrator for his congressman, a gentleman of leisure who cheerfully turned his duties over to his eager young assistant. Johnson was phenomenal in this role and established a reputation for his knowledge of how to get things done in Washington. He demanded that letters from constituents be answered the same day they were received with a letter-perfect, personalized response. Technically only a secretary, he signed the letters. To the people back home, he was their man in Washington. He was a slave driver to his staff, requiring eighteen-hour days with a half-day off on Sundays. Nonetheless, those who stayed did not feel exploited: They felt they were part of something important.

When the congressman died, a scramble for his office ensued, with Johnson and the congressman's widow as the top contenders. While custom favored the widow, powerful interests in Texas that year needed a man who could get things done; Johnson was that man. In Congress, he was instrumental in getting funding for dam building and the electrification of rural Texas. He had limited interest in national affairs that did not impact his district or Texas and voted *against* significant civil rights legislation including an antilynching bill, integration of the armed forces, and the end of the poll tax.

He now had his eye on a Senate seat and was looking to build statewide recognition. Always searching for an angle, Johnson would not dance with the attractive single women at Washington parties but with the wives of senators. He befriended them and gained access through them. At the same time, he began plying and flattering powerful men, particularly FDR and Speaker of the House Sam Rayburn. Rayburn was an aloof, forbidding man with few friends and no family, and a towering figure in Washington. He was so successful in currying the favor and affection of these men and others that he became known as a "professional son."

Johnson waged a flashy, highly expensive campaign for senator but alienated voters with his domineering manner and unpleasant speaking voice. He eventually modified his approach and was even expected to win, but in the end, the election was stolen from him. Johnson's main opponent, the popular governor "Pappy" O'Daniel, announced support for laws restricting liquor sales, making him a bane on the local liquor manufacturers' business. But O'Daniel's "promotion" to the Senate would eliminate this threat. The liquor lobby conspired to delay the vote counts in some rural counties, not reporting the totals until they knew how many votes they needed to shoo in Pappy. For Johnson, it was a crushing, ironic defeat.

Johnson went on to win a Senate seat in 1948, earning the nickname "Landslide Lyndon" for his narrow victory brought about by another late vote count in South Texas. He had a meteoric rise in the Senate, virtually becoming its master by 1957. He opposed President Truman on a number of measures and then reversed his early record by engineering passage of the Civil Rights Acts of 1957 and 1960. Explaining his reversal to other Southern Democrats, he stated "We'll have the niggers voting with us (Democrats) for the next 200 years!"[4] This should be read with knowledge of Johnson's preference for crude language and his capacity for selecting phrasing to suit his audience. Nonetheless, he did have a tendency to degrade the people he championed, as when he referred to the South Vietnamese as "those poor little boogers."

As vice president under Kennedy, Johnson found himself left out of the White House inner circle. Kennedy had looks and charisma and had attained power and adulation with seeming ease. Jealous of his boss, Johnson felt intimidated by the Eastern intellectuals in the administration. As vice president, he fathered the U.S. space program and for a while was its principal spokesperson. After serving out the remainder of Kennedy's term and being elected in 1964 in his own right, he declined to run for another term. He died of a heart attack enroute to a hospital in San Antonio on January 22, 1973, at the age of sixty-four.

Personality

Six specialists, who generally agreed among themselves, rated Johnson. Many extreme scores, reflecting strong personality, mark his profile. His score on Character (0.10th percentile) is the lowest of all presidents. On the Big Five factors, he scored very low on Agreeableness (0.07th), low on Openness to Experience (7th), and high on Extraversion (99.4th) and Neuroticism (95th). There was a significant diversity of opinion on his standings on Neuroticism and Openness, hence the diamonds in Chart 5.3. Unlike the specialists, generalists saw Johnson as higher in Openness than most presidents. Both groups rated Johnson high on Negative Valance, with the specialists' ratings being very high.

On the NEO Facet Scales, Johnson showed a remarkable number of very high or low scores relative to typical Americans. His very low score on Straightforwardness was more extreme than any score of any president in our study. It portrays a man exceptionally willing to use any means available to get his way, who

CHART 5.3

Lyndon Johnson's Scores on Character and the Big Five Traits

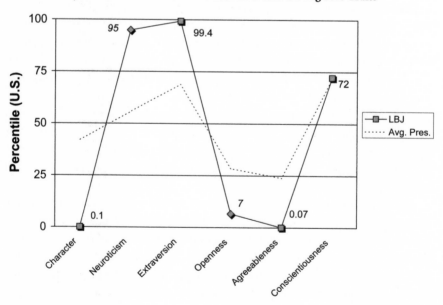

was not polite or "nice" (low Altruism), humble (low Modesty), or trusting (low Trust). He was forceful (high Assertiveness), irritable (high Angry Hostility), and had a very high energy level (Activity). He scored second highest among presidents on Assertiveness, Impulsivity, Activity, and on the Negative Valence (evil, sick, dangerous) scale. His scores were the lowest of all presidents on most measures of Character and on Straightforwardness, Altruism, and Modesty.

High	Percentile	Low	Percentile
Assertiveness (E)	99.7	Straightforwardness (A, Ch)	0.005
Impulsivity (N, − Ch)	99.6	Altruism (A, Ch)	0.16
Angry Hostility (N, − Ch)	99.0	Modesty (A, Ch)	0.18
Activity (E)	98.6	Trust (A, Ch)	1.4
Achievement Striving (C, Ch)	97.8	Openness to Ideas	3
Openness to Feelings	95	Openness to Aesthetics	4
Gregariousness (E)	93	Deliberation (C, Ch)	5
Anxiety (N)	91	Dutifulness (C, Ch)	5
Self-Consciousness (N)	90	Compliance (A, Ch)	8
Excitement Seeking (E)	90		

The items receiving the most extreme ratings amplify and flesh out these findings. Without question, Johnson was a bully. He was dominant and forceful and gave the air of being high-ranking and powerful—not commonplace. He was faultfinding, unsympathetic, and unforgiving; his "feedback" sessions with subordinates could reduce even hardened men to tears. Glancing at the messy desk of his assistant press secretary, he once remarked, "Kilduff, I hope your mind isn't as cluttered as your desk." The next day, after adjustments had been made, Johnson responded to the change with "Kilduff, I hope your brain isn't as vacant as your desk." He used strong-arm tactics, flattery, and trickery to get his way more than any other president. He showed an exceptional willingness to distort facts or lie, and was markedly deceitful, unscrupulous, underhanded, cunning, and sly. He prided himself on his ability to "handle" people, and he was highly persuasive, using virtually any means to his ends. On the Senate floor, "the Johnson treatment" might include a large arm around the shoulder accompanied by a kick to the shins.

Johnson definitely did not live true to his personal convictions and values; he was not at all "ethical, honest, moral, principled or sincere." He was also exceptionally greedy, literally robbing the White House as he left office, according to Ronald Kessler.[5] Leading people to become dependent on him, he then took advantage of them. When he first came to Washington, he recruited his former high school students and then pocketed a large portion of their allotted salary. Clearly not moralistic, he also failed to show moral courage.

Many who knew Johnson disliked him—to an exceptional degree. He was exceedingly intrusive, meddlesome, and nosy, NOT courteous, diplomatic, or polite. He very often argued with family or coworkers. Stewards aboard Air Force One reported that he would throw meals or drinks he did not like on the floor. Exceptionally boastful, conceited, egotistical, and vain, he wore only shoes made of the softest leather and, as a young man, annoyed others by his incessant hair combing and primping in mirrors. He attributed his successes to his talents or personal qualities. Markedly "demonstrative, exhibitionistic, flamboyant," Johnson was good at calling attention to himself. He always tried to do most of the talking in a conversation and liked to discourse on his own achievements. A gifted storyteller, "he was forever improvising, embroidering, and exaggerating." But if he was obliged to listen to others, he literally fell asleep. He *clearly* thought himself superior to others.

Johnson was remarkably explosive, tempestuous, and volatile and was self-defensive and humorless about his own faults. He was embarrassed by teasing or ridicule and did not forgive and forget. He was unable to control his emotions, expressed anger freely, and often mistreated others during outbursts. Though he usually tried to make amends afterwards through gifts or special treatment, he neither seemed embarrassed at the time nor apologized later.

Even compared to other men who later became president, Johnson was *not* lazy or slothful, and very often appeared to be rushing or short of time. He moved quickly, lived at a fast pace, and felt energetic and vigorous. During the 1964 campaign, he gave twenty-two speeches in one day; in 1968, he visited five countries in Latin America in one day. He did not work slowly but steadily, was not forgetful or absentminded, and was a workaholic. He was concerned with excellence and unique accomplishment.

Not at all effeminate, as a young man he was nonetheless a pathetic fighter, falling to his back and "kicking like a girl" when attacked, according to Caro. He swore profusely, was *not* indecisive or wishy-washy, and had a hunger for excitement. He often acted without thinking and was rebellious and nonconforming, not inhibited or restrained. Johnson personally integrated the Forty Acres Club at the University of Texas in Austin. He simply walked in with a handsome black woman from his staff, violating the club's whites-only policy—which was subsequently dropped.

Johnson enjoyed sensuous experiences but lacked sophistication. His culinary tastes ran to basic farm and country food. Very self-indulgent, he was known as a grabby, greedy eater who sometimes ate until he got sick. Art and beauty were unimportant to him, and he had a poor memory for melodies. He clearly lacked appreciation for the visual arts, such as paintings or sculpture, and he was unaffected by poetry. But he valued and paid attention to his feelings and experienced a broad range of emotions. He was not interested in philosophy or talk about theories or ideas, and he was not wise. Despite other traits reflecting low Openness to Experience and Values, Johnson believed social policies should evolve to meet current needs.

Known for currying the favor of powerful men, he was decidedly suspicious when someone did something nice for him. He was NOT naturally trusting. Yet, he believed society should do its utmost to help the disadvantaged, and that political leaders should be more attuned to the personal side of issues.

Miscellaneous Observations

Johnson was a complicated man who embodied contradictions. He believed that government should help the disadvantaged, but he was not personally Altruistic (NEO Facet Scale). Recently released tapes catch him, by then a multimillionaire, haggling with a merchant because "I'm not a rich man." Yet, he always remembered birthdays and anniversaries of staff, sent flowers to those in the hospital, and lent money to newsmen despite his feuds with them. One source asserted that he was impulsive yet dilatory, meticulous but careless, gregarious yet cold and aloof.

Working for Johnson was a wrenching, all-involving experience. He did not trust anyone if he did not have "his pecker in my pocket." One expert described his method of coping with stress as "Food. Alcohol. . . . Yelling at subordinates." When Johnson entered Air Force One and was out of sight of the press, he would turn to his staff and proclaim, "I piss on you all."[6] He expected his staff to work as hard as he did and to be just as effective as he was: "I didn't ask you to get me a negative answer! Say that I want this done for certain and get an affirmative answer!" He was said to be a good judge of other's abilities and character, able to identify those who would put up with his dictatorial style. Lastly, Johnson made it clear he could not stand having fat or ugly women around him. His imperious manner continued in the White House, where he talked of "*my* Supreme Court" and even "the State of *my* Union."

Despite his overbearing manner, Johnson had many close friends with whom he kept in contact over his life, though he was reserved in sharing close confidences. Hunting was an especially prized pastime. As a husband and father, he was often inconsiderate, expecting Lady Bird to "whip up" food for a dozen people on short notice; the family's schedule was always subordinated to his work. Yet, he was said to have become a good father later in life, and Lady Bird apparently never publicly complained.

No description of Johnson would be complete without mention of his crudity. Despite the wide coverage of our questionnaire, there were no items that included terms such as "vulgar" and "uncouth"—terms frequently applied to Johnson. Yet, many sources report such things as: "He scratched himself freely, and belched loudly whenever he felt like it. He used four letter words freely. . . . If in the midst of a conference, he had to go to the bathroom, he sometimes made his conferees join him there." He talked about his gonads and of how he needed more room for them in his pants. When he ordered trousers, he thoughtfully provided the tailor with coordinates from his "bunghole."

Lastly, he had a sex life as president that rivaled Kennedy and far surpassed Clinton. He walked around Air Force One in his underwear or even naked in full view of his mixed staff, and locked himself in rooms with female secretaries even when Lady Bird was on the plane. Johnson recruited a whole stable of beautiful women, whose primary job requirement was that they be attractive and service their boss; some had to be sent to secretarial school. After being caught with one of his assistants by Lady Bird, he had a buzzer installed so the Secret Service could warn him if his wife approached.[7]

Johnson Quoted

"I do not want to be the President who built empires or sought grandeur or extended dominions. I want to be the President who educated young children, . . . who helped to feed the hungry, . . . who helped the poor find their own way and who protected the rights of every citizen to vote in every election."

"Well, it's probably better to have him inside the tent pissing out than outside pissing in." (rationalizing the inadvisability of forcing J. Edgar Hoover out as director of the FBI)

Johnson Described

"He may have been a son of a bitch but he was a colossal son of a bitch."—Press Secretary George Reedy

"He absorbed power like a sponge."—Ken Hendricks

"Lyndon was always prodding me to look better, learn more, work harder. He always expects more of you than you think you are really capable of putting out. It is really very stimulating. It is also very tiring."—Lady Bird Johnson

"Lyndon will go the way the wind blows." "Maybe, but if he does, he'll probably beat the wind there."—two Johnson friends discussing his possible stance on an issue

"He hasn't got the depth of mind or the breadth of vision to carry great responsibility. . . . Johnson is superficial and opportunistic."—Dwight Eisenhower

"He can be as gentle and solicitous as a nurse, but as ruthless and deceptive as a riverboat gambler."—Journalists Rowland Evans and Robert Novak

"Lyndon Johnson's public life was filled with controversy because he was a man who cared, a man of action, a man of decision."—Hubert Humphrey

"He tells so many lies that he convinces himself after a while that he's telling the truth. He just doesn't recognize truth or falsehood."—Robert F. Kennedy

President Johnson

"I knew from the start that if I left the woman I really loved—the Great Society—in order to fight that bitch of a war . . . then I would lose everything at home. All of my hopes . . . my dreams."

Johnson was ranked as the twelfth best president overall by Ridings and McIver, just behind Polk and ahead of Monroe. He obtained high marks for his Political Skill (3rd), but low scores on Character and Integrity (37th). He is remembered for his Great Society programs, for the passage of civil rights legislation, and for becoming ensnared in Vietnam. He provided the nation a strong, capable leader after the assassination of JFK. Edward Kennedy proclaimed that Johnson's legislative achievements "earned him a place in the history of civil rights alongside Abraham Lincoln." He modeled himself on FDR and believed that government should help people, not rule them. On the other hand, Kessler reports that when he left office, he shipped planeloads of booty from the White House, including much of the furniture, at government expense.[8]

On Vietnam, Johnson saw the dangers initially, but gradually came to regard himself as the Great Emancipator of South Vietnam. Once committed, his ego would not permit him to be remembered as the first president to lose a war. Controversy over Vietnam eventually persuaded him not to run for reelection, although biographer Robert Dallek suggests that disillusionment with his social programs also played a part. Johnson was greatly troubled by protests against the war, which he took personally.

Johnson's personality, unpleasant as it sometimes may have been, was well suited for the presidency (see Chart 5.4). Scoring lowest of all presidents on Straightforwardness, he was a master of getting his way, whether through trickery or outright domination. He scored high on Activity, Assertiveness, Tender-Mindedness, and Achievement Striving—all assets for a successful chief executive. Though a bit more rattled by stress (Vulnerability) and less "Intelligent and Smart" than some other presidents, even those scores are near average.

CHART 5.4

Personality Assets and Liabilities of Lyndon Johnson as President

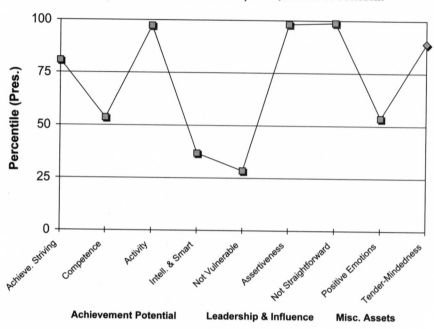

Behavior as President (our data)

As chief executive, Johnson clearly did not show good moral character, was very given to emotional outbursts, and showed true artistry in manipulating his staff. He did *not* keep them informed on matters involving other departments and did not choose advisers based on their competence and knowledge. Loyalty was the prime qualification, and outsiders would sometimes be shocked by the dullness of some high level Johnson officials.[9] He did not permit discussion of issues among his cabinet and was intolerant of disagreement or advice.[10] He initiated many programs and much legislation, was a dynamo of energy and determination, was not suspicious of reformers, and had a vision of what he wanted to accomplish. Though ultimately unable to maintain popularity, he recognized the need for a consensus when pressing for change and had a gift for theatrics.

Johnson in Perspective

Johnson's personality was most similar to Jackson (r = .56), Nixon (r = .51), and Andrew Johnson (r = .33). He was least similar to Fillmore (r = −.50),

Madison (r = − .47), and Hayes (r = − .40).[11] Johnson saw himself as a champion of the common man, and often acted like one, but he had little real respect for the average citizen. He was portrayed in very different lights by two quality biographers. In *The Years of Lyndon Johnson*, Robert Caro presented one of the most negative character portraits imaginable. In *Big Daddy from the Pedernales*, Paul Conkin acknowledged Johnson's faults but did not dwell on them. Conkin saw Johnson as a sentimental idealist who used indirect means to meet his noble ends. Our data generally supports Caro's portrayal without contradicting Conkin's.

Johnson presents a classic dilemma when the issue of character is considered. He was a consummate politician, with all the negative features that the stereotype implies. But this also means that he was flexible and versatile, able to appeal to many different perspectives, and able to serve varied interests. He had noble aims and was great at getting things done. Aside from Vietnam, he was very successful, passing landmark social programs that, more than any other president, brought about a revolution in social equality.

In 1965 Johnson hosted a Festival of the Arts at the White House. One participant, a black jazz singer, was found sobbing in her dressing room. Asked what was wrong, she replied, "It's just that twenty years ago when I came to Washington I couldn't get a hotel room. And tonight I sang for the President of the United States at the White House—and then he asked me to dance with him. It is more than I can stand!"

RICHARD M. NIXON

Brief Biography

Richard Nixon was born into a struggling, working-class family in Yorba Linda, California, second of five children. His father, Frank, was of Scotch-Irish descent. He dropped out of grade school to work at farming and various odd jobs before operating a gas station and market. He was known as quarrelsome and temperamental, and frequently engaged in heated political discussions with his customers. Nixon's mother was of English–Irish heritage. A devout Quaker, she saw young Richard as a future missionary. Nixon described her as "a saint" and exceptionally kindhearted, but others perceived her as cold and undemonstrative. Nixon acknowledged his mother was not given to hugs or outward displays of affection, but he felt she conveyed her love nonetheless. Still, he would later speak of his childhood in terms of poverty and sacrifice.

Nixon had several early experiences with death. At age three he fell from a carriage and suffered a serious cut to his forehead, nearly bleeding to death. He described running after the carriage after his fall as his earliest memory. He nearly died again the next year from pneumonia. His brother, Arthur, died of tuberculosis at age seven, which was especially tragic since his father was partly to blame. Cow's milk was a common source of TB infection, and Frank had obtained a cow because of his distrust of pasteurization. He disregarded the warnings of the family doctor and eventually lost two sons because of his obstinacy.

Dick Nixon was a hardworking, devoted, well-behaved boy who worked in the family store and was an exceptional student. In high school he won the Constitutional Oratorical Contest, the California Interscholastic Federation Gold Seal Award, and the Harvard Award for Best All-Around Student. He graduated first in his class and won a scholarship to Yale, but even with the stipend he could not afford to go. Disappointed but stoic, he attended local Whittier College where he majored in history and was captain of the debate team. He was elected class president his senior year and was active in drama and glee club.

The Whittier campus had social clubs for the well heeled, but not for those of working-class background. For the first time, Nixon felt the sting of class discrimination. He helped found a social club for students of modest means and served as its first president. After graduation, he attended Duke University Law School on a scholarship. He found that the boardinghouse he was assigned was noisy and distracting, so he moved into a vacant shack near the campus. Though it lacked heat or running water, he lived there for the rest of law school. Despite being viewed as overly serious, he was elected president of the 1937 class, graduating third of twenty-five students. He was reportedly shocked by racial segregation in North Carolina, which ran counter to his Quaker upbringing and courageously spoke out against it. In an astonishing portent, Nixon and several law school classmates broke into the dean's office to get an early look at their grades when they were not posted on time.

After graduating from law school, Nixon returned to Yorba Linda without clear career prospects. He joined a law firm and rose to junior partner in two years. He joined several Whittier businessmen in forming the Citra-Frost (frozen orange juice) Company, which went broke under his two-year reign as its president. In early 1942, he worked in the U.S. Office of Price Administration, where he became disillusioned with government bureaucracy. He quit to join the Navy, where he rose to the rank of lieutenant commander while serving as officer in charge of air transportation, an administrative position. In his off time, he played poker and regularly won a great deal of money.

Nixon did not date much, which one biographer attributed to lack of money.

He had been engaged once before he met Thelma "Pat" Ryan. While working as a lawyer, he learned that a pretty new teacher, who had appeared in minor parts in motion pictures, had moved into town. Pat was trying out for a part in a local play; Nixon auditioned opposite her and proposed to her that night. She refused, but they began to date. Winning her hand was testimony to his tenacity. At first she continued to date other men and would occasionally not answer the door when he came to call. She fell for his dog before falling for him.

Pat Ryan, even more than Nixon, came from a hard life and was difficult to get to know. She was an agnostic who, as a teacher, made twice the salary of her lawyer husband. Nixon and his wife were fully in love by the time of their marriage and regained a special closeness after his resignation from the presidency. They had two devoted daughters.

Nixon was elected to represent Whittier and parts of Los Angeles in the U.S. House of Representatives in 1946, upsetting a five-term incumbent. He became a member, and later chair, of the House Committee on Un-American Activities and took the lead in a high profile investigation of suspected Communist Alger Hiss. When Hiss was later convicted of perjury, Nixon's reputation as an anti-Communist grew. When he ran for the Senate in 1950, he distributed half a million fliers tying his opponent's voting record to the ambitions of the Communist movement and labeling her the "Pink Lady." This behavior earned him the nickname "Tricky Dick," which stayed with him throughout his career. When questioned about his tactics, Nixon replied tellingly: "They didn't understand. I had to win." As a senator, he was the political nemesis of President Truman, criticizing his restraint during the Korean War and his dismissal of Gen. Douglas MacArthur.

Now the rising star of the Republican Party, he was tapped as Eisenhower's vice president in 1952. Eisenhower never liked or trusted him, however, and when Nixon came under attack for accepting unethical gifts, Eisenhower made it clear that Nixon would have to come through "clean as a hound's tooth" to remain on the ticket. He went on television, a radical move at that time, and in a thirty-minute speech salvaged his career. Ironically, it was the only time Nixon ever appealed for public understanding, and he initially thought he had performed poorly.

After eight years as vice president, Nixon was expected to receive a hearty endorsement from the still-popular Eisenhower, but Ike remained silent until Nixon pressed the issue. Kennedy defeated him in 1960 in a very tight contest; Nixon also lost his bid for California governor in 1962. The two defeats were stunning reversals that led him to lash out at reporters with his infamous vow, "You won't have Nixon to kick around anymore." He purportedly withdrew from politics and practiced law between 1963 and 1968, though his exile may have been a shrewd and temporary withdrawal. He campaigned for Barry Goldwater in 1964, earning additional exposure and credit within the party.

America in 1968 was in cultural and political turmoil. Two idealistic leaders, Robert Kennedy and Martin Luther King, had been assassinated. President Johnson had been exposed as lying to the public on numerous occasions and was driven to retire by the pressures of the Vietnam War. Cynicism toward "the establishment" had become epidemic. Historians have rated those years as the third most unstable and threatening period in the country's history.[12] If crisis creates the potential for a great president, the ground was as fertile in the late sixties as it had been for Washington, Lincoln, or FDR.

Nixon returned to politics and won the 1968 Republican nomination over Nelson Rockefeller and Ronald Reagan. The Democratic Party was divided over the war. As a moderate running on a law-and-order platform and a staunch anti-Communist, Nixon had broad appeal that others did not.

Personality

Compared to most Americans (Chart 5.5), Nixon scored very low on Agreeableness (0.02th percentile) and Character (0.9th), and quite high on Conscientiousness (98th) and Neuroticism (97th). He was also quite introverted compared to other presidents (7th percentile on Extraversion), though there was disagreement on this issue, as well as on Nixon's level of Neuroticism and Conscientiousness. Despite these discrepancies, his four raters were consistent in describing the overall pattern of his personality. And although they paint a bleak portrait, as you will see shortly, specialists gave Nixon much higher job performance ratings than did our generalists and than did historians in the major polls of presidential greatness. Specialists also rated Nixon lower in Neuroticism and higher in Conscientiousness than did generalists.

On the NEO Facets, Nixon repeatedly scored much higher or lower than average Americans, describing a devious (low Straightforwardness), suspicious (low Trust), hard-hearted (low Tender-Mindedness), and surly (Angry Hostility) man. Very prone to embarrassment (Self-Consciousness), he was anxious and aloof around people (low Warmth). He liked to be in charge (high Assertiveness) and was uncooperative with others (low Compliance). He scored highest of all presidents on Negative Evaluation (e.g., evil, sick), on Simonton's Pettiness scale, and on one measure of Neuroticism; he was second highest on Anxiety and Self-Consciousness. He scored lowest of all presidents on most measures of Agree-

CHART 5.5

Nixon's Scores on Character and the Big Five Traits

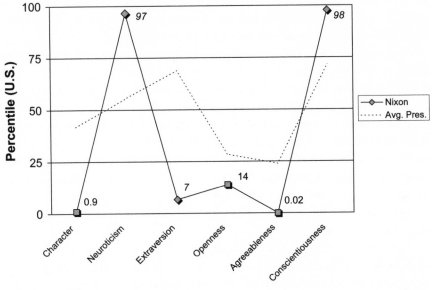

ableness, Character, and Tender-Mindedness, and second lowest on Trust, Warmth, and Altruism.

High	Percentile	Low	Percentile
Angry Hostility (N, −Ch)	99.0	Straightforwardness (A, Ch)	0.07
Achievement Striving (C, Ch)	99.0	Trust (A, Ch)	0.10
Self-Consciousness (N)	98.6	Tender-Mindedness (A)	0.11
Anxiety (N)	98.2	Altruism (A, Ch)	0.4
Assertiveness (E)	96	Warmth (E)	0.7
		Compliance (A, Ch)	0.8
		Positive Emotions (E)	1.8
		Modesty (A, Ch)	1.9
		Openness to Values	3

Nixon was rated as extraordinarily "treacherous, disloyal" and, to nearly the same extreme, seen as deserving of hatred. He was described, to an exceptional degree, as "cruel, ruthless, vindictive" compared to other chief executives, and to a marked degree, "evil."[13] He disregarded the rights and feelings of those not on his side to a degree unmatched among presidents, and played on people's fears and insecurities. Nixon encouraged people to rely on him so that he could exploit them much more than other presidents. He clearly valued power, wanted to have impact and prestige, and was assertive, dominant, and forceful. He definitely bullied people. He preferred getting compliments to giving them, liked talking about his achievements, and did not mind bragging.

His personality was *not at all* well defined and consistent, and he was markedly hypocritical. He was intensely self-pitying and felt cheated by life to an extreme degree. A remarkably "bitter, joyless, melancholic, moody, morose, pessimistic, somber" man, he lacked a sense of life's purpose. When a sympathetic journalist asked Nixon, then retired nearly ten years, if he had had a good life, he replied, "I don't get into that kind of crap."[14]

Extremely jittery and tense, he was prone to feeling inferior to others, had many fears, and worried excessively. He blamed others for his problems to an exceptional degree but attributed successes to his talents or personal qualities. Surprisingly, given his aloofness, he sought reassurance from others considerably more than most presidents.

Extremely "deceitful, dishonest, underhanded, unscrupulous," Nixon was not at all "ethical, honest, moral, principled, sincere, truthful" or "direct, frank, or straightforward." He definitely did not believe that honesty is the best policy and took pride in his ability to handle people shrewdly. Unethical behavior in subordinates and colleagues was tolerated or endorsed.

He was unmistakably hostile toward others and would much rather compete than cooperate. He was very "antagonistic, argumentative, combative, quarrelsome," and quite frequently angered by the way others treated him. He did not forget a slight and let people know if he did not like them. Self-defensive and humorless about his shortcomings, he had a well-earned reputation as touchy and temperamental and was ready to fight if attacked.

Condescending, Nixon was also seen as "abusive, disrespectful, impolite, impudent, rude, scornful" and "faultfinding, harsh, unforgiving, unsympathetic" to a remarkable degree. He was decidedly not affectionate, compassionate, sentimental, or warm, and often felt disgusted with people. When asked what he was thinking as he shook hands with hundreds of *supporters*, he responded, "I felt like I would like to kick them in the ass." Remarkably cynical, distrustful, skeptical, and suspicious, he did *not* believe in the goodness of human nature, assume the best about those he met, or believe that most people around him were honest and trustworthy. He was disliked and rejected much more than most presidents; even people in Nixon's circle were not moved to nurture or take care of him.

Nixon himself had very little sympathy for the less fortunate, being not at all benevolent, charitable, or generous. He did not believe that human needs take priority over economic considerations and was hardheaded and tough-minded.

He enjoyed sensual pleasures a great deal less than most presidents. He had remarkably little interest in women, few sexual encounters, and probably no extramarital affairs. Though he sometimes acted before thinking and did not delay in taking a position or action, he planned carefully when taking a trip and would think his answer through before responding to a question. He did not endanger others by reckless behavior or failure to observe safety rules. He was not "extravagant, frivolous, impractical" nor nonchalant and easygoing. A workaholic, Nixon was productive and got things done, and he did not give up when things went wrong. His lifestyle was fast-paced—but devoted to work, not family or leisure.

Nixon abhorred small talk and *did not* like being with people. Nor was he at all warm or compassionate, and he did NOT invest in close relationships. In fact, he decidedly avoided them. He definitely did not make friends easily and did *not* like most people; he had a well-known reputation for being distant, cold, and calculating. Markedly "detached, reserved, secretive," he much preferred working and doing most things on his own. Nixon was NOT enthusiastic, spirited, vivacious, or zestful. He may have never literally "jumped for joy."

Clearly not attracted to bright or flashy styles, he was decidedly un-cheerful, -jovial, -merry, and -optimistic; he was not charming. *Not* adventurous, mischievous, playful, or rambunctious, he overcontrolled his needs and impulses. He was not "down-to-earth, earthy, folksy, homespun, simple," and did not laugh easily.

Nixon certainly was not "religious, spiritual; committed to a personal faith," despite occasional references to his Quaker upbringing. He also clearly lacked an interest in science and was not good with figures. He strongly believed that normal people have a firm grasp of themselves and their goals by age twenty-five. Markedly indifferent to questions of values, philosophy, or religion, he had little taste for painting, sculpture, or other visual arts. Though mindful of people's motivations when evaluating situations, he did not usually empathize with the views or feelings of others. He was rarely aware of the "mood" of different settings and was proud to be objective and rational. Comfortable with uncertainties and complex issues, he did not have difficulty grasping new ideas and problems.

Miscellaneous Observations

In addition to poker, Nixon golfed in the low 90s and bowled around 175. Typically a lifelong loner, he became friends with his roommates in law school and several colleagues in the course of his career. As he rose higher in politics, his associations became more businesslike and he became more remote. Two later-life friends, Bebe Rebozo and Bob Abplanalp, were "Totally discreet men who wanted nothing from Nixon. . . . Uncomplicated men too content with their own successful roles in life to be overwhelmed." With Rebozo, Nixon could relax and work at a legal pad without talking for hours at a time. Little conversation was needed between them.

Before his entry into politics, Nixon apparently had no reputation for the rancor and combativeness that would characterize his later life. Some have attributed this development to injustices he suffered from the Kennedy campaign, including wiretaps by the FBI and investigation by the IRS. Another author cites the mesmerizing influence of John Mitchell, a dedicated partisan whose boundless self-confidence left Nixon in awe. In contrast to the impression left by the White House tapes, Nixon rarely swore until later in life. He did have a strong personal sense of right and wrong, but not when it came to politics.[15]

Nixon himself provided some explanation for his obsession with winning and his occasional ruthlessness toward opponents. "[What really drives it] are the laughs and slights and snubs when you are a kid. But if . . . your anger is deep enough and strong enough, you learn that you can change those attitudes by excellence, personal gut performance."[16] Nixon was said to love to confound his critics, which suggests a motivation based on hostility but also creativity, such as his opening relations with China.

Though generally portrayed as aloof and self-absorbed, some anecdotes show his capacity for graciousness. Bob Dole, whose right arm is paralyzed, recalled Nixon as the only man in Washington who offered him a left-handed handshake. Jackie Onassis had dreaded attending the dedication of John Kennedy's official portrait in the White House, but Nixon's hospitality and graciousness transformed the affair and provided her with fond memories. Lastly, the Chinese were reputed to be obsessed with protocol and highly sensitive to questions of status and respect. Nixon broached these issues with skill and tact, leading to a visionary rapprochement with the People's Republic. Seemingly, then, he had the capability to be sensitive and considerate but was rarely motivated to behave so.

There are mixed reports about his use of alcohol. He was observed to be intoxicated in public on several occasions. However, this may have been due to alcohol interacting with the prescription medication Dilantin, which he regularly took to control his anxiety.[17]

Nixon is one of few modern presidents to be profiled in a major motion picture. Oliver Stone's *Nixon* struck some as an unfair and overly negative portrayal (as well as lacking historical accuracy). John Dean, Nixon's lawyer, thought Stone's portrayal was not sufficiently cold.[18] It seems to us that Stone's version of Nixon was more helpless and vulnerable than our data suggest, while Nixon's intelligence, duplicity, combativeness, malevolence, and capacity to get things done were not fully depicted.

Nixon Quoted

"I have never been a quitter."

"I want a break in. . . . I want the Brookings (Institution) safe cleaned out. And I want it cleaned out in a way that makes somebody else look bad."[19]

"Could we please investigate some of those c_____ suckers?"[20]

Nixon Described

"I am always struck by the President's breadth and depth of knowledge . . . and his ability to articulate significant considerations in so many fields."—George Romney

"A terribly proud man, he detested weakness in other people."—Gerald Ford

"Richard Nixon is a no-good lying bastard. He can lie out of both sides of his mouth at the same time, and if he ever caught himself telling the truth, he'd lie just to keep his hand in."—Harry Truman

"Making up his mind and then pretending that his options were still open— that was a Nixon trait that I'd have occasion to witness again."—Gerald Ford

"In two hundred years of history, he's the most dishonest President we've ever had. I think he's disgraced the Presidency."—Jimmy Carter

President Nixon

Nixon got an overall rating of thirty-second in the Ridings and McIver poll, a significant rise from earlier assessments. He was ranked just behind Benjamin Harrison and ahead of Coolidge. His highest rating was in Political Skill (eighteenth) and he polled a respectable nineteenth on Accomplishments and Crisis Management. He got the lowest rating of any president on Character and Integrity.

Nixon showed considerable strengths as president, his most prominent being the trait that led to his being labeled "Tricky Dick"—low Straightforwardness (see Chart 5.6). He worked hard in pursuit of his goals (high Achievement Striving) and was very Assertive. On the negative side, he lacked concern for others (low Tender-Mindedness), was low in Positive Emotions, and was more sensitive to stress (Vulnerability) than most presidents. Overall, his personality was a reasonable match for the job—about average among presidents.

CHART 5.6
Personality Assets and Liabilities of Nixon as President

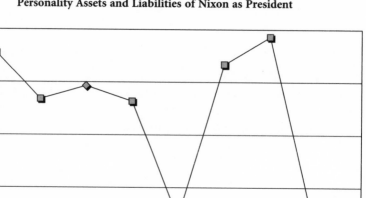

Usually, scandals occur among presidents low on Conscientiousness—a result of lax morals or oversight. This was not the case with Nixon; the relevant personality factors for him appeared to be low Agreeableness and Dutifulness (devotion to principles) and high Neuroticism. Our item pool does not capture much of his more notorious behavior. We delve into this here because of his notoriety, its historical significance, and because his biography does not prepare us for what followed.

Nixon chose his advisory staff to be as tough and as cynical as he was—and to a man, they generally were. This promoted a culture where toughness was valued above all else, where ethical concerns became a liability, and where there was no voice of conciliation. It quickly established an "us-versus-them" mentality and created a climate ripe for enemies lists and abuse. Recently released tapes catch Nixon prescribing his specifications for the next commissioner of Internal Revenue:

> I want to be sure he is a ruthless son-of-a-bitch, that he'll do what he's told, that every income tax return I want to see I see, that he'll go after our enemies and not our friends. Now it's as simple as that. If he isn't, he doesn't get the job.[21]

The eventual choice, John Walters, recalled being handed a list of hundreds of people the White House wanted investigated, including staffers and contributors to Democratic candidate George McGovern.[22]

While discussing the Pentagon Papers, Nixon's special assistant H. R. Haldeman once suggested, "You can blackmail Johnson [LBJ] on this stuff, and it might be worth doing." Harry Truman would have thrown Haldeman out of his office. Nixon's response? "How?"[23] In *Go Quietly . . . or Else,* Vice President Agnew claimed that he resigned not to avoid prosecution, but out of fear that Nixon's chief of staff, Alexander Haig, would have him murdered.[24]

John Ehrlichman, one of his close assistants (and one of our raters), reported that Nixon would approach him in the hallways days after ordering a questionable action and seek assurance that it was not actually being carried out. According to him, Nixon would relieve stress by "popping off" in this way with no intent that action should be based on his bombast. However, he also berated staff when similar orders were not carried out.

Nixon avoided challenges to his authority by dividing responsibility for many issues between two government departments. This allowed for Henry Kissinger's rise as national security adviser while the State Department was largely kept in the dark about his activities. It also impelled the Joint Chiefs of Staff to literally spy on the White House to discern policy issues they believed vital to performing their mission.

Nixon the introvert attempted to govern by memo as much as possible. Many of these have been preserved, including communiqués from staffers to Nixon that were returned with his comments. Often these included aggressive, action-based directives like, "Hit them on this." These were not always directed against purely political opponents. A university researcher who found that participation in football did not build "character" was also singled out for harassment—Nixon's beliefs about football apparently being to the contrary.

Behavior as President (our data)

Nixon scored highest of all presidents on Simonton's Creative presidential style scale. He definitely did not keep in frequent contact with his advisers and Cabinet, and clearly did not give credit to others for their work. Not surprisingly, he did not endear himself to his staff through courtesy and consideration. He clearly placed political success over effective policy, did not regard his relationship with the press as challenging and enjoyable, and did *not* evince good moral character. Unfortunately, he nonetheless viewed the presidency as a vehicle for self-expression. Though his personality hardly seems to have been desirable at any time, it was an especially poor match for the needs of a divided country. Despite these problems, Nixon was an innovative chief executive who sponsored many new programs and legislation.

Nixon in Perspective

Nixon most resembled LBJ ($r = .51$), John Adams ($r = .43$), and Hoover ($r = .40$). He was least like Hayes ($r = -.40$), Ford ($r = -.36$), and Fillmore ($r = -.35$).[25] He was a self-made man of unusual ability and industry who, throughout his early life, was limited by his background. He became deeply resentful of those who had inherited wealth, power, and popularity without earning it and felt the Eastern elite looked down on him. John Kennedy personified everything Nixon was not and, on one occasion, flatly stated that his one-time Senate colleague had "no class." Kennedy narrowly defeated him in an election that may have been subject to tampering and used government agencies to harass him and his family. If that were not enough, the press clearly preferred his rival. Though not vanquished, Nixon was left embittered and fatally flawed. The acts that would stem from his wrath would eclipse the historical opening to China in his legacy. More than any other president, Nixon illustrates that Character may, in some cases, be important in a president.

Dominators Compared

As can be seen in Chart 5.7, all three Dominators were very low on Character, Openness, and Agreeableness. Nixon and Johnson had strikingly similar profiles except on Extraversion, where Nixon scored low. Jackson differed from the other two by scoring low on Conscientiousness and average on Neuroticism. Lyndon Johnson was closest to being a prototypical Dominator, although he scored higher than average on Neuroticism and Extraversion.

The three exhibited numerous differences on the more specific scales. Nixon and Johnson were both rated highly on Simonton's Machiavellian Scale (sly, deceitful), and on our measure of Need for Power, while Jackson did not. Johnson and Jackson both scored low on Poise and Polish, while Nixon was about average. In several cases, one scored high, while the others did not. Nixon scored off the chart on Pettiness (greedy, self-pitying), Jackson was high on Inflexibility, and Johnson scored moderately high on Wit. Lastly, Jackson was Charismatic, Nixon decidedly not.

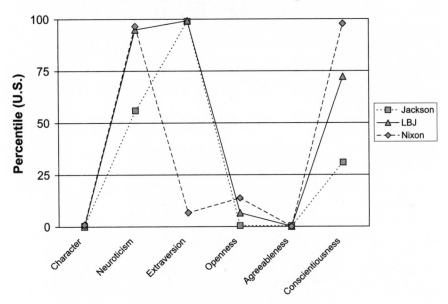

CHART 5.7
Jackson, Johnson, and Nixon Compared

CHAPTER 6

Two Introverts—John Adams and Woodrow Wilson

Morphed image of John Adams and Woodrow Wilson.
Library of Congress

AS REPORTED in Chapter 4, Introvert presidents share a number of characteristics not necessarily related to sociability. Traits shared by Adams and Wilson are shown in Table 6.1. Both were famously difficult person-

TABLE 6.1
Adams and Wilson Compared

	Adams High	*Adams Low*
Wilson High	Achievement Striving, Angry Hostility	*Pacifism*
Wilson Low	**NONE**	Modesty, Openness to Values, Compliance, *Moderation, Friendliness, Interpersonal Presidential Style*

alities—Adams driven for achievement and recognition, Wilson in the service of his ideals. As presidents, both scored low on the Interpersonal style of governing and dramatically failed to appreciate their own limitations.

To be listed in Table 6.1, *both* presidents had to score in the upper or lower 15 percent of average Americans for NEO Scales or the upper or lower 15 percent of presidents for other scales.

We now turn to their individual lives and personalities.

JOHN ADAMS

Brief Biography

Descended from John and Priscilla Alden, John Adams was born to Deacon John Adams and his wife, Susanna Boylston, on October 19, 1735, at Braintree, Massachusetts. The eldest of three sons, he enjoyed a happy childhood in the outdoors. He was especially fond of hunting and disliked school. This may have stemmed from daydreaming, boredom, and a clash with a teacher, who was strong-willed, like his parents.

Adams recalled a lot of bickering between his parents in his youth. His father saddled John with the responsibility of getting a college education. At Harvard, he came into his own as a student. On graduation, he rejected his father's choice of career for him as a clergyman and tried teaching for two years before reading law.

His cousin, Samuel Adams, was a firebrand who tried mightily to stir up opposition to Britain's increasingly harsh treatment of its American colonies. Eventually, John was totally transformed, in part by his cousin's rhetoric. He went from being a rather conservative town councilman in the 1760s to a delegate to the Continental Congress in Philadelphia by 1774.

Painfully separated from his wife and children for the next decade, he worked nonstop for the Revolutionary cause. He served on the War and Ordnance Board, the panel assigned to draft the Declaration of Independence, and the Committee on Foreign Correspondence, charged with getting foreign aid. He nominated George Washington as General of the Army and Thomas Jefferson to draft the Declaration of Independence. Later, Adams sometimes claimed to have "made Washington" by his nomination.

Though short and obese, "Adams exuded a certain rustic masculinity and intellectual vigor that made him popular with girls." He waited to marry until his finances and career allowed it; he was proud to have remained a virgin until marriage. An early love, Hannah Quincy, got tired of waiting and married another. At age twenty-eight, he married nineteen-year-old Abigail Smith, a sickly child with no formal education. She became one of the most intellectually vivacious women ever to serve as First Lady and is considered an early hero of the Women's Movement.

As minister to Holland, he played a pivotal role in raising much needed cash for the Revolution. He took his son John Quincy Adams with him to France in 1778 where the elder Adams served in a delegation with Benjamin Franklin. Adams disapproved of Franklin's womanizing and was jealous of his popularity. His blunt manner irritated the French and he achieved little before returning home the next year. In a little over two months, he was ordered back to France. He remained in Europe as a peace delegate, and later served as the first minister to Great Britain until 1788.

He was elected Washington's vice president by the Electoral College and assumed the presidency in 1797. It was as vice president, while serving as president of the Senate, that he came to first be accused of monarchical tendencies. Adams believed in government by "the rich, the wise, and the well-born." Having been exposed to the royal courts of Europe for the previous decade, he suggested that the president be addressed as, "His Highness, the President of the United States and Protector of their Liberties." Hooted down by the senators, he was thereafter disparaged as "His Rotundity, the Duke of Braintree."

Once friends, Jefferson and Adams took opposing sides in the Republican–Federalist conflicts during Washington's administration. Their dislike of each other deepened when they were forced to serve together during Adams's presidency. Adams was very bitter over his defeat by Jefferson, his vice president, in 1800. He created numerous federal judgeships and other offices and staffed them with loyal Federalists before leaving office; he then left Washington before dawn to avoid Jefferson's inauguration.

Reconciled with Jefferson via correspondence in old age, his lifelong adversary may have been, in the end, his closest friend. Adams's dying words in Boston on July 4, 1826, were "Thomas Jefferson survives." In fact, Jefferson had died just a few hours earlier the same day in Virginia. Incredibly, the only two signers of the Declaration of Independence to become president both died on the fiftieth anniversary of its signing.

Personality

The five experts rating Adams agreed well on his overall personality style. However, they had substantial difference of opinion on all traits except for Openness and Agreeableness (Chart 6.1). Adams scored very low on Character (1.9th percentile) and Agreeableness (1.5th), low on Extraversion (9th), high on Conscien-

CHART 6.1
John Adams's Scores on Character and the Big Five Traits

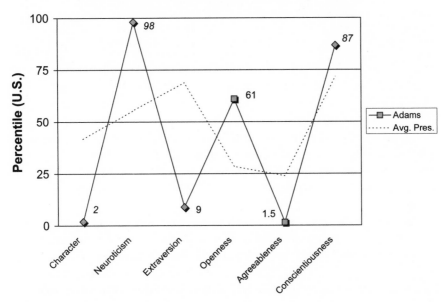

tiousness (87th), and very high on Neuroticism (98th). Specialists indicated less respect for Adams's job performance than did generalists (and the historians who completed the surveys of presidential greatness) and rated Adams higher in Neuroticism and lower in Conscientiousness than did generalists.

Adams's low score on Character reported here requires some explanation, since this differs dramatically from his reputation. It derives from his very low scores on the NEO Trust, Altruism, and Modesty scales and his high score on Angry Hostility (see table below). Yet when asked to describe him on the single item, "has good moral character," the same experts rated him highly, at about the 80th percentile among presidents. The generalists rated him second highest on character on two similar items. When allowed their own definition of character, raters apparently focused on Adams's honesty and fairness in positions of power, where he was accused of many things, but not corruption.

On the NEO Facet Scales, below, Adams had many extreme scores relative to current Americans. His scores denote a suspicious (low Trust), self-centered (low Altruism), vain (low Modesty), and irritable (Angry Hostility) man who was also very self-conscious. He was rated the second lowest of all presidents on Charisma. In the following paragraphs, we paraphrase individual questionnaire items to form our descriptions.

High	Percentile	Low	Percentile
Angry Hostility (N, -Ch)	98	Trust (A, Ch)	0.3
Self-Consciousness (N)	98	Altruism (A, Ch)	0.9
Anxiety (N)	96	Modesty (A, Ch)	1.7
Depression (N)	96	Tender-Mindedness (A)	3
Openness to Ideas (O)	91	Warmth (E)	3
		Openness to Values (O)	4
		Compliance (A, Ch)	6

Adams was exceedingly uncomfortable around his superiors and was decidedly *not* capable and unfazed in the face of a crisis. To an exceptional degree, he compared himself to and was envious and jealous of others. Proud of his role in the Revolution, he fretted that:

> The essence of [it] will be that Dr. Franklin's electrical rod smote the earth and out sprang . . . Washington. . . . Franklin electrified him with his rod—and thenceforward [they] conducted all the policies, negotiations, legislatures and war.

Particularly prone to self-pity and feeling cheated by life, Adams was very "bitter, joyless, melancholic, moody, morose, pessimistic, somber," as well as defensive, fretful, insecure, negativistic, and self-critical. He often became disgusted with people and was angered by how they treated him (both to a marked degree). He was very temperamental, touchy, and unstable, *not* even-tempered, and clearly unable to keep his emotions under control. He was defensive and could not laugh at his own quirks or faults.

Highly anxious and fearful, he very readily felt guilt and worry, had frightening and preoccupying thoughts, and tended to overcomplicate matters. Much more than most people, situations often appeared bleak to him. He frequently felt sad, dejected, or alone.

Adams did *NOT* have faith in human nature or assume the best about those he met. Nor did he believe that most people have good intentions: "The people, when they have been unchecked, have been as unjust, tyrannical, brutal, barbarous, and cruel as any king or senate possessed of uncontrollable power," he wrote. He very much saw people as ready to exploit others if permitted, and he was clearly cynical, critical, skeptical, and not easily impressed. He was not courteous, polite, or respectful; he tended to compete rather than cooperate with others. He did *not* try to be humble and thought he was superior to most people. He was notably "boastful, conceited, egocentric, egotistical, vain." Remarkably condescending, he did *not* prefer complimenting people to being praised. Highly antagonistic, argumentative, and combative, he was very often hostile toward people and could be sarcastic and cutting. He definitely lacked personal magnetism and *was not* charismatic.

Nor was he at all optimistic and cheerful. He clearly did not like most people, *was not* outgoing or friendly to strangers, and shied away from crowds. He definitely was *not* generous or giving toward others. Though his lifestyle was not fast paced, his manners were not leisurely. He was not casual, easygoing, informal, natural, or relaxed. He was sensitive to and resentful of anyone making demands of him and did not forgive and forget. He valued his independence and autonomy and took little personal interest in his colleagues. Not surprisingly, then, he did not want or value close relationships (aside from that with his wife).

Adams very much enjoyed pondering abstract ideas and theories and talking about them. He was particularly interested in the nature of the universe and the human condition and unusually introspective of himself. Much more than most presidents, he fantasized and daydreamed. However, he had a particularly bad sense of direction and a lesser problem recognizing faces—both of which require spatial ability.

He was talented, gifted, intellectually curious, and "bright, intelligent, smart." He was complicated, complex, and deep. He valued intellectual matters, had many interests, and thought in unusual ways. He had an exceptional vocabulary and could express ideas well. Despite his philosophical bent, he thought there was something wrong with those who did not know themselves and their life goals by their mid-twenties. He was conservative, did not see himself as broadminded or tolerant, and did not empathize easily with the feelings of others.

Adams was ambitious, enterprising, opportunistic, and set high goals for himself. He was very concerned with excellence and making unique personal accomplishments. Though Conscientious, he tended to answer questions before thinking them through. He was not extravagant, frivolous, or impractical. Despite his negative qualities, he did not cheat on taxes, at sports, or in business, and was "ethical, honest, moral, principled, sincere, truthful."

Miscellaneous Observations

Adams was not handsome or attractive. By the time of his election, he was bald, "so very fat," in the words of his wife, and missing most of his teeth. Though a Puritan, he began each day with a glass of hard cider. A voracious reader of history and politics, he had little interest in art or music. He had "few but very close friends" according to one source—none at all according to another—but a wide circle of acquaintances.

Despite his prickly personality, he had a warm relationship with his wife, Abigail. When she chided him in a letter that even a man of sixty years of age "ought not live more than three months at a time from his family," he wrote back, "Oh, that I had a bosom to lean my head upon! . . . If I were near I would soon convince you that I am not above forty."

Adams Described

"Whether he is spiteful, playful, witty, kind, cold, drunk, sober, angry, easy, stiff, jealous, cautious, confident, close, open, it is always in the wrong place or to the wrong person."—James McHenry, Adams's secretary of war

"He is vain, irritable, a bad calculator of the force and probable effect of the motives which govern men. This is all the ill that can possibly be said of him. He is as disinterested as the Being who made him."—Thomas Jefferson

"He means well for his country, is always an honest man, often a wise one, but sometimes, and in some things, is absolutely out of his senses."—Benjamin Franklin

"You stand nearly alone in the history of our public in having never had your integrity called into question or even suspected."—Benjamin Rush

President Adams

Adams was rated as the fourteenth best president in the Ridings and McIver poll, behind Monroe and ahead of Kennedy. He ranked third in Character and Integrity but seventeenth in Leadership Qualities and twenty-first in political skill. These latter ratings may be inflated by his Founding Father status. An avid Federalist, he was instrumental in enacting the Alien and Sedition Acts, which greatly jeopardized freedoms guaranteed under the Bill of Rights. This further contributed to his reputation as a monarchist. In fact, Adams greatly mistrusted the electorate and favored lifelong terms for senators.

Adams's personality was less well suited to being president than most of his colleagues'. His single strength for presidential successful was his intellect (Intelligent and Smart); he had four liabilities: low scores on Competence, Tender-Mindedness, and Positive Emotions, and a very high score on Vulnerability.

Behavior as President (our data)

Adams scored second lowest of all chief executives on Interpersonal Style. As president, he eschewed teamwork to an exceptional degree and lacked close relationships with his associates. He *did not* select advisers for their professional

CHART 6.2

Personality Assets and Liabilities of Adams as President

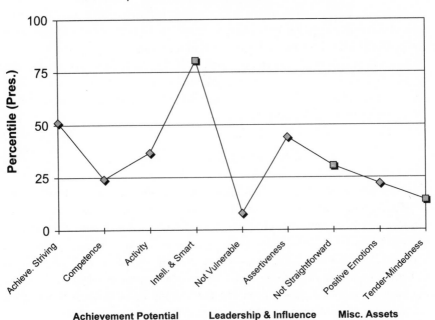

competence and knowledge, failed to tend to his public image, and plainly lacked charisma. He was impatient and abrupt in meetings, given to emotional outbursts, and did not endear himself to his staff through courtesy or consideration.

Like Nixon, whom he resembled closely, Adams did not like dealing with the press and lacked the ability to remain popular. Unlike Nixon, he allowed opponents to outflank him. More than most presidents, he served during a time of crisis and opportunity for the country.

Adams in Perspective

Adams was most like his son, John Quincy Adams (r = .54), Nixon (r = .43), and Andrew Johnson (r = .39). He was least like Ford (r = −.38), Hayes (r = −.35), and Harding (r = −.32).[1] None of the men Adams most resembles were particularly effective presidents, as judged by their rankings by historians. It was said of Adams's son, John Quincy Adams, that the presidency was the least successful facet of his career. The same could be said of Hoover.

Adams's similarity to Nixon is also provocative: In fact, it provoked a burst of indignation from one of our specialists who reviewed this chapter. Certainly,

Adams's and Nixon's reputations for integrity in office are at the opposite ends
of the spectrum. David McCullough's recent biography has spurred something
of an Adams revival, with talk of a monument in Washington, D.C. But aside
from their differing character in office, Adams's personality similarities to Nixon
could fill the next three pages. Chart 6.3 is more concise.

Adams's and Nixon's scores are nearly identical on four of the five Big Five
traits, whereas Adams scores considerably higher in Openness. A major difference, one of relatively few, is on the facet scale of Straightforwardness. Adams
scores relatively high, Nixon very low.

(THOMAS) WOODROW WILSON

Of all the presidents, Wilson's personality was probably the most shaped by family experiences, particularly by his father and grandfather. His mother, Janet
Woodrow Wilson, came from England at age four and attended the Female Seminary in Chillicothe, Ohio, where she lived most of her life. Though quarrelsome
with outsiders, she was a warm and giving mother. Woodrow recalled, "I clung
to her (a laughed-at mama's boy) till I was a great big fellow," and "The love of
the best womanhood came to me and entered my heart through those apron
strings." They maintained an intimate correspondence until her death.

CHART 6.3
Adams and Nixon Compared

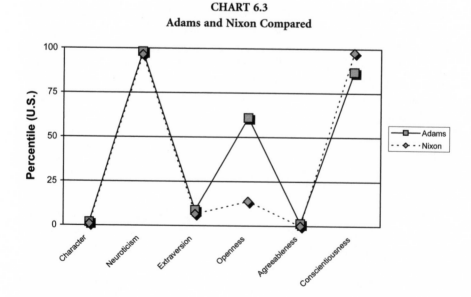

The Wilson family had a tradition of intellectual accomplishment running through Wilson's grandfather and his father. Tommy was awed by his larger-than-life, affectionate, but demanding father, Joseph Ruggles Wilson. A strikingly handsome man, he was also a Presbyterian minister and the undisputed lion of his congregation. A stirring orator, and a staunch supporter of the South during the Civil War, he taught theology at a seminary and a university. By age four, Tommy was expected to express his thoughts in organized and proper English and was made to try again if he failed. The pressure was psychological (no physical punishment), but it was constant and unavoidable for a shy, imaginative boy. His father was also known, within his extended family, for "painful teasing [that] sometimes left barbs in the wounds he made." A niece described him as "a cruel tease, with caustic wit and a sharp tongue," and recalled hearing how Wilson had suffered under his attacks.

A description of Wilson by a childhood friend presents the sad picture of a little boy old before his time:

> A boy of good moral character and attainment, precise, slow-spoken, dignified and very orderly. He never, like the rest of the boys, went barefoot. When they went riding, [he] preferred a reliable nag to a more spirited ride.

Wilson did not endure his childhood without pain. Speaking years later at the pinnacle of his career, he recalled his grandfather with tears in his eyes: "I remember how much he required. I remember the stern lessons of duty he spoke to me. I remember also painfully the things which he expected me to know which I did not know." Even as president and until the day he died, he regarded his father as a greater man than himself and never openly criticized him. Yet consider this portion of a 1904 address:

> Those who have read that delightful book of Kenneth Graham's entitled "The Golden Age," the age of childhood, will recall the indictment he brings against the Olympians, as he calls them,—the grown-up people—who do not understand the feelings of little folks . . . who do not live in the same world, who are constantly forcing upon the young ones standards and notions that they cannot understand, which they instinctively reject. They live in a world of delightful imagination; they pursue persons and objects that never existed; they make an Argosy laden with gold out of a floating butterfly—and these stupid Olympians try to translate these things into uninteresting facts. I suppose that nothing is more painful in the recollections of some of us than the efforts that were made to make us like grown-up people. The delightful follies that we had to eschew, the delicious nonsense that we had to disbelieve, the number of odious prudences that we had to learn.

Perhaps because of the extraordinary pressure placed on him, Wilson developed a rich inner life but was a slow learner. He could not read until age eleven and had trouble with basic arithmetic. Poor health and eyesight may have compromised his performance but by college he had a 90 average, though he remained weak in science and math. He enjoyed debating and writing, publishing historical articles in some professional journals and better magazines.

He attended the University of Virginia Law School, but did not like it and dropped out, he said, due to poor health. He practiced law briefly, primarily as a means to enter politics, but never had a taste for it. He decided to return to graduate school at Johns Hopkins, where he studied political science and became the only president to earn a Ph.D.

He joylessly played golf for exercise and took up horseback riding as president. He enjoyed theater, especially vaudeville and musical comedies, and was a voracious reader of poetry, novels, and essays. He was a gifted mimic who delighted in telling dialect jokes in English, Irish, Scottish, and black accents, or in imitating a drunk.

At twenty-eight, he married Ellen Louise Axson, then twenty-five. Like Wilson, her father was also a Presbyterian minister. Ellen was a refined lady with a taste for art, music, and literature. As First Lady, she painted, donating the proceeds to charity, and lobbied Congress to fund slum clearance. She died of Bright's disease in the White House in 1914. Wilson was so distraught that he confided to an aide that he hoped to be assassinated.

The White House hostess introduced Wilson to his second wife. Edith Bolling Galt was an intelligent, attractive, forty-three-year-old widow. Wilson, then fifty-eight, was immediately taken with her, and they became engaged only eleven months after Ellen's death. The courtship was partially concealed from the press, though a typographical error in the *Washington Post* sensationally reported that, "The president spent much of the night entering [entertaining] Mrs. Galt." The rapid pace of events led to rumors that he had cheated on Ellen and even that he and Edith had murdered the First Lady.

After earning his Ph.D., Wilson taught political economy and public law at Bryn Mawr College in Pennsylvania, then taught history at Wesleyan in Connecticut. While there, he organized a debating society and coached the football team. From 1890 to 1902, while a professor of jurisprudence and political economy at Princeton, he wrote political and historical works that earned him a national reputation for scholarship. For the next eight years he served as president of Princeton, where he revised many of its venerable institutions, including the sterile lecture hall environment. One of his proposals, to abolish the traditional, anti-intellectual "eating clubs," aroused bitter opposition. Wilson was unmovable, refused to compromise, and was defeated. It was one of two major policy defeats in his life where psychoanalysts accused him of self-defeating and even pathological stubbornness.

After Princeton, Wilson ran for governor of New Jersey. After his victory, he declared war on the party bosses. He was a progressive who instituted election reforms, established price controls on utilities, and saw the states' first worker's compensation law passed. His reputation as a reformer eventually helped land him the nomination in the 1912 presidential race. He was hailed as "the ultimate Democrat, a genius of liberty and the very incarnation of progress." With the Republican Party badly split by TR's break with Taft, he easily won with 42 percent of the vote.

Wilson's supporters got a clear message of his position shortly after his election. Meeting with the officers of the Democratic National Committee, he told them, "Before we proceed I wish it clearly understood that I owe you nothing." When the chairman reminded Wilson of the assistance provided in getting him elected, Wilson responded, "God ordained that I should be the next president of the United States. Neither you nor any other mortal could have prevented that!"

Wilson's upbringing had infused him with "a fervent belief in religious destiny: His own, America's, and the world's." In time, his manner came to resemble his father's to a remarkable degree, completing his identification with this powerful figure. This may have been one source of his occasional dogmatism: Speaking with the voice of his incomparable father, how could he be wrong?

Personality

Three specialists rated Wilson. There was overall agreement about his personality, but a range of opinion regarding Neuroticism and Extraversion, and generalists indicated higher Neuroticism and Extraversion than the specialists did as a group. Wilson's profile on broad personality factors is notable for a very high score on Conscientiousness (99th percentile) and a low score on Agreeableness (13th). His score on Openness (64th) is significantly above other presidents; he might qualify as a Philosophe if he were not so disagreeable. On the NEO Facets, he scored as shown in the table on page 130 compared to current Americans.

Wilson's most prominent trait was his very high score on Openness to Feelings, indicating a very passionate, emotional man despite his achievement drive, order, control, and self-discipline. Two of the raters saw Wilson as conservative in his moral outlook (low Openness to Values) despite being a social reformer, while the third saw him as rather liberal. He was not modest or cooperative (low Compliance)—again with some disagreement among raters. He scored highest

CHART 6.4
Wilson's Scores on Character and the Big Five Traits

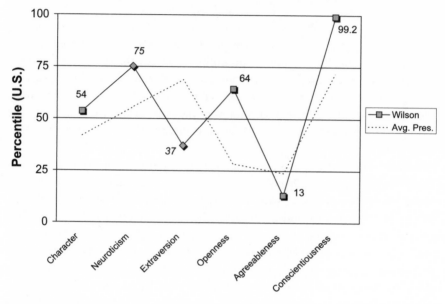

High	Percentile	Low	Percentile
Openness to Feelings	98.7	Openness to Values	5
Achievement Striving (C)	98.3	Modesty (A, Ch)	5
Assertiveness (E)	97	Impulsiveness (N, -Ch)	6
Order (C)	93	Compliance (A, Ch)	7
Self-discipline (C, Ch)	90	Openness to Actions	8
		Gregariousness (E)	9

of all presidents on Simonton's Inflexibility scale, on the generalists' estimate of intelligence, and on Conscientiousness. He was second highest on the generalist's ratings of Neuroticism and on the NEO Order scale. He was second lowest on the NEO Scales of Impulsivity and Gregariousness.

Unlike Adams, most of Wilson's salient features were related to Introversion. He was undeniably inhibited and restrained, had great difficulty making friends, and according to one biographer, eventually broke with all of them. He did *not* enjoy big parties *nor* did he like being with people. He was detached, reserved, secretive, bashful, and shy. He liked to do things alone and would likely prefer a cabin in the woods to a crowded beach. He did not live a leisurely lifestyle, but neither did he do things for excitement. Despite his introversion and austerity, he rarely failed to assert his position. He also was interested in women and wrote many highly personal letters to a number of female friends throughout his life.

He had sympathy for the less fortunate and an exceptionally strong belief that human needs outweigh economic considerations. Yet, these were attitudes toward people in the abstract. He very often thought himself superior to those around him, and blamed them for his problems. He was bullheaded, obstinate, and stubborn, though not prejudiced.[2] He was autonomous, independent, and individualistic, slow to forget a personal slight. When people did something nice for him, he wondered what they were up to. When a Republican senator visited him after his incapacitating stroke and said he and his colleagues would be praying for him, Wilson shot back, "Which way?"[3]

He was exceptionally able to let his mind wander and had a very vivid imagination. He believed that social policies should change with the times. Passions gave his life purpose, and he attended to and valued his feelings. But he was also moralistic, idealistic, and spiritual: Interested in topics of philosophy, religion, and values. He was not "commonplace," and could speak publicly without preparation better than most presidents.

Wilson was markedly thin-skinned and sensitive to insults or slights. He was humorless about his own faults and often felt profoundly guilty or sinful. In one of his essays at age twenty, he warned that every act must be performed "as an act of which we shall some day be made to render a strict account, as an act done either in the service of God or in that of the Devil." Whatever the costs of his religion, he did not think himself inferior to others (except to his father), was not anxious, and did not lack a sense of purpose in life. But he did not have an even temper, and occasionally spoke of himself as carrying around a volcano inside of him—a seeming reference to bottled up anger.

Lastly, Wilson had a number of characteristics associated with Character. He took pride in his good judgment and was not one to cheat at solitaire or to indulge his cravings. Rarely late to appointments, he did not waste time before getting down to work, and did not give up when things went wrong. He was "meticulous, perfectionistic, precise" and attended church regularly. He kept his promises and did not lead people to become dependent on him in order to exploit them.

Miscellaneous Observations

Wilson, the boy mature beyond his years, sometimes displayed a decidedly boyish side as a man. As president, while accompanied by a Secret Service agent, he encountered a child who made a face at him; Wilson made one back. He knew his austere manner inspired respect but not affection, and once complained that he wanted people to love him but knew they never would. When a supporter shouted, "That was a good one, Woody!" he turned to his aide and gushed, "Did you hear that? They called me 'Woody'!"

Besieged by an advocate for a position he did not support, he plugged his ears and ran from the room. This was a variation of another Wilson tactic—refusing to respond to critics. It is not hard to see how the little boy who could not talk back to his father would transfer his anger, and his silence, toward a less exalted antagonist.

Yet he also had a kind and democratic side. While accompanying General Pershing on an inspection, the American commander picked up a folding tent pole from a soldier's kit to explain how it worked. When he was finished, he threw the pole down on top of the other carefully arranged equipment. "Are those boys not likely to be inspected further after we have passed?" Wilson asked Pershing. "Yes, sir, they may be." "One other thing, General," continued Wilson, "I am the Commander-in-Chief of the Army and authorized to give you orders, am I not?" "Certainly, sir." "Then General, you will replace that tent pole as you found it." The General did so with a smile, and the soldiers said that Wilson winked at them.

The outside world saw only the aloof, confident man, but Wilson had a profound need for reassurance and admiration that centered on his wife:

> You are the indispensable thing in my life. I wish you knew how often and with what feeling I read the dear words of tenderness and love in your letter! They seem to put life and hope into me. There is a sense in which it may be said that I keep alive on them when I am away from you.

Wilson Quoted

"The world must be made safe for democracy."

"It is not men that interest or disturb me primarily; it is ideas. Ideas live; men die."

Wilson Described

"He thinks he is another Jesus Christ come upon the earth to reform men." —French president Georges Clemenceau

"[His] mind was richly stored and disciplined to an almost perfect precision [and] was never deflected to . . . any question that did not head up in how government should be best administered . . . to advance the common weal." —Josephus Daniels, secretary of the Navy

"He was more than just an idealist; he was the personification of the heritage of idealism of the American people. He brought spiritual concepts to the peace table. He was a born crusader."—Herbert Hoover

"For Heaven's sake never allude to Wilson as an idealist or militaire or altruist. He is a doctrinaire when he can be so with safety to his personal ambition. . . . He hasn't a touch of idealism in him. . . . [He's] an utterly selfish and cold-blooded politician always."—Teddy Roosevelt[4]

President Wilson

Wilson was rated sixth best in the Ridings and McIver poll, just behind TR and ahead of Truman. All of his rankings were in the range of sixth to eighth, except for Political Skill where he was judged thirteenth. His personality was well suited to being president. He scored in the upper quarter of presidents on six of the nine scales in our index (Chart 6.5): Intelligent and Smart, Assertiveness, Achievement Striving, Activity, Tender-Mindedness, and Competence. He had no real weaknesses, at least as measured by our scales.

CHART 6.5
Personality Assets and Liabilities of Wilson as President

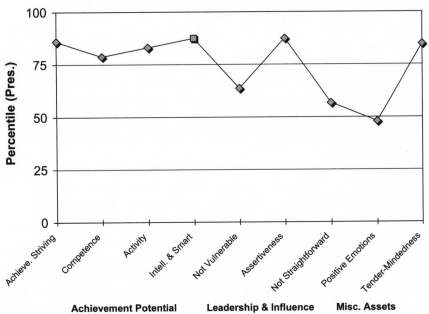

Wilson's administration reformed banking and eased currency problems with passage of the Federal Reserve Act. Other programs targeted trusts and child labor. Wilson also distinguished himself by his inaction as Southern members of his cabinet imposed segregation in federal agencies. He helped settle a rail strike by persuading Congress to pass legislation for an eight-hour workday, effectively undercutting the position of the railroad owners. When Germany announced that its U-boats would sink any ship engaged in trade with the Allies, Wilson armed merchant ships and began preparing for war, although he continued negotiations. He brought America into World War I with the greatest reluctance:

> Once lead this people into war, they'll forget there ever was such a thing as tolerance. To fight you must be brutal and ruthless, and this ruthless brutality will enter into every fibre of our national life, infecting the Congress, the courts, the policeman on the beat, and the man on the street.

Wilson's most famous battle was one he lost. A League of Nations, in the aftermath of the War to End All Wars, was to be his legacy. But his opponents knew his weakness. They accused him of selfish motives and made quibbling objections to his plan. With his righteous ire roused, he refused any modifications, despite urgings of virtually all around him, including his wife. As a result, the United States never joined the League. Wilson's defiance and rigidity were so blatantly self-defeating that they have been attributed to deep psychological disturbance or stroke-induced brain damage.

Wilson was severely disabled by the stroke he suffered in 1917—the most physically impaired president ever to remain in office by some accounts. Though he continued to make high-level decisions, his wife decided which problems were important enough to warrant his attention. He served out his term and later attempted to practice law, but was unable to do more than discuss legal matters from home. His speech was unimpaired and his righteousness was unshaken. He died on February 3, 1924. In his last public statement, he thundered:

> I am not one of those that have the least anxiety about the triumph of the principles I have stood for. I have seen fools resist Providence before, and I have seen their destruction, as will come upon these again, utter destruction and contempt.

Behavior as President (our data)

Wilson scored lowest of all presidents on Interpersonal Style. He was not at all flexible,[5] but he initiated many programs and was not suspicious of reformers. He was not cautious or conservative in his actions, was emphatic in asserting his judgments, and had a vision of what he wanted to accomplish. He suffered health problems during difficult periods in office and did not keep his staff informed on matters concerning other departments.

Wilson in Perspective

Wilson was most like Adams (r = .33), Carter (r = .26), and John Quincy Adams (r =.21). He was least like Harding (r = −.44), Ford (r = −.26), and Taft (r = −.22). He stands out among all presidents by his combination of idealism and occasional but absolute inflexibility. The only modern president with any similarity to him is Jimmy Carter, whose reputation as president is mixed. Wilson is remembered as visionary, a man ahead of his time, whose dream did see eventual fulfillment in the United Nations. He is also recalled as a man whose inability to compromise at critical times led to devastating defeats.

Adams and Wilson Compared

Next, we present the graphs of the Introverts we profiled together. Chart 6.6 shows Wilson was more Extraverted and less Neurotic than Adams. Their largest

CHART 6.6
Adams and Wilson Compared

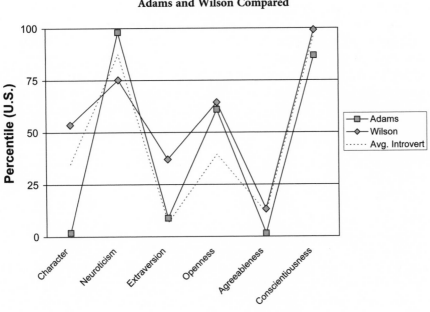

difference is on Character, where Adams scored very low for the reasons discussed earlier.

On more specific scales from our study and Simonton's, Wilson and Adams showed notable differences. Adams was much higher on Anxiety and Impulsiveness than Wilson and moderately higher on Self-Consciousness. Wilson scored high on Tender-Mindedness, Competence, Dutifulness, Trust, Pacifism, Spatial Ability, and Creative Style relative to Adams—but also very high on Inflexibility.

CHAPTER 7

Two Good Guys—Dwight Eisenhower and Gerald Ford

Morphed image of Dwight Eisenhower and Gerald Ford.
National Archives and Gerald Ford Library

THE GOOD GUYS include Hayes, Taylor, Eisenhower, Tyler, Fillmore, Cleveland, Ford, and Washington (in order). Washington is presented as a special case in Chapter 13 because of his preeminence and his limited resemblance to other presidents. Below, we profile two prominent Good Guys: Dwight Eisenhower and Gerald Ford. Aside from similarities in their personalities, they were both very good football players. Both scored relatively low on Neuroticism and high on Conscientiousness and Character. Table 7.1 shows the NEO Facets and other traits where they were similar; they differed on no traits.

One scale in this table needs explanation. Both scored low on Tender-Mindedness, though neither had a reputation for being callous or hard-hearted. Both also scored about average among presidents on the item "has sympathy for the less fortunate" but lower on items that imply government aid to such people or that specify sympathy for panhandlers.

TABLE 7.1
Eisenhower and Ford Compared

	Ford High	Ford Low
Eisenhower High	*Friendliness, Conservatism, Interpersonal Presidential Style,* Achievement Striving	**NONE**
Eisenhower Low	**NONE**	Openness to Values, Vulnerability, Tender-Mindedness, Depression

As presidents, both clearly relied on a staff system, deciding among options formulated by advisers. They kept their staffs informed on matters concerning other departments, emphasized teamwork, and knew their own limitations.

(DAVID) DWIGHT EISENHOWER[1]

Brief Biography

Named after his father, David Dwight Eisenhower was called by his middle name from childhood. His father, David Jacob Eisenhower, was an aloof, bad-tempered man who believed in physical punishment. His mother, Ida, was a taskmaster, too, but she was also warm and giving. The children were spanked on the spot for poorly done chores, with referral to their father for more serious offenses. When he was twelve, Eisenhower stepped in to physically restrain his father, who was beating his younger brother with a leather harness. Eisenhower would later defend his dad's discipline as, "deserved and beneficial," but on this occasion he risked his father's wrath by asserting that, "no one deserves to be beat like that—not even a dog."

David Dwight Eisenhower was born in 1890 near Denison, Texas, but grew up in Abilene, Kansas. With five other brothers in cramped quarters, there was a lot of roughhousing and fighting; something his parents did not discourage. When one brother sought to intervene as another pounded Eisenhower's head on the kitchen floor, Ida waived him off. She wanted them to fight their own battles, and the Eisenhower boys had more than their share of fights.

Abilene also instilled ideals of self-reliance and fear of God. A town of farmers and engineers, it produced doers, not thinkers or artists. Few distinctions of class or wealth existed, and there was little culture beyond a church social. The Eisenhower family was traditional and fit well in this milieu. They read the Bible every night, each child taking a turn and earning praise for clarity and smoothness of recital. There was never any discussion of the reading—never a question of why. It was God's word—to be accepted, not analyzed. Eisenhower could not remember his parents ever having an argument because Ida invariably bowed to her husband's point of view.

From an early age, Eisenhower had a temper. When told he could not go trick or treating with his brothers at age six, he punched a tree in frustration until his hands were bloody. Ida bandaged his hands and told him that conquering his anger would be his greatest achievement—something he struggled with all his life. He had a chip on his shoulder as a teen but avoided any real trouble. At fifteen his knee became infected. Blood poisoning developed, and the doctor recommended amputation. Eisenhower protested forcefully and secured a promise from his brother to keep him from the knife. The doctor became increasingly agitated, muttering about neglect and even murder, but the family backed Dwight. The leg healed.

During adolescence, Eisenhower developed a keen interest in military history. He especially admired Hannibal and Washington. His interest was so intense that his pacifist mother took to hiding his books to keep him focused on his schoolwork. He was an enthusiastic football player, notable for fair play and sportsmanship. He would not tolerate cheating and disliked those who sought individual glory over team play. In one memorable incident, another team fielded a black center. None of his teammates would line up across from the boy, but Eisenhower did. He also shook hands with him before and after the game. By then, a ready smile on his face had replaced the chip on his shoulder.

After high school, Eisenhower was intent on getting a college education but lacked the money. He made a deal with his brother to alternate years of working and school, with each helping to support the other during school years. Eisenhower let his brother take the first year at college—then the second. He initially worked doing hard labor but later got a soft, supervisory job with lots of down time. Friends would drop by to talk, and Eisenhower began the first of his political discussions. He showed a talent for trapping opponents with Socratic logic and using his luminous smile and humor to extricate himself from similar traps.

A friend persuaded him to apply for Annapolis in 1910, but at twenty-one, Eisenhower was too old to be accepted. After winning a local scholastic competition, he got an appointment to West Point. When he left for the Academy, he was broad shouldered, 175 pounds, agile, handsome, and supremely self-confident. Having conquered the entrance exams, he knew he could do the schoolwork and could succeed at sports and with people. He knew who he was and where he was going.

Most of his classmates at West Point were similar to Eisenhower—the best from their hometowns—and West Point would burst their bubbles. Plebes were given impossible tasks without enough time to do them and were harassed by upper-classmen. The food was bland; the rooms were hot in summer and cold in winter. The coursework was rigorous and based on math and technical skills, taught and absorbed by rote drill. As in Abilene, the issues were "what" and "how," not "why?" The goals were proficiency and the building of character. Eisenhower fit in but was not a blind convert. His overall ranking reflected demerits for smoking, messiness, and tardiness. He was ranked 125th of 164 in Discipline, and remained suspicious in later life of anyone afraid to break a rule. He received some traditional hazing but gave almost none of it back.

Eisenhower showed some indications of a broader mind-set than his class-mates. He was not paying attention one day as a young instructor detailed a cal-culus problem and its solution on the board. When called on to repeat the process, Eisenhower struggled for an hour until he found a solution. It was right, but not the prescribed method; the instructor accused him of cheating. Eisen-hower indignantly defended himself and was at risk of being expelled for insub-ordination. A senior officer from the math department overheard the argument, reviewed the solution, and pronounced it superior to the one in use. West Point adopted it as the new "correct" one.

Eisenhower developed rapidly as a star halfback and played against the leg-endary Jim Thorpe in one game. However, he suffered a catastrophic knee injury in 1912 that not only ended his football career but also nearly prevented him from being commissioned an officer. He seemed much more concerned with how the injury would impact his ability to hunt and play sports—his goal at West Point had been a college education, nothing more.

Aside from football, he excelled at history and English composition, which at West Point stressed logical presentation. Recuperating from the knee injury, he grew depressed and irritable. He viewed football as a metaphor for manly achievement—a model for successful problem solving and teamwork. When he could not play, he became a cheerleader. He had developed an interest in the strategy of the game and after his injury put this knowledge to use by coach-ing—a skill that would hamper his future career. He graduated in 1915, was com-missioned a second lieutenant, and was assigned to the 19th Infantry.

He met Marie "Mamie" Geneva Dodd, his future wife, in San Antonio that same year. The daughter of a wealthy meatpacker, she was attractive and viva-cious. Eisenhower's first attempt to make a date with her met with a month of previous engagements, but she hinted at other good times to call. They mainly went to dollar-per-couple Mexican restaurants, vaudeville shows, and movies. During the first week of their marriage, while staying with his parents, Eisenhower was gone most of the day playing poker. Against the advice of her mother-in-law, Mamie called him to come home; he remained out until 2:00 A.M. They fought the rest of that night.

The two families each took well to the young couple. Mamie's father regarded Eisenhower as the son he never had, and the rest of the family soon was enthusiastically cheering his football team, though previously they had no interest in sports.

Eisenhower's military career got off to a slow start. He spent much of it training troops and, later, officers. His workload was light and there was much time for recreation and socializing, of which he took full advantage. He and Mamie entertained so often that their apartment was dubbed "Club Eisenhower."

He was assigned to one of the newly formed tank corps, which at that point, not only had no tanks but no other modern weapons. Eisenhower lobbied energetically and got the corps into respectable shape. He earned glowing recommendations for his organizational ability and was to take command of a unit going into combat.

Instead, the Army decided that his abilities would best be used at home, where he was to attend and teach at the nation's first tank training program. There he met George Patton and the two became fast friends. Under Fox Conner, they developed advanced strategy for tank warfare that was dramatically validated in the Second World War. Eisenhower was given another combat command, but Germany negotiated a cease-fire before he shipped out. A career soldier, he sat out World War I. He grew bitter and wondered what he would tell his son about what he did in the "War to end all wars."

To add to the insult, the Army censured Eisenhower and Patton after they published their views on tank warfare in military journals and ordered them not to disseminate their views again. Eisenhower obeyed but learned a bitter lesson about the Army's attitude toward freethinkers.

Later, he attended Command and General Staff School at Fort Leavenworth, competing against 275 officers handpicked to represent the honor of their units. He graduated first in his class—then reported to coach football. He found himself captive to a commanding officer whose football team's record was more important than his subordinate's desire to transfer. After running a camp and giving orders to thousands of men at age twenty-eight, he would not make a significant military decision until he was fifty-one.

The Eisenhowers' first son David Dwight, nicknamed "Icky," was an energetic, charming boy who was the delight not only of his parents but also of the base. But at age three, he contracted scarlet fever and died. Eisenhower recalled it as the greatest tragedy of his life. For a long time, "it was as if the light went out in his life," recalled Mamie. They blamed themselves, grieved, and became distant and formal toward each other. Eisenhower regained his outlook through a transfer and his work. The couple had another son, John Sheldon Doud Eisenhower, in 1922.

Eisenhower's reliability, good nature, and ability to organize made him an ideal staff officer, and he served under the most illustrious generals of his day—Douglas MacArthur, John Pershing, and George Marshall.

His assignment in the Philippines under MacArthur from 1935 to 1941 was a trial. Mamie in particular suffered from the heat, humidity, and mosquitoes, but the local government supplemented their Army pay generously. MacArthur was a difficult boss; he was lavish with his praise but brutal with his criticism. Eisenhower disliked MacArthur's grandstanding and his lack of subordination to civil authority, but the general depended on him for reports, speeches, and innumerable other services. Eisenhower had made the mistake of being indispensable, and MacArthur would not let him go. In fact, he ordered Eisenhower not to even request transfers, which prevented him from pursuing a command position and nearly locked him into a staff officer career path.

MacArthur had called Eisenhower "the best officer in the Army," but as Eisenhower's star rose and challenged his own, he became jealous and caustic. Though he did his best to maintain a cordial relationship, Eisenhower's opinion of MacArthur diminished. His loyal service and competence put him in great demand as a staff officer, further diminishing his opportunities for command. Yet, at the start of World War II he was called to Washington.

Gen. George Marshall was a very different man than MacArthur—aloof and slow to praise, but reasonable, modest, never abusive. After working with MacArthur, Eisenhower found Marshall to be the ideal boss and became a fervent admirer. Marshall initially insisted that he remain a staff officer but later sent Eisenhower to London to head the American military headquarters for the European theater. This change of semantics freed Eisenhower for a command career path, and Marshall assigned him to head Operation Torch in North Africa. He worked furiously, was ill tempered and insecure, and performed poorly in his first command. Nonetheless, he grew in experience and wisdom, and was given command of Operation Overlord (D-Day), the largest invasion in history.

As Supreme Commander of Allied Forces, he had to coordinate the air, sea, and land forces of the United States, Canada, and Britain against a well-organized, experienced, and powerful enemy. Despite his title, he had far from absolute authority. Generals like Montgomery showed less than complete deference, and Eisenhower had to balance military matters, political considerations, demands from civilian authorities, and the weather. He was chosen for his organizational skill and zeal, his popularity with the British, and his ability to work with difficult prima donnas (including Montgomery and DeGaulle) and because Marshall and Churchill trusted him. Eisenhower put great emphasis on morale, insisting that officers and enlisted men get equivalent food and quarters.

He and Mamie generally had a warm and affectionate relationship but were separated for much of the war. She worried about the newspaper pictures she saw of him with his English driver, Kay Summersby. He reassured her, but an affair apparently developed over time. Truman claimed to have seen correspondence from Eisenhower, informing Montgomery that he intended to divorce Mamie and marry Kay. Marshall allegedly threatened to run him out of the Army and make his life miserable forever after; no divorce took place. The Eisenhower family denies this account, and at least one prominent biographer also dismissed it as untrue.

The end of World War II ushered in the atomic era. Eisenhower abhorred the bomb and the talk of "the next war" with the Soviet Union that circulated soon after Germany had been defeated. He was deeply moved by the destruction and the human suffering that he saw in postwar Europe. He initially advocated cooperation with the Russians but gradually hardened into a cold warrior as their tyranny over Eastern Europe proceeded.

Eisenhower was not always comfortable in the Army. For years, his career stagnated, his pay was low, and superiors used him for their own purposes. Until World War II he was frustrated by his low rank and expected to retire as a colonel. He was also frustrated with the lack of imagination he observed. Yet, he passed up a number of lucrative offers from the private sector and retired as a five-star general in 1948.

In a mismatch of person and job, he served as president of Columbia University (1948–1950), where he was expected to raise funds. He was neither happy nor popular there. On one occasion, when told that Columbia had some of the best scientists in the world, he asked, "But are they good Americans?" He then served as Supreme Commander of NATO (1951–1952) before entering politics. President Truman had courted him, even offering to stand aside to let him take the top spot on the Democratic ticket. When Eisenhower declared himself a Republican, Truman was incensed and rarely spoke to him thereafter.

Personality

The three experts rating Eisenhower showed moderate levels of agreement among themselves, but they had considerable differences of opinion on Neuroticism and Openness, where one expert rated him high and another quite low. He got a very high score on Conscientiousness (98th percentile) and almost as high on Character (89th). His score on Neuroticism (30th) was relatively low, both compared to average Americans and to other presidents. He was very close to the presidential average on the other Big Five factors. Our specialists rated Eisenhower higher on Intellectual Brilliance than did Simonton's raters and produced higher scores than Simonton's did for Forcefulness.

On the NEO Facets, Eisenhower received some extreme scores (below) compared to Americans now.

High	Percentile	Low	Percentile
Self-Discipline (C, Ch)	96	Vulnerability (N, -Ch)	1.8
Achievement Striving (C, Ch)	94	*Openness to Values (O)*	6
Competence (C, Ch)	94		
Assertiveness (E)	91		
Order (C)	91		

These scores are consistent with those one would expect from a successful military man with a strong administrative background: capability, drive and

CHART 7.1

Eisenhower's Scores on Character and the Big Five Traits

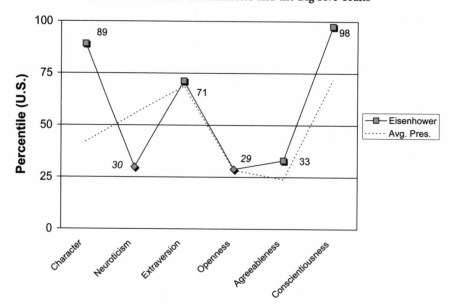

resilience, organization, and conservative values. He scored second highest of all presidents on Self-Discipline and second lowest on Vulnerability.

Eisenhower did not score highly on Openness to Aesthetics, yet our raters noted that art and beauty were very important to him. This may reflect his enjoyment of painting—a hobby he adopted later in life. He typically did not go to art galleries, and items reflecting enjoyment of music, poetry, and dance were not endorsed. Only two other items related to Openness or ability met our criteria: He would not let his mind wander but had a good sense of direction.

He definitely did not "get too discouraged when things went wrong" and made good decisions under adversity—he was capable and unfazed in a crisis. He was not anxious and rarely if ever felt worthless. He was not troubled by preoccupying thoughts and felt able to handle most of his problems.[2] He tried to do his work carefully and held to a standard of personal excellence. He did not have trouble motivating himself or getting down to work; he was productive and "always got the job done." He thought things through when making a decision and was known for his good judgment. He followed through on promises and was reliable and dependable. Duty, Honor, and Country, the motto of West Point, were Eisenhower's guiding principles. Yet he apparently had at least one extramarital affair.

He was trusting and optimistic and did not believe people would exploit others if given the chance. During World War II, he briefed a room full of reporters on specifics of the upcoming assault on Italy. "General," gasped one of the stunned reporters, "if one of us leaked the plan, couldn't it be disastrous?" Eisenhower nodded and added, "But I'm not going to censure you fellows. I'm just leaving it up to each man's sense of responsibility." He did not avoid close relationships, was not reclusive, unsociable, or withdrawn, and did not have trouble taking charge. He was very concerned about relations between the United States and England and sent home an American officer who commented about some "British SOB." Eisenhower did not dramatize or call attention to himself; he often referred reporters to his subordinates so they could receive some credit and glory.

Is This the Real Eisenhower?

In his well-regarded biography, Stephen Ambrose emphasized several traits: a hot but usually controlled temper, likeability, a positive outlook, and competitiveness under challenge combined with lassitude when not. He also wrote of Eisenhower's moodiness and irritability during his commands—especially the early ones. Lastly, he reported that Eisenhower gave the impression of always agreeing with the last man he talked to as Patton, Montgomery, and Bradley vied for supplies and priority in the grand strategy. Ambrose's work served as the primary source for the brief biography given above and the descriptions contained in it. Yet, many of these qualities do not appear in our data—either on the scales or items. Why is this?

Some qualities Ambrose depicted contain important qualifications (a hot but controlled temper), so that our raters might reject a global statement about anger and its expression. It is also possible that Ambrose simply perceived these qualities as more salient than did our raters. Regarding Eisenhower's temper, two out of three raters said he was *less* "quick-tempered or hot-blooded" than other presidents, though two of them indicated that he was not especially "even-tempered." Though all three raters thought Eisenhower was "liked by others," the scores they assigned were quite moderate compared to other presidents. Neither the overall score nor the level of agreement among raters was sufficient to meet our criteria.

Our sources simply may have seen Eisenhower differently than did Ambrose. For one thing, they were not comparing him to other generals and emphasized his reliability, self-discipline, and ability to tolerate stress. Ambrose portrayed officer training and promotion as designed to build these qualities and ensure that military leaders have them. If virtually all senior military officers have these traits, then Eisenhower could rank low on these characteristics among his military peers, yet higher than most Americans or presidents.

Miscellaneous Observations

Eisenhower was a well-rounded man accomplished in many hobbies. He was a devoted golfer, liked fly-fishing and hunting, and painted landscapes. He was a skilled chef and a shrewd poker player; retiring in middle age, he said, because his fellow officers were losing more than they could afford. He smoked four packs of cigarettes a day until he quit, cold turkey, on the advice of his doctor in 1949. He could swear like a sergeant, but avoided doing so in mixed company. He read paperback westerns and drank moderately, usually an old-fashioned, scotch, or martini before dinner. His tastes were conventional, but he demanded top quality. Lastly, while a successful politician, Eisenhower retained a distrust of partisanship and politics. Despite frequent absences, his family was central to his life. Though a stern, demanding, and critical father, he had a generally positive relationship with his son. He was somewhat superstitious, often carrying with him a collection of lucky coins. If someone crossed him, he would "write off" that person, rather than nurse a grudge, by printing his name on a slip of paper and throwing it into the lowest drawer of his desk.

Eisenhower Described

"The sturdy and enduring virtues—honor, courage, integrity, decency, all found eloquent expression in the life of this good man and noble leader." —Lyndon Johnson

"He don't take shovin'."—"A close aide" quoted by William Bragg Ewald Jr.

"He was a far more complex and devious man than most people realized, and in the best sense of these words. Not shackled to a one-track mind, he always applied two, three, or four lines of reasoning to a single problem and he usually preferred the indirect approach where it would serve him better than the direct attack on the problem. His mind was quick and facile."—Richard Nixon

President Eisenhower

Eisenhower's stock with historians has risen steadily since he left office. In one of the first polls after his term, he was ranked twenty-second, behind the then-unpopular Truman. Subsequently, it was learned that Eisenhower was far more active than originally believed—that his advisers had not really run foreign policy or the White House. The 1997 Ridings and McIver poll gave him an overall ranking of ninth—in the upper quarter of presidents—flanked by Jackson at eighth place and Madison at tenth. His highest rankings were in three categories of performance: Leadership, Accomplishments and Crisis Management, and Character and Integrity. His lowest ranking, sixteenth, was in Appointments.

Eisenhower had two major personality assets as president: good resilience under stress (Not Vulnerable) and high Competence (Chart 7.2). He was at somewhat of a disadvantage because of his honesty (Straightforwardness) and his lack of Tender-Mindedness. Yet, at news conferences, he often gave scattered, rambling answers that were vaguely reassuring. This may have been a conscious strategy to duck tough questions, but it contributed to a perception of him as disengaged and maybe even a bit doddering. It certainly contrasted with his talent in logical, written expression. Some thought him too influenced by the rich with whom he spent most of his time. He clearly did not appear to be working hard; he played golf 150 days a year and let his advisers explain many important decisions.

True to his campaign promise, he went to Korea and negotiated an armistice. He initiated the policy of massive retaliation as a deterrent to attack and presided

CHART 7.2
Personality Assets and Liabilities of Eisenhower as President

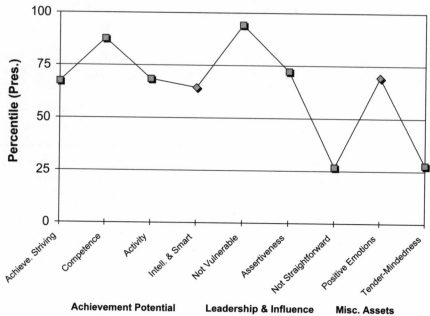

Achievement Potential   **Leadership & Influence**   **Misc. Assets**

over a massive weapons buildup. He was slow to embrace the civil rights movement and reluctant to confront Senator Joseph McCarthy, whom he privately
detested. Recently, it was discovered that Eisenhower helped bring about McCarthy's downfall through back channels. This was typical—he was a conciliator by
nature and disliked open confrontation. Perhaps defending his reputation, he
commented on his accomplishments as president, "The United States never lost
a soldier or a foot of ground in my administration. People ask how it happened—by God, it didn't just happen, I'll tell you that!"

Behavior as President (our data)

In addition to the qualities shared with Ford, Eisenhower carefully considered
his opinions before making them public. Though aware of his limitations, he
understood the implications of his decisions and had a depth of comprehension;
he did not force premature decisions. Like most historians, our raters thought
he performed well on the job. Lastly, Eisenhower accepted recommendations
without undue protest or resistance.

Eisenhower in Perspective

Eisenhower was simultaneously the conquering hero and the common man. He was perhaps the last generally accepted father figure in the role of president—someone that most members of both parties liked and looked up to. He was also the last clearly successful president who was undeniably high in character.

In our analyses, he was most similar to two generals, Washington (r = .42) and Hayes (r = .33). He also resembled Fillmore (r = .31). He was least like Andrew Johnson (r = −.39), Nixon (r = −.24), and Lyndon Johnson (r = −.23).[3]

GERALD R. FORD

Brief Biography

Gerald Ford shares two distinctions as president: He is the only one *appointed* to office, and he is one of only two presidents born with a different name (Clinton's last name was Blythe). Ford was born Leslie Lynch King Jr. on July 14, 1913, in Omaha, Nebraska, to Dorothy Ayer Gardner, whose tumultuous marriage to King Sr. ended in divorce two years later. Within a year, she remarried Gerald Rudolf Ford Sr., who adopted his wife's young son and gave him his name. Ford Sr. was the only dad Jerry knew until his biological father walked into the restaurant where seventeen-year-old Ford was working. This meeting left him shaken and in tears and was remembered as the most traumatic incident of his youth. He always resented his birth father for his lack of paternal and financial support and only met with him on one other occasion.

After their divorce, Jerry and his mother went to stay with her parents. She had many health problems but was active in church and civic affairs. Her son described her as selfless and solicitous of other people's problems. His adoptive father owned a paint store in Grand Rapids, Michigan, and was active in the Republican Party. Ford recalled him as the strongest influence on his life—a man of impeccable integrity, in great contrast to his natural father.

Attractive, bright, and a well-adjusted doer from an early age, Jerry was a National Honor Society member, an Eagle Scout, and the captain of an undefeated high school football team. Working part-time in high school, he still was in the top 5 percent of his class, was named to the Official All-State Scholastic Gridiron Team, and was voted the most popular high school senior in Grand Rapids. The latter honor carried with it a free trip to Washington, D.C.

Ford attended the University of Michigan on a football scholarship and continued to work part-time (including washing dishes at his fraternity, DKE). An intense competitor, he captained the freshman football team and won the Chicago Alumni Trophy for being the most promising freshman football player at

Michigan. His team voted him the most valuable player in 1934, when he also played center in the College All Stars game against the Chicago Bears. He received contract offers from the Green Bay Packers and Detroit Lions but decided instead to pursue law. His coach described him as "a smart guy with no fear." Finishing in the top 25 percent of his class, he was named to the Michigamua Honor Society.

Following college, he accepted a coaching position at Yale University. There he met many future politicians and got involved in professional modeling. In fact, he was a partner in a successful modeling agency but sold his shares to study law part-time at Yale. He received his law degree and passed the Michigan Bar exam in 1941.

The Japanese bombing of Pearl Harbor disrupted Ford's career plans. By April 1942, he had accepted a Navy commission and saw combat in the Pacific on a light aircraft carrier (converted cruiser), USS *Monterey*. He served as athletic director and gunnery division officer, where he directed the firing of a 40mm antiaircraft gun. His commanding officer called him "the best Officer of the Deck of my cruiser." He was discharged from the Navy in 1946 with the rank of lieutenant commander and a host of medals including ten Battle Stars, the Philippine Liberation Ribbon with two Bronze Stars, and various special citations.

He joined a law firm in Grand Rapids after the war but soon was very active in the Republican Party and numerous civic organizations. In 1948, he was elected to the U.S. House of Representatives, where he represented the Grand Rapids area for the next twenty-four years. The first person to welcome him to Washington was Richard Nixon, whom Ford supported during the attempt to oust him from the 1956 vice presidential candidacy and during the 1960 campaign. Ford also served on the Warren Commission that investigated the assassination of President Kennedy. He became intrigued by the emotionally unbalanced Lee Harvey Oswald, a man so different from him, and published a psychological portrait of him in 1965.

In Congress, Ford drew criticism from black leaders for attempts to weaken civil rights legislation, though he voted for the final bills. In 1967 he attacked Lyndon Johnson's handling of the Vietnam War, calling on the president to either commit to victory or get out of Vietnam. He served as House Minority Leader from 1965 to 1973. His most memorable action was to launch an impeachment effort against Justice William O. Douglas, the Supreme Court's most liberal member. In the course of defending this action, he made a comment that would turn out to have historic significance in 1999: "An impeachable offense is whatever the majority of the House of Representatives considers it to be."

Under the provisions of the 25th Amendment, Ford was appointed vice president under Nixon when Spiro Agnew resigned in 1973. A year later, he assumed the presidency when Nixon resigned. He lost his effort to be elected to a second term in 1976 to Jimmy Carter, who became a close friend.

About the time he announced his first congressional candidacy, he fell in love with Betty Warren, a divorced fashion consultant at a Grand Rapids department store. Due to her divorcee status, they waited until he was elected before marrying. He took her to a Michigan football game on their honeymoon. They remain married and have four grown children. They live near Vail, Colorado.

Personality

Three experts rated Ford (Chart 7.3). He scored low on Openness (8th percentile) and Neuroticism (15th); there was good agreement among raters on these traits. His high scores on Extraversion (91st) and Character (85th) were more controversial. There was some disagreement between the specialists and the generalists on these factors. The latter saw Ford as slightly *less* Extraverted than most presidents, and not nearly so low on Neuroticism. His score on Agreeableness (53rd)

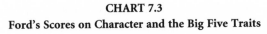

CHART 7.3
Ford's Scores on Character and the Big Five Traits

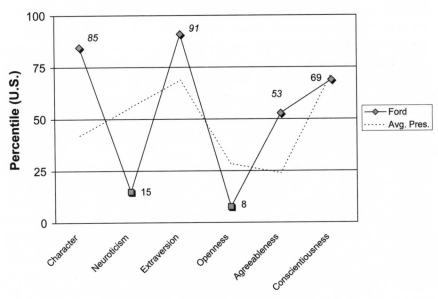

was not much different from the average American's but significantly higher than most presidents'.

High	Percentile	Low	Percentile
Gregariousness (E)	98	Openness to Values (O)	4
		Tender-Mindedness (A)	7
		Angry Hostility (N, -Ch)	8
		Impulsiveness (N, -Ch)	10
		Vulnerability (N, -Ch)	10

On the NEO Facet Scales, Ford obtained the scores shown in the above table.

Consistent with his Good Guy image and our classification, Ford's scores suggest a conservative, sociable, patient, steady, and confident man. He received the highest score of all presidents on the single item "is of good moral character" and the lowest rating on the Negative Valence (evil) factor. He scored second highest of presidents on Gregariousness and Altruism (about 85th percentile among typical Americans).

Despite his low score on Openness to (liberal) Values, Ford did NOT believe that all people should have a firm grasp of their goals and themselves by age twenty-five. But he himself *was not* nonconforming or rebellious. He kept focused on his work much more than most presidents and clearly preferred to travel the same route day after day. Conventional, traditional, and uncomfortable with uncertainty or complex issues, he accepted religious authority on moral issues. He was rarely aware of the emotional climate of different places and settings, and used gestures (related to emotional expression) awkwardly.

He liked being with people, enjoyed big parties, and definitely felt the need for company if alone for long. Outgoing and friendly toward strangers, he greatly enjoyed just talking with people. Unlike many presidents, especially Extravert ones, he did not do most of the talking, and let his actions speak louder than his words. Despite his other Extravert traits, he did not crave excitement, though he sometimes literally "jumped for joy."

Ford definitely was embarrassed when associates did foolish things—probably more because of his empathy for friends than out of self-consciousness. He almost never got disgusted with people, was not frustrated by minor problems, had an even temper, and was rarely hostile toward others. Yet, inexplicably, our raters still said that he was known as touchy and temperamental.[4] He did not worry, rarely felt depressed, dejected, or alone, and was not fearful. He resisted temptation easily and rarely indulged his impulses or ate too much of his favorite foods.

Consistent with his Republican politics, Ford did *not* believe that people's needs should come before economic concerns or that society cannot do enough for the disadvantaged. But he was not miserly or stingy in his personal life (despite an anecdote about Dan Quayle and him once tipping their golfing caddies a dollar). Ford tried to be modest and clearly felt he was no better than anybody else. While Ford was president, his golden retriever, Liberty, soiled the rug at his Vail condominium. When a White House steward rushed to clean up the mess, he abruptly stopped him, saying, "Nobody should have to clean up after someone else's dog." He did not try to take advantage of circumstances by bending the rules, and few if any thought him cold or calculating,

A last theme involves orderliness and character. Ford liked to keep everything in its place, did not overcomplicate issues, and even relative to other presidents, was not "confused." He did not endanger others through reckless or dangerous behavior (despite hitting them with errant golf balls), kept promises, and rarely swore. He respected the rights and feelings even of his opponents.

Miscellaneous Observations

Though Ford had generally amiable relations with everyone, including the press, his image suffered by media attention to his stumbles—both physical and verbal. His press secretary fumed that this active and athletic man, a former college all-star, was portrayed as an oaf—but some Secret Service agents did think him clumsy. When he declared Poland free of Soviet influence, he created an impression of a president seriously lacking in international knowledge or intelligence. Yet, one of our sources described Ford as "highly intellectual but self-effacing about [his] intellect." Ford's self-deprecating sense of humor may have left him more vulnerable than most presidents to such attacks. When asked years later how his golf game was doing, he noted that he was getting better and hitting fewer spectators.

As president, Ford remained unpretentious and even a bit too earthy for some. In the presence of a Secret Service agent, he reportedly passed gas and playfully passed the blame to the agent. "Jesus, did you do that? God, show a little class!"[5]

Ford Described

"A common-sense, unpretentious Midwesterner with a balanced personality."—W. Pederson, Louisiana State University

"He just doesn't have enemies."—Senator Robert P. Griffin

"He never in his life tried to outsmart anybody. But if intellectual hubris from a tormentor gave him a chance, Jerry would out-dumb him, swiftly and deadpan. It might take days before the attacker would realize he'd been had."—Bud Vestal, Grand Rapids reporter

"I can get tears in my eyes when I think about Jerry Ford. We love him." —Congressman Paul McCloskey, political opponent

"In all the years I sat in the House, I never knew Mr. Ford to make a dishonest statement nor a statement part true and part false. He never attempted to shade a statement, and I never heard him utter an unkind word."—Representative Martha W. Griffiths

President Ford

It is probably too soon to assess Ford's standing with history, given the lack of perspective of time. Nonetheless, the historians in the Ridings and McIver poll ranked him twenty-seventh overall, just behind Reagan and ahead of Arthur. His highest ranking was in Character and Integrity (seventeenth), his lowest in Leadership Qualities (thirty-fourth).

Our raters indicate that Ford was an average match for the job. Enthusiastic and cheerful (high Positive Emotions), he was not unnerved by pressure (Not Vulnerable). He was not rated as one of the brightest men to hold the office and was not especially concerned with people down on their luck (low Tender-Mindedness).

His greatest accomplishment as president was the stabilization of the office after the resignation of both the president and vice president. "[He] restored to the office of the presidency the decency, the integrity, the honor, and the nobility which that office must have," said Hubert Humphrey.

Ford can claim several other accomplishments during his brief tenure. It was under his administration that the Vietnam War ended. When Vietnam succumbed to the Communists and Congress refused any aid to prevent a debacle, he took the initiative and ordered an immediate rescue of fifty thousand Vietnamese who had assisted the Americans. Those memorable helicopters taking off from the roof of our embassy were sent by Gerald Ford himself.

He soon thereafter had to confront the seizure of the American merchant ship *Mayaguez* by the Khmer Rouge rebels in Cambodia. President Ford ordered an air and amphibious assault on the port of Koh Tang, which retrieved the vessel and its thirty-eight crewmen at the cost of forty-one American lives. These actions demonstrated that our failure in Vietnam did not indicate a general unwillingness to respond to overt threats to U.S. sovereignty.

CHART 7.4
Personality Assets and Liabilities of Ford as President

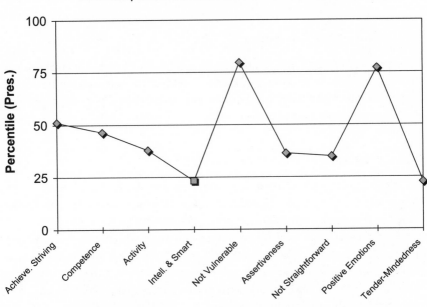

His negotiations with Leonid Brezhnev led to an agreement that the United States and the Soviet Union would abide by the provisions of SALT I, which had expired, and to the successful SALT II agreement. Both of those pivotal strategic arms limitation agreements were concluded after Ford's term, however. He also was less successful in handling runaway inflation and oil prices and in reducing unemployment; voluntary efforts did not produce the effects for which he had hoped.

More controversial was his pardon of Richard Nixon before any indictments of him were filed in the Watergate break-in and cover-up. He said he felt the country could not get beyond the crisis in leadership that the scandal had created if indictments and trials were to drag on for years. Perhaps it was the right decision, but it likely cost him a second term.

Ford also was the target of two assassination attempts. Lynette "Squeaky" Fromme, one of Charles Manson's followers, attempted to shoot him at point blank range with a .45-caliber pistol in 1975 in Sacramento, California. Secret Servicemen grabbed the gun before she could fire it. Seventeen days later in San

Francisco, Sara Jane Moore fired a shot at Ford with a .38-caliber pistol. Luckily, she missed her target and was immediately subdued.

Behavior as President (our data)

As president, Ford endeared himself to his staff through courtesy and consideration. He believed in freedom from government interference for businesses. His health was robust and did not fail during difficult or critical periods in office. He was willing to make compromises.

Ford in Perspective

The men most similar to Ford in personality were G. H. W. Bush ($r = .33$), Eisenhower ($r = .26$), and Hayes ($r = .20$).[6] Ford was least like John Quincy Adams ($r = -.39$), John Adams ($r = -.38$), and Nixon $= -.36$).

Ford seems to be remembered for being a nice guy who filled in until a "real" president came along. However, we both found him to be an impressive man, possibly underrated because of his affability and modesty. It may say something of the job, the media, and our demands of our leaders that a man who graduated in the upper third of his law class could be considered dumb; that an all-star athlete could be perceived as a stumblebum. On the other hand, his low standing on Openness may relegate him to a caretaking presidency—not one requiring vision. Though such men rarely stand in the first ranks of glory (Washington is an exception), they seem essential at critical times in history.

EISENHOWER AND FORD COMPARED

Chart 7.5 shows the scores of Eisenhower and Ford. Eisenhower scored higher on Conscientiousness and Openness than Ford, while Ford was more Agreeable and Extraverted. On more specific scales Eisenhower was higher on Charisma, Positive Valence, and measures of intelligence, particularly Spatial Abilities and Intellectual Brilliance. Ford scored very low on Angry Hostility, while Eisenhower was a bit above average. Eisenhower was rated as more Competent, Orderly, and more likely to think before acting (Deliberative).

CHART 7.5
Eisenhower and Ford Compared

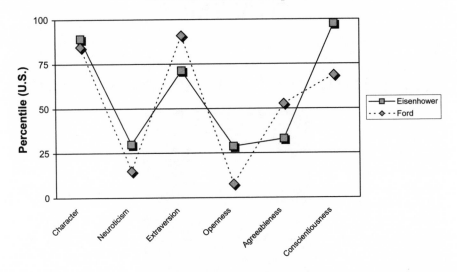

CHAPTER 8

One Innocent—Ulysses S. Grant

Morphed image of Ulysses Grant and William Taft.
Library of Congress and National Archives

THOUGH A competent general and the foremost hero of the Civil War, Ulysses S. Grant was a clear failure as president, rated as low as Harding in some historians' polls. But he was still extremely popular as he ended his second term and even contemplated a third term. We profile him next, while Harding is presented in the chapter on Actors, where he also belongs.

Brief Biography

Ulysses Grant yearned for the admiration of others and never tired of getting it wherever he went. He never got it from his father, Jesse; he spent his entire life trying to earn his father's love and simultaneously repudiating all he stood for. Jesse Grant did not have much to offer his son emotionally. He had been separated from his own childhood family at age eleven and apprenticed to an Ohio tanner after the death of his mother. His father, a cobbler and failed farmer, was once put in debtor's prison. Perhaps because of his own unstable childhood, Jesse never saw a family as a secure joining of people in mutual affection. He turned to his grown children to bolster his own self-esteem and, at times, embarrassed the would-be president with various schemes he concocted to profit from his son's name. Grant's mother was an aloof figure about whom virtually nothing is known. She was barely mentioned in his *Memoirs*. Nonetheless, he was closer to her than to his father, and she was proud of her son.

Despite (or because of) his great need to prove himself, Grant failed at virtually everything he attempted. Sent alone at the age of eight to bargain for a horse, he told the owner, "Papa says I may offer you twenty dollars for the colt, but if you won't take that, I am to give you twenty-five." The horse sold for twenty-five dollars, and Grant became a laughingstock of his neighborhood. This incident reportedly deeply wounded him for the rest of his life, setting the stage for his repeated failures as a farmer, wood seller, rent collector, railroad owner, and leather merchant.

The oldest of six children, Grant was expected to work hard even as a young boy. "When I was seven or eight years of age," he wrote, "I began hauling all the wood used in the house and the shops." Unlike virtually every boy in rural Ohio, he did not hunt for sport and was squeamish at the sight of blood, whether animal or human. He came to love horses, trained them skillfully, and became a gifted horseman.

Grant was horrified when his father arranged his West Point appointment through Representative Thomas Hamer, fearful that he would flunk out. He did not but distinguished himself primarily by his horsemanship and earned many demerits for tardiness and sloppy dress.

Julia Dent, the future Mrs. Grant, was plain and cross-eyed, but educated. Her father was a slave-owning planter and merchant. The couple was engaged over the objections of both families. Julia's father did not like Grant's prospects as a career soldier, and Grant's father objected to the slave-owning Dents. His parents refused to attend the wedding but eventually warmed to their daughter-in-law. The couple saw each other only once during their four-year engagement. The marriage bore four children, to whom Grant and Julia were devoted.

Grant depended on Julia and his friends for continued self-esteem. When he was without Julia for even a few days, he became bored and sometimes turned to drink. He resigned his commission in the U.S. Army after the Mexican War because of the loneliness and despair he felt away from his wife. While waiting for transit back to Ohio, he allegedly stayed drunk for weeks in San Francisco.

A quiet man who smoked incessantly, Grant was anxious to see battle in the Mexican War. Instead, he served as a quartermaster who quietly watched and learned much from his superior officers. When the Civil War broke out years later, his reputation for drunkenness may have kept him from being recommissioned. Finally, by going through Congressman Elihu Washburne, Grant was commissioned as a colonel. In his first Civil War command, he was assigned to lead a group of rowdy and insubordinate volunteers. Introduced to his new company by two flowery politicians, Grant issued his first order: "Go to your quarters!" A few days later, when one of the men returned to camp drunk and belligerent, Grant decked him. He ordered the man gagged and tied to a post, then returned to cut him loose himself. He ordered the man to salute him and go to his quarters. He did.

During the Civil War, Grant applied all that he had learned to one successful battle after another. Assigned to prevent Missouri and the other Border States from going over to the Confederacy, he did what most generals were reluctant to do in the early years of the war—he pursued the enemy. Julia and the children often accompanied him to the battle sites. While other generals pondered what Napoléon would do, Grant's philosophy was simple: "Find out where your enemy is. Get at him as soon as you can. Strike at him as hard as you can, and keep moving on." Moving farther south, he won bloody battles at Shiloh and Vicksburg that, by the summer of 1863, split the Confederacy in two, making communication and supply difficult for the rebels.

Searching for an effective general, Lincoln called Grant to Washington to pursue Lee's soldiers through the swampy Wilderness north of Richmond, the Confederate capital. After many battles, Grant forced Lee to surrender at Appomattox Court House on April 9, 1865. Ironically, Grant barely escaped capture himself by rebel soldiers en route to Lee's surrender ceremony.

Lincoln and Grant hit it off from the start. Both were from poor frontier families, and both had troubled relationships with their fathers. They understood and trusted each other and might have been able to change the social structure of the South if Lincoln had not been assassinated within a week of Lee's surrender. Grant, too, was to have been assassinated that night; he reluctantly turned down an invitation to sit beside Lincoln, because Julia, like much of Washington society, could not stand Mary Lincoln.

After the war, Grant found himself in an awkward political situation. The national hero of the Civil War and General of the Army (the first since Washington), he was subordinate to Democratic president Andrew Johnson. Johnson was undoing much that had been achieved in the South and was at war with Congress. By turning over local government positions to white supremacists throughout the South, he virtually assured renewed suppression of African Americans. Through brutality and various involuntary-servitude plans, white supremacists intimidated blacks into virtually the same degree of subordination they had suffered under slavery. There they would languish for another century.

Though personally infuriated by this, Grant believed that anarchy, chaos, and another terrible conflict might ensue if Federal troops were used to suppress the killing of blacks throughout the South. Gradually, Grant distanced himself from Johnson, while remaining in his cabinet. He dreamed of purchasing the island nation of Santo Domingo as an entirely black U.S. state. He persisted in this plan despite the unlikelihood that African Americans would ever voluntarily move there or that the island's economy could support them if they did. He saw Santo Domingo as an alternative to the intimidation blacks faced in the South and felt that if many emigrated, the value of those that remained (and their treatment) could only improve.

Major leaders of both parties were sullied as the crisis between Johnson and Congress led to his impeachment. By removing himself from the fray when he did, Grant was virtually the only national leader unblemished by the major conflict of his time—the role of Southern social systems after the Civil War. He had few enemies and was universally loved as the common man who had saved his country.

These were years of great social and political upward mobility for the Grants. Wealthy patrons bestowed investment funds and homes upon the man who they felt had saved the Union. Julia never thought it was enough and may have been influential in getting Grant to resign from the Army to pursue the presidency. He was not wealthy and would give up a good Army salary and pension for only four to eight years of glory. Still, he sought the presidency out of a sense of duty.

Unfortunately, he embraced the values of his benefactors, coming to equate gold with good in the years surrounding his presidency. Repudiating the financial and emotional poverty of his youth, he and Julia increasingly deferred to the "better" class of people with whom they associated. Not surprisingly, his administrations, especially the second, were plagued with scandals involving much of his cabinet and several close friends.

Personality

Three experts rated Grant. While they indicated average levels of respect for him, generalists did not and rated him very low in this regard. Generalists also gave Grant quite high ratings on Negative Valence (evil), in contrast to specialists who rated him low, and very low scores on Intellectual Brilliance compared to other presidents. Returning to specialists and their ratings, low scores on Openness to Experience (2nd percentile), Conscientiousness (9th), and Neuroticism (21st) distinguished Grant's personality. He scored far below most presidents on Conscientiousness. Though the raters agreed moderately well on his overall profile, opinion was more divided regarding Extraversion, Openness, and Conscientiousness.

High	Percentile	Low	Percentile
Trust (A, Ch)	92	Openness to Aesthetics	0.2
Self-Consciousness (N)	91	Openness to Ideas	0.5
Depression (N)	90	Anxiety (N)	5
		Tender-Mindedness (A)	6
		Competence (C, Ch)	6
		Vulnerability (N, Ch)	7
		Achievement Striving (C)	8

On the NEO Facets, Grant obtained the scores shown in the above table.

Grant scored lowest of all presidents on measures of achievement drive, Openness to Aesthetics, and on Musical Ability. He was second lowest on Religiousness, Competence, and Openness to Ideas.

To a degree unparalleled among presidents, Grant did *not* strive for accomplishment. He definitely *did not* work hard to achieve his goals. This lack of ambition may have stemmed from being coaxed into cleaning stables as a young

CHART 8.1

Grant's Scores on Character and the Big Five Traits

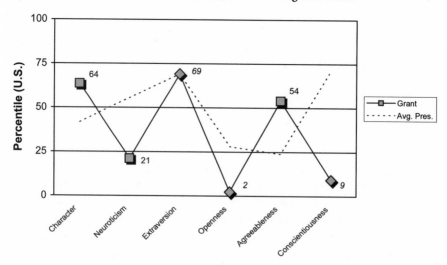

boy by his father. Jesse acknowledged the job was perhaps too big for such a young boy, but offered his son the immense prize of a silver dollar. Ulysses said he would try and went to work, straining his endurance to the limits. After hours of huffing and puffing, he finished. His father was pleased. "Ulysses, you did it splendidly, and now that I find you can do it so nicely, I shall have you do it every morning this winter."

Grant had an exceptionally poor memory for melodies and sense of rhythm; he had trouble keeping step when marching at West Point. He had practically *no* interest in music. Asked if he enjoyed a concert as president, he responded, "How could I? I only know two tunes. One is Yankee Doodle and the other isn't." He sang awfully and clearly had no ear for musical tone. Intensely bored by ballet and dance, he was decidedly unaffected by poetry or music and was not a good dancer. He had *no* interest in abstract, theoretical, or philosophical discussions, and was not intellectually curious. Despite this, he was elected president of the West Point literary society, and saw himself as broad-minded and tolerant. He preferred to approach problems scientifically or with numbers. As was expected of a field commander, he also had a very good sense of direction.

Unlike most presidents, Grant definitely *did not* offer advice, and much more than other presidents, preferred to simply go his own way rather than be a leader. He preferred not to talk about himself or his accomplishments and did not like to draw attention to himself; few thought him self-centered or egotistical. He clearly failed to assert himself at times, and he *did not* think himself better than others. Rarely sarcastic, he was not condescending toward others. He was perceived as an ordinary, everyday person and as "average, unremarkable"—both to an exceptional degree among presidents. On the way to a reception in his honor, he shared an umbrella with another guest who did not recognize him. The man commented, "Between us, I have always thought that Grant was a very much overrated man." "That's my view also," Grant responded. He was not crafty or sly, did not bully, flatter, or trick people to get his way, and did not lead people to become dependent on him to exploit them.

He definitely stifled outward expression of his emotions and was reluctant to show anger or hostility. One of the few times he lost his temper was when he observed a civilian beating his horse. Grant seized the man, shook him violently, and ordered him tied to a post for six hours. He was not moody, definitely did not worry too much, was calm and relaxed, and "brave, courageous, daring." But he was very self-conscious. After graduating from West Point, he headed home in full uniform. On the way, a boy mocked him with a limerick. In his hometown, a stable hand pinned stripes to his livery pants that mimicked Grant's uniform.

Stung by these taunts, he nearly always favored unpretentious clothing in the future.

Relative to other presidents, Grant did *not* think before responding to a question, and *did not* consider consequences before acting. Though decisive, firm, and purposeful, he was not known for good sense and judgment.[1] He was certainly not economical or thrifty, and he had a well-known drinking problem.[2] Nonetheless, Grant had a well-defined, consistent personality and was not unpredictable or changeable.

He was naturally trusting and clearly did not perceive people as ready to exploit others. He assumed the best about the people around him—when people did things for him, he did not question their motives. And, for the most part, others wanted to take care of and nurture this agreeable man.

Grant showed mixed qualities related to Extraversion. He probably would have preferred a crowded beach to an isolated cabin, but he rarely appeared to be rushing or short of time. Casual, informal, and natural, he was still charismatic. Though cool and aloof in public, he was warm and easygoing in private.

Miscellaneous Observations

Grant was superstitious and refused to retrace his own steps. He did *not* attend church services regularly.[3] He was prudish—reluctant to be seen naked and not amused by dirty jokes. One biographer felt he had a strong feminine streak.

Grant Quoted

"A military life had no charms for me and I had not the faintest idea of staying in the Army even if I graduated, which I did not expect."

Grant Described

"Often foresighted, always democratic in his evaluations of people and events."—R. Goldhurst (biographer and data source)

"A brilliant general who hated things military . . . an imaginative and aggressive commander . . . he was devoted to his family and to his country . . . doted on his children and loved his wife . . . he put enormous emphasis on loyalty."—David L. Wilson (biographer and data source)

President Grant

Ridings's and McIver's historians ranked Grant the fourth worst president overall, just behind Pierce and ahead of Andrew Johnson. He received a respectable ranking of twenty-seventh in Leadership Qualities but was rated third last in Political Skill and Appointments.

According to our data, his personality was a very poor match for the presidency—the worst of any president thus far. His only strength: a low score on Vulnerability. This was more than offset by his very low scores on Achievement Striving and Competence and low scores on Activity, Assertiveness, "low Straightforwardness," and Tender-Mindedness.

Though honest, Grant was also at risk, based on his personal qualities, for severe ethical problems on the job. He had railed early in his career against corruption in filling government contracts. Yet his associates were doing similar things that Grant could not bring himself to see despite clear, overwhelming evidence. He was not dishonest; rather, he seemed blinded either by his needs for admiration and approval or by loyalty.

He was cheered, during his extensive travels around the world after his presidency, as the common man who had become a hero. In fact, Grant had long before turned his back on his origins. The failures of his administration, be they the nearly total loss of black civil rights within a decade of the Civil War or the numerous scandals defrauding Native Americans and the nation's fighting men, seemed to stem from a determination to see no evil.

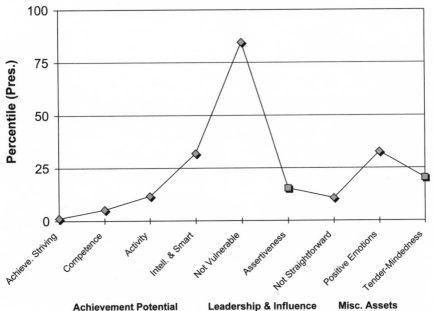

CHART 8.2

Personality Assets and Liabilities of Grant as President

Grant was successful in ending many long-sputtering conflicts with Great Britain and was deeply concerned about preventing the extinction of Native Americans. He appointed the first Native American as commissioner of Indian Affairs. Still, Grant was a dependent man who relied excessively on admiration, his wife, and his cigars. It was the cigars that got him. He died of throat cancer in 1885 at age sixty-three.

Behavior as President (our data)

Like Ridings's and McIver's historians, our raters gave low marks on the items tapping job performance, particularly the quality of his work. Grant was very much a middle-of-the-roader and *not* an innovative executive. He definitely encouraged independent judgment by his aides and did not view the presidency as a vehicle for self-expression. He was able to maintain his popularity despite the serious scandals that rocked his administration. He was rated the lowest of all presidents in Creative presidential style, and was assessed as the least Charismatic leader by Simonton's raters.

Grant in Perspective

Grant was not much like any other president. He was most like Harding (r = .18), G. H. W. Bush (r = .17), and at least by our preliminary data, G. W. Bush (r = .16).[4] He was least like John Adams (r = −.25), LBJ (r = −.21), and Nixon (r = −.20). Grant is psychologically interesting because he was a highly successful general, but unsuccessful at nearly everything else. In Ken Burns's epic documentary *The Civil War*, Grant is introduced as "a failure at everything except marriage" who was selling firewood on the streets for his father-in-law at the start of the Civil War. Typically passive and even sluggish as a man and a president, he came alive in battle where he behaved with courage and decisiveness. His only true success in life, aside from his pivotal role in the Civil War and his family, was the literary and financial success of his *Memoirs*. Grant struggled to complete them, often in great pain from his throat cancer. He did so shortly before his death.

As president and before, Grant was easygoing, naïve, overly trusting, and loyal to friends who did not warrant his devotion. Much the same could be said of Harding, who found himself in a similar predicament fifty years later. In both cases, failure as president seemingly evinced deep moral weaknesses. Both were dependent men who were unable to see evil in others. As we will see with Reagan, these qualities don't necessarily lead to failure.

CHAPTER 9

Two Actors—Warren Harding and Ronald Reagan

Morphed image of Warren Harding, Ronald Reagan, and William Clinton.
National Archives, Library of Congress

HERE, WE PROFILE two of the Actors with quite different reputations. Warren Harding is generally regarded as the least successful of all presidents in both his job performance and his intellect. He seemed overwhelmed by the job. Though not prominent, he is interesting, like Grant, as an ineffective president. Ronald Reagan, though similar to Harding in personality, has a different reputation. The only president reelected between Nixon and Clinton, he seemingly did not attend to details but was a master of political themes. A professional actor, he also understood how to articulate them effectively.

Harding and Reagan shared a number of personality traits. Our experts perceived them both as "shallow, nonintellectual, unreflective," although Harding was much more so. Both saw themselves as unusually lighthearted, they did not overcontrol their needs and impulses, and were not thin-skinned or overly sensitive. Their feelings showed on their faces and through body language; both were

TABLE 9.1
Reagan and Harding Compared

	Harding High	Harding Low
Reagan High	*Attractive*, Positive Emotions, Excitement Seeking, *Friendliness*, Gregariousness, Openness to Fantasy & Feelings, Trust	**NONE**
Reagan Low	**NONE**	Openness to Values, Openness to Ideas, Competence, Deliberation, Dutifulness, Self-Consciousness, Angry Hostility

charismatic and reluctant to express anger. As presidents, both encouraged the independence of their aides, often with unhappy results.

WARREN HARDING

Brief Biography

The eldest son of two physicians, Warren Harding was descended from a Puritan fisherman who settled in Massachusetts in 1623. His great-grandfather was an officer in the Continental Army during the Revolutionary War. Officially of English, Irish, Scottish, and Dutch heritage, Harding was dogged by the rumor that this latter ancestor was a West Indian Black. Not at all defensive, he said, "How do I know? [Somebody] may have jumped the fence."

Harding enjoyed a happy childhood near Marion, Ohio. He loved public speaking from an early age and spent his teen years working part-time at the local newspaper. He was well liked and delivered the commencement address at Ohio Central College when he graduated in 1882. He taught school for one term and tried his hand at insurance sales before buying the nearly defunct *Marion Star*. With the help of his wife, Flossie, he built the newspaper to financial success during the years before he entered politics.

Florence (Flossie) Kling was a dowdy, headstrong divorcée several years his senior. She was also heir to a prominent Marion banker. Taken with the handsome Harding from the moment they met, she chased him until he agreed to marry her. Immediately, she took over running his life in her somewhat masculine, martial manner. It was not a happy union.

Usually cheerful and pliable, Harding suffered occasionally from "severe doubts." He suffered his first nervous breakdown at age twenty-four and was treated several times over the course of his life at the sanitarium of Dr. J. P. Kellogg.

Flossie suffered from a kidney problem that required her to sleep attached to elaborate, bedside medical equipment. She and Harding slept in separate rooms, allowing him to sneak out at night for several romantic affairs, two of which became enduring. He enjoyed an affair for many years with his best friend's wife, Carrie Phillips. Then he met Nan Britton, a teen with a crush on him. Both women pursued him relentlessly. Though he and Flossie had no children, he fathered a daughter with Nan while president.

He enjoyed the company of businessmen at his regular poker and golf games as well as watching baseball, burlesque, and boxing. He drank, smoked, and read little but a daily news summary. He would have been happy to remain in local politics in Marion the rest of his life, but his wife and a coterie of corrupt "kingmakers" persuaded him to seek higher office.

He entered national politics after undistinguished terms in the Ohio Senate and as lieutenant governor. He was an equally undistinguished U.S. senator before running for president. With his handsome face and charm, he hoped to capitalize on the female vote. He realized that with several strong candidates, the Republican convention might deadlock and was shrewdly positioned for that eventuality. His plan worked, and he was a comfortable second choice. He died in office in the midst of scandals, while traveling on the West Coast.

Personality

Generalists gave Harding little respect and even rated him quite high on Negative Valence compared to the three specialists that rated him. The specialists perceived Harding as much more Extraverted, and about average (versus low) in Openness, compared to generalists. Two of the specialists showed exceptionally high agreement with each other on Harding's overall profile, while the last specialist sharply disagreed. This latter rater perceived Harding as much more capable than did the other two and the generalists. All specialists thought that he was very extraverted and a generally agreeable man, but they agreed on little else. Chart 9.1 shows that like most Actors, he scored high on Extraversion (99.9th percentile) and low on Conscientiousness (4th) and Openness (10th). Though he did not rate that high on Agreeableness (66th) compared to most Americans, he was quite high relative to other presidents. His score on Conscientiousness was much lower than most presidents, and generalists thought it even lower.

On the NEO Facets, Harding received the scores shown in the table on page 170 compared to today's Americans.

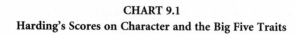

CHART 9.1

Harding's Scores on Character and the Big Five Traits

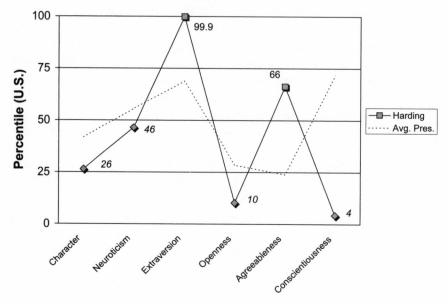

High	Percentile	Low	Percentile
Gregariousn ess (E)	99.3	*Competence* (C, Ch)	*1.7*
Compliance (A, Ch)	96	Openness to Values	*1.9*
Warmth (E)	96	*Deliberation* (C, Ch)	*5*
Trust (A, Ch)	*94*	*Openness to Ideas*	*6*
Positive Emotions (E)	*94*	*Dutiful* (C, Ch)	*10*
Excitement Seeking (E)	*93*		

These scores indicate a highly sociable (Gregariousness and Warmth), cooperative (high Compliance), and trusting man who lacked common sense, prudence, and good judgment (low Competence). He was very traditional in his moral beliefs (low Openness to Values) and not interested in intellectual matters (low Openness to Ideas). He was cheerful and enthusiastic (high Positive Emotions) and Excitement Seeking.

Harding was rated highest of all presidents on Gregariousness and on Simonton's Friendliness scale, as well as on several measures of Agreeableness. He was rated second highest on the NEO Warmth, Compliance, and Vulnerability scales, on Simonton's Pacifism and Moderation scales, and on Optimism and Physical

Attractiveness. He was rated lowest of all presidents on Positive Valence, Intellectual Brilliance, Competence, and several measures of achievement drive. He scored second lowest of all presidents on Achievement Striving and on several measures of Openness and Conscientiousness.

Exceedingly shallow and unreflective for a president, he was decidedly *not* "contemplative, intellectual, introspective, meditative, philosophical;" his thinking was plainly uninspired and mainstream. He was conventional and traditional and clearly did not believe that social policies should change with the times. Though by no means complicated, he nonetheless had a vivid imagination.

Harding scored extraordinarily low on items relating to Positive Valence, including "Important, significant," "Excellent, first rate," and "Impressive, remarkable." Our raters found him to be an average, unremarkable man.

Harding had great difficulty resisting temptation and was not inhibited or restrained. *Not* liking to do things alone, he very much enjoyed big parties, spending time with people, and being part of a crowd. Definitely not known as cold or distant, he welcomed close relationships and was warm and self-disclosing. He was outgoing and friendly toward strangers, "casual, easygoing, informal, natural, relaxed," and made friends easily. Harding clearly saw himself as a lighthearted person and very plainly showed it when he was happy. His feelings showed in his facial and body language; his gestures were adroit. He often felt very energetic and vigorous.

He was exceptionally lenient, uncritical, and undemanding. In three decades as a newspaper publisher, he never fired an employee. He *did not* let people know if he did not like them, was not sarcastic or cutting, and was reluctant to express anger. He had an even temper. He was not stubborn or hardheaded, and virtually nobody considered him cold or calculating. Nor was he defensive or lacking in humor about his faults. He empathized easily with others, believed most people were honest and trustworthy, and assumed the best about those he met.

Clearly not self-conscious, Harding thought of himself as good-looking. But he was concerned with his adequacy as a person, and did not think himself better than most people. "I am a man of limited talents from a small town," he once said.

Miscellaneous Observations

Harding always tried to maintain a positive approach and could not stand to see anybody hurt or offended by anything he said or did. His father once told him, "Warren, it's a good thing you wasn't born a girl. Because you'd be in the family way all the time. You can't say, No!"

Denied admission to the convention that elected him president by a doorman who was a stickler for detail (Harding technically was not a delegate), he compliantly waited in a nearby bar, where he was found sitting alone at 4:00 A.M., after many of the delegates had already left for the night.

Harding Quoted

"I don't know what to do or where to turn in this taxation matter. Somewhere there must be a book that tells all about it, where I could go to straighten it all out in my mind. But I don't know where the book is, and maybe I couldn't read it if I did find it! And there must be a man in the country somewhere who could weigh both sides and know the truth. Probably he is in some college or other. But I don't know where to find him. I don't know how to get him. My God, this is a hell of a place for a man like me to be!"

Harding Described

"I like Harding. I like him very much, but I can't conceive of his being President of the United States. He's done nothing to deserve it."—Hiram Johnson, California senator

"He was a man of the people, indulging no consciousness of superiority, incapable of arrogance, separated from neither by experience nor pride nor eccentricity."—Charles Evans Hughes, secretary of state, 1924

"Harding wasn't a bad man. He was just a slob."—Alice Roosevelt

"He was not a man with either the experience or the intellectual quality that the position needed."—Herbert Hoover

President Harding

Harding received the lowest overall rating of all presidents in the Ridings and McIver poll and has placed near the bottom in every presidential poll ever conducted. He ranked lowest of any president in Leadership Qualities, Appointments, and Character and Integrity, and second lowest on Accomplishments and Crisis Management.

Despite this, he was a well-liked president. But his popularity was starting to unravel by the time he died in office. He gradually learned of schemes by his staff, one of who looted the country of two hundred million dollars (in 1922 dollars!). He passively allowed the chief perpetrator to flee the country but did have others arrested. There is no evidence that he participated in any of the corruption. Yet even as amiable a president as Harding had his breaking point. He was observed with his hands around the throat of the director of the Veterans Bureau yelling, "You yellow rat! You double crossing bastard!"

Harding was known for his way with words—or rather his lack of verbal poise. Consider this sample: "Progression is not proclamation nor palaver. It is not pretense nor play on prejudice. It is not of personal pronouns nor perennial pronouncement." "An army of pompous phrases moving over the landscape in search of an idea," concluded one critic. Despite his limitations, he was the first president since the Civil War to speak on Southern soil for the rights of African Americans.

Harding's enthusiasm and optimism were his real assets as president, as shown by his high score on Positive Emotions in Chart 9.2. But other, more important qualities were lacking: He scored very low relative to other presidents on Achievement Striving, Competence, and Intelligence. Summing up his assets and liabilities, his overall score is the third lowest among presidents—only Grant and Taft scored lower. His personality also presaged very low ratings for Ethics on the Job, which he did in fact receive.

Behavior as President (our data)

Harding enjoyed the ceremonial aspects of his job and, despite his limitations, was charismatic. He very much enjoyed and felt challenged by his relationship

CHART 9.2
Personality Assets and Liabilities of Harding as President

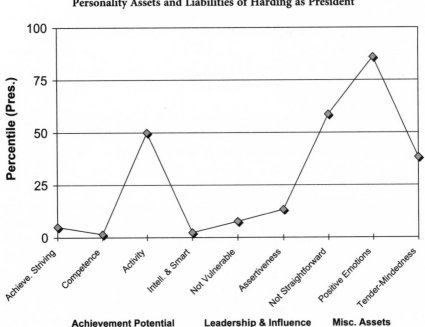

with the press, struggling to get the image he wanted to come across. Unlike many other presidents, he did *not* believe he knew what was best for people and was suspicious of reformers. He maintained close relationships with a wide circle of associates and was a dyed-in-the-wool middle-of-the-roader. He kept his staff informed on matters concerning other departments, encouraged their independent judgment, and was not abrupt or impatient in meetings.

Harding in Perspective

Harding was most similar to Reagan ($r = .48$), William Henry Harrison ($r = .36$), and according to our preliminary data, G. W. Bush ($r = .32$).[1] He was least like Wilson ($r = -.44$), Washington ($r = -.39$), and Madison ($r = -.38$). He is remembered as a failure as president—a man in over his head. He was an amiable, likable guy of average abilities who was maneuvered into a job beyond his depth. He was a near-perfect tool of those who placed him there: popular, trusting, not very bright, cooperative, and yet personally honest and without ambition. Such a person is ill suited for the snake pit of presidential politics.

RONALD REAGAN

Brief Biography

Ronald Reagan's father, John ("Jack"), was an alcoholic shoe salesman; his mother was a devout Christian fundamentalist. The family moved nearly every year as he was growing up, which resulted in Reagan's loss of childhood friendships. "Dutch" (as he was nicknamed) was the younger of two boys. His older brother Neil ("Moon") became an advertising executive in Los Angeles and is now deceased.

Reagan's mother, Nelle Wilson Reagan, "took great care that her children realized that their father's alcoholism was a disease, for which they should not resent him."[2] Despite the poverty of his youth and his father's drinking, Reagan recalled his childhood as the happiest time of his life, "as sweet and idyllic as it could be."

Jack Reagan made a leap into the managerial class when he and a partner opened the Fashion Boot Shop in Dixon, Illinois, but their business went broke during the Great Depression. He was a liberal Democrat and a supporter of FDR. Following Roosevelt's election, he directed several relief and construction projects in and around Dixon. Firmly against bigotry, he refused to let his children see *Birth of a Nation* because it glorified the KKK, and he once walked out of a hotel because it refused lodging to Jews.

In high school Reagan lettered in sports and was elected president of the student body. Working part-time as a summer lifeguard, he personally pulled dozens of people, few of whom ever thanked him, from the waters of the Rock River. Years later, as Alzheimer's disease robbed him of memories of Washington and Hollywood, he sometimes would tell visitors, "You know I was a lifeguard. I saved seventy-seven people." Several biographers considered this hero role as his life motif; only once in fifty-five films did he play a villain.

At college, Reagan studied sociology and economics but was only an average student. He received a partial scholarship and earned the rest of his tuition by washing dishes. In his first job after college, he was a sports announcer for WHO radio in Des Moines, Iowa. He has told of broadcasting to his audience play-by-play dramas that, working from only telegraph information, sprang almost entirely from his own imagination. However, Walter Cronkite wrote that he told Reagan a very similar broadcasting story before this story began appearing in Reagan's speeches. In *The Character Factor,* a number of similar apparent fabrications are cited.[3]

In Hollywood, Reagan played the lead in many B movies before making the A list as a major star. For a brief period in 1943, he was Hollywood's biggest box-office draw. Unlike many stars, he showed up on time and took direction graciously. In 1940 he married actress Jane Wyman; they became a wholesome and appealing Hollywood couple at a time when the film industry needed such an image.

When World War II broke out, Reagan was called from the Army Reserves to active duty as a second lieutenant. Though barred from combat due to poor eyesight, he rose to the rank of captain and narrated military training films for the Army Air Force. Following the war, he was elected president of the Screen Actors Guild and testified about Communists in Hollywood before the House Committee on Un-American Activities.

In the early 1950s, with his film career in decline, he hosted *GE Theater* on television, which brought him into millions of American homes on a weekly basis. Part of his job involved giving speeches for GE, and this became his first broad political forum. He increasingly was drawn to politics, but his wife was not; their marriage eventually broke over this issue. The first divorced president, he was despondent for months over this "personal failing."

While in Hollywood, Reagan had changed from a liberal New Dealer to a right-wing Democrat. He was not the first to warn of Communists in the film industry and had initially dismissed the issue. Then, in 1946, he observed labor riots at the gates of his studio, saw buses set on fire, and peered into the face of anarchy. An anonymous caller threatened to disfigure him. His liberal convictions changed overnight, though he did not switch to the Republican Party until 1962.

Nancy Davis was a twenty-eight-year-old MGM starlet when she was mistakenly identified as having leftist Hollywood connections. Fearful for her career, she turned to Reagan for help in November 1949. In 1952 they were married, and their first child, Patti, was born seven months later. They were near opposites in personality, and as such, became a famously complementary marital and political team.

Reagan's entry into big-time politics came when he served as California co-chair for Barry Goldwater's 1964 presidential run. His television address in support of Goldwater drew more contributions than any other political speech in history. Shortly thereafter, having never held a public office, he ran for governor of California and won. Stepping down after two successful terms in 1975, he began his bid for the presidency, nearly unseating President Gerald Ford at the 1976 convention. By 1980 he was unstoppable, winning a 489 to 49 electoral vote landslide over Jimmy Carter.

Reagan and Wyman had a daughter and adopted a son. He fathered two more children, Patti and Ron, in his second marriage. Three of the children have written books portraying their family as emotionally distant. Patti recalled Nancy as raging and abusive toward her. Yet, there is no doubt that she and Reagan shared a deeply loving and enduring marital partnership.

Personality

Six specialist experts rated Reagan. Both they and generalists indicated low levels of respect for Reagan, with specialists giving very low scores. There was good agreement between the two groups of experts, with no significant difference on Big Five scores. Turning to the specialists' ratings, Reagan scored very high on Extraversion (98th percentile), low on Neuroticism (4th), Openness (10th), and Conscientiousness (9th). This latter score was far below the average of other presidents but with a great range of opinion (1st–85th percentile). Raters also disagreed on Character, Openness, and Agreeableness. Character ratings ranged nearly as widely as for Conscientiousness but centered more on the U.S. average.

On the NEO Facets, Reagan scored as shown in the table on page 177 compared to current-day Americans:

Reagan's very low score on Openness to Values is a reflection of his tendency to look to the church and tradition for guidance on moral issues. He scored highest of all presidents on the NEO Openness to Fantasy scale and on Simonton's Conservatism scale. So, though very reluctant to try new things (low Openness to Actions), he was very prone to daydream and fantasize (Openness to Fantasy).

CHART 9.3

Reagan's Scores on Character and the Big Five Traits

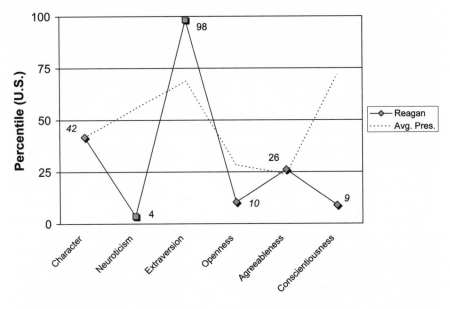

High	Percentile	Low	Percentile
Openness to Fantasy	98.3	Openness to Values	0.5
Positive Emotions (E)	98	*Tender-Mindedness* (A)	2
Excitement Seeking (E)	95	Depression (N)	2
Assertiveness (E)	90	*Anxiety* (N)	3
		Openness to Ideas	3
		Openness to Actions	4
		Self-Consciousness (N)	7
		Dutifulness (C, Ch)	10

He also scored high on Excitement Seeking and was second highest on Simonton's Wit scale.

Reagan definitely had a leisurely style and was very carefree, happy-go-lucky, and spontaneous. "Show me an executive who works long, hard hours, and I'll show you a bad executive," he once quipped. He was undeniably humorous, laughed easily, and was happy and high-spirited. When an opponent charged that teenage births had increased alarmingly while he'd been in office, he joked that he had never felt so young and virile. He appeared aware of the impression he made on people, but he showed his feelings and did not keep a tight rein on his needs or desires. He was optimistic and cheerful, laughed at the antics and jokes of those around him, and was enthusiastic, spirited, vivacious, and zestful. Strong emotions gave his life meaning. Charismatic, Reagan radiated personal magnetism and was greatly admired and held his followers in awe. He was talkative, good-looking, and was a bit of a thrill seeker. He dramatized and called attention to himself and was assured, confident, and proud.

Reagan did *not* worry excessively and had fewer fears than other people. Situations rarely seemed hopeless to him, and he was seldom sad, dejected, or lonely. He was not thin-skinned, sensitive to personal slights, or moody. He had a clear sense of meaning in life, rarely if ever felt worthless, and was not self-conscious. "A man of almost supernatural calm and self-certainty," commented his official biographer. He did not sabotage his own goals through self-defeating behavior. He coped well under stress, did not blame himself if things went wrong, and did not let minor problems upset him.

Reagan was decidedly shallow, nonintellectual, and unreflective,[4] yet clearly skilled at imaginative play. He had an active imagination and often viewed his problems as president in terms of movie plots and motifs. His only contribution during a high-level discussion of the MX missile was to relate the lesson of the movie *War Games.* He did not approach problems in a quantitative, scientific manner, was not good with numbers, and quickly lost interest in abstract, theoretical discussions. Reagan tended to "accept as fact any opinion, story, or rumor that tended to support his own view."[5] He did not believe that the values of other cultures or people might be valid for them and looked to traditional religious authority on moral issues. Nonetheless, in day-to-day dealings, he liked to keep his options open. He was able to persuade others but he lacked an exceptional vocabulary.[6]

Reagan did not feel that "society can never do too much for the elderly and poor."[7] Yet, at the same time he was slashing human service benefits, he would write personal checks to people who approached him with their problems. His son Ron offered insight on how to sway his father on a social issue: Bring him a real live person with that problem. Ironically, other people wanted to take care of and nurture *Reagan.* He was trusting of others and reluctant to express anger, "lenient, uncritical, undemanding," and not condescending.

Miscellaneous Observations

Despite his friendly exterior, Reagan was "emotionally shy" and had few close friends aside from his wife. In the view of some, he used his charm to keep people at a distance. More than most presidents, Reagan remains an enigma. He once protested this assessment to Edmund Morris, his official biographer, stating that his life is an open book. Morris responded, "Yes, Mr. President, but all the pages are blank." Even Nancy has professed not to really know him.

This is one common outcome of growing up in a family with an alcoholic parent—put on a good face and do not let anyone know anything is wrong. Though he preached family values, Reagan was a distant, emotionally unavailable father. His daughter Patti Davis wrote poignantly of trying to tell him of her embattled relationship with her mother. According to Patti, Reagan would accuse Patti of lying. Patti drew a parallel between her father's inability to face problems in their home and his attitude toward social problems as president. Both could be seen as a form of denial—and of personal distance. Reagan's son Ron recalled that he and his father never once had a conversation. Reagan and Nancy constituted an inviolable unit within the family, separate and self-sufficient. There have never been any credible allegations of infidelity.

Reagan had a problem remembering names and often made gaffes in this regard. He once greeted his HUD secretary as "Mr. Mayor" and introduced Diana, Princess of Wales, as "Princess David," apparently thinking ahead to his upcoming trip to Camp David.

As president, Reagan was a master of stagecraft and enjoyed the ceremonial aspects of the job. He enjoyed delivering polished speeches and giving a confident salute as Commander in Chief. He also kept up an active exercise routine in the White House and once bested a professional bodybuilder in arm wrestling.

Reagan Quoted

"There *are* simple answers, just not easy ones."

"What I'd really like is to go down in history as the president who made Americans believe in themselves again."

"Freedom is not the prerogative of a chosen few; it is the universal right of all God's children."

Reagan Described

"He could act decisively when presented with clear options, but he rarely initiated a meeting, a phone call, a proposal, or an idea."—Lou Cannon, Reagan biographer

"Ronald Reagan is by profession a performer, and it is the single most important fact about him."—Robert Lindsey

"[He] . . . has always felt hands on his shoulders, keeping him safe, and he has never doubted that they belong to God."—Patti Davis, daughter, in *Angels Don't Die*

President Reagan

Reagan received an overall ranking of 26th in the Ridings and McIver poll, scoring 9th in Political Skill but a lowly 39th in Appointments and Character and Integrity. Chart 9.4 shows our profile of Reagan's strengths and weaknesses as president. It is quite similar to Harding's. A high score on Positive Emotions is more than offset by low ratings in Achievement Striving, Competence, and Tender-Mindedness. Taken together, Reagan's personality scores predict a president who eventually is rated in the lower third of his peers.[8] His low score on Conscientiousness is interesting for another reason. The conservative values of hard work, competence, and devotion to principle are all parts of this factor. Reagan, the hero of conservatives, seemed not to fully embody the virtues he represented.

CHART 9.4

Personality Assets and Liabilities of Reagan as President

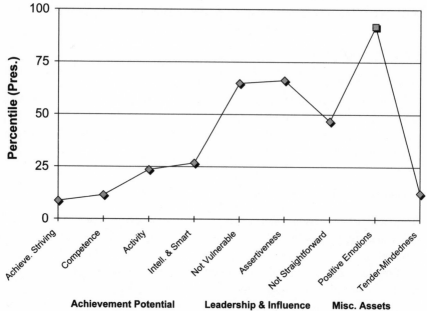

Reagan came into office on the heels of Jimmy Carter and a period of economic and spiritual stagnation. America had started to lower its expectations, to doubt itself. Reagan explicitly rejected that stance. He believed in America as God's shining example to the rest of the world, destined to spread democracy and defeat the forces of tyranny. In terms of his personality and mission, he was much like FDR, but Reagan was a conservative looking backward in time as well as forward. He had several avowed goals for his administration: to cut taxes, lower the deficit, and restore military readiness. He soon found that, as many had warned, he could not meet all his economic goals while outspending the Soviet Union on weapons. Yet, he chose to focus on the Soviet Union.

Reagan's approach to the Soviet Union was a dramatic break with previous administrations. Nixon had established détente, a means of peaceful coexistence. Ford and Carter followed suit, concerned above all with not losing the Cold War. Reagan set out to *win* the war, branding the Soviet Union "an evil empire." Using CIA analyses, he concluded that the USSR economy was fragile and could not support another arms race. Subsequent arms buildups would serve to strengthen the U.S. negotiating position while simultaneously striking at the fibrillating heart of the Soviet Union. It was a daring and potentially dangerous plan. Despite these intentions, he struck a friendly relationship with Mikhail Gorbachev and insisted on telling his counterpart the mildly anti-Soviet jokes that he himself found so amusing.

We may never know for sure if Reagan's actions brought about the defeat of the most formidable enemy the United States ever faced without firing a shot, or if the Soviet Union would have fallen apart from its own weight. His legacy may be already undergoing a revision similar to that of Eisenhower. A recent article portrayed Reagan pouring over detailed intelligence data on the economy of the Soviet Union for hours each day, always looking for another stress point to exploit.

There is little doubt that Reagan delegated a great deal of authority to his staff and took more naps than any president since Coolidge. Though it is unclear how much he really knew or remembered about the incident, the Iran-Contra arms for hostages scandal threatened his administration and raised concern about his management style.

Reagan was very nearly killed by John Hinckley Jr. when a bullet fragment missed his heart by only an inch. Hinckley was found not guilty by reason of insanity for his assassination attempt, a verdict that prompted more stringent guidelines for this defense in a number of states. Reagan maintained his sunny demeanor even as he was wheeled into the emergency room, telling his doctors he hoped they were all Republicans. Though he returned to work only nine days later, he began to show a decline in his mental and physical capacities.

After leaving the presidency, he was diagnosed with Alzheimer's disease. It is likely that his mental functioning had been affected, at least periodically, while still in office. At one point, Chief of Staff Howard Baker considered invoking the 25th Amendment to relieve him from office after a staff member noted that the president appeared dazed and confused. However, when they went to discuss the issue with Reagan, they found him "his same old self."[9] Incredibly, they apparently did not consult a physician. People with early Alzheimer's often show only such occasional periods of confusion.

Lastly, Reagan's Star Wars initiative deserves comment. Taking office, he found that he had only two options in the case of a nuclear attack: to do nothing or to attack in return. He wanted a third, nonaggressive option. From the beginning, the scientific community was skeptical that the Star Wars system could work. But with just a proposal, the United States trumped the Soviet Union where it had little ability to compete, while giving Star Wars the image of a purely defensive weapon. Reagan was sometimes heard to talk about his initiative as if it were an online, finished system rather than a set of proposals. As a result some observers concluded that the president occasionally had a hard time distinguishing fantasy from reality.[10]

Behavior as President (our data)

As president, Reagan definitely had a flair for the dramatic, was charismatic, and conveyed a distinct, public personality. He relied on a staff system, deciding among options formulated by advisers; cabinet members were given considerable independence. He was patient and polite in meetings and endeared himself to his staff through his courtesy and consideration. He had the ability to maintain popularity and kept in touch with the public and its moods. Not a middle-of-the-roader, Reagan had a vision of what he wanted to accomplish. Despite his Alzheimer's, he showed less personality change after assuming office than most other presidents.

Reagan in Perspective

In terms of personality, Reagan was most like Harding ($r = .48$), G.W. Bush ($r = .38$), and FDR ($r = .34$).[11] He was least like John Q. Adams ($r = -.34$), Hoover ($r = -.30$), and John Adams ($r = -.28$).

He was not the most intellectual of presidents and likely suffered at least occasionally from the effects of Alzheimer's. But like FDR, Reagan possessed "people smarts," political skills, and the ability to communicate a vision that was clear and appealing (to many). While his predecessors had many goals, Reagan had but a few, and he clearly failed one of them—reducing the deficit. But the mood of the country changed while he was in office. The popular song "I'm Proud to

Be an American" captured this rebound in spirit. Reagan may well have brought about the end of the cold war and its accompanied threat of nuclear war. But he remains controversial, largely along party lines. If he is eventually viewed as a great president, it will be in defiance of our predictions based solely on his personality.

Reagan's presidency raises serious questions regarding the public's right to know about the physical and mental health of its leader. Consider these facts about a man with his finger on the nuclear button: Reagan had a rich fantasy life, suffered intermittent confusion from Alzheimer's, and occasionally had difficulty distinguishing fantasy from reality. He demonized the Soviet Union, reflected on major problems from the standpoint of what John Wayne would do, believed his generation could be the one to see Armageddon, and was stubborn and obdurate when his mind was made up.

HARDING AND REAGAN COMPARED

Chart 9.5 compares the two Actors. Both Reagan and Harding are lower in Openness than the average Actor, as well as a bit lower on Conscientiousness (not

CHART 9.5
Reagan and Harding Compared

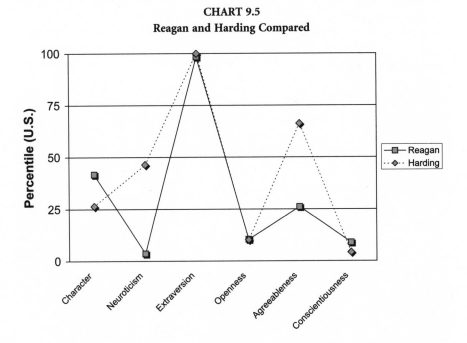

shown). Reagan differs from both Harding and other Actors by his very low score on Neuroticism. Harding stands out by his high score on Agreeableness.

The two differed on quite a few of the narrower facet scales. Harding scored very low on all measures of achievement drive, while Reagan was about average. Reagan received the highest rating of all the presidents on Simonton's Wit scale, while Harding got a low score. Reagan was Assertive and Forceful (energetic, active) but Conservative; Harding high on Pacifism (peaceable) and Moderation (modest, gentle). Harding also scored higher than Reagan on spatial abilities and on one measure of general intelligence, but lower on Intellectual Brilliance (interests wide, artistic, inventive). Though Harding was more Optimistic, he also scored higher on Depression, indicating he could become very discouraged. (Recall his sanitarium stays.) Reagan scored low on Impulsivity and Vulnerability, while Harding was high. Finally, Reagan scored higher than Harding on a number of indexes of character.

CHAPTER 10

Two Maintainers—Harry Truman and George H. W. Bush

Morphed image of Harry Truman and George H. W. Bush
Library of Congress and George H. W. Bush Library

THE MAINTAINERS include (in order) McKinley, G. H. W. Bush, Ford, and Truman. Three of these men followed a more prominent president, and McKinley preceded one. We profile Truman and Bush, who shared only two traits on the NEO: low scores on both Openness to Values and Straightforwardness. Though each was easily identified as traditional in his moral tenets, their low scores on Straightforwardness are surprising, especially for those of us who have read David McCullough's Pulitzer Prize–winning biography of Truman. This is one of the times that the meaning attached to a scale may be questioned. Low Straightforwardness usually indicates a willingness to deceive or manipulate, but this is not invariably so. In the case of Truman and Bush, it may refer to an ability to manage or "handle" others effectively.

TABLE 10.1
Truman and Bush Compared

	Bush High	Bush Low
Truman High	NONE	NONE
Truman Low	NONE	Openness to Values, Straightforwardness

HARRY TRUMAN

Harry S. Truman was born May 8, 1884, at his parents' home in Lamar, Missouri. He was their first child. His first memory was of playfully chasing a frog as it hopped in his yard. Truman's father, John, was a compact, muscular, hardworking, ambitious man with a streak of ingenuity. He was greatly protective of his family and fought like a buzz saw, remembered Truman. His mother, née Martha Ellen Young, was an unreconstructed Confederate; Union soldiers during the war had pillaged her family farm, and she never forgave them. When her son went to the White House, she refused to sleep in the Lincoln bedroom—holding the ex-president personally accountable for her family's losses.

By his mother's account, little Harry "tended toward a girl." He loved hanging around the kitchen as his mother cooked, tenderly cared for his little sister, sometimes braiding her hair for hours and singing her to sleep. At age five, he got his first set of the thick glasses that he wore the rest of his life. He was something of a curiosity, as few children in Missouri had glasses, and perhaps none of them were as young as Truman. They magnified his eyes and gave the alert, affable boy a wide-eyed appearance. He took to school naturally and skipped the third grade.

When he was ten, his mother gave him *Great Men and Famous Women*, a collection of biographies etched in gold leaf. He would remember this gift as the formative moment of his childhood. He loved history, "to know the real facts." He and a friend vowed to read every book in the local library, and he later claimed to have completed all two thousand volumes, including the encyclopedias. He came to believe that men like Hannibal and Robert E. Lee make history, as opposed to history making great men. As an adult, he showed an encyclopedic knowledge of historical facts.

Perhaps because of his expensive glasses, Truman avoided sports. In his own words, he was "not one of the fighters" and "kind of a sissy." He was always very neat and clean—unnaturally so at times—and unfailingly polite. He took piano lessons, which almost no other boy did, and cheerfully practiced two hours each morning. He was good enough for his music teacher to raise the possibility of a career as a concert pianist.

Heading off with his music scrolls under his arm, he suffered the indignity of being referred to as a model boy by other mothers. He was shy around girls except for his two female cousins, who read widely, were loyal and unaffected, and were not particularly attractive. They would read parts of Shakespeare to each other and remained close throughout life.

Truman learned early how to please people to get what he wanted—and to be liked. Independence, Missouri, where he moved at an early age, was a small town set in its ways, but it also hosted literary discussion groups and other cultural events. In the Midwestern tradition, people did not talk about their feelings. When someone asked you how you were, your stock answer was, "Fine, how are you?" And as Truman would say later, "Right was right and wrong was wrong—you didn't need to talk about it."

His extended family included a number of good-natured, unpolished examples of manhood. Though he and his father shared few interests, John supported Harry in his interests. Later, father and son would discover a mutual love of politics. John did not physically discipline his son but could deliver a scalding rebuke; Truman's mother used a switch. Truman remembered his childhood as the best imaginable.

In the major health trauma of his youth, Truman was struck with diphtheria and paralyzed for two months. His family was financially comfortable, his father making a good living dabbling in wheat futures and trading horses. He patented an invention and was offered two thousand dollars by a railroad company for another, an automated switching device. A second company offered twenty-five hundred dollars—four times the annual income of an average family—but John held out for five thousand dollars. Both companies adopted an alternative design, and he got nothing. Still, times were good, and the family prospered. But in his attempts to get rich, John invested in increasingly risky crop futures. In 1912 he lost everything—even his house. At age fifty-one, he was broke.

Truman began working outside the home at age fourteen, tending the counter at a local drugstore. There, he got his first glimpse of adult hypocrisy. Independence, like many towns of the era, had a strong church and temperance community. The store he worked in catered to some of those customers, who could have a shot of whiskey in a private back room, checking a peephole before leaving to make sure the coast was clear. This left young Truman with a lifelong distaste for pretense and "high hats." He graduated from high school at seventeen without distinction. He did well in history and Latin, less well in science. He had ambitions of attending West Point, or another college, but these fell with the family's finances.

He went to work at a bank in Kansas City, then transferred to another, eventually earning one hundred dollars a month. This handsome salary allowed him to take in theater and other shows, as well as lead an urban lifestyle. Then his father called him home to work on the family farm, which John had taken over after his losses in the stock market. Friends did not think Truman, an owlish bank clerk, would last a week doing hard labor. He could not have been happy about this turn in his career (and the loss of his independence), but he did not complain.

John loved being a farmer, and his family thought him the happiest they had ever seen him; he would sing while doing his chores. Harry's opinion of farmwork ranged from dislike to hatred. And his father was a taskmaster—"If a row was plowed crooked, I'd hear about it all year." Still, farming had a near-spiritual significance for the family. They saw themselves as the culmination of Thomas Jefferson's plan for a nation of farmers, each a caretaker of his own parcel of the country. Truman, the farmer, took tips from sources as varied as the Roman writer Cato and modern scientific agriculture. The Truman farm implemented many developments and was among the first in the area to rotate crops.

He met his future wife, Bess Wallace, in Sunday school. It took him five years to work up the nerve to talk to the attractive, athletic, popular girl. She was everything Truman was not and from a prominent family. Over the years he would write her hundreds of letters, often self-effacing. He eventually proposed this way; she turned him down, but he "understood" and continued his pursuit. She was apparently the only woman he ever cared for. But she came at a cost. Bess's father committed suicide when she was a teenager, leaving a confused, humiliated family. Her mother never got over the shock and never thought Truman worthy of her family. She made her opinion of her daughter's suitor known to those around her, including the Secret Service agents who protected him as president. Bess apparently did not intercede, and in a phenomenal demonstration of self-control and character, Harry was never known to speak ill of his mother-in-law.

With similar forbearance, he put in ten years of hard labor on the family farm. His father, drawn to politics, took a job as a road construction supervisor, a job that paid little and promised a further decline in the family's social standing. He injured himself moving a large rock and never recovered. As he lay dying, much of the community came to pay respects to this man they liked and admired. But John Truman felt he was a failure, a fact his son would remember forever.

Like his father, Truman was eager to get rich. At one point, he invested most of his time and energy in a mine, in partnership with two men and with some money from Bess. They lost everything. Truman began to think of himself as a failure like his father.

When America entered World War I, nearly everything changed for him. He decided to enlist, despite his duties on the farm and the fact he could have been exempted from service on at least three grounds. He had to memorize the eye chart to pass the physical. On news of his enlistment, Bess finally agreed to marry him, but Truman now refused, insisting they wait until he return home "whole." Like Lincoln, he was elected captain by the men of his squad and was given advanced training as an artillery officer. He was then assigned to command the notorious Company D, a group of 192 rowdy Irish Catholics who had run off three previous captains.

At their first inspection, Truman was too scared to speak, and after he ordered them dismissed, they gave him a Bronx cheer. The next day, a notice was posted busting many of the noncommissioned officers, including the first sergeant. Truman told the remaining ones, "I'm not here to get along with you. You'll have to get along with me." He asked if anybody could not live with that, and no one objected. But the men noticed also that the food improved and that their new commanding officer took a personal interest in them and their problems. He lent them money to go on leave and occasionally bucked orders to see to their needs. When he also proved his courage and capability under fire, they were his forever. Truman's experience in the military remade him. Going into the war as a business failure without prospects or money, he proved that he could do the college-level work of the artillery school, that the boy who had been a sissy could stand tall in battle, and that he could lead men. Years of farmwork and combat produced a "tough son-of-a-bitch of a man" sharing space inside the body of the sensitive boy.

Truman and Bess were married soon after he returned. At thirty-five, he had never dated another woman. They moved into Bess's home, supposedly only long enough to get her mother used to her being married. He opened a men's store with a Jewish friend from the Army, but after a promising start, the haberdashery went bankrupt. "Lost all I had and all I could borrow," reflected Truman. His ticket into politics was through the brother of another soldier from Company D. Tom Pendergast was an old-time, Irish ward politician who ran the Kansas City rackets, gambling, prostitution, and narcotics. A returning war hero, Truman was an attractive candidate for county commissioner for the Pendergast "machine."

Although he was a terrible speaker, his men from Company D provided a

noisy but effective booster group. He was elected and earned a reputation for
efficiency and honesty. However, he also found he had to turn his back on Pendergast's corruption—a conflict that along with other job stresses led to headaches and insomnia. "Am I just a crook?" he asked himself in his diary, but he
was scrupulously honest about his own finances. He even denied his mother
eleven thousand dollars in compensation from the county for highway land that
would've been granted to anyone else. By his own estimate as well as others', he
could have pocketed over a million dollars during his days as a county judge.

When Truman wanted to run for county commissioner, for Congress, and for
governor, Pendergast blocked him. He did not think Truman could be elected,
and at least a few people considered the jobs too big for him. In 1935 he went to
the Senate, only to be derided as "Pendergast's bellhop." Truman came with an
inferiority complex, which was not too surprising given his instructions from the
boss before he left: "Work hard, keep your mouth shut, and answer your mail."
Yet Truman admired Pendergast as "all man" and hung a picture of him in his
office even after Pendergast was convicted of tax evasion and sent to prison in
disgrace.

His own financial situation remained austere. Running for his second term
for the Senate, he was forced to sleep in his car some nights because he could
not afford a hotel room. Bess and their daughter, Margaret, stayed in Washington only five months before returning to Independence. Mrs. Truman did not
like the spotlight and feared her father's suicide would be exposed. Her departure
left Truman desolate and lonely but was repeated when he later became president.

After Pendergast's fall, Truman came into his own in the Senate. Responding
to letters from constituents about government waste, he got in his car and took
a fact-finding tour. With the country gearing up production for the coming war,
he found men and their supervisors standing around and equipment left out in
the rain to rust. He formed a committee that investigated these abuses, as well as
the quality of weapons and goods provided by major companies. He became a
feared inquisitor but was also renowned for his fairness. His committee work
earned him a national reputation and journalists named him one of the ten most
important men in Washington. He was tapped for vice president in 1944 but
demurred, convinced that FDR did not like him. The president had given him
good reason to think so over the years, on one occasion directly calling Pendergast to "tell Harry how to vote"—a consummate insult to an honest politician
living under a shadow. Truman met alone with Roosevelt only twice before
FDR's death eighty-two days into his fourth term.

Personality

Seven experts rated Truman. Though in general agreement, there were significant differences on four of the six dimensions. Truman scored high on Extraversion (95th percentile) and Conscientiousness (90th) and very low on Openness to Experience (2nd), but generalists did not agree on this last assessment (low Openness). Specialists indicted only average appraisals of Truman's job performance, while generalists expressed a much better opinion. They also rated him higher, although still average, on Intellectual Brilliance and Openness and lower on Neuroticism.

On the NEO Facet Scales, Truman scored as shown in the table on page 192.

There were also some differences between our data and Simonton's scores. Although rated high in Warmth and low in Assertiveness by our raters, Simonton's data shows average ratings on Friendliness and Forcefulness.

Truman's very low scores on Openness to Experience and Openness to Ideas require some explanation. These would not be expected from a man who spent much of his childhood reading and taking piano lessons and reciting Shakespeare with his female cousins. Truman did score about average on Openness to Aes-

CHART 10.1

Truman's Scores on Character and the Big Five Traits

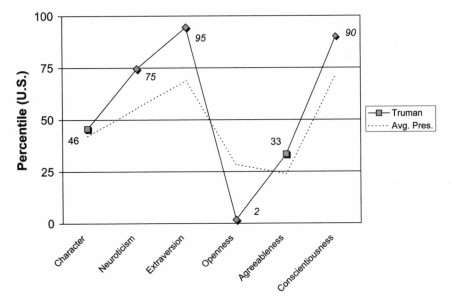

High	Percentile	Low	Percentile
Achievement Striving (C)	96	Openness to Ideas	1.4
Self-Discipline (C, Ch)	91	Openness to Actions	1.4
Activity (E)	89	Openness to Values	2
		Openness to Fantasy	4
		Compliance (A, Ch)	6
		Deliberation (C, Ch)	8

thetics. Though he had a deep love for classical music and art, he had a decided distaste for modern works, including the jazz of Kansas City. He embraced the traditional values of his family and hometown (low Openness to Values) and was a commonsense (low Openness to Fantasy) kind of guy.

Turning to Truman's low score on the Openness to Ideas scale, it is important to know that the items on this scale reflect two general themes. One refers to enjoyment of philosophical conversation, the other to enjoying doing puzzles and brain-twisters. Not known for deep conversation, Truman was not fond of puzzles either. Though the Openness to Ideas scale correlates with curiosity and breadth of interests, there are no items about these qualities on it. Lastly, Truman scored above average (70th percentile) on Openness to Feelings. Truman was the highest-rated president on Musical Intelligence and on Winter's Need for Power. He was third lowest on Simonton's Poise and Polish Scale.

Truman sometimes became completely absorbed in music, and some forms of art fascinated him. He had a good ear for tones and a good memory for melodies. Yet, he did not pursue other sensual pleasures (touch, taste, smell, physical contact). Nor did he see situations in sexual terms; he believed in the traditional morality of sexual restraint. On one occasion, he indignantly chastised a driver who offered to set him up with a prostitute. He did not have many sexual partners.

Though he had an exceptional tendency to swear frequently, Truman did not cuss or even drink in the presence of women. He was "bullheaded, obstinate, stubborn" and did not hesitate to express anger; he was ready to fight if anyone picked on him. He generally kept focused on his work and was not interested in developing hobbies. He was uncomfortable with uncertainties or complex issues and did not enjoy pondering abstract ideas or theories. He was not moved to strong emotions by many things and did not indulge in elaborate daydreams and fantasies.

Few considered him cold or calculating. He believed that human needs outweigh economic considerations and was not "greedy, selfish, self-indulgent." He laughed at people's jokes or antics and did not obstruct or undermine others' goals. He was not hypocritical, and did not lead others to become dependent on him to take advantage of them.

Truman would not miss work unless he was really sick. He was industrious, persistent, tenacious, and thorough. He did not suffer from preoccupying thoughts or have trouble making up his mind. Not self-indulgent, he did not eat too much even of his favorite foods, and he resisted temptation easily. Lastly, he did not see himself as good-looking or attractive.

Miscellaneous Observatons

Harry Truman, the simple man from Missouri, showed a number of contradictions and complexities. He was humble yet cocky, gentle but tough, honest yet accepted dishonesty in associates, anti-intellectual but well read in history, personally unimaginative but innovative in office. He could become angry quickly but did not become violent. A "common man," he saw himself as Cincinnatus, the Roman citizen/political leader. He could talk bluntly and sometimes indiscreetly to the press, yet, as a senator, he was never known to snap at a staff member. He was a reformer who was both personally conservative and hailed from a corrupt political machine; a racist by upbringing who split his party by backing civil rights legislation.

In his youth, he firmly expressed his opinion that white men belonged in Europe and America, yellow men in Asia, and black men in Africa, and he was in favor of deportation. He was particularly hostile to the Chinese in America, and even put up ten dollars for membership in the Ku Klux Klan, although he refused to join when told he could not appoint Catholics (which included most of Company D) to county jobs. Eventually the Klan became a bitter political enemy, and Truman reported he received a death threat from them. He would later champion equality under the law and embrace "the Brotherhood of Man" but not social equality.

Bess and Margaret were the center of his emotional life—they were a very tight-knit family. Some have suggested the marriage was hardly a fairy-tale romance, and Bess never showed the exceptional devotion to Harry that he did to her. Perhaps her mother's opinion over the years made some impact. One of our sources stated that Truman "was brutalized by his mother-in-law, who was backed up by his wife."

People were the most important thing in the life of Harry Truman. Though he had many casual friends to whom he disclosed bits of himself, he had no true confidants other than Bess. He was easily persuaded to do what his friends wanted, and loyal to the point of irrationality to his associates. Perhaps because of his trusting nature and personal purity, he was a poor judge of character. He did not appear to recognize class distinction: He treated the service staff at the White House like real people, not servants.

Some sources saw Harry Truman as a different man after assuming the presidency, both growing into the job and insisting on being treated with a dignity suitable to the office that he did not always command as a person. With his strong sense of history, he knew what was expected of a president and was proud to serve in that capacity. He viewed the government as owned by the average man; Andrew Jackson and Wilson were among his role models. When Douglas MacArthur failed to salute him as Commander in Chief, he gave him a dressing down. Later, he fired the popular general for insubordination.

The presidency was "dropped" on him, much like his father calling him back to the farm years earlier, so his sense of duty may have played a role, as well. As before, he may have acted more confident than he felt. This might have contributed to his occasional brusqueness and his tendency to sum up complex issues with the simple conclusion "and that's all there is to it."

Despite his well-known quotation about standing the heat in the kitchen, Truman was prone to psychosomatic problems under stress in the Senate. He frequently complained of headaches, fatigue, and nausea, despite outward indications of good health. However, he did not display any tendency to get sick during periods of stress while president. We can only wonder if this reflected his missing his family in the Senate more than the stress of office.

Lastly, there is his transformation from the boy who wanted to please to the man who scored below ninety-four out of one hundred Americans on Compliance. Though Truman's experience of command in the Army undoubtedly contributed, during his early days in the Senate he was known as, "Go along, get along Harry." He had come into the Senate under a cloud, and freshmen senators were not expected to make waves. As he rose through the political ranks, he inevitably faced more criticism, and he responded pugnaciously. He was unyielding on issues involving the public trust but was much more accommodating to his friends and associates. Hence, his low score on Compliance may reflect his political more than his personal life.

Truman Quoted

"I tried never to forget who I was, and where I came from and where I'd go back to."

"When Franklin Roosevelt died, I felt there must be a million men better qualified to take up the presidential task. But the job was mine to do and I had to do it. And I tried to give it everything that was in me. . . . I felt like the moon, the stars and all of the planets had fallen on me."

Truman Described

"[Truman was] a vindication of the democratic ideal of leadership . . . a man of common sense and personal decency."—"Harry Truman," *The American Experience*, PBS TV.

"[Truman] is vastly concerned with being right; he does not seem sufficiently concerned with getting the right things done."—columnist Samuel Grafton

"A lot of people admired the old bastard for standing by people who were guilty as hell."—Richard Nixon

President Truman

FDR had been president for twelve years and towered above all the nation's presidents since Lincoln, even in his own time. Truman doubted his ability to fill those great shoes and said so. At the time of FDR's death, he had met with him alone only twice. He had little knowledge of the Manhattan Project that was shortly to deliver the first atomic bomb, yet he would have to decide how to use it. Though this was long touted as his most momentous decision, there was little debate about whether to use it, only how. He hoped it would be used on a military target, but he approved its use on Hiroshima and Nagasaki.

Soon after the conclusion of the Second World War, Truman faced the prospect of a new and powerful enemy in the Soviet Union. He wasted little time in confronting Soviet foreign minister Vyacheslav Molotov with the Soviet Union's failure to respect the autonomy of Poland and hold free elections. "I've never been talked to like that in my life," exclaimed Molotov.

His other initiatives were momentous. He sponsored the Marshall Plan to help rebuild western Europe and head off political crisis as European Communist parties were on the rise. He sent aid to Turkey and Greece to help put down Communist insurgencies there, and proclaimed what became known as the Truman Doctrine: "I believe that it must be the policy of the United States to support free people who are resisting attempted subjugation by armed minorities or by outside pressures." He helped champion the United Nations and sponsored the creation of Israel. In 1950 he convinced the United Nations to intervene in Korea, the first time the world body acted to confront an aggressor. The cold war had begun.

Ironically, Truman, the tough anti-Communist, came under attack by Joe McCarthy as soft on communism. Though skeptical of charges of Communists in the government, Truman initiated a program including loyalty oaths. But he also took on McCarthy directly, with his characteristic bluntness. Nor did he back away from a fight when steelworkers threatened to strike during the Korean War. Threatening to draft the strikers, he ordered federal seizure of the mills. The Supreme Court later reversed his actions as unconstitutional.

In 1949 Communists won the Chinese civil war. Truman unfairly received some of the blame for "losing China." Another crisis came when the Russians blockaded West Berlin, in a gambit that could have led to war. Truman chose to avoid confrontation by airlifting in needed supplies. This was a tremendous effort, barely adequate to meet the needs of a city of millions, but the Soviets backed down.

Truman left the presidency in 1953 practically in disgrace, largely due to the unpopular Korean War. Republican campaign slogans, even in 1946, proclaimed "To err is Truman" and "I'm just mild about Harry." Early historians' polls showed a similar opinion, but Truman has recently undergone a dramatic upsurge in popularity. David McCullough's Pulitzer Prize–winning biography portrays him as an admirably honest and principled man, loyal to a fault, modest yet feisty, brighter and more intellectual than he was ever credited for. His newly refurbished reputation earned him one of the most sentimental popular songs ever addressed to a president: "America Loves You, Harry Truman".

Truman produced an earlier reversal of his reputation in the 1948 election. Every newspaper and poll gave him *no* chance of reelection, even as he barnstormed across the country to large and enthusiastic crowds. One paper even printed the headline "Dewey Defeats Truman" before the polls closed. It was the biggest electoral upset in the history of the presidency.

By the 1990s, Truman ranked seventh among the presidents, just behind Wilson and ahead of his hero, Jackson. His highest ranking was in Accomplishments and Crisis Management, where he ranked sixth. This is somewhat better than predicted given his personal assets on our questionnaire. Overall, he would be expected to be a bit better than the average president and to be clearly in the upper half on Ethics on the Job. His strengths included his high activity level, Tender-Mindedness, and Achievement Striving. His biggest liability was his low Assertiveness—in contrast to his popular "Give 'em hell" image. Truman could be combative when his authority was challenged and take decisive action when the responsibility was his; but he did not seek out positions of leadership and was more comfortable with collegial relations than with domination. He was the only successful president to have a clearly below-average score on Assertiveness.

Behavior as President (our data)

Truman was not charismatic; he had a direct, uncomplicated approach. He relied on his staff, deciding among options they recommended, while asserting his own judgments.

Truman in Perspective

Truman was not much like any other president. He was most like Ford (r = .19), G. W. Bush (r = .19), and McKinley (r = .16). He was least like Jefferson (r = −.20), Garfield (r = −.19), and Kennedy (r = −.19).[1] He stands out from other modern presidents, especially Democrats (except for Carter), by his high scores on Conscientiousness and Character. Even more than Carter, he spoke his mind. People may have thought him crude and unpresidential, with his loud

CHART 10.2

Personality Assets and Liabilities of Truman as President

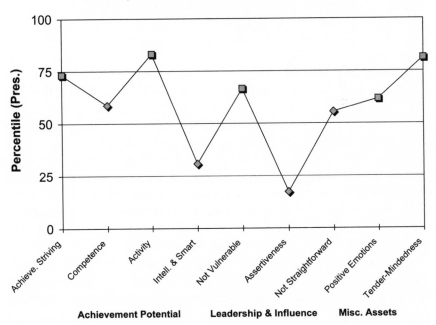

shirts and poker games with reporters, but they did not doubt his sincerity or integrity. In time, the feisty man who said exactly what he thought came to be seen as an admirable president even by Republicans.

GEORGE HERBERT WALKER BUSH

George H. W. Bush is related to several notables, including Benedict Arnold; Presidents Pierce, Lincoln, Theodore Roosevelt, and Ford; his own vice president, Dan Quayle; Winston Churchill, Queen Elizabeth II; and Marilyn Monroe. He is also the only president born in June. He was born the second of five children on June 12, 1924, in Milton, Massachusetts; his family moved to Greenwich, Connecticut, where he grew up. His father, Prescott, was a successful businessman and U.S. senator. Active in sports and charitable causes, George Bush was taught that people of wealth and privilege have an obligation to give something back to society.

Bush's mother, Dorothy Walker, was born in Kennebunkport, Maine. She was a remarkable athlete, who hit a home run in a family softball game moments before going to the hospital to deliver her first child. Her father was also very athletic and established golf's Walker Cup competition. A strict disciplinarian, she instilled in her children competitiveness without boasting or other self-promotion. As a senator's wife, she wrote a newspaper column published in twenty Maine newspapers.

Raised amid wealth, Bush was driven to school and on his first dates by the family chauffeur. An early baseball fan, he once caught a foul ball at Yankee Stadium. Fiercely competitive, he ordered an aunt off the tennis court at age ten for being too noisy. He spent summers at Walker's Point, an eleven-acre peninsula in Kennebunkport where he fished, boated, and beachcombed.

He attended Greenwich Country Day School, where he played baseball, football, soccer, and tennis. At age thirteen, as family tradition dictated, he entered Phillips Academy in Andover, Massachusetts. He was president of his senior class, editor of the school newspaper, and a leader in baseball and soccer. He was voted second most influential (with the faculty), third best athlete, third most popular, and third most handsome in his 1942 graduating class.

On his eighteenth birthday he enlisted as a seaman in the Navy. As a single engine carrier pilot in the Pacific during World War II, he flew fifty-eight combat missions. Rising to the rank of lieutenant (junior grade), he was one of only four pilots in his original fourteen-man squadron to survive. He crashed at sea twice but was rescued with only minor injuries both times. The second time, he narrowly escaped capture by the Japanese on one of the Bonin Islands. (Ironically, his distant relative, President Franklin Pierce, nixed Commodore Perry's plan to annex the Bonin Islands, thereby making them available for Japanese annexation.) After the war, the Japanese on Chici Jima were convicted of war crimes including torture, decapitation, and cannibalism of those they took prisoner. Bush was awarded the Distinguished Flying Cross for completing his bombing run over the island after being hit by shrapnel.

After the war, Bush married Barbara Pierce, daughter of the publisher of *Redbook* and *McCall's* magazines. In striking contrast to their wealthy home lives, when they moved to Odessa, Texas, a few years later, George and Barbara were forced to share a bathroom with a mother-daughter team of prostitutes.

Bush attended Yale University, where he played first base and completed a degree in economics and sociology in two and a half years. As team captain, he had the honor of accepting from Babe Ruth the original manuscript of his autobiography for Yale Library. In an impromptu gesture, he led the terminally ill Ruth to the Yale dugout to meet his teammates. He lettered in soccer at Yale and was a member of the Delta Kappa Epsilon fraternity and the venerable Skull and Bones secret society. He won the Francis Gordon Brown Prize for his junior grades, made Phi Beta Kappa, and graduated with honors in 1948.

Eschewing positions in several family businesses, he joined Dresser Industries to learn the oil business in Texas. In 1950 he started his own oil development company, which later merged to form Zapata Petroleum Corporation. In 1959 he bought out the Zapata Offshore subsidiary and moved it from Midland to Houston. In 1966 he sold his interests in Zapata Offshore for a reported one million dollars.

He had become active in Republican Party affairs and in 1963 was chosen chairman of the Harris County (Houston) Republican Party. In 1964, he ran unsuccessfully for a seat in the U.S. Senate and was a Goldwater delegate to the Republican National Convention. In 1966 he won election to the House of Representatives, where he served until 1971, representing a mostly black, Republican district in northwestern Houston. Defeated for the U.S. Senate again in 1970, he was appointed UN ambassador by Richard Nixon (1971–1973). He was national Republican Party chairman (1973–1974) and Chief U.S. liaison in China (1974–1975). Quietly lobbying for the vice presidency in those years, he instead served as head of the Central Intelligence Agency (1976–1977). In 1980 Reagan selected him as his vice president. As Reagan's heir, he was elected president in 1988.

After his defeat by Bill Clinton in 1992, he settled in Houston, where he actively supported his sons' political dreams. George W. Bush, who successfully campaigned for the presidency, is one of six children. The death of a daughter, Robin, at age four of leukemia, led the Bushes to be very active in anticancer causes. Barbara's hair became gray at age twenty-eight while she cared for her terminally ill daughter. Both she and George reported Robin's death as the single greatest challenge to their marriage. Second son Jeb was elected governor of Florida, while Neil, Marvin, and Dorothy are all active in business.

Personality

Only two experts rated Bush, so we must be cautious with our interpretations. In addition, these two raters indicated considerably lower appraisals of Bush's job performance than did other groups. Conversely, specialists gave moderately low ratings on Negative Valence, while generalists' ratings were moderately high. On the Big Five traits, the two groups of experts were in general agreement. Simonton's study rated presidents only through Reagan, so we do not have this alternative data to corroborate our results. Given these limitations, the results presented here should be regarded as somewhat tentative.

Though Chart 10.3 shows Bush received low scores on Openness (18th percentile) and Conscientiousness (23rd), only one of our two raters thought so. The generalists agreed with the specialists on most factors but portrayed Bush as considerably more Extraverted and Conscientious. This latter score still was below that of the average president, however.

CHART 10.3
G. H. W. Bush's Scores on Character and the Big Five Traits

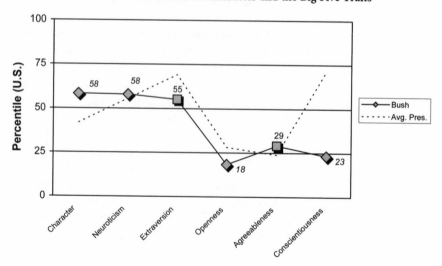

Because of the limited data, we will report only NEO Facet Scales on which there was agreement among specialist raters. Since Bush received mostly moderate scores, we broaden our usual criteria and present scales on which his score was in the upper or lower 15 percent of today's Americans.

On the NEO Facet Scales, raters showed reasonable agreement on the following scales:

High	Percentile	Low	Percentile
NONE		Openness to Ideas	9
		Straightforwardness (A, Ch)	9
		(Openness to Feelings	14)

NB: () – Does not meet the criteria for inclusion used for other presidents.

These scores suggest a practical (low Openness to Ideas), persuasive (low Straightforwardness) man who does not typically attend to or value his emotions. For those who saw the *A&E* documentary on Bush, this may come as a surprise. In it, he choked and teared up as he described telling his father of his plan to go to war and how his father saw him off on the train. But his emotions appear unwanted and even confusing to him. He tried to stop the tears, smiled, and then appeared embarrassed. He did not acknowledge his emotions nor elaborate on the feelings he obviously experienced, however.

Instead of presenting a narrative personality portrait, as we did for other presidents, we show the dozen items that met a revised and stringent set of requirements in a table.[2] The direction in which they were answered ("Yes" or "No") is indicated in the second column, though all items were actually answered on a five-point or nine-point scale. Those answers that are in bold are above the 95th percentile or below the 5th percentile among presidents and would qualify for amplification (e.g., "strongly," "very," "not at all") if we wrote them out as for other presidents.

G. H. W. Bush Described

"I've always felt that if there's one thing you can count on George Bush for, it's decency and fairness."—Mayor Andrew Young of Atlanta, 1988

"George is a damn good guy, but he doesn't come through well. It's a case of choking. It takes eleven hours to get George ready for an off-the-cuff remark." —Robert Strauss, former chairman of the Democratic Party, 1988.

TABLE 10.2
Personality Items Rated High or Low for G. H. W. Bush

Item	Answer
Values intellectual and cognitive matters.	**No**
Wants to be where the action is.	**Yes**
Expresses ideas fluently/masterfully.	**No**
Sometimes feels resentful, bitter.	**No**
Thinks he's superior to most people.	**No**
Uses gestures awkwardly.	Yes
Willing to manipulate others.	No
Gets disgusted with people he interacts with.	No
Anxiety leads to physical symptoms.	No
Dependable, reliable, responsible	Yes
Worries.	No
Financially successful.	Yes
Is a good family man (husband and father).	Yes

President Bush

Though it is too early to accurately place his standing in history through polls of historians, Bush ranked twenty-second in the Ridings and McIver study, just behind Van Buren and ahead of Clinton. His highest ranking was eighteenth in Accomplishments and Crisis Management, perhaps referring to his masterful forging of an alliance to confront Saddam Hussein. His lowest rating was in Political Skill at twenty-seventh.

His inaugural address looked beyond the collapse of totalitarianism around the world, anticipating what he later called "A New World Order." Unemployment worsened and more businesses failed under Bush than under any president since the Great Depression. Interest rates, however, reached their lowest level in two decades.

Bush ordered U.S. forces to invade Panama in 1989 to capture dictator Manuel Noriega and led allied forces in the Persian Gulf War against Iraq in 1990–1991. In 1992, he dispatched U.S. troops to Somalia to assist in feeding the starving victims of their civil war. Other Bush administration accomplishments include bailing out the Savings and Loan Crisis in 1989, maintaining global stability as communism collapsed in Eastern Europe and Central America, preventing destabilization of Third World countries by urging international bankers to forgive some of their debts, cleaning up the *Exxon Valdez* oil spill in Alaska in 1989, and signing the Americans with Disabilities Act and the Clean Air Act in 1990.

Bush's profile of personality strengths and weaknesses for the job is presented in Chart 10.4. Again, it must be cautioned that his scores are based on only two raters, who did not always agree and expressed very low levels of respect for their subject relative to another group of experts. With these limitations in mind, Bush is portrayed as poorly suited, personally, to being president.

Bush's score on our Presidential Success index, if accurate, places him in the lowest 10 percent of presidents—lower than any recent chief executive back to Harding. The only personality asset attributed to him is his low standing on Straightforwardness. He scored high on Vulnerability (reversed in the chart) and quite low on Competence and Assertiveness. This is not the portrait of a natural leader and often portends problems in such a role. He scored in the lower third of presidents on all of our performance predictors as president, including for Ethics on the Job. If the personality scores reported above are accurate, we would predict George H. W. Bush ultimately to be considered one of the less successful presidents of the twentieth century, comparable to Coolidge or Harding. For the reasons given above, however, we need more data before making such a prediction.

Behavior as President (our data)

Bush scored high on the Interpersonal style of management. He was reported to be extremely cautious and conservative in action—"That wouldn't be prudent—

CHART 10.4
Personality Assets and Liabilities of George H. W. Bush as President

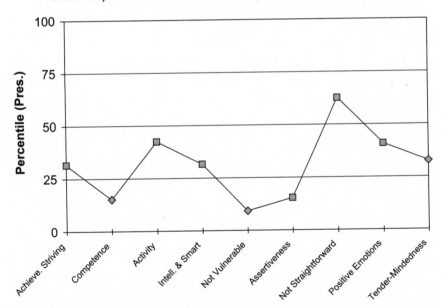

not at this junction," mimicked comedian Dana Carvey. He did not spark much new legislation compared to other presidents and was not charismatic.

G. H. W. Bush in Perspective

In personality Bush most resembled Ford ($r = .33$), Eisenhower ($r = .28$), and Fillmore ($r = .26$). He was least like John Q. Adams ($r = -.35$), LBJ ($r = -.35$), and Nixon ($r = -.34$). George H. W. Bush's presidency differed markedly from that of Harry Truman's, although both entered office in the shadow of their predecessors. Bush faced one big challenge in the Gulf War, Truman, a half dozen. Truman's reputation benefits from these enormous challenges and the low expectations initially people had of him. But he was also personally better suited to the job. Bush will likely be remembered for his decisive role in Desert Storm and as a transition between two very different, activist presidents.

G. H. W. Bush and Truman Compared

As can be seen in Chart 10.5, Truman and Bush received very similar ratings on Character and Agreeableness. Truman was higher on both Neuroticism and

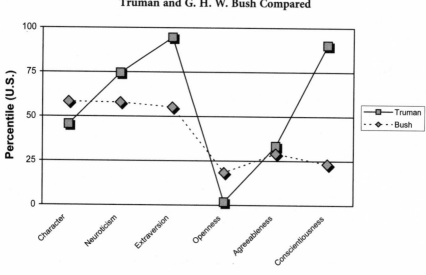

CHART 10.5
Truman and G. H. W. Bush Compared

Extraversion, and much higher on Conscientiousness. Truman is also a closer match for the typical Maintainer, differing from the group only by a higher score on Neuroticism. Differences between the two must be offered tentatively, because Bush was assessed by only two raters who did not closely agree on some traits. However, Bush scored lower on Angry Hostility but higher on Vulnerability. Truman was more appreciative of art and beauty (Openness to Aesthetics), more Open to Feelings, but very set in his ways (low Openness to Actions) and less imaginative (low Openness to Fantasy). He received higher scores than Bush on Self-Discipline, Competence, Dutifulness, Altruism, and Tender-Mindedness.

Three Philosophes—Thomas Jefferson, Abraham Lincoln, and Jimmy Carter

Morphed image of Thomas Jefferson and Abraham Lincoln.
National Archives

THE THREE MEN we profile here shared high scores on Achievement Striving and Openness to Aesthetics. Each was emotionally moved by art, yet understood advanced mathematics and was interested in science. Each manifested his Openness in a somewhat different way.

THOMAS JEFFERSON

Brief Biography

Jefferson's mother, Jane Randolph, could trace her ancestry back to Charlemagne. Thomas fell somewhere in the middle of ten children, born on April 13,

1743, in what became Albemarle County, Virginia. His sister, Jane, cared for him as much as his mother. His father, Col. Peter Jefferson, was a strapping, industrious surveyor who gained clear title to thousands of acres of land in western Virginia. He served in the House of Burgesses and was a sheriff, county court judge, and leader of the county militia. He died of unknown causes when Thomas was fourteen years old.

Jefferson received an excellent education, was an avid reader and note-taker, and mastered architecture, science, archeology, languages, politics, foreign affairs, and agriculture. At the College of William and Mary, he was introduced to the Enlightenment writings of Bacon, Newton, and Locke, who remained his heroes for life. Bacon taught him to respect and trust his own observations and to apply reason to all matters, including government, rather than unquestioningly accepting tradition or the word of experts. From Newton, Jefferson learned about the harmony of God's mechanistic universe, from which humans might deduce laws to guide their own lives. And from Locke, he learned that each mind is a blank tablet at birth, written on only by one's experiences. He also learned that legitimate authority comes only from the consent of the governed. Putting this together, Jefferson constructed the ideal of an agrarian democracy wherein people were elevated through education to better govern themselves. He never gave up on that ideal, though he grew discouraged at times based on his political experiences.

Jefferson was a gifted conversationalist and a good fiddler even as a young man. He was frequently invited to the households of wealthy planters and the governor's palace, which allowed him to meet and converse with the great men of Virginia. These men served as role models for him, and in times of difficulty, he would stop and reflect on what they would do in similar situations.

If he played hard, he studied even harder, rising at dawn and often studying well past midnight with John Tyler, father of the tenth president. When he completed his college studies in 1762, he remained in Williamsburg to study law. He took a roundabout approach that included further studies in Greek, Latin, French, and English. He was fond of literature, especially Homer and Shakespeare, but it was Horace's portrayal of supreme contentment in a country estate amid books and friends that caught his imagination.

Shy around women in his teens, Jefferson fell hard for Rebecca Burwell, a classmate's sister. Unable to choke out a proposal to her, he suffered his first of many severe headaches when she married another.

Jefferson turned twenty-one in 1764 and inherited five thousand acres of land, which he planted with the help of slaves. By 1766, he was keeping a gardening journal in an effort to scientifically improve his production. He also assumed leadership of his family, keeping records of even the most trivial expenditures. Though "penny wise" he was also "pound foolish" when it came to his love of books, entertaining, good wine, and scientific equipment. At his death, he left debts in excess of one hundred thousand dollars.

He entered the practice of law in 1767 in the higher courts. There the other planters, who often composed juries, appreciated his meticulous attention to detail and Enlightenment ideas. In 1768 a longtime friend and neighbor asked him to watch over his wife while he was away on business. Jefferson, apparently, took too good of care of Betsey Walker. When she confessed her apparently minor infidelity to her husband many years later, he challenged Jefferson to a duel. Though Jefferson talked his way out of dueling, the issue haunted him for years. The matter was brought up, for example, to politically defuse Alexander Hamilton's lengthy, consummated affair with a married woman.

In 1765, Jefferson watched Patrick Henry give a fiery speech in the House of Burgesses against the Stamp Act. Inspired by Henry, he was elected to the House of Burgesses in 1769 and was quickly drafted to write a response to the new governor's message. Though reverential in tone, the ideas expressed were so revolutionary that the governor immediately dissolved the legislature.

The next year the family home at Shadwell burned to the ground, and he lost all his books and papers. In 1772 he married a young widow, Martha Skelton, and they moved into an outbuilding at Monticello while the main house was being built. He would continue remodeling his home throughout his life, creating one of the most elegant, innovative buildings in North America.

Before the year's end, Martha delivered a daughter, who was named after her. Other daughters followed in 1774 (Jane), 1778 (Mary), and 1780 (Lucy). A son was born in 1777, but died within a few weeks, apparently unnamed. Only Martha and Mary lived to adulthood. Jefferson was happy in his home life, despite events that challenged the colonists in the early 1770s.

Parliament ordered the closing of Boston Harbor after the infamous Boston Tea Party. Jefferson proposed a day of fasting and prayer, "to inspire us to support our rights, and to turn the heart of the King and Parliament to moderation and justice." Yet another colonial governor dissolved the House of Burgesses as soon as they adopted this measure. Jefferson then composed lengthy, spirited resolutions that he hoped to present at the Continental Congress in Philadelphia. Without his knowledge, his ideas were published as "Summary View of the Rights of British America." They attracted much attention because of the excellent case they made against Parliament's authority over the colonies and contributed to Jefferson's growing reputation as a wordsmith.

By the time he arrived in Philadelphia, the war had escalated with bloodshed at Lexington and the burning of Norfolk. The Virginia Convention instructed its delegates to declare the colonies free and independent states. Though Jefferson thought the Convention lacked the legal authority to adopt a constitution, he drafted one when asked to do so. By the time his draft reached Williamsburg, the Virginia Bill of Rights of 1776, mostly written by George Mason, already had been approved in committee. Jefferson's preamble was tacked on to it just before passage. This important document became the template of virtually every other declaration of liberty in the world.

Back in Philadelphia, Jefferson was asked to chair a committee to draft the Declaration of Independence. He composed the classic document over seventeen days in June, unaided by any reference works. To quote historian Alf Mapp, the results, "have a rhythmic grace, a processional stateliness. . . . They carry with them the sense of inevitability, of cosmic harmony, that distinguishes so much of the style of the King James Version of the Bible and the noblest passages of Abraham Lincoln's oratory."[1] They also reflect his exposure to the works of Enlightenment writers. Years later, Jefferson said his guiding purpose was simply "to place before mankind the common sense of the subject, in terms so plain and firm as to command their assent, and to justify ourselves in the independent stand we are compelled to take."

Concerned about his wife's health, Jefferson declined reelection to the Congress and appointment to the Court of France to return to Virginia. As a member of the Virginia House of Delegates, he worked to promote religious freedom, education, and greater opportunity for the underdog. In 1779, he was elected governor of Virginia and spent the next two years avoiding British troops and accomplishing little.

After the death of his wife in 1782, Congress reappointed him minister to the Paris peace talks with Great Britain, but he was unable to sail due to the severity of the winter weather and the British patrols of Chesapeake Bay. A few months later he returned to the (Second) Continental Congress in Annapolis. He was a ratifier of the Treaty of Paris, ending the Revolutionary War, and created our decimal monetary system. A metric system of weights and measures he later proposed was voted down.

In 1784 he sailed for France, where he was to replace Benjamin Franklin as minister. As he waited to assume that position, he developed a model trade agreement featuring humane treatment for seamen and prisoners of war. Knowing that Frederick the Great, king of Prussia, prided himself on being an enlightened monarch, Jefferson, Adams, and Franklin persuaded him to be the first world leader to sign the document. Many other European nations soon followed suit.

Jefferson was skillful (some would say sly) about using the law to his advantage. For example, he realized that, unless a formal treaty was in effect, foreign commerce remained in the hands of the individual states. Believing that a strong federal government was essential to good trade, he hurried to sign as many trade agreements as he could while in Paris, knowing that he was depriving states of their rights with each treaty he signed. This side of Jefferson would surface repeatedly, leading to his estrangement from George Washington during his last years of life.

Despite his hatred of large cities, he came to love the arts and culture of Paris. He acquired a fine wine collection and apprenticed his servant, James Hemings, to a gourmet chef. He attended many theatrical and musical shows and spent part of most days shopping for books. Taking advantage of printing costs lower than costs in America, he published some of his own writings. This, as well as his friendship with Lafayette, afforded him entrée to some of Paris's most prestigious salons. Glowing in the conversational feasts they provided, he developed close friendships by drawing others out about their specialties.

An especially close friendship of another kind developed between Jefferson and Marie Cosway, the beautiful, twenty-seven-year-old wife and model of English miniaturist Richard Cosway. Jefferson became deeply infatuated with her during her lengthy stay in Paris and spent most of every day with her. Forgetting that he was forty-three, he permanently crippled his wrist jumping over a fence to impress her. His right hand withered, leaving him unable to fiddle for the rest of his life, though he learned to write again after some time.

Also, while in Paris, he helped revise entries about the United States in the great *Encyclopedie Methodique* and a French history of the American Revolution, and he designed the Virginia capitol building with French architect Charles-Louis Clerisseau. He also toured parts of France, Germany, and Italy.

It was an exciting time to be in Europe. Through his friendships with Lafayette and La Rouchefoucauld, he was in the unusual position of knowing what was happening on both sides of the French Revolution. He took copious notes that remain invaluable to historians. He witnessed the opening of the Estates General and the declaration of the National Assembly in 1789 and saw some street fighting after the fall of the Bastille that same year. He returned home before the Reign of Terror began, however.

When he landed at Norfolk, Jefferson was greeted with news that he had been appointed the first secretary of state, although he did not even know what that office entailed. He accepted after careful consideration, despite his longing for Monticello. In the years that followed, he clashed continually with Alexander Hamilton, secretary of the treasury, whom Jefferson saw as a closet monarchist in favor of strong central government, a central bank, enhanced commerce with Great Britain, and the development of large cities. In contrast, Jefferson's ideal remained that of an agrarian democracy of farmers and small businessmen. He mistrusted the concentration of wealth in hands that tilled paper instead of soil. Their wrangling led to the first embryonic political parties, Jefferson's Republicans (later Democrats) and Hamilton's Federalists.

Despite U.S. neutrality, the French repeatedly outfitted and manned warships in U.S. ports and seized British ships, sometimes in U.S. waters. The situation called for clever diplomacy, and as secretary of state, Jefferson handled it beautifully, maintaining good relations with France while remaining out of its wars.

Jefferson also was an accomplished inventor and served, in effect, as the nation's first supervisor of the patent office. Among his creations were the swivel chair, the folding ladder, a folding music stand, the lazy susan, and a cipher wheel for cryptography. Another, the moldboard plow, provided a significant boost to American agriculture.

At the start of the nineteenth century, though a candidate for president, Jefferson found himself, like Lincoln, simultaneously one of the most revered and hated men in America. Like Lincoln, the issue was the rights of states versus a strong central government. Unlike Lincoln, though, Jefferson sided with the states' rightists. Just months before assuming the presidency, he called for Nullification, committees of correspondence, and secession of the South from the Union.

At the end of his term as president in 1809, he retired to Monticello where he was plagued by bill collectors and rheumatism. He planted his fields, rebuilt his home, and remained president of the American Philosophical Society, an office to which he was inaugurated the night before he was sworn in as vice president under John Adams.

Personality

Jefferson scored exceptionally high on Openness to Experience (99.1th percentile). He was less Extraverted (23rd) than most Americans or presidents but more Agreeable (51st). Eleven experts rated Jefferson, the second most number of raters for any president in our study. They showed agreement only on Openness to Experience; they differed substantially on the other Big Five traits and on Character. Also, generalists portray Jefferson as moderately Extraverted, in contrast to the scores assigned by specialists.

On the NEO Facet Scales (see table), Jefferson showed relatively few extreme traits, which probably contributes to the difficulty people have grasping his per-

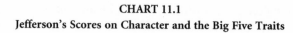

CHART 11.1

Jefferson's Scores on Character and the Big Five Traits

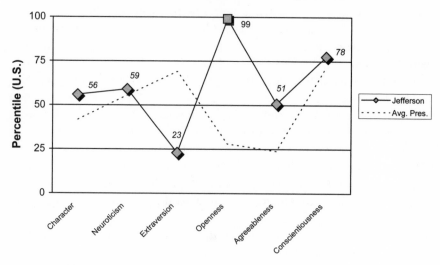

High	Percentile	Low	Percentile
Openness to Aesthetics	99.1	NONE	
Openness to Ideas	98.1		
Achievement Striving (C)	92		
Openness to Actions	87		

sonality. (The subtitle of a recent biography is *American Sphinx*.) The scores reported clearly reflect his broad interest in art (Openness to Aesthetics), philosophy (Openness to Ideas), and his willingness to try new approaches (Openness to Actions). As indicated by his high score on Achievement Striving, he also was ambitious and worked hard to achieve his goals. He was rated highest of all presidents on Intellectual Brilliance (Simonton), Openness to Actions, and Openness to Ideas, and second highest on Science and Math Ability and Musical Ability. Simonton's raters assigned a very high rating on Tidiness, while our raters gave only an average score on Order.

Compared to other presidents, Jefferson had an extraordinary willingness to modify his home and spent much of his life building and rebuilding Monticello, which contained many original inventions and novel conveniences. He did not like to keep everything in its place. He greatly enjoyed sampling foreign foods, and art and beauty were very important to him. He clearly appreciated and was touched by works of visual art, beautiful music, and drama. He had a definite appreciation for musical talent and had a good ear for musical tone. Much more than most presidents, he sometimes became completely absorbed in music. Our raters described him as cosmopolitan, cultured, refined, sophisticated, and worldly.

Jefferson was extremely artistic, creative, imaginative, and inventive, and thought in unusual ways to a degree remarkable among presidents. He found new hobbies fascinating, had an extremely active imagination, and loved pondering abstract ideas and theories. He clearly excelled in science, relished solving brain-teasers, and preferred to approach problems in a quantitative, scientific manner. He was intellectually curious and had many interests. Once, a fellow traveler, after a short conversation with Jefferson about mechanics, believed he must be an engineer. After touching on agriculture, the man assessed him to be a farmer. And so on for law, medicine, and the clergy. He enjoyed philosophical conversation and was interested in the universe and human nature. He was "contemplative, intellectual, introspective, meditative, philosophical."

Jefferson definitely did not subscribe to religious authority on moral issues and was not conventional or traditional. He encouraged a faithful but critical reading of the Bible and distrusted clergy and formalized religion. He did not lack a sense of meaning in life and believed that social policies should change with the times. Speaking on the issue of slavery, he once proclaimed, "I tremble for my country when I reflect that God is just." Though a lifelong slaveholder, he saw himself as broad-minded and tolerant. He thought that all people, no matter their circumstances, deserve respect and consideration. He believed in the essential goodness of humanity. Perhaps because of these qualities and his broad-mindedness, people looked to him for advice and reassurance.

Miscellaneous Observatons

Jefferson was tall and thin with large hands and feet. He attended to his dress with a studied negligence that mixed various styles fashionably. He did not dread making a social mistake. On one occasion, he met (and offended) His Majesty's minister in his robe and slippers. He was not athletic and took to bed with headaches in times of stress. He never developed a thick skin and maintained an emotional core that made him appear reserved at first meeting. Still, he was admired by men and adored by women. Though an Introvert, he entertained often and lavishly, as was the custom for a man of his station in Virginia. He offered gourmet food and wine, as well as conversation touching on virtually the whole range of human experience. More than anything else, his entertainment expenses kept him in debt.

Jefferson Quoted

"Nature intended for me the tranquil pursuits of science, by rendering them my supreme delight. But the enormity of the times in which I have lived has forced me to take a part in resisting them, and to commit myself on the boisterous ocean of political passions."

"Education . . . engrafts a new man on the native stock, and improves what in his nature was vicious and perverse into qualities of virtue and social worth."

Jefferson Described

"His talents were of the highest order, his ambition transcendent, and his disposition to intrigue irrepressible."—John Quincy Adams

"The immortality of Jefferson does not lie in any one of his achievements, but in his attitude toward mankind."—Woodrow Wilson

"Jefferson thinks he shall get a reputation of a humble . . . man, wholly without ambition or vanity. He may even have deceived himself into this belief. But if a prospect opens, the world will see and he will feel, that he is as ambitious as Oliver Cromwell."—John Quincy Adams

President Jefferson

Participants in the Ridings and McIver poll rated Jefferson as the fourth best president, behind Washington and ahead of Theodore Roosevelt. His highest rating was for Appointments (4th) and lowest for Character and Integrity (7th). Yet, he was only an average match for the job in terms of his personality, although he would be expected to show above average Ethics on the Job. He did. He had only one true personal asset as president—his intellect—although he was also above average on Tender-Mindedness. He had no clear weaknesses, though he was below average on Assertiveness and more vulnerable than average.

Jefferson served two terms as president. The first one was nearly lost to Aaron Burr, his vice presidential candidate, who tied him with seventy-three electoral votes. The House of Representatives selected Jefferson as president and Burr as vice president. During Jefferson's terms, Ohio entered the Union as the seventeenth state, Congress prohibited the importation of slaves (1808), the United States defeated Tripoli in a confrontation with the Barbary Pirates of North Africa who had long extracted tribute from passing ships (1805), and the U.S. government embargoed

CHART 11.2
Personality Assets and Liabilities of Jefferson as President

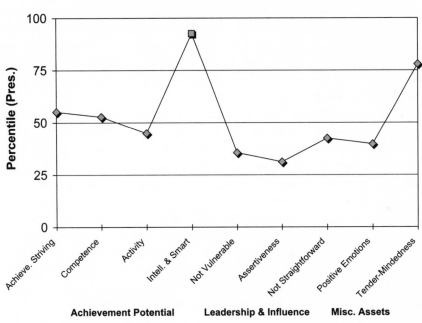

foreign ships and ports in a failed attempt to stop ship seizures during the Napoleonic Wars. Most noteworthy of Jefferson's accomplishments, however, was doubling the land area of the United States for three cents an acre through the Louisiana Purchase (1803) and sending Lewis and Clark to explore this new land between the Mississippi River and the Rocky Mountains (1803–1806).

Behavior as President (our data)

Jefferson showed few distinguishing characteristics as a president, although he scored second highest among chief executives on Simonton's Creative style of governing. He was not abrupt or impatient in meetings and did not have emotional outbursts. He championed personal freedom and was perceived as a world figure.

Jefferson in Perspective

Jefferson was most similar to Madison (r = .43), Lincoln (r = .31), and Garfield (r = .28). He was least like G. W. Bush (r = −.39), Jackson (r = −.32), and Andrew Johnson (r = −.29).[2]

DNA findings have shown that a member of Jefferson's family fathered at least one child of Sally Hemings, a teenage slave girl. This issue has been the basis of an ongoing dispute between two camps of Jefferson scholars. While we cannot offer any direct evidence on this issue, we do find the defense of Jefferson based on his noble character naive and unconvincing. Sexual relations with slaves were hardly uncommon, and Jefferson was probably less restrained by traditional moral codes and more willing to try new sensual experiences ("enjoys sampling new or foreign foods") than most people.

Jefferson was clearly a liberal in his day, as defined by a tendency to challenge old values and religious authority. Yet, he is also one of the most revered Founding Fathers of our country. (Successful liberals tend to turn into traditional icons over time.) Both liberals and conservatives admire him today, though there has been increasing discomfort with his apparent hypocrisy. For his contribution to the philosophical underpinnings of the New World's first democracy, he is a titan of history and political thought. His written works are soaringly idealistic and elegant, yet skirt the contradictions that the words, and the man, represented.

He bore the abuse of the new two-party system better than Adams. A visiting baron noticed scurrilous attacks on his host in a paper in Jefferson's home. He asked him why these libels were allowed; the editor not imprisoned. Jefferson smiled and said, "Put that paper in your pocket, baron. And should you hear the reality of our liberty, the freedom of the press questioned, show them this paper and tell them where you found it."

ABRAHAM LINCOLN

Brief Biography

Lincoln's parents were "both born in Virginia of undistinguished families," as he put it. His father, Thomas, was seventh-generation American, descended from Samuel Lincoln who emigrated from County Norfolk, England, to Massachusetts in 1637. He and many of his descendants became wealthy, some as Pennsylvania Quakers. His grandfather, Abraham, moved from Virginia to Kentucky in the early 1780s. Lincoln was born in a one-room log cabin near Hogdenville, Kentucky, on February 12, 1809; when he was two, the family moved to Knob Creek Farm, ten miles away. There he recalled "working the big field" of about seven acres and learning the alphabet when he accompanied his sister to a local school to keep her company.

When he was seven, the family moved to Indiana to get away from slavery. They spent that first winter in Indiana huddled in an unchinked log "half-faced camp" surviving on the game they could hunt. Several family members, including his "angel mother," died in the following months from "milk sickness" (probably brucellosis). His sister was unable to handle the household, so his father promptly married Sarah Bush, a widow with three children of her own. She and Abraham became very close; childhood went from being harsh, deprived, and sad to joyous and loving. He called her "Mama" and spoke of her as his "best friend in this whole world."

At age fifteen Lincoln attended school for one term and learned to read. From then on, he was largely self-taught. An avid reader who committed himself to learning in many areas, he was often asked by neighbors to draft their letters and (later) legal documents.

There seems to have been more than the usual adolescent rebellion in his distancing from his father. Strong and tall, Abe was increasingly expected to run the family farm and even to work for others. As with most boys in this time and place, he was to turn over all of his wages to his father until he was twenty-one. At that age he left, never to speak well of his father again. His father reportedly was *not* a harsh disciplinarian but was described as an easygoing storyteller who encouraged his son's education and reading. Many neighbors said Abe was just lazy, preferring reading to labor.

A man of paradoxes, Lincoln could not stand to hurt a living thing and yet once accepted a duel, choosing broadswords as the weapon. The duel never occurred because the seconds intervened. Lincoln chose broadswords because his long arms would be an advantage in such a contest. A man who never exercised, he reputedly had incredibly strong arms throughout his life. Growing up, he was said to be both the strongest and smartest boy in town, and the most formidable wrestler. Though he later weighed as little as 160 pounds, as a young man he weighed over two hundred pounds and at six feet, four inches tall, was very large and imposing for his time.

When he was seventeen, his sister Sarah married and died within eighteen months in childbirth. Lincoln blamed his in-laws for negligence in sending too late for a doctor. The resulting controversy further estranged him from his home folk, so he welcomed an opportunity to accompany a merchant's son on a flatboat trip to New Orleans. They had a leisurely journey, trading at the sugar plantations they passed in Louisiana. One night seven black men attacked them with the intent to rob and kill them. They drove the men from the boat, hastily cut the line, and drifted off without serious injuries. On his return, Lincoln dutifully handed his father all of his wages.

Lincoln yearned for a life on the river but remained legally bound to his father until age twenty-one. He handled his frustration with a number of pranks, the most memorable of which involved mixing up the brides' and grooms' bedrooms when two brothers married. He remained obedient to his parents, even helping them relocate to Illinois in 1830. When asked to take another flatboat downriver, he eagerly accepted, never to live in his parents' home again. He had little idea what career to pursue.

Within a year of "drifting" into New Salem where his riverboat got stuck, Lincoln entered politics, announcing his candidacy for the Illinois legislature. He had greatly impressed the residents of New Salem with his eagerness to learn, his great ability to reason and debate, and his painstaking attention to the needs of others. He had taken an active interest in town affairs and had made many friends who encouraged his candidacy.

When he lost his first race for the legislature, he enlisted in the brief Black Hawk War, chiefly to have a means of support. Elected by his men as their leader, he taught himself to drill troops. He was elected to the legislature in 1834 and re-elected in 1836. He had met several leading men during his brief military campaign, and they helped him find a variety of jobs including postmaster, store manager, and surveyor. He incurred large debts as a partner in a failed local store that took him many years to repay, but he never complained.

Despite such setbacks, he was a popular, up-and-coming bachelor in a frontier town. But he was incredibly shy around women and frightened of sex and intimacy. He came to spend much time with Ann Rutledge, the daughter of his landlord in New Salem. Ann was safe because she was betrothed to another man who had gone to New York to fetch his family for the wedding.

As postmaster, Lincoln noticed how her correspondence dwindled over the months the man was gone and then fell off entirely. Lincoln approached Ann and they agreed to announce their betrothal if her fiancé did not return in the next year. Though her fiancé never returned, Ann died before the year ended. Lincoln fell into a profound depression, the first of many in his life. (At other times, he would also experience periods of unusual confidence and unwarranted exuberance.)

The town of New Salem was dying, having been bypassed by the railroad and, like the rest of the country, crippled by the Panic of 1837. It was time to move on to Springfield. He was licensed to practice law after an intensive course of self-study and was asked to join the prestigious law firm of John Todd Stuart. Stuart was interested in pursuing a political career and provided Lincoln's entrée to the aristocratic society of Springfield. He became a regular guest at the home of the snobbish Ninian Edwards and ended up marrying Mrs. Edwards's sister, Mary Todd.

Lincoln's friends realized how deeply he thirsted for distinction. He told a friend once that he needed to be remembered for "something that would resound to the interest of his fellow man." He also, unwittingly, revealed his own fear of descending into madness, when he spoke in the same talk about a classmate of his who had "unaccountably become furiously mad" at age nineteen. Lincoln struggled to bring coherence to his own still unshaped and conflicted personality and to master his mood swings, through strict application of "cold, calculating, unimpassioned reason."

Elected to the House of Representatives, Lincoln moved his family to Washington at the end of 1847. The boys, Robert and Edward (Edward died soon afterward, Willy and Tad were not yet born), were unruly and elicited complaints from other boarders. Lincoln was proud that he never beat his children, but neither did he set appropriate limits. Mary was also lonesome for female companionship, so she took the boys to stay at her father's home in Lexington, Kentucky, for the rest of the congressional session. At first Lincoln was so busy that he hardly missed his family. He tried, unsuccessfully, to emancipate the slaves of Washington, D.C., with a proposal that offered compensation to their owners.

As was the custom in his district, he returned to private life after his one term in Congress. Lonely for his family and home, he turned down appointments as the secretary or the governor of Oregon Territory. From 1849 to 1854, he was at the head of Illinois's legal society, trying important cases in the higher courts. "He was a wonderfully inventive lawyer on the side of the truth . . . a lousy lawyer when he believed his client to be guilty."[3] His law practice required him to be away from home often, and he often joked about the unfortunate lodgings he and his fellow attorneys and judges were forced to accept. Once when he showed up late for dinner at an inn, a cabbage was all there was to eat. Without complaint, he sat down and went to work eating the cabbage whole. Lincoln seemed impervious to discomfort or finery. He would eat whatever was put in front of him and would sleep in barns or under wagons, or share beds with other travelers, when on the road. On the other hand, the possibility that he visited prostitutes during those trips is now seriously entertained.[4]

In 1854, he was reelected to the Illinois legislature but refused to serve. There were two reasons for this: He ran only to help a fellow Whig win election to another office, and Illinois's own Stephen Douglas unleashed a typhoon of resentment when he introduced a bill in the U.S. Senate to rapidly establish local governments in Kansas and Nebraska. Lincoln challenged Douglas, one of the most prominent politicians of the time, for a Senate seat.

The famous Lincoln-Douglas debates were held at various towns around Illinois during the 1858 Senate race. Lincoln's acceptance speech at the Republican State Convention that year came to be known as his famous "House Divided" speech. "A house divided against itself cannot stand," he told the abolitionist group. "I believe this government cannot endure permanently half-slave and half-free."

In 1860, he accepted an invitation to speak to the Young Men's Central Republican Union at Coopers Union in New York City. He was anxious to win the Republican presidential nomination without appearing to seek it, and this was his opportunity to impress kingmakers in the East. After a great deal of research and preparation, he argued that a majority of the thirty-nine signers of the Constitution believed that the federal government had the power to control slavery in the territories. Republicans were, therefore, the conservative party on this issue because they demanded that it be so controlled.

His performance won him great kudos both in the hall that evening and the next day. The *New York Tribune* exclaimed, "He's the greatest man since St. Paul." Meeting in Chicago three months later, the Republican Party offered him the nomination for president, just as he had hoped, when they became deadlocked. When he also won the general election that fall, the South immediately began to secede. Lincoln spent his entire presidency, and the rest of his life, defeating the newly formed Confederate States of America.

Though not religious in a conventional sense, Lincoln was deeply spiritual and believed in the Doctrine of Necessity. "That the human mind is impelled to action, or held at rest by some power, over which the mind itself has no control" was the way he once put it. During the Civil War he came to see himself as an instrument of Divine Purpose. "Doesn't it strike you as queer," he asked a friend, "that I . . . who was sick at the sight of blood, should be cast into the middle of a great war, with blood flowing all about me? . . . Surely He intends some great good to follow this mighty convulsion." Perhaps he was able to wage the war aggressively and stick with it through incredible setbacks because he had long seen God's hand at work in his life.

Personality

Seven specialists who rated Lincoln showed moderate agreement on his overall profile. There were significant levels of disagreement about his standing on Character, Neuroticism, and Openness. His most notable score was on Openness (95th percentile), followed by Character (85th), Neuroticism (82nd), and Agreeableness (76th). Generalists perceived Lincoln as considerably higher in Conscientiousness than did specialists.

On the NEO Facet Scales, shown in the table, Lincoln had many scores that were high or low compared to modern Americans. His scores show a strong ten-

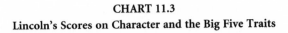

CHART 11.3
Lincoln's Scores on Character and the Big Five Traits

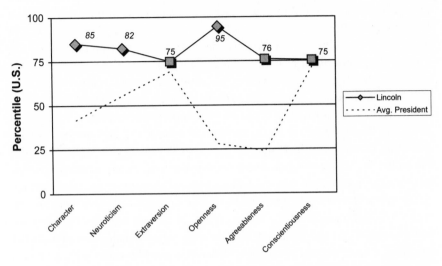

dency toward occasional sadness and discouragement (Depression) and, to a lesser degree, tension and worry (high Anxiety). Although ambitious and hardworking (high Achievement Striving), he was not organized (low Order). He was a natural leader (high Assertiveness) who used a variety of tactics to persuade people (low Straightforwardness). He generally thought well of others (high Trust) and was quite capable (high Competence). He scored lowest of all presidents on Pettiness and was the second highest on Depression. Simonton's data portrays Lincoln as low on Forcefulness, while our raters gave him higher than average marks on Assertiveness. Similarly, our raters gave very low scores on Order, while Simonton's scores for Tidiness were more moderate.

High	Percentile	Low	Percentile
Depression (N)	*98.9*	Order (C)	4
Openness to Feelings	*97*	*Straightforwardness* (A, Ch)	8
Assertiveness (E)	*94*		
Achievement Striving (C)	*93*		
Anxiety (N)	*91*		
Trust (A, Ch)	*90*		
Competence (C, Ch)	*90*		

Compared to other presidents, Lincoln was occasionally very sad, dejected, and depressed. He worried excessively about the future, and at times things looked hopeless to him: "If what I feel were equally distributed to the whole human family, there would not be one cheerful face on earth. Whether I shall ever get better, I cannot tell; I awfully forebode that I shall not. To remain as I am is impossible; I must die or be better." And he was moody. This was most apparent at home, where he was often silent to the dismay of his lonely, talkative wife.

Well-known for his homely appearance, Lincoln clearly shared the public's opinion about his looks. When accused by his opponent, Stephen A. Douglas, of being two-faced, he turned to the crowd and asked, "If I had another face, do you think I would wear this one?" He was *not* self-defensive or humorless about his faults, nor did teasing or ridicule embarrass him. Rarely angered by other people's conduct toward him, he had an even temper and minor problems did not upset him. One evening, Lincoln and his advisers called on Gen. George McClellan, commander of the Union Army. McClellan was upstairs when his butler announced the president was calling. After a half hour, the butler informed the visitors that General McClellan had retired for the evening. Lincoln did not protest, left, and apparently bore no grudge.

He was decidedly not obsessive about cleaning, *not* fastidious, nor "orderly, organized, systematic." Lincoln often kept large, unsorted stacks of legal papers in his office and stowed current work in his stovepipe hat.

He greatly preferred going to places that he had never been before for vacation. He was deeply moved by poetry, empathized with others' feelings, and took notice of the "moods" of different settings. He thought in unusual ways and did not judge others in conventional terms. He was complex, deep, and complicated as well as "artistic, creative, imaginative, innovative." He also enjoyed solving puzzles and challenges. When traveling to New Salem, Lincoln's flatboat got hung up on a dam. He bored a hole in the bow and unloaded the stern. The stern rose, the water flowed to the bow and out the hole, and the boat floated free. Lincoln later patented a flotation device to allow ships to traverse shallows. He was curious and inquisitive, skilled at imaginative play, and "foresighted, insightful, perceptive."

Of all the abilities we measured, Lincoln most stood out from other presidents by his decided lack of dancing ability. Nonetheless, he easily grasped new ideas and problems. In what might seem a contradiction, he was simultaneously analytical, imaginative, and wise. He cultivated his image as a sage from the time he was a young man. He was communicative, expressive, and verbal—"the only literary genius among presidents" in one writer's estimation. Lincoln developed his ability to express himself from an early age, focusing especially on the majestic style of the Bible. Though he did not attend church services regularly, he was religious and read the Bible frequently as president. He did not believe that controversial speakers mislead and confuse students, being such a speaker himself.

Lincoln was completely abstinent from alcohol, and he did not eat too much even when having his favorite dishes. He was not hypocritical and did not gamble. Despite his tendency toward depression, he was also humorous and witty. "He could make a cat laugh," claimed a friend. "Adventurous, mischievous, playful, rambunctious," he was also carefree, happy-go-lucky, and spontaneous. He showed his feelings openly, laughed easily at the jokes or antics of others, and was "down-to-earth, earthy, folksy" as well as casual, easygoing, informal, natural, and relaxed.

Even if it was inconvenient, Lincoln went out of his way to help others, and people wanted to nurture and take care of him. He was quick to forgive and forget—not bullheaded or stubborn, not boastful, egocentric, greedy, or selfish. Though subjected to incredible verbal abuse from both sides during the Civil War, few ever accused him of being self-centered and egotistical. He seemed unable to be sarcastic or cutting, and rarely blamed others for problems. He trusted their motives. He was not "faultfinding, harsh, unforgiving, unsympathetic," and was respectful of the rights and feelings of others—even of his opponents. When a general's inaction again dashed Lincoln's hopes for a decisive Union victory, he wrote how disappointed he was. He then folded the letter and put it in his desk, never to be sent.

Miscellaneous Observations

Lincoln had few close, intimate friends, despite his warm and gracious manner toward all. His marriage was troubled, partly due to his moodiness, but largely due to his difficult wife. He was also emotionally estranged from his oldest son. Neither father nor son could break the awkward silences when they met for visits at the White House.

He was referred to as the "Chief Jokester of the Land" by a London paper, and numerous books such as "Old Abe's Jokes" were circulated in the 1860s. His humor could range from the profound ("You can fool some of the people some of the time . . .") to the lowly pun. He was said to have a crude and corny sense of humor, but one that produced sore ribs in his traveling companions. His jokes were usually gentle, but the sanctimonious were frequent targets. Meeting with a dozen self-described "weighty men" from Delaware, he asked, "Did it ever occur to you gentlemen that there is danger of your little state tipping up during your absence?" His storytelling was not only a gift for entertainment but also a strategy to distract favor-seekers and impart moral lessons. Once, a foreign diplomat found him polishing his own shoes. "What, Mr. President, you black your own boots?" "Yes," replied Lincoln, "whose do you black?"

He retained a number of backwoods habits as he advanced socially and intellectually, which doubtless contributed to his image as a hick. Yet he "constantly strove for self-improvement," according to one of our sources. His role models included the Founding Fathers, especially George Washington and Henry Clay.

Lincoln Quoted

"Die when I may, I want it said of me by those who know me best, that I have always plucked a thistle and planted a flower when I thought a flower would grow."

Lincoln Described

"He is . . . full of wit, facts, dates—and the best stump speaker, with his droll ways and dry jokes, in the West."—Stephen A. Douglas

"He is a barbarian, Scythian, Yahoo, a gorilla in respect of outward polish, but a most sensible, straight-forward old codger."—George Templeton Strong, New York lawyer and friend of Lincoln

"His heart was as great as the world, but there was no room in it to hold a memory of a wrong."—Ralph Waldo Emerson

"Although he cared little for simple facts, rules and methods, it was on the underlying principle of truth and justice that Lincoln's will was firm as steel. . . . No man can move him. No set of men can."—William H. Herndon, Lincoln's law partner

President Lincoln

Ridings and McIver's historians rated Lincoln the greatest of all presidents, with top marks for Character and Integrity and Accomplishments and Crisis Management. His lowest mark was in Appointments, where he ranked third.

Lincoln had no outstanding personality assets as president but was above average in almost everything that counts. His scores on Tender-Mindedness, Positive Emotions, and Competence were all near the 75th percentile for chief executives. His only weakness was lower than average Activity. Lincoln's personality was better suited than most of his peers to the job but not as outstanding as his reputation with history.

Assuming the presidency at the outbreak of civil war, Lincoln had to be smuggled into Washington, D.C., aboard a high-security train. When he arrived, he

CHART 11.4
Personality Assets and Liabilities of Lincoln as President

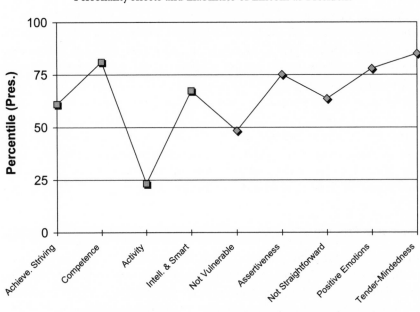

Achievement Potential   **Leadership & Influence**   **Misc. Assets**

found a death threat on his desk. His immediate task was to mobilize the country for war and forestall provisioning of the South by blockading its ports. Because the North had an overwhelming advantage in population and industry, most expected a quick Union victory. It was not to be.

Though Lincoln opposed slavery, the Civil War was fought over secession, to preserve the Union. In the eyes of Lincoln and many of his contemporaries, America was the shining example of democracy, "the last, best hope for mankind." For it to divide would be to lose this promise for future generations and the whole of the world. Though he advocated the rights of African Americans, he did not see them as social or political equals.[5] (It would be hard to find a Caucasian contemporary of Lincoln who did.) Still, he appeared to value the opinion of black rights leader Frederick Douglass over that of all other men. As the war dragged on, Lincoln grew ever more able to see African Americans as ellow citizens. He was especially touched by black crowds' demonstrations of enthusiasm and affection toward him and by the service of black soldiers. He abandoned his earlier plans to resettle freed slaves in African or Central American colonies and boldly redefined the purpose of the war as the elimination of slavery.

As president, he reserved hours each day to meet with ordinary people in his office. He was extraordinarily generous to many and often turned away the less worthy with a parable. He nearly always found reasons to pardon those condemned for desertion, sometimes to the exasperation of his generals.

During the war, he often visited battlefields while battles were being waged and even sat in Jefferson Davis's chair after Grant took Richmond. He seemed oblivious to his personal vulnerability, despite several attempts to harm, kill, or kidnap him during and immediately after the Civil War. Given his symbolic and very real importance, this might be seen as a considerable lapse of judgment. He was shot in the head at close range by John Wilkes Booth at Ford's Theater in Washington on April 14, 1865, and died the next day.

Behavior as President (our data)

Lincoln served during the greatest crisis in the country's history. Consistent with all the polls of historical greatness, he was rated very highly on both the quantity and quality of his work as president. He knew his limitations but was innovative in his role as chief executive. He used rhetoric effectively and found dealing with the press challenging and enjoyable. He was patient when meeting with advisers and did not make decisions based on willfulness, nervousness, or egotism. Told one prospective cabinet member "thinks himself a great deal bigger that you," Lincoln asked if the informer knew any other such men "because I want to put them all in my cabinet." More than most presidents, he understood the implications of his decisions and exhibited a depth of comprehension.

Lincoln in Perspective

Lincoln was most similar in personality to Jefferson, ($r = .31$), Madison ($r = .31$), and Garfield ($r = .29$). He was least like Buchanan ($r = -.34$), Hoover ($r = -.33$), and Andrew Johnson ($r = -.33$).[6] He is probably the best loved and the most respected of presidents.

Ironically, his gaiety and humor have largely been forgotten in his popular image. Portraits and the statue at his memorial portray a solemn figure, almost Christ-like in his suffering for his country. This was true: Lincoln worried endlessly and was appalled by the carnage of the war, which no doubt darkened his mood. But the black suit he was typically photographed in was not his usual garb—it was a popular fashion. Also missing from his popular image are his inventiveness, intellectualism, and ability to persuade using variations of the truth. "Honest Abe" did not tell outright lies, but his version of the truth might vary from time to time.

Lincoln's preeminence changed the image of the successful president from the austere and dignified Washington and the wild man Andrew Jackson. Far from formal in manner, Lincoln was as approachable and folksy as Harry Truman. His obvious concern for the well-being of individual citizens would not be found in a popular president until FDR.

Lincoln suffered incredible personal and political attacks during his term. General McClellan regularly referred to his Commander in Chief as a baboon, and he was not alone. Franklin Pierce assessed him to be "of limited ability and narrow intelligence," as well as responsible for the catastrophe of the Civil War. Lincoln's hometown paper exclaimed, "How the greatest butchers of antiquity sink in insignificance when their crimes are contrasted with those of Abraham Lincoln!" These assessments, so absurd to our sensibilities, show how subjective the perception of personality and political performance can be.

JAMES EARL CARTER

Brief Biography

Carter was the oldest of four children and the first president born in a hospital. His father was of English descent, a successful farmer and insurance salesman, and employed as many as two hundred black workers. A conservative Democrat and a devout Baptist who opposed the New Deal, he was elected to the Georgia Legislature in 1952. Carter's mother was much more liberal, more interested in politics than her husband, and made service to others a focus of her life. She was home so little that the desk where she left the children notes came to be called "Mother."

Though born in Plains, Georgia, Carter grew up in a predominantly black, rural farm community without electricity or running water. He helped with family chores and income beginning at the age of five. Although generally well behaved, he once stole a penny from a church collection plate and once shot his sister with a BB gun. Carter had several role models as a boy, including his uncle, who was a radio operator in the navy, and his English teacher who introduced him to literature. Carter played basketball in high school and graduated second in his class. He would have been valedictorian had he not once cut class to go to a movie and received zeros for the day (and a paddling from his father).

He initially went to Georgia Southwestern College (1941–1942) then to Georgia Institute of Technology (1942–1943). After boning up on his math, he was accepted to the U.S. Naval Academy in 1943, where his constant smile and Southern accent brought him unwanted attention. He underwent a brutal, traditional hazing. But when he was ordered by some upperclassmen to sing "Marching Through Georgia," which celebrates Sherman's devastating march to the sea, he refused. He graduated 59th of 820 despite putting in less than his best effort. Carter read three to four books per week, studied Spanish intensely, read poetry, and liked both classical and popular music.

He was married at age twenty-one to Rosalynn Smith, his sister's longtime best friend. She graduated valedictorian of her high school class and attended two years of college. Carter took little notice of her until home on leave from the Naval Academy, when he asked his sister to set them up. They fell in love on their second date and married after his graduation. During the first six years of their marriage, the couple lived in Virginia, Connecticut, Hawaii, California, and New York, where Carter was stationed. He was an electronics instructor and later served as an engineering officer on the *Sea Wolf*, one of the first nuclear submarines. However, when his father died, Carter resigned his commission to take over the family business. This caused conflict between the newlyweds, as Rosalynn had hoped, as the wife of a naval officer, to see more of the world than the small patch of rural Georgia where she was raised. They had three sons and a daughter.

As a peanut farmer, Carter made use of modern agricultural developments and earned a handsome living. In Plains he gradually adopted more civic roles and positions, including chairman of the board of education and deacon of his church. He was defeated in a primary for state senator in 1962 but was able to prove voter fraud and eventually won. Placing third in a run for governor in 1966, in 1970 he ran as a conservative Democrat. He opposed busing and invited George Wallace to campaign for him. Yet, when a neighbor brought him racist brochures, Carter walked to the toilet, tore them up, and flushed. In his inaugural address, he announced that, "the time for racial discrimination is over," stunning some of his former supporters. He went on to promote racial equality and civil rights in Georgia.

Carter was an obscure Southern governor at the beginning of the 1976 presidential race and ran on the promise to restore trust in government following Watergate. He achieved stunning early primary victories that proved irreversible. He again made controversial statements on racial relations, defending the rights of neighborhoods to maintain "ethnic purity," but later adopted themes of unity and harmony.

Personality

Eight specialists rated Carter and they showed very high agreement on the Big Five traits. Carter scored very high on Conscientiousness (98th percentile) and moderately high on Character (82nd), Openness to Experience (77th), and Neuroticism (76th). Like Jefferson and Lincoln, he scored above most presidents on Agreeableness (56th). However, only his Conscientiousness ratings showed high consistency across raters.

High	Percentile	Low	Percentile
Achievement Striving (C)	99.7	Impulsiveness(N, -Ch)	10
Openness to Aesthetics	97		
Openness to Activity	97		
Tender-Mindedness (A)	95		
Order (C)	93		

On the NEO Facet Scales, Carter scored as shown in the above table.

Carter clearly was hard-working and dedicated to achieving his goals, as indicated by his extremely high score on Achievement Striving. He was unusually attuned to art and beauty (high Openness to Aesthetics) and willing to try new

CHART 11.5
Carter's Scores on Character and the Big Five Traits

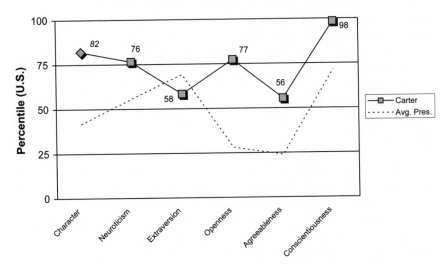

experiences and ways of doing things (high Openness to Activity), yet he was also very organized (high Order). He was sympathetic (Tender-Mindedness) and not Impulsive. He scored highest of all presidents on Simonton's Achievement and Pacifism scales and on our scales of Science and Math Ability and Religiousness. He scored lowest of all presidents on the charisma of his public messages.

He understood advanced mathematics much better than most presidents, and clearly excelled in science. Not surprisingly, he strongly preferred to approach problems in a quantitative, analytical manner, and he was good with numbers. He definitely followed through on attempts to change himself and his behavior. He was meticulous, perfectionistic, and precise, as well as "concise, exacting, efficient, fastidious, self-disciplined." The high moral demands he placed on himself were at least once placed on his son, Chip. Other boys hostile to Johnson ripped an LBJ button off Chip's shirt several days in a row at school and finally roughed him up so that he came home in tears. "Put the button back on," his father ordered. "What if they tear it off again?" asked Chip. "Put it on again, . . . you just put it on again, if you want to wear it. Do what you want to do—and learn to box."

Carter kept his possessions neat and clean and was orderly, organized, and systematic. He was also prompt and punctual. Seldom overindulging in anything, he had little difficulty resisting temptation, and overcontrolled his needs and impulses. Perhaps because of his demanding moral code, he sometimes felt deeply guilty and sinful. He attended church services regularly and was active in his church. He was religious, spiritual, and committed to a personal faith. His religious beliefs entailed "a very close, intimate personal relationship with God, through Christ." He and Rosalynn took turns reading the Bible to each other at night, and Carter cited biblical authority throughout his 1996 book, *Living Faith*.

Art and beauty were important to Carter, and some types of music held an endless fascination for him. Hobbies, philosophical issues (religion, values), and the patterns of art and nature all interested him. Despite his Openness, Carter rarely played games of make-believe as a child. He saw himself as broad-minded and tolerant. He felt we can never do too much for the poor and elderly and believed political leaders should focus more on the human side of problems. He was a giving person who would personally help others even if it were inconvenient. He believed that all people deserve respect and had sympathy for the less fortunate. He did not think people would exploit others if given a chance and was not cynical, distrustful, skeptical, or suspicious. Nor was he prejudiced. He tried to be humble and was rated as modest, selfless, and unassuming. He led a fast-paced lifestyle, but even as a busy presidential candidate did his own sewing, helped with the cooking, and did the shopping. In 1979 with his administration facing severe criticism, a reporter asked him if his daughter ever bragged about her father being president. "No," he replied, "she probably apologizes." He believed that being perfectly honest is the wisest policy, although perhaps he reevaluated this view after he suffered the fallout from telling *Playboy* that he had "committed adultery in my heart many times." He was optimistic and cheerful and attributed his failures to circumstances or temporary problems. Nevertheless, his administration was blamed, in part, for the "crisis of confidence" and malaise of the late 1970s. Despite his ability and energy, he typically did not become a leader of groups he belonged to throughout his life.

Though humble, Carter strove to achieve personal excellence and unique accomplishment. "Show me a good loser," he once said, "and I'll show you a loser." He implied that he had not always been that way, though his nickname as a boy was "Hotshot." He recounted his meeting with Admiral Rickover, the architect of the nuclear navy. Quizzing Carter, Rickover asked if he had done his best at Annapolis. Carter admitted he had not. Deeply impressed by this incident, he later entitled his campaign autobiography *Why Not the Best?*

Carter Described

"When it came to understanding the issues of the day, Jimmy Carter was the smartest public official I've ever known. The range and extent of his knowledge was astounding."—Former Speaker of the House Tip O'Neill

"He's got courage . . . He's got a religious tone in what he says and maybe we should have a little more religion in our community. . . . The man talks about true values."—Richard Daley, mayor of Chicago

President Carter

Carter was the first president from the Deep South since the early nineteenth century. He was ranked as the nineteenth best president overall by the Ridings and McIver poll—just behind J. Q. Adams and ahead of Taft. He received a ranking of fifth in Character and Integrity but rated twenty-eighth in Leadership and thirty-second in Political Skill. This is an unusually broad spread of ratings and may reflect the short time since his administration.

On the face of it, Carter was well suited to be president. He had both intelligence and integrity. He scored quite high on Achievement Striving, Activity, Intelligent and Smart, and Tender-Mindedness. In fact, all of our personality predictors are above average except two—but they appear to be critical. Carter was not a natural leader, as indicated by his low Assertiveness score. And with his relatively high score on Straightforwardness (reversed on the chart), he was not willing to manipulate people or stretch the truth as much as most presidents.

Carter's presidency is remembered for a number of achievements and policies. For the first time, a moral stance on human rights was made a cornerstone of international policy. No longer did the United States blindly support repressive governments for political advantage. Carter came to power during the height of the energy crisis, and this issue remained a focal part of his agenda until eclipsed by the Iranian Hostage Crisis. Perhaps his greatest achievement was securing a peace settlement between Egypt and Israel, ending a thirty-one-year state of war. When the Soviet Union invaded Afghanistan, Carter led opposition in the United Nations and declared the United States would not send a team to the 1980 Olympic games. He also returned the sovereignty of the Panama Canal, TR's prize and one of the greatest and costliest engineering projects of all time, to the control of the Panamanian people. In 2002 he was awarded the Nobel Peace Prize.

Behavior as President (our data)

Carter's manner as president was distinguished on only two items, where he was rated as "skilled and self-confident as negotiator" and as a "dynamo of energy and determination."

CHART 11.6
Carter's Personality Assets and Liabilities as President

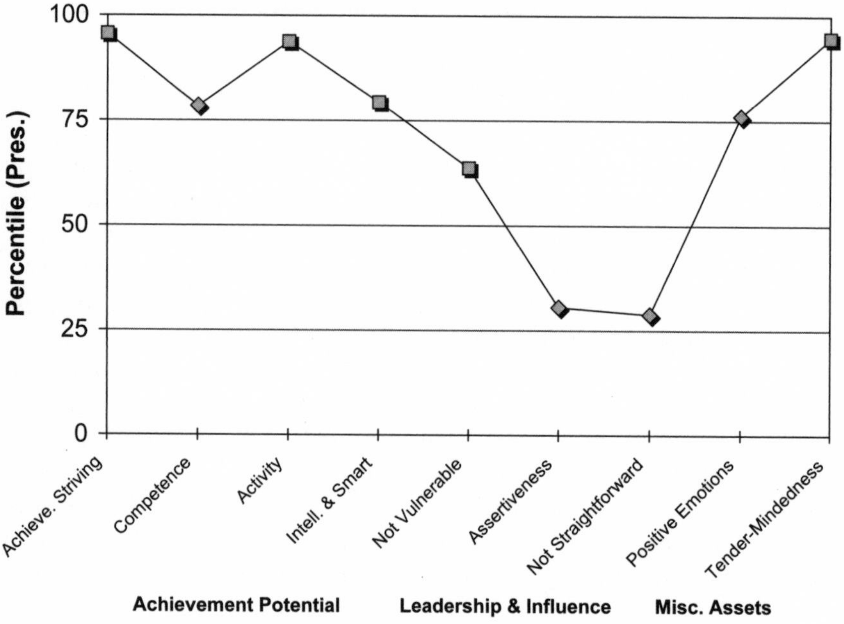

Carter in Perspective

Carter was most similar to Madison (r = .31), Jefferson (r = .27), and Wilson (r = .26). He was least similar to Jackson (r = −.41), G. W. Bush (r = −.30), and LBJ (r = −.30).[7]

His character may have been both his strength and greatest weakness as president. Observers have argued that he acted on his conscience rather than on public opinion polls and squarely faced up to difficult problems requiring unpopular measures. However, character can also imply lack of flexibility and charisma. For example, there was a striking contrast between Carter and FDR as leaders during periods of economic downturn. While the latter always had a reassuring twinkle in his eye, Carter appeared, at times, to be a beaten dog. He did not play the game in Washington and ultimately paid the price. Many admired him, but they did not embrace his leadership. His tendency to micromanage came in for considerable criticism, too. He reportedly oversaw the time schedule of the White House tennis courts, wrote corrections to the briefing papers he reviewed, and personally chased down hot water leaks in the White House. Concern with such small problems suggests he did not always use his resources wisely.

JEFFERSON, LINCOLN, AND CARTER COMPARED

As shown in Chart 11.7, Carter, and especially Jefferson and Lincoln were all high on Openness and Conscientiousness. Relative to most presidents, they were also quite high in Agreeableness. Jefferson stood out as the most introverted and the lowest in Character,

Lincoln was the most Agreeable, while Carter was highest on Conscientiousness. They also had notable differences on specific scales. Jefferson and Carter both excelled at Science and Math, while Lincoln, though an inventor, was just above average. Jefferson was far above the rest on Intellectual Brilliance (interests wide, artistic, inventive), but Lincoln far exceeded the other two on Wit. He also was Warmer and more Gregarious but much lower on Order and Simonton's Tidiness (methodical, thrifty). Carter was by far the most Active but also the least imaginative (low Openness to Fantasy). Jefferson was the most willing to try new things (Openness to Actions). Lincoln and Carter were high on Positive Emotions while Jefferson was below average. Lincoln also scored high on Anxiety and Depression compared to the others. Both he and Carter were moderately high on Self-Consciousness while Jefferson was low.

CHART 11.7
Jefferson, Lincoln, and Carter Compared

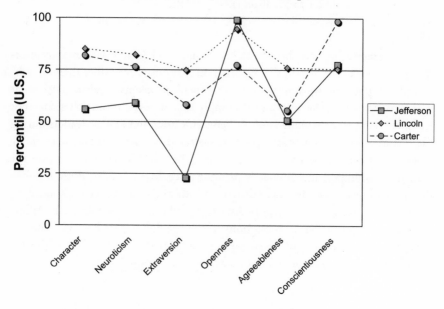

CHAPTER 12

Three Extraverts—
Theodore Roosevelt, Franklin
Delano Roosevelt, and
John Fitzgerald Kennedy

Morphed image of John Kennedy and Franklin Roosevelt.
John F. Kennedy Library and Franklin D. Roosevelt Library

ALL THE MEN profiled in this chapter are, or were at one time, considered to be in the first ranks of the nation's leaders. Kennedy's reputation has declined in recent years as disclosures about his reckless sexual behavior have continued to leak out. The perspective of time has removed some of the glimmer of Camelot, and the martyrdom of assassination has paled as the programs he helped sponsor are taken for granted. The other two Extraverts we profiled did not share Kennedy's sexual adventurism, but they did have many common traits.

All were enthusiastic and happy (Positive Emotions) and liked being around people (Gregariousness). They were drawn to thrills and adventure (Excitement

Seeking) and valued a wide range of emotions (Openness to Feelings). All three were willing to use indirect means or deceit to influence others (low Straightforwardness) and scored high on Charisma. As presidents, they found dealing with the press challenging and enjoyable, shared a flair for the dramatic, were charismatic, and carefully crafted their public images. None was shy or awkward in public, and all viewed the presidency as a vehicle of self-expression.

We begin with our portrait of Theodore Roosevelt, quite possibly the most dynamic personality of all the presidents.

THEODORE ROOSEVELT

Brief Biography

Theodore and Franklin Roosevelt descended from a common Dutch colonist of the mid-1600s; Claes Martinszen van Roosevelt died shortly after arriving in New Amsterdam, leaving his children orphans. The family name was shortened to Roosevelt. Two of Claes's grandsons, Johannes and Jacobus, launched the family on its journey toward wealth and power and produced two competing family lines, each producing a president. Johannes's heirs established country estates on Long Island and yielded Theodore and Eleanor Roosevelt. Jacobus's heirs settled along the Hudson River Valley and produced Franklin Delano Roosevelt.

TR's father, "the first Theodore," was a philanthropist with a reverberating social conscience and a love of humanity. He was involved in founding the American Museum of Natural History, the Metropolitan Museum of Art, and other cultural institutions in New York City. But his primary focus was on the oppressed and underprivileged. TR revered and loved his father and would remember him as "the best man I ever knew." His father's instructions when he left for college were revealing: "Take care first of your morals, then your health, then finally your studies." Throughout his life he sought to never make a decision, without reflecting on what his father would think.

TR idealized his father, but the first Theodore had one major failing in his son's eyes. When the Civil War broke out, TR's father did not enlist in the Army; he limited himself to relief work. The Roosevelt household was divided by the conflict: TR's father opposed slavery and supported the North, but his wife had brothers who fought for the Confederacy. As a compromise, the elder Roosevelt did not take up arms against his wife's family. What TR understood of this is unclear, but he later became a vociferous advocate of war.

TR's mother, Martha "Mittie" Bulloch, was a Southern belle from Roswell, Georgia, near Atlanta. She was given to mood swings and poor health and had an obsession with cleanliness. Huddled with her mother and sister under a Confederate flag, she rolled bandages and packed supplies for Confederate soldiers when her abolitionist in-laws were not looking.

Born on October 27, 1858, TR was his parents' second child and first son. From an early age, he suffered near-fatal asthma attacks for which his parents sought cures from one end of the earth to the other. When young Theodore suffered from asthma attacks in the middle of the night, his father would summon the carriage and take him into the night air. Content to be the center of attention, TR resigned himself to a life of the mind until his father encouraged him to build up his body at age eleven. He began working out in a gym his father built in the family home and took up wrestling, boxing, rowing, riding, and running. He did nothing halfway. He was already an avid reader and student of natural history who regularly mounted and dissected catches in his home laboratory, making impressive sketches of his subjects. However, even after two years of determined bodybuilding, he still found himself easily manhandled by two bullies his age. David McCullough, a Roosevelt biographer, argued that TR never blossomed physically until he separated from his family, a dynamic the author contends is common among asthmatics.

At Harvard one woman described him as "a campus freak with stuffed snakes and lizards in his room, with a peculiar violent vehemence of speech and manner and an overriding interest in everything." He would run to classes and take an eight-mile walk every afternoon. Agitated over a point in class, he would sometimes jump up and talk so long and intensely that one professor protested, "See here, Roosevelt, let me talk. I'm running this class."

While TR was at Harvard, his father died suddenly of stomach cancer. TR was devastated for months and retreated into nature and solitude. With his father's loss, he became the head of the family at the tender age of nineteen. While studying law full-time, he also wrote his first book, *The Naval War of 1812*, considered by many to be a minor classic. Unlike his later epic, *The Winning of the West*, this work was a dry recital of the weaponry and specifications of warships. TR also read voraciously, often one or two books a night. He reportedly could quote whole paragraphs from his readings five years later.

When he met his wife, Alice Lee, he confided to a friend, "She won't have me, but I will have her." Obsessed with self-discipline and personal virtue, he proudly remained a virgin until he married in 1880. The couple became a prominent part of the New York social scene. TR then made a dramatic decision for someone from his social class: to enter politics. Politics was not considered an honorable or suitable profession for a gentleman. But TR wanted to be in charge; before

1881 was over, he had won election to the New York State Assembly from the Twenty-first District.

Arriving in Albany in 1882, he parted his hair in the middle and assumed alternately pince-nez, perched precariously on his nose, or a monocle with a gold chain thrown over his ear. He carried a gold-handled cane and a black silk top hat. Caring little that the other legislators thought him a fop and an eccentric, he intended to occupy center stage and use it to his advantage. From his first day, he spoke at length on every issue, with his high pitched, patrician accent, and went after the Tammany Hall Democratic machine with a fury.

In the summer of 1883, told by physicians that his childhood asthma had left him with a weak heart, he decided to go buffalo hunting in the Badlands. He enjoyed two weeks of privation before downing a bull in the Dakota Territory. Then he broke into an improvised war dance, whooping with abandon before sawing off the bull's head for mounting. He often performed such war dances after hard-earned victories.

In 1884 his daughter Alice was born. Notified of the news, TR boarded a train for home. When he arrived, both his wife and mother were mortally ill. They died on the same day. Roosevelt never spoke of or wrote about Alice Lee again nor displayed her pictures. Bereft, he left his daughter to be raised by his sister Bamie and retreated to the Badlands, whose landscape mirrored his inner desolation.

TR invested in a North Dakota cattle ranch where he took up the everyday life of a cowboy. With his Tiffany knife, silver spurs, pearl-handled revolvers, and a custom-made, frilled leather shirt that cost today's equivalent of nearly fifteen hundred dollars, the hardened men of the area did not know what to make of him. When TR shouted, "Hasten forward quickly there!" at his first roundup, his companions nearly fell out of their saddles laughing. What's more, he used a toothbrush and did not drink. But they came to respect him for his stamina and grit.

Looking for strays one cold day; he rode into the town of Mingusville and went to the hotel bar for a cup of hot coffee. Just before he arrived, a drunken cowboy had shot holes in the bar clock and was now dangerously brandishing his two smoking six-shooters. Turning his guns on TR, he demanded that "Four Eyes" buy a round for the bar. Roosevelt smashed him in the nose with both fists and disarmed him. Though both revolvers went off as the cowboy fell, nobody was hit.

Another time, while tracking a boat of his that had been stolen, he captured Redhead Finnegan and his gang of horse thieves, brought them to justice, and collected a reward. The first president to know how to use the media to his advantage, he made sure that these and many other successes of his were abundantly covered by the press. In other respects, too, TR was not a typical cowboy; discussions around a campfire usually don't include medieval history, literature, astronomy, European politics, and socialism. But at his campfire, they did.

On a trip home to New York in 1885, he ran into an old girlfriend and long-time family friend, Edith Carow. Although Roosevelt fought the attraction (he did not believe in second marriages) and told his sister to keep them apart, she disobeyed. TR and Edith rekindled their romance and married in 1886. She functioned as a censor for his sudden enthusiasms and a governor for his appetites, without extinguishing the "eternal boy" within him.

His daughter, Alice, rejoined the family at that time and became a notorious political maverick. Asked about her antics years later, President Roosevelt responded, "I can do one of two things. I can be President of the United States or I can control Alice. I can't possibly do both!"

After his marriage, he wrote the four-volume *The Winning of the West* to rave reviews and began maneuvering to reenter politics. President Benjamin Harrison appointed him to the Civil Service Commission where he immediately created a stir with his pugnacious commitment to reform. He gained admittance to the salons of notables like Henry Adams, of the famous political family. Adams saw TR as "chewing his way through his future like a buzz saw, always busy and fully engaged, exploiting his chief quality, which was the ability to live intensely every thought."

TR had six children and relished entertaining and playing with them. He helped them shoot holes in the ceiling with their new rifles, encouraged and took part in regular pillow fights, and spent hours reciting poetry and songs to them that he had stored in his prodigious memory. When away from them, he would write nearly every night, developing original stories that he would illustrate lavishly to keep their interest.

Meanwhile, he was appointed assistant secretary of the Navy. At a time when the United States was realizing its economic might, the Navy was an important guarantor of the freedom of trade. TR was where the action was. Although second in command, as tensions rose with the Spanish he cabled contingency battle plans to naval commanders during his boss's day off. He was reprimanded, but his plans were left in place.

At the outbreak of the Spanish-American War, Roosevelt resigned his post and raised a volunteer regiment. He took his troops, a motley collection of cowboys and Indians, Ivy League athletes, and sportsmen, to Cuba and led them in the capture of San Juan Hill and nearby Kettle Hill. He recalled it as the best day of his life. Though he and his "Rough Riders" performed heroically and broke the Spanish resistance, he was denied the Congressional Medal of Honor for political reasons.

As a result of his Cuban adventure, TR became a national war hero and was tapped by Boss Platt to become the governor of New York. In exchange, TR was expected to moderate his reformist tendencies; he did not. Eager to be rid of a troublesome governor, Platt helped orchestrate his nomination as vice president in 1900. Roosevelt did not want the job, knowing it was without any real power, and Platt believed he had killed TR's political career with this master stroke. Others, more foresighted, noted, "Now there's only one life between that madman and the presidency!" The next fall, an anarchist assassinated President McKinley in Buffalo, New York. Climbing Mount Marcy, a couple of hundred miles to the east, TR was called to Buffalo. He was not yet forty-three when he became president.

Personality

TR's personality stands out as much on our graphs as it did in real life. He scores at the top of the chart on Extraversion (99.97th percentile), high on Conscientiousness (89th), and very low on Agreeableness (2nd). The seven experts who rated him showed exceptional levels of agreement, both on his overall profile and the separate Big Five and Character scales. Only on Openness to Experience was there disparate opinion, both among specialists and compared to generalists, who rated TR considerably higher. High scores on Impulsiveness and Angry Hostility, and low scores on Deliberation, Compliance, and Straightforwardness, account for his relatively low score on Character. Lastly, although our sources rated TR high on Warmth, Simonton's raters assigned low scores on Friendliness.

On the NEO Facet Scales, TR received scores on eighteen scales (out of thirty) that were in the top or bottom 10 percent of Americans, tied for the most of any president. He scored highest of all presidents on measures of Extraversion, Activity, Assertiveness, and Positive Emotions, and second highest on general intelligence and Openness to Feelings. (His score on Conscientiousness also is very high for Extravert presidents.)

TR used superlatives, such as his trademark "That was bully!" a great deal more than most presidents, and he often would literally "jump for joy." Strong emotions clearly gave his life meaning, and he was not always able to keep them under control. He was uncommonly carefree, happy-go-lucky, and spontaneous, and clearly showed his emotions. He experienced periods of intense joy and laughed easily.

He definitely did things just for thrills and had a prodigious appetite for

CHART 12.1

Theodore Roosevelt's Scores on Character and the Big Five Traits

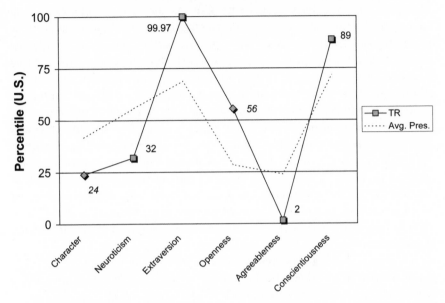

High	Percentile	Low	Percentile
Activity (E)	99.9	Modesty (A, Ch)	0.5
Assertiveness (E)	99.9	Vulnerability (N, − Ch)	4
Positive Emotions (E)	99.8	Compliance (A, Ch)	4
Achievement Striving (C)	99.7	Deliberation (C, Ch)	6
Openness to Feelings	99.5	Anxiety (N)	6
Excitement Seeking (E)	97	Openness to Values	6
Impulsiveness (N, C)	96	Straightforwardness (A, − Ch)	8
Gregariousness (E)	93		
Self-Discipline (C, Ch)	92		
Angry Hostility (N, − Ch)	90		
Competence (C, Ch)	90		

excitement. Adventurous, mischievous, playful, and rambunctious, he went on safari to Africa, climbed mountains, swam among sharks, and explored remote, piranha-infested rivers. He frequently appeared to be rushing or short of time, moved very rapidly, and regularly felt very energetic and vigorous. He had a fast-paced life and did not work slowly and steadily.

He was *not* calm and relaxed, but quick-tempered and hot-blooded—ready to fight back if someone picked on him. And yet, he was not known as touchy and temperamental, nor was he defensive or insecure. His emotion came from Extraversion—not Neuroticism. Though very concerned about his health,[1] he otherwise had fewer fears than most people, rarely experienced frightening thoughts, and did not worry about the future. He did not get overly discouraged when things went wrong and coped with stress or strain better than most. He did not do things that would undermine or sabotage his goals and did not see feelings and motives in others that he preferred not to recognize in himself.

TR did *not* try to be humble; he called attention to himself and dramatized incessantly. He was extremely demonstrative, exhibitionistic, and flamboyant— "He wanted to be the bride at every wedding and the corpse at every funeral," quipped his nephew, Nicholas. He thought highly of himself, liked to talk about himself and his accomplishments, and did not mind bragging. It was rumored that his publisher had to place a special printing order for more capital *I*'s each time he turned in a manuscript. Some contemporaries thought him self-centered and egotistical.

TR *often* played make-believe games as a child and as an adult continued to have an active and vivid imagination. He was artistic, creative, imaginative, inno-vative, and inventive—"A very symbol of the creative will in man," said H. G. Wells. He was also extremely "nonconforming, rebellious, unconventional," but he believed in traditional morality and sexual restraint. Still, he thought social policies should change with the times. He excelled at science and was quick to grasp new ideas and problems. He found it interesting to take on new hobbies and was interested in many different things.

TR did most of the talking in conversations. A famous British big-game hunter was invited to the White House to give a few pointers. Asked afterward what he had told the president, the dazed and weary visitor said, "I told him my name." Roosevelt rarely failed to assert himself when appropriate, and was force-ful and dominant. He was not inhibited or restrained, nor "bashful, shy, timid." Willing to bully or flatter to get his way, he possessed personal magnetism and valued power in himself and others.

Relative to other presidents, TR did not think before acting.[2] He exposed him-self to gunfire, even on horseback, as others around him prudently kept their heads down. He did not delay before committing himself or taking action, nor did he have trouble making up his mind. He sometimes answered questions before thinking issues through and acted impulsively, only to regret it later. For example, he pledged not to run for president again as he began his second term, weakening his administration and denying him the office he loved for the rest of his life.

More than most presidents, he kept promises and did not tolerate unethical behavior in his staff or colleagues. While a rancher, he observed one of his best hired hands placing the Roosevelt brand on a cow found on another man's land. TR fired the man on the spot.

Miscellaneous Observations

His approach to life was one of energetic opposition; he was a fighter! Henry James once called him "a wonderful little machine" running almost on perpetual motion. A Renaissance man touched by a "divine fire," he was an ornithologist, big-game hunter, taxidermist, collector, explorer, author, traveler, poet, military hero, athlete, and politician. He did it all well and at full throttle; he wrote thirty-six books and was the first American awarded the Nobel Peace Prize. He embodied the turn-of-the-century ideal of muscular Christianity. He was opinionated regarding his deeply held beliefs and had special contempt for atheists.

His low score (24th percentile) on Tender-Mindedness suggests that his advocacy for a Square Deal for workers was probably motivated more by disgust at the greed and lack of public spirit of the upper class than compassion for the less fortunate. TR greatly feared a class struggle erupting in the United States, as it was in other parts of the world, and believed he could head it off by reasonable reforms.

His trademark was his optimism and machismo; yet these qualities were not present in his youth or in his parents. Psychoanalysts have long recognized the defense mechanism of reaction formation—acting in a manner exactly opposite to one's inner tendencies. TR could be a textbook example. Nothing is more important to a prepubescent boy than strength and daring—qualities that young Roosevelt decidedly lacked. When he finally became a powerful man, he reclaimed these core juvenile virtues.

TR suffered profound grief at the loss of his father, wife, and mother. Certainly, his sense of "all is well with the world" must have been profoundly shaken. He subsequently lived a frenetic life of activity and disdain for injury, coupled with a vigorous defense of any challenge to his courage. An entry in his journal states, "Black care rarely sits behind the rider whose pace is fast enough." While he did not suffer from depression apart from bereavement, "Black Care" did appear to stalk him and may have caused him to redouble his pace.

TR Quoted

"I like to drink the wine of life with brandy in it."

"Speak softly, but carry a big stick."

TR Described

"He was a walking day of judgment."—John Burroughs

"The monstrous embodiment of unprecedented and resounding noise."—Henry James

"He is the most dangerous man of the age."—Woodrow Wilson

"You must always remember that the president is about six [years old]."—British diplomat Cecil Spring Rice, a friend of the Roosevelt family

President Theodore Roosevelt

A reform-minded president who hated the plutocracy, TR set about abolishing corporate trusts, invited Booker T. Washington to the White House, and tried to provide a "Square Deal" in every way possible for the working people of America. He was an early defender (at least in principle) of women's rights, made possible the building of the Panama Canal, and easily won reelection in 1904. Shortly thereafter, he won the Nobel Prize for negotiating the peace at the end of the Russo-Japanese War. He also bullied Congress to pass pure food, drug, and meat inspection laws and initiated the Forest Service and Fish and Wildlife Services.

He wasn't just aggressive toward domestic foes—when Colombia refused a modest offer of ten million dollars for rights to the Panama peninsula, he entered negotiations with Panamanian rebels and used the U.S. Navy to block intervention by the Colombians. Defending his actions to his cabinet, he asked if he had successfully acquitted himself. "You certainly have, Mr. President," he was told. "You have shown that you were accused of seduction and you have conclusively proved that you were guilty of rape."

As president, he invited professional boxers and wrestlers to challenge him, and loud crashes could be heard throughout the newly remodeled and renamed White House (before TR, it had been known as the Executive Mansion). His children rollicked through the grounds, often chased by their father; they even dropped water balloons on the security detail. The White House teemed with energy as never before.

TR was rated the fifth best president in the Ridings and McIver poll of historians, just behind Jefferson and ahead of Wilson. He was ranked fourth in Leadership Qualities, Accomplishments and Crisis Management, and Political Skill, but twelfth in Character and Integrity. As we report in Chapter 3, the match of his personality with the demands of the office was the best of all presidents. He scored exceptionally high, even among presidents, in Activity level, Assertiveness, Positive Emotions, and Achievement Striving (see Chart 12.2). He had no real weaknesses, only relative ones. He had limited concern for people down on their luck (low Tender-Mindedness) and was not much more prone to stretch the truth than most chief executives (i.e., a bit too Straightforward). Depending on which estimate is used, TR was average or less likely than other presidents to behave in an unethical manner on the job.

Behavior as President (our data)

In addition to the qualities shared with FDR and Kennedy listed at the beginning of this chapter, as president TR was not conservative in action. He was "a dynamo of energy and determination" who indulged in emotional outbursts.

TR after the White House

Unlike most presidents, TR had a long and active political life after his presidency. He reluctantly left the White House after two terms, to keep the rash promise he made early in his accidental presidency, turning his progressive agenda over to William Howard Taft, his hand-picked successor. Returning in

CHART 12.2

Personality Assets and Liabilities of Theodore Roosevelt as President

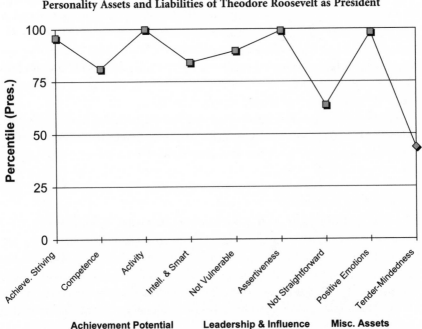

1910 after a yearlong safari in Africa, he was so alarmed at Taft's reluctance to stand up to corporate America that he denounced his old friend as a "fathead." In 1912, denied the Republican nomination, he formed the Progressive or Bull Moose Party and ran for president as its candidate. Woodrow Wilson, a Democrat, became president in large part because of this split between Taft and TR.

At a campaign stop in Milwaukee, John Schrank, a deranged former saloon owner, shot TR in the chest at point-blank range. TR insisted on giving his entire speech after giving Schrank a dismissive stare of contempt. Bleeding heavily, he told the stunned crowd, "I have just been shot, but it takes more than that to kill a Bull Moose." Apparently, his text and a case in his vest pocket slowed the bullet.

He almost died on a 1914 expedition as well—tracing the River of Doubt, an uncharted Brazilian stretch of remote white water. Far from civilization, he suffered an infected leg wound, became feverish, and slipped in and out of delirium for days. Intermittently lucid, he insisted that he be left without food to die in the jungle. His son and the others he traveled with would not hear of it. He continued to the end of the river despite losing thirty-five pounds, but his robust health never returned. Now an old man, he reflected on the ill-fated trip: "I had to go. It was my last chance to be a boy."

Unable to hold together his Progressive Party or win forgiveness for deserting the Republicans, he contented himself with writing a magazine column and nine books about politics, his expeditions, and the letters he wrote his children when they were young. Gradually, though, time and age took their toll. The times that he had personified were rapidly changing. With the onset of the First World War, he reported feeling as though the kaleidoscope through which he had viewed the world had been shaken. Others now found him a caricature of what he had been—his previous quirks magnified into fatal flaws.

In 1918, he had a recurrence of the fevers that nearly killed him on the River of Doubt (now renamed Río Roosevelt), and he died quietly in his sleep on January 6, 1919, at his home at Oyster Bay, New York.

Theodore Roosevelt in Perspective

TR was most like FDR ($r = .49$), Kennedy ($r = .40$), and Jackson ($r = .33$). He was least like Taft ($r = -.40$), Coolidge ($r = -.40$), and Buchanan ($r = -.34$). Like FDR, TR defined his times in a way few other presidents have. Though seen as eccentric wherever he went before the presidency, he proved himself bigger than every job he ever held. He was the first president to actively intervene on the part of the common man against big business monopolies; the first intellectual in the White House since John Q. Adams, yet also the most physical and vigorous of all presidents. His combination of extreme Extraversion, high Conscientiousness, and high morals is not found in any other president.

While Roosevelt was ahead of his times on many issues, he now seems downright anachronistic on several. He was an unabashed warmonger, believing that a man's soul is uniquely tempered in battle and that civilization was softening and weakening the upper classes. As an ex-president, he beseeched Woodrow Wilson to give him a command in World War I. He was a hunting enthusiast on a scale almost unimaginable by today's standards. His one safari to Africa took the lives of nearly 450 large animals including elephants, rhinos, and lions. TR was not particularly sympathetic to Native Americans either, arguing that the Europeans had merely done more effectively what the various tribes had done to each other in battle. He was an unabashed nationalist, at a time when the word had positive connotations, and a believer in Manifest Destiny. His acquisition of the rights to the Panama Canal was a windfall for this country but marked a low point in U.S. international morality.

FRANKLIN DELANO ROOSEVELT

Brief Biography

Franklin Delano Roosevelt lost his father at nineteen, the same age, he noted, as did TR. He was not, however, expected to take over as head of his family. That position had always been the province of his mother, Sara Delano Roosevelt, who dominated him from an early age. Born January 30, 1882, FDR was a gentle and overprotected boy with an active imagination. Throughout his life he exaggerated, made up, manipulated, denied, and distracted others from facts at odds with the dramatic image of himself he wished to convey.

He met President Grover Cleveland at age five and was told somewhat mysteriously, "My little man, I am making a strange wish for you. It is that you may never be President of the United States." FDR went on to be the nation's longest-tenured and one of its most beloved presidents. In doing so, he patterned himself on his older cousin, TR, who became a surrogate father to him. His real father, James Roosevelt, was much older than his mother. A man of wealth and power, he took the family with him when he toured his railroad holdings. He suffered a heart attack when FDR was age eight and gradually sank into invalidism.

Already overprotected by his strong-willed mother, FDR soon became her sole focus. She did not cut his hair until he was four and then enshrined his braids in a satin box. She kept him in dresses until he was six, a fad among the upper classes during this time. Told by his father's doctors that virtually any stress could kill the elder Roosevelt, FDR and his mother formed "a loving conspiracy" to keep him alive by shielding him from even the hint of any problems.

Not surprisingly, FDR grew up both with a great need for love and attention from others and a corresponding discomfort with true intimacy. His solution was to create a strong, confident, hearty persona that few ever penetrated. And when the facts did not support that image, he altered the facts.

At Groton prep school as a gangly fourteen-year-old, he felt miserably alone. Yet when he wrote home, his letters told of imagined camaraderie. In truth, he was totally unable to hold his own in the rough-and-tumble sports that were the key to success at Groton. The one thing that kept him afloat socially was his relationship to TR, who often gave Chapel Speeches to the students and who, along with Woodrow Wilson, remained his role model through life.

Galvanized by his cousin's exploits in Cuba, FDR told others that he had been on his way to Florida to volunteer when illness forced him to return home. In fact, he had never left Groton. Later in life he would refer to injuries he imagined sustaining in football games and boxing matches that never occurred.

When his father died during FDR's freshman year at Harvard (where he did make the lowest of eight football teams), his mother moved to Cambridge to be close to him at all times. He was denied admission to the prestigious Porcelain Club (which had had TR as a member) but was eventually made editor in chief of the Harvard *Crimson*. Nonetheless, one classmate remembered him during this time as being "like a dog whose tail wagged too much."

FDR stayed on an extra year to keep his job at the *Crimson* and took graduate courses in history and economics. He attended Columbia Law School but continued to be a mediocre student and even failed two courses. He passed the bar exam and promptly dropped out of law school. He did practice law at various times in his career. He served two terms in the New York Senate and had a progressive voting record. President Wilson rewarded him for his early support with an appointment as assistant secretary of the Navy, a position that TR had held and that FDR occupied from 1913 to 1920.

Eleanor Roosevelt was the daughter of TR's alcoholic brother, Elliott. Her mother died when Eleanor was eight years old, and various relatives kept her, but none provided her with a true home. She was buck-toothed and unattractive and felt that she embarrassed her family simply by existing. Schooled at Allenwood, an all-girls boarding school in London, she was loved and appreciated by its famous and cosmopolitan headmistress. Madame Souvestre recognized Eleanor's intelligence and sensitivity and taught her that true happiness came from focusing on and helping others with their problems rather than by dwelling on one's self. Eleanor never forgot this lesson, and it became the focus of her life and an important part of FDR's presidential legacy.

Her great caring and compassion, as well as her closeness to TR, attracted her cousin FDR, then a handsome young man at Harvard. They married in 1905 with TR giving away the bride. FDR seemed the fulfillment of Eleanor's childhood fantasies, Prince Charming come at last to awaken Sleeping Beauty. Sex was an ordeal to be borne.

If Eleanor came with neurotic residue from her grim childhood, FDR came with his domineering mother. Failing to break their engagement, Sara bought adjoining town houses and had the walls between them removed, so she could control both households. Eleanor was so intimidated that she dared not even rearrange her own furniture.

FDR began a romantic affair with Lucy Mercer, Eleanor's secretary, during World War I. He had hired her at the Department of the Navy, where he was assistant secretary. Returning home from a tour of American bases in Europe in 1919, FDR was so ill with the flu that he had to be taken from the boat by ambulance. While unpacking his suitcase, Eleanor came upon love letters from Lucy.

FDR's boss promptly fired Lucy, and his mother forced him to end the affair, but the damage had been done to his relationship with Eleanor. They were never again close, though they remained close political allies. Eleanor embraced various women's causes and began to associate (and even live) with lesbians she met in the woman's movement. Those closest to her swore she was not at all a sexual being and was repulsed by lesbian sexual practices.

Franklin accepted what he called the "she-males" and, in characteristic fashion, made them his friends as well. He was very skillful at building bridges to others, making allies he could use to his own ends. Much of the time, however, he was away from his family on his houseboat in the Florida Keys or at the Warm Springs Resort near Bullochville, Georgia.

FDR was a rising star in the Democratic Party and the vice-presidential nominee in 1920. But the next year, he was struck with polio while sailing near Campobello, Maine. He soon was almost totally paralyzed from the waist down. His mother arranged for him to move back in with her—her plan was that he would spend the rest of his life as a shut-in. Eleanor saw the danger to her husband of his mother's plan and shored up her courage to defy her imposing mother-in-law. She won and increasingly articulated her husband's unspoken wishes. Yet, FDR also found it necessary to flee his family, escaping to Florida for months at a time.

Refusing to give in to this incurable disease, FDR embraced water cures almost mystically and began to struggle back to walking and running, politically.

With Missy LeHand, his secretary and companion, he spent most of each year cruising the warm waters of Florida or exercising at Warm Springs, Georgia. Though he enjoyed the sun and relaxation, he also experienced depression, no doubt mourning the loss of his body and perhaps his future. There were days when it took him until noon to recover his smile sufficiently to join his companions. FDR invited Eleanor to join him many times, but she was now deeply into her causes and helping to lay the base for her husband's return to politics. Besides, FDR was with Missy.

FDR invested two-thirds of his personal fortune to purchase Warm Springs, aptly named for its 90-degree waters, and developed it into the first modern clinic for polio victims. "Dr. Roosevelt" was an inventive and charismatic director, often rollicking with his young patients in the spa's pools. He personally devised a new form of crutch and a means for measuring muscle strength that are still used today; he also personally rigged his car so he could operate it with hand controls. Yet, the lure of Warm Springs was as much in its director as in any "healing waters." "Whether they got better or not, they felt better," summarized one biographer. Franklin was determined and creative, but he was not a scientist. The Warm Springs waters did not cure him, or presumably anyone else.

The response of both FDR and his mother to his paralysis was denial. They never talked about it and always "kept their chin up" as they had for FDR's father. Roosevelt spent seven years trying everything to regain use of his legs and was still trying fanciful cures as he neared the end of his life. At the time, being an invalid was thought to be an absolute barrier to public office.

Facing reality as he prepared to run for office, he devoted his energy to finding ways of appearing to have recovered his ability to walk. With the help of his strong sons, leg braces, and a cane, FDR was able to "walk" across the stage at the 1924 and 1928 Democratic conventions to nominate Al Smith for president. In both cases he rehearsed extensively, teaching his sons how not to show in any way that they were supporting most of his weight. So impressive was this apparent return to health and politics that he easily won the 1928 New York governor's race.

Though he remained largely confined to a wheelchair, few outside the White House and the Roosevelt family ever fully recognized that he was crippled. He was quick to cover his atrophied legs with a newspaper when strangers approached and was masterful at using witty banter, puns, and gossip to create a heightened social ambiance in which he appeared quite robust. For his 1928 gubernatorial campaign, he had a specially designed bar installed in the backseat of a convertible that let him "stand" and wave at the crowds for many hours each day.

In 1932 with the country mired in the Great Depression, FDR was elected president. The "Dr. Roosevelt" persona took over, doing for the crippled country what he had done for the patients at Warm Springs.

Despite his mastery of the political arena, FDR was unable to face down two people: his mother and his contrary White House cook. Sara Roosevelt continued to control FDR's money throughout his presidency. "She would not let her son call his soul his own," recalled a family acquaintance. His cook, Mrs. Nesbitt, for years offered "plain foods, plainly prepared" and defied desperate requests for change. Roosevelt talked of firing her but never did.

He died suddenly of a stroke on April 12, 1945, at Warm Springs while posing with Lucy Mercer for a portrait she had commissioned. He and Lucy had been reunited in his final days through his daughter Anna, who was concerned at the toll the war effort had taken on him. Eleanor, who had just approached him about reconciliation, again lost her dream.

Personality

Thirteen experts rated FDR, the most of any president. They showed high levels of agreement, differing significantly only in their assessment of his Agreeableness. On the Big Five factors (see Chart 12. 3) FDR scored very high on Extraversion (99.8th percentile), and moderately low on Agreeableness (10th), Neuroticism (14th), and Character (19th). Generalists agreed in most respects but not with the low score on Conscientiousness. Unlike TR, FDR's profile is a close match to that of the average Extravert president.

On the NEO Facet Scales, FDR got the scores listed in the table on page 252.

FDR scored highest of all presidents on several measures of charisma and job performance and nearly equaled TR on measures of Extraversion and Positive Emotions. He definitely saw himself as cheerful and jocular and experienced intense happiness and joy; he laughed easily. Carefree, happy-go-lucky, and spontaneous, he was also "adventurous, mischievous, playful, rambunctious" and had a good sense of humor.

As outstanding as FDR's upbeat temperament was his clear willingness to trick people to get his way. He prided himself on his ability to handle others shrewdly and was willing to manipulate people. Crafty and sly, he was able to persuade others to his viewpoint but would also employ bullying or flattery. Not surprisingly, some perceived him as egotistical and self-centered. He would bend or break rules to his best advantage. He was alert to clues that reveal how others are thinking or feeling and seemed aware of the impression he made on others. Yet he wouldn't let others know if he did not like them.

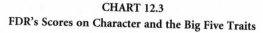

CHART 12.3
FDR's Scores on Character and the Big Five Traits

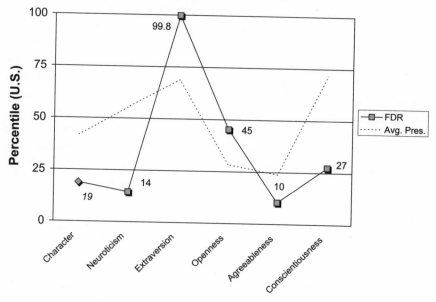

High	Percentile	Low	Percentile
Positive Emotions (E)	98.7	Straightforwardness (A, Ch)	0.5
Assertiveness(E)	98.6	*Dutifulness* (C, Ch)	4
Openness to Feelings	97	Vulnerability (N, -Ch)	6
Gregariousness (E)	96	*Modesty* (A, Ch)	7
Achievement Striving (C)	92	Depression (N)	10
Tender-Mindedness (A)	90		
Activity (E)	86		

Roosevelt was looked to for leadership—he was charismatic, and he liked to be the boss. He did not have difficulty taking charge and was able to persuade others and control social situations. He called attention to himself and was not "docile, passive, submissive" nor "an ordinary, everyday person." He acted vigorously and was successful in his endeavors.

FDR was not conservative in values and believed social policies should change with the times. He saw himself as broad-minded and tolerant. Nonetheless, he preferred to take vacations in familiar spots rather than going some place new. He was good at imaginative play, took notice of the ambience of different locales, and was emotionally expressive. Comfortable with uncertainties and complex issues, FDR had an active imagination and was able to readily grasp new ideas or problems. But he did not approach problems in a scientific or quantitative manner and rapidly lost interest in abstract or theoretical discussions. After meeting with him, economist John Maynard Keynes expressed disappointment in his lack of interest in economic theory. FDR commented, "Men and women are becoming mere units in statistics. This is not human progress." He similarly lacked interest in examining himself or his deeply held beliefs. When Eleanor asked if they should allow their children to choose their own faith, implying that reason should play a role, FDR replied emphatically that he believed it better not to think too deeply about such things.

He liked having many people around. He was talkative, outgoing, and friendly toward strangers, and he enjoyed chatting with people. In keeping with his people orientation, FDR sympathized with panhandlers and thought that political leaders should be more concerned about the human consequences of issues. He was not miserly or stingy, and he empathized easily with others. In turn, people wanted to take care of and nurture him.

A number of descriptors come from FDR's low Neuroticism. He was not self-defensive or unable to laugh at his own faults, nor was he thin-skinned or sensitive to slights. Apart from the first years of his paralysis, he rarely felt depressed, alone, or worthless, and was less moody than other presidents. He had a clear sense of meaning in life and was not bitter or morose. Seldom embarrassed when associates did foolish things, he was rarely self-conscious and was satisfied with himself as a person. He was capable in a crisis and did not feel overwhelmed under stress. Not anxious, fearful, or nervous, he rarely suffered from preoccupying thoughts. Lastly, FDR showed only two characteristics of low Conscientiousness: He was not prompt or punctual, and he liked to keep his options open.

FDR Described

"A second class intellect—but a first class temperament."—Supreme Court Justice Oliver Wendell Holmes Jr.

"[A] chameleon on plaid."—Herbert Hoover

"He was the only person I ever knew—anywhere—who was never afraid."—LBJ

"If [FDR] becomes convinced tomorrow that coming out for cannibalism would get him the votes he so sorely needs, he would begin fattening a missionary in the White House backyard come Wednesday."—H.L. Mencken

Miscellaneous Observations

FDR had an extensive network of friends and was a profoundly social animal. Yet, he had no close friends. He was at his best learning from others during conversation, "a genius at handling people and in learning from them." His relationship with Eleanor was troubled and not intimate, but they had a great mutual admiration, and he was loving toward other family members. He saw himself as "a Democrat and a Christian." Still, he liked to gossip about and manipulate his opponents.

President Franklin D. Roosevelt

At the depth of the Great Depression, Roosevelt's inaugural address came like a call to arms. For the first time in years, there was energy, warmth, and optimism in a voice from Washington. One of his first acts as president was to direct that whenever someone called the White House asking for help, a staff member be available to take the call and to do something. He instituted his radio "Fireside Chats" to encourage the country not to give in to fear as he took them through the Depression and a dangerous world war. Along the way he developed a plethora of "New Deal" programs, greatly expanded and redefined the role of the federal government, and helped shape the world order leading to the cold war.

Before that came the dire threat of Nazi Germany—Hitler had bullied and finally taken virtually all of Europe by force. Now Britain, in terrible shape and short of supplies, faced the mightiest war machine the world had known. The United States, like much of the rest of the world, abhorred the prospect of another world war. Roosevelt worked behind the scenes to provide materiel and financing and then dramatically won the public over with his radio appeal for the Lend-Lease Act. Congress had prohibited the sale of arms to Britain unless paid in cash, but FDR found a way to do it and a way to sell it. The Lend-Lease Act proposed that the United States would lend England the weapons it needed, like a neighbor lending a hose to another to put out a fire. The analogy was shaky, since (unlike hoses) weapons would be lost, and if they survived, they would likely be obsolete. But FDR infused his proposal with his charm and, as a result, probably saved Great Britain from Nazi conquest.

More than most, FDR saw the Nazis as a long-term threat to the United States as well as to the rest of the world. While the country remained officially neutral, he ordered American warships to accompany supply vessels and to not shrink from any clashes with Nazi U-boats. This policy was calculated to create an incident that would stir public opinion.

When the Japanese attacked Pearl Harbor, FDR was aghast at the losses. The Pacific Fleet lay in ruins. Yet, he recovered his composure to give a rousing call to arms the next morning. During the war, he developed a close relationship with Winston Churchill and tried to charm Stalin, with modest success. As he looked toward the end of the war, he envisioned guaranteed jobs and homes for everyone and college educations for returning soldiers.

Eleanor had become the most active and controversial First Lady in history. More liberal than her husband, she was an unfailing champion of the underdog, pressing for civil rights for African Americans and for the right to collective bargaining. Like her husband, many despised her as a traitor to her class.

FDR rated as the second best president overall in the Ridings and McIver poll, behind Lincoln and ahead of Washington. He received the highest rating in Leadership Qualities and Political Skill, but was only fifteenth in Character and Integrity. Although his lowest rating, this probably was still inflated by a halo effect (the tendency to rate qualities all good or all bad).

Franklin Roosevelt's personality matched the office nearly as well as TR's. He was average or above on every quality of our prediction index (see Chart 12.4). He scored in the upper quarter of all presidents on "Not Straightforward," Positive Emotions, Assertiveness, Tender-Mindedness, and "Not Vulnerable." Only on Achievement Striving and Competence did his scores fall near the average. His level of Ethics on the Job, given his personality scores, was expected to be about average. It was.

CHART 12.4
Personality Assets and Liabilities of FDR as President

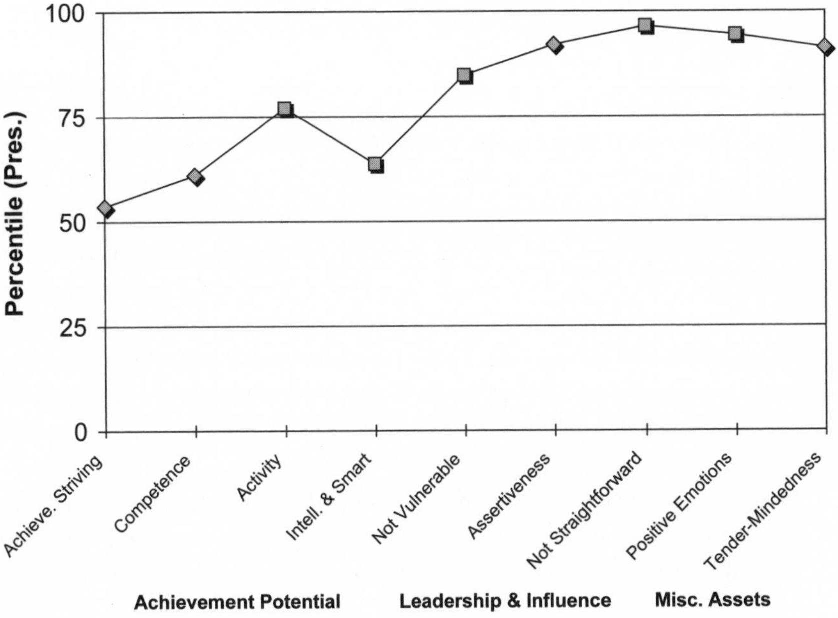

Achievement Potential   Leadership & Influence   Misc. Assets

Behavior as President (our data)

FDR was rated the second most charismatic of presidents on our two measures and on Simonton's. His public addresses were rated the most compelling of any president. An exceptional number of items regarding his behavior in office met our criteria. Only those not given at the beginning of the chapter are listed here. As president, he initiated new legislation and programs and was given top marks in the quantity of his accomplishments. His first hundred days produced an unprecedented rush of government activity. He exhibited artistry in manipulation, had the ability to maintain popularity, and rarely permitted opponents to outflank him. "A master conjurer," summarized one commentator. At a meeting with reporters, H. L. Mencken made brief but prepared comments critical of the New Deal. FDR took the podium, referred with a smile to "my old friend Henry Mencken," and then spoke at length on the stupidity and arrogance of journalists. The crowd was not amused, but they did notice the face of the previous speaker grow crimson. FDR was quoting from Mencken's essay *Journalism in America*. He paused to shake Mencken's hand on the way out.

Roosevelt did not believe in unfettered business freedom but was innovative in his own executive role. He kept in touch with the mood of the American public and maintained close relations with a wide circle of associates. He conveyed a clear-cut, highly visible personality, used rhetoric effectively, and was characterized by others as a world figure.

FDR in Perspective

FDR most resembled Kennedy ($r = .66$) and Clinton ($r = .51$), and to a lesser degree, his cousin Theodore ($r = .49$). He was least like Coolidge ($r = -.50$), Hoover ($r = -.45$), and Buchanan ($r = -.37$). He was president longer than anybody, reelected to a fourth term, and saw the country through two of its greatest crises, the Great Depression and World War II. At a time when the United States lacked hope and was indifferent to the fate of Europe, FDR's booming, confident voice inspired and made everything seem OK. There was some snake oil in the potion, but the medicine seemed to work. When Japan and the Nazis threatened, America rose to the challenge and became a military as well as an economic world power.

FDR's personality and leadership style reshaped America's view of a successful president and politician. Speaking the night of FDR's death, a young soldier said, "I felt as if I knew him. . . . I felt as if he knew me—and I felt as if he liked me."

JOHN F. KENNEDY

Brief Biography

Kennedy's father, Joe, had groomed his oldest son Joe Jr. to be president someday. A self-made man with a social conscience, Joseph Sr. graduated from Harvard and was the youngest bank president in Massachusetts by twenty-five. He
made money in the stock market, sometimes pooling with other insiders to draw
in the unwary, and sold off before the 1929 crash. He was a millionaire by thirty-
five. He later made millions as a liquor importer, in real estate, and as a Hollywood producer. He had a long-term affair with Gloria Swanson, the era's leading
sex goddess and the most influential woman in Hollywood. Joe Sr. was bold,
brash, handsome, profane, anti-Semitic, and an incessant social climber. Despite
his money and accomplishments, the Kennedys were excluded from society
because of prejudice against the Irish and the nouveau riche.

When Franklin Roosevelt needed the right man for the newly formed Securi-
ties and Exchange Commission, Joe Kennedy was tapped. Explaining his choice,
Roosevelt quipped, "It takes a crook to catch a crook." Joe Sr. was an early supporter of FDR and at times claimed to be decisive in securing his nomination.
Yet, after the election, he was denied many desirable posts in the new administration. Later he proposed that he be ambassador to Great Britain, where he eventually served. He and his family enjoyed celebrity befitting a "first family" of the
Americas until he disgraced himself by openly admiring Nazi military might and
siding against Winston Churchill. When he was quoted as declaring democracy
in Britain dead, his political career was over. This pugnacious, larger-than-life
man left England with the nickname "Jittery Joe" amid accusations of cowardice.

But he infused a fierce competitive spirit in his children and a moral obligation to contribute to society. If he couldn't become president, then maybe one
of his sons could. "My father wasn't around as much as some fathers when I was
young," Kennedy later said, "but . . . he made his children feel that they were the
most important things in the world to him. He was so terribly interested in
everything we were doing. He held up standards for us, and he was very tough
when we failed to meet those standards."[3] He also held up a prodigious model
for both achievement and sexual conquest. Many visitors to the Kennedy home
recalled a lot of razzing and teasing—like a bunch of chickens pecking at you,"
recalled one guest.

Kennedy's mother, Rose Fitzgerald Kennedy, was educated in convents and
studied piano at the New England Conservatory of Music. When her father was
mayor of Boston, she acted as hostess for the city. She later took an active role
in her son's political campaigns. Having a retarded daughter herself, she became

an activist for the developmentally disabled. She maintained her piety and manners even as Gloria Swanson accompanied the family on trips abroad, apparently never suspecting the affair.

Despite his outward appearance of health, John F. "Jack" Kennedy was sickly as a child and as an adult. His brothers joked that a mosquito took a big risk in biting him. As an adult, he was given last rites on two widely separated occasions. His health, though, did not prevent him from scrapping frequently with his older brother Joe, who was something of a bully and a bigot. Jack was not, but he got himself into a fair amount of trouble in the private schools he attended by pulling pranks. Though he finished forty-sixth of 112 students at Choate prep school, he was voted "most likely to succeed"—but he had fixed the vote. His headmaster noted, "Jack has a clever, individual mind," but added that he needed to learn "the right place for humor and . . . to use his individual way of looking at things as an asset instead of as a handicap."

During his school years, he twice had to withdraw from school, once because of appendicitis and another time for jaundice. His poor health kept him thin to the point that he was known as "rat-face." Kennedy majored in political science, especially international relations, while at Harvard (1936–1940). His senior thesis was later published as *Why England Slept* and earned forty thousand dollars and wide acclaim for its young author. It was notable also for its break with his father's position, portraying Churchill as a visionary leader. At Harvard he played freshman and junior varsity football, participated on the freshman golf and swim teams, and was part of the 1938 championship sailing crew. He also served on the staff of the Harvard *Crimson*. When he turned twenty-one, he claimed a one million-dollar trust fund established by his father.

According to a friend from Choate, Kennedy had his first sexual experience in a Harlem brothel at the age of seventeen. He reputedly retained a preference for "professionals" into his presidency (though there were also many "amateur nights"). While Nixon crammed with cue cards before their famous 1960 television debate, Kennedy allegedly "relaxed with a prostitute," according to Nixon biographer Jonathan Aitkin. Despite his warmth and charm, Kennedy reportedly did not like to be touched during sex. Some of his affairs were dangerous and politically fatal. Among them were Inga Arvad ("Inga Binga"), an actress and former Miss Europe who was a friend of Hitler and other high-level Nazis, and Judith Campbell, girlfriend to mob boss Sam Giancana. His relationship with Inga brought him under the surveillance of the FBI during World War II and cost him his post at navy intelligence when recordings caught him talking unguardedly about his job to the suspected German spy. The affair also provided J. Edgar Hoover with leverage on the future president.

When World War II broke out, Jack volunteered for the Army but was rejected because of back problems. His father did what he could to discourage him from going to war, but when he couldn't be dissuaded, helped secure him the command of a Navy PT boat. On patrol in 1943, the little ship was rammed and sunk by a Japanese destroyer. Two of the crew were killed. Kennedy received a Purple Heart and the Navy and Marine Corp medals when he managed to swim four miles to safety, towing an injured crewman despite his bad back. The account of the incident was published in the *New Yorker* in 1944 and made Kennedy a bona fide war hero. He was rotated home afterward due to having aggravated his back in the rescue.

Kennedy's stardom came at a cost. His older brother Joe, heir to the Kennedy throne, was temporarily overshadowed. Shortly thereafter, he volunteered to pilot what was essentially a flying bomb and died when the plane malfunctioned and blew up. According to biographer Shneidman, when Joe Jr. was alive, Jack was number two in a family where only number one counted. "Once . . . daddy recognized him as No. 1, then nothing would stop him."

After his release from the military, Kennedy worked briefly as a journalist, then ran for and won a seat in the House of Representatives. His father pulled the strings, financially and otherwise, persuading editors to write endorsements or print yet another version of the *PT 109* saga. More than almost anyone else, Joe Kennedy understood the developing power of the media. "It's not what you are that's important," he counseled his son. "It's what people think you are that's important." Jack took the lesson to heart. As he partied with the stars, he consciously studied those with "presence," what today is called charisma, with an eye to developing it in himself.

Although Jack generally supported Truman's programs, he joined Republicans in blaming the president for "losing China." He was something of an iconoclast. His most memorable moment in the House was his lambasting of the American Legion, a dangerous political target, over its opposition to public housing. Kennedy refused to retract or apologize for his statements, despite the urging of his own supporters.

During this time, he lived like a college student, often showing up for work in spotted, rumpled clothes. His apartment was strewn with women's underwear and an occasional moldy hamburger, and he had no sense of financial responsibility. He refused to carry money and constantly borrowed money from his staff and did not repay them. Once he lectured a staff member on how he should be able to support himself and his family, plus go to law school, on his five-thousand-dollars-a-year salary. His father, who had been listening, angrily broke in: "God damn it, Jack! You spend ten times that much on incidentals!"

In the Senate from 1953 to 1961, his most notable act was his support for the Saint Lawrence Seaway, which promised to divert ship traffic away from his own state. He consistently supported pro-labor legislation. Kennedy's Senate term was during the reign of terror precipitated by Joseph McCarthy, a family friend of the Kennedys. Personally, Kennedy liked McCarthy for his crude sense of humor and willingness to challenge authority. He eventually recognized his duplicity but avoided a confrontation and was absent during the vote on his censure.

In fact, Kennedy was seriously ill at this time. His weight had dropped by forty pounds, and his back continued to plague him. The mysterious wasting illness that had afflicted him all his life was finally diagnosed as Addison's disease. Not long before the McCarthy vote, he agreed to an operation on his back for which he had been given no more than a 50 percent chance of surviving. He nearly did not, and the operation was not successful. A second one was, however, and dramatically changed his life and his outlook. He no longer was obsessed with death and began to see himself as lucky rather than cursed.

During his medical leave, he wrote *Profiles in Courage*, a series of biographies of American politicians who championed unpopular but principled positions. Most of his subjects were conservative. Kennedy was later awarded the Pulitzer Prize for his work, but there were persistent rumors that he had hired a ghostwriter.

Kennedy met Jacqueline Bouvier at a dinner party hosted by a mutual friend. She had been named "Queen Deb of the Year" when she made her debut and earned a degree in art from George Washington University. She later worked as a photographer for the *Washington Times-Herald*. Like Kennedy, she was raised among wealth and privilege, and her father was the equal of Kennedy's in rakish behavior. Jackie, as a teenage girl, had turned the story of her father's infidelity forty-eight hours into his marriage into a lusty tale for her friends. Her own wedding was performed by the local archbishop with a special blessing bestowed by Pope Pius XII. The wedding was a Joe Kennedy production, with the patriarch controlling details down to the wedding dress. The overriding goal was to make a fitting impression on the country for his son's political career. In fact, Kennedy would rather have remained a bachelor.

The real marriage bore little resemblance to the fairy tale. Kennedy acknowledged that he loved the chase and lost interest after the conquest. On their honeymoon, he got bored and suggested Jackie return home while he went on to visit a friend. He was unfaithful from the start, and after a year, Jackie appeared dazed. During one of her several miscarriages, he was off sailing somewhere, with a mixed crew, and could not be located for three days. Jackie did not take this treatment passively. She began staying away from home and refused to do more than the minimum expected of a politician's wife. She went out publicly with other men, including Aristotle Onassis. The marriage became closer in time, based on mutual respect and affection. Jackie became the most fashionable First Lady of the century and was especially admired for her courage and dignity in the aftermath of her husband's assassination.

When Kennedy ran for president in 1960, he won all seven primaries he entered. Lyndon Johnson, who he eventually tapped to be his running mate, was his only real rival and added Southern appeal to the ticket. Kennedy held liberal Democrats, such as Adlai Stevenson, in contempt. He ran against Nixon, earning one of the narrowest popular vote victories in history (49.7 percent to 49.5 percent).

Both before and after becoming president, Kennedy partied with the stars, including Frank Sinatra. But his health remained so poor that he rarely drank alcohol, often keeping a friend nearby to discreetly dispose of the drinks people would hand him. Kennedy's brother-in-law, Peter Lawford, was asked to introduce Kennedy to a number of stars and starlets, including Marilyn Monroe.

More troubling, Kennedy had come to rely on "vitamin shots" from a physician of questionable competency who took his own medicine. On at least one occasion, the doctor was observed to have slurred speech as he went to minister to the president. Robert Kennedy, worried about his brother's care, had a spent syringe analyzed, and found that it contained amphetamines. Kennedy had these injections before meeting with Khrushchev on at least one occasion.[4]

Personality

Like the other three Extraverts, Kennedy scored off the top of the chart on Extraversion (99.6th percentile), but he also scored high on Openness (82nd), low on Character (5th) and Conscientiousness (4th), and moderately low on Agreeableness (11th). The five experts that rated him showed good agreement on his overall profile but showed a wide range of opinion on Conscientiousness and Neuroticism. Smaller but still appreciable differences were observed for Character and Agreeableness. Specialists gave Kennedy substantially lower marks for job performance than did historians, and generalists did not perceive him to be nearly so low in Conscientiousness as did the specialist.

On the NEO Facet Scales, Kennedy received the scores shown in the table on page 262.

Kennedy scored second highest of all presidents on Openness to Fantasy, Openness to Values, Excitement Seeking, and Intellectual Brilliance. He was lowest of all presidents on Dutifulness and second lowest on Self-Discipline.

Kennedy undeniably had extramarital affairs and a great many sexual encoun-

CHART 12.5

Kennedy's Scores on Character and the Big Five Traits

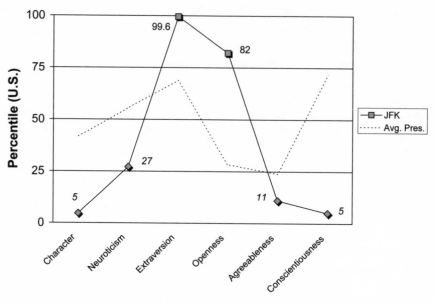

High	Percentile	Low	Percentile
Excitement Seeking (E)	98.5	Dutifulness (C, Ch)	0.13
Positive Emotions (E)	97	Straightforwardness (A, Ch)	0.5
Openness to Fantasy	96	*Deliberation* (C, Ch)	2.5
Impulsiveness (N, -Ch)	94		
Tender-Mindedness (A)	93		
Openness to Feelings	93		
Activity (E)	90		

ters. He did *not* believe in the traditional morality of sexual restraint and perceived many situations in erotic terms. His lovers often included two hookers at a time, sometimes procured by high-ranking local law enforcement officers. The Secret Service, sworn to give their life in the protection of the president, watched helplessly as he disappeared behind closed doors with women they did not know. Two White House secretaries, nicknamed Fiddle and Faddle, were said to routinely skinny-dip with him in the White House pool. Jack clearly did things just for excitement, in keeping with the Kennedy family culture, and was adventurous, aggressive, and competitive. Though he played hard, he was not aimless or (un)ambitious, even compared to other future presidents.

Much more than most presidents, he had sympathy for the less fortunate and felt we could never do too much for the poor and elderly. Yet, he found it easy to deceive others, and sometimes encouraged their dependence in order to take advantage of them. But he wasn't faultfinding, harsh, unforgiving, or unsympathetic; he did not blame others for his troubles.

When Kennedy used physical gestures, they were undeniably stylish and graceful. He freely expressed his feelings through expressions on his face and body, experienced a wide range of moods. Strong emotions lent his life meaning—but he was not always able to keep them in check. He was lighthearted, lively and quick, carefree, happy-go-lucky, and spontaneous. He was also humorous and witty: When speaking at a businessman's luncheon, he quipped, "It would be premature to ask you for your support in the next election, and it would be inaccurate to thank you for it in the past." When Vice President Johnson was unenthusiastic about traveling to Saigon, Kennedy said, "Don't worry, Lyndon. If anything happens to you, Sam Rayburn and I will give you the biggest funeral Austin, Texas, ever saw." He laughed easily, was demonstrative, exhibitionistic, and flamboyant, and friendly and outgoing toward strangers.

Kennedy was not embarrassed by teasing or ridicule and did not fear making a faux pas. He was not defensive, insecure, negativistic, or self-pitying, and did not feel cheated by life. He did not believe that controversial speakers mislead or confuse students; he valued open-mindedness over devotion to ideals and principles. He saw himself as tolerant and broad-minded. Perceptive and observant, he was quick to comprehend new ideas and problems but liked to keep his options open. He was intellectually curious, was skilled at imaginative play, and had many interests.

Kennedy got high ratings on items reflecting Positive Valence as well as a low rating on Negative Valence. He was charismatic, handsome, and "special"—not an ordinary, everyday person. Less even than other presidents, he did not steal and wasn't seen as "disgusting, sickening."

President Kennedy

In 1957, America was shocked by the ability of the Soviet Union to place a satellite in earth orbit. Kennedy announced the formation of a "New Frontier" and set the goal of putting a man on the moon before 1970. It was the beginning of a stupendous engineering effort and NASA's glory days.

Cuba was a focal point for two crises, the ill-fated Bay of Pigs invasion and the Cuban Missile Crisis. The CIA sponsored a small invasion force, expecting Cuban rebels to rise up and overthrow Castro. When they did not, the venture was a disaster. Later, the decision-making process that led to the invasion found its way into social psychology textbooks as Groupthink. In Groupthink, a group, acting from a similar frame of reference, discounts the abilities and resources of their opponents and minimizes the risk to the group's venture, failing to raise valid objections and problems. Kennedy took responsibility for the Bay of Pigs fiasco but bitterly exclaimed of his advisers, "I was a fool to listen to them."

The Cuban Missile Crisis brought the world closer to nuclear war than ever before. CIA satellite photos revealed the Cubans were establishing a base with nuclear missiles that could reach the United States in minutes. Though the United States had similar missile sites in Europe and Turkey, Kennedy demanded that the missiles be removed and stated that any missiles launched from Cuba would be regarded as a strike from the Soviet Union. Behind the scenes, he made an agreement to remove similar missiles deployed in Turkey. When the Soviets seemingly backed down, Kennedy had redeemed himself as a strong and capable leader.

It is now known that the CIA attempted to assassinate Castro through contacts with the American Mafia. During this time, Judith Campbell acted as a courier between Kennedy and mobster Sam Giancana (both were her lovers). Some have speculated that Kennedy's own assassination resulted from these efforts; others point to Robert Kennedy's war on organized crime. It was well known that RFK and Lyndon Johnson detested each other, and many assumed that RFK would immediately be replaced as attorney general if Johnson became president.

During the 1960s, civil rights became a pressing issue, and Kennedy was sometimes an eloquent spokesman. During the election, he called Martin Luther King's family after his arrest in Atlanta and had RFK arrange bail. This gesture may have been politically motivated and quite possibly won him the election. But Kennedy was far from a dedicated civil rights crusader. He held to the discredited view that Reconstruction after the Civil War led to excesses by the black population, which justified harsh repression in the South. Still, sensing the mood of the country, he issued an executive order to end discrimination in federally funded housing, appointed blacks to federal positions, and established the President's Committee on Equal Employment Opportunity.

President Eisenhower had sent two thousand military advisers to Vietnam. The number grew during Kennedy's administration to sixteen thousand and included Special Forces. At the time of his death, his administration's policy in Southeast Asia was unclear. Some advisers contend that he intended to withdraw troops after the 1964 election.

Kennedy was ranked as the fifteenth best president, behind John Adams and ahead of Cleveland. His best marks were in Appointments (seventh), his worst in Character and Integrity (thirty-fourth). Kennedy's assets as president included intelligence, compassion, optimism and cheerfulness, and low Straightforwardness. However, he was rated lower in Competence and as less goal oriented than his peers (see Chart 6).

Behavior as President (our data)

Kennedy's qualities as president have largely been described in the first part of this chapter—almost all of which he shared with the Roosevelts. However, much more than most presidents, he liked meeting the press. He also stood out from the other two with a low rating on "has good moral character."

Kennedy in Perspective

Kennedy was highly similar to FDR ($r = .66$) and Clinton ($r = .57$), less so to TR ($r = .40$). He was least like Coolidge ($r = -.41$), Buchanan ($r = -.40$),

CHART 12.6
Personality Assets and Liabilities of Kennedy as President

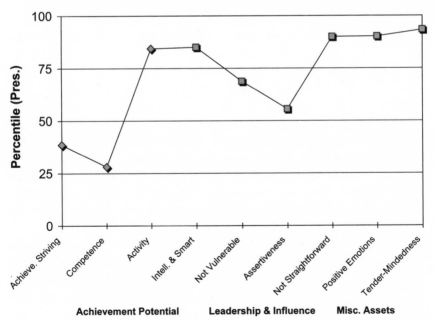

and Hoover (− .39). He had numerous gifts that made him very attractive as a public figure. He was eloquent, witty, pragmatic, open-minded, yet championed some traditional virtues such as courage. Men with qualities like Kennedy often receive high ratings by historians. But Kennedy's sexual appetite probably would have been his undoing were he president today, as it was for Clinton.

Kennedy and his administration retain a patina of celebrity and idealism unjustified by recent revelations. In him, idealism was mixed with deception, vitality with lust, optimism with constant pain and illness. His assassination was a national trauma—almost everyone past childhood at the time remembers where they were when they heard the news. He was the first president struck down in a half-century, and in the years after his death, Kennedy was among the most idealized of all presidents, even by some historians. He served during an especially dangerous time, when cold war adversaries probed relentlessly for personal weaknesses of any official that could be exploited. Had he lived and faced hard investigation of his affairs, he might have had a very different reputation. As it was, he was the only president between Eisenhower and Reagan to leave office with his reputation enhanced.

This seems due not just to his martyrdom but also to dedicated efforts by his family to shape his memory. Jackie created and promoted the portrayal of Kennedy's administration as "Camelot," while Robert Kennedy allowed his own idealistic advocacy for migrant workers and civil rights to be viewed as extensions of his brother's unfinished work. In fact, Kennedy had been much more pragmatic and conservative. As his father had counseled, image counted above all.

EXTRAVERT PRESIDENTS COMPARED

As can be seen in Chart 7, the Extravert presidents profiled closely resemble each other in most respects. The largest departure from the group is TR's high standing on Conscientiousness. There were also differences on more specific scales. TR rated low on Openness to Values, and Simonton's Moderation, Poise and Polish, Wit, and Physical Attractiveness, and relatively low on NEO Tender-Mindedness—in contrast to FDR and Kennedy. He was also rated relatively high on Angry Hostility, Dutifulness, Order, and Simonton's Pettiness scale.

There are some moderate differences between Kennedy and Franklin Roosevelt. Kennedy showed more willingness to try new things (Openness to Activity) and scored higher on Openness to Ideas but lower than FDR on Self-Discipline.

CHART 12.7
Personality Scores of FDR, Kennedy, and TR

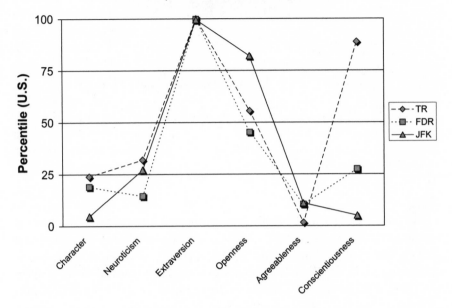

CHAPTER 13

Special Cases—George Washington and Bill Clinton

I N THIS SECTION, we profile two men who don't fit cleanly into one of the eight types. George Washington did not closely resemble any other president; Bill Clinton resembled three types. For Washington, we follow the same format as the rest of the profiles. For Clinton, whose personality is now quite familiar, we take a different approach. Not only does Clinton fit with Extraverts, Actors, and Dominators, he closely resembles four other prominent presidents we profiled in other chapters: John Kennedy, Lyndon Johnson, Franklin Roosevelt, and Warren Harding. Our goal will be to place Clinton's personality in this context.

GEORGE WASHINGTON

Brief Biography

George Washington was born in Westmoreland County, Virginia, in 1732. His father, a moderately successful farmer and planter, was frequently away from home on business. He had ten children, four by his first wife and six by his second, Mary Ball Washington. Mary's oldest son remembered his father only vaguely as a tall, kind man, who passed away when Washington was just eleven.

Washington's relationship with his mother was strained. She was extremely demanding and a burden to him through most of his life. While General of the Army, he had to contend with her public complaints of neglect, and even worried that she might betray military secrets to get attention. He got along well with most of his siblings, though he disapproved of some of their lifestyles. He nonetheless was supportive, contributing financially when warranted.

Washington attended grammar school irregularly and did not receive any formal education beyond that. His early training came mostly in outdoor activities, such as horseback riding, surveying, and painting. His lack of formal education was at times evident in his writing; he often used incorrect grammar, and his spelling was atrocious.

After his father's death, he was left in the custody of his elder half-brother, Lawrence, whom he greatly admired and loved. Lawrence was interested in intellectual pursuits, and exposure to the atmosphere created by Lawrence greatly compensated for Washington's limited book learning. Though limited in most academic areas, he was good in math. He was especially interested in surveying land, and at the age of fifteen went to work with a group of surveyors in the Shenandoah Valley. He later worked as a public surveyor for Fairfax County, Virginia, before beginning his military career at the age of twenty-one.

Washington's military service began in 1753 when the governor of Virginia sent him to order French soldiers to leave the Ohio area. The French refused, and a year later, British general Braddock, with Washington as his aide, led a small army against them. They were ambushed and badly defeated. During the fighting, however, Washington showed great leadership qualities and later was appointed commander of all Virginia troops. For several years, he led armies in small frontier battles against the French and Indians.

Washington was awkward and tongue-tied with girls, and most of his early romances were disappointing. He developed an infatuation with Sally Fairfax, the wife of his friend and neighbor, and there was some reciprocation of feeling and an exchange of letters. Aside from romantic misadventures, others have reported the young Washington to be headstrong and impetuous, sometimes ordering the Indians accompanying his division around like slaves.

At age twenty-six, he quit his military post to marry a rich young widow named Martha Dandridge Custis—possibly for her money. Another of his romantic interests, Mary Phillipse, was the daughter of a wealthy landowner.

Sometime between his youth and his emergence as a national figure, Washington's character was transformed. He was an admirer of Roman virtues, and he quoted from the play *Cato* (which dramatizes Caesar's rise and fall) throughout his life. One of his heroes was the general Cincinnatus, who after saving his country, retired to his farm, forsaking politics or any advantage from his military glory. As such, he was the opposite of Caesar, whose personal ambition brought an end to the republic. The Roman virtues of patriotism, duty, and self-sacrifice became Washington's own.

Possibly because of his lack of formal education and the lowly social standing of his mother, Washington also devoted himself to mastering etiquette and manners that set apart the upper classes. He learned and mastered *110 Rules of Civility and Decent Behavior in Company and Conversation*, which he may have been required to write as a penmanship drill. This guide dealt with matters such as not killing vermin in front of guests. However, most of its rules taught the social graces of gentlemen and were summarized by the first of the adages: "Every action done in company ought to be done with some sign of respect to those that are present." Washington's devotion to courtesy and manners undoubtedly contributed to the social success of this reserved man.

For the next fifteen years, he spent most of his time at Mount Vernon, his home. He became a wealthy tobacco farmer and raised horses, cattle, apples, peaches, and pears. Never having any children of his own (he was probably sterile[1]), he doted and lavished attention on Martha's two children from her previous marriage. He had a difficult time with his stepson, who reportedly cheated and stole from him. He was faithful and loving toward his wife and their marriage was stable and fulfilling. They entertained lavishly and frequently, as was the custom for their social station. Washington enjoyed the company of his friends, liked socializing, and was an exceptionally good host. So many guests passed through their home that husband and wife did not dine together alone for nearly twenty years. Though his tastes were sophisticated, Washington also had an earthy sense of humor growing out of his experiences as a planter and was not put off by sex.

A man of extraordinary height, strength, and bearing, at 6 feet, 2 inches, he was taller by a head than the average man of his day. There are mythical accounts of his physical strength—throwing a silver dollar across the Potomac, crushing walnuts in his bare hands, throwing a rock atop the 215-foot high Natural Bridge rock formation. Thomas Jefferson deemed him "the best horseman of his age" and "the most graceful figure that could be seen on horseback." Lafayette commented that he was "straight as an Indian" and that his "graceful bearing on horseback, his calm deportment which still retained a trace of displeasure . . . were all *calculated* [emphasis added] to inspire the highest degree of enthusiasm. . . . I thought then as now I have never beheld so superb a man." Benjamin Rush commented, "[He] has so much dignity in his deportment that you would distinguish him to be a general and a soldier from among ten thousand people."

Washington often rode as much as six to ten miles a day and was able to stay awake and in the saddle for days at a stretch. He also enjoyed watching horse races and placing bets. He took pleasure in playing billiards and cards, breeding dogs, going to the theater, dancing, and listening to music. He also had a particular fondness for fashion, almost to the point of dandyism. He meticulously attended to his grooming and dress, and he fretted if his clothes did not fit perfectly. One caller, visiting him at his home, spoke of him dressed in "purple satin, and his levees . . . were clad in black velvet; his hair in full dress, powdered and gathered behind in a large silk bag." With age, he dressed softer and more modestly.

Trouble was brewing as England refused to loosen its bonds on the colonies. On April 19, 1775, the Revolutionary War broke out. John Adams nominated Washington as Commander in Chief of the army, partly because of his previous military experience but also because of his reputation and character, because he was from Virginia (the largest colony), and because he had an independent fortune. Judging by his military record alone, he was grossly underqualified for such a high command. About to face the mightiest army in the world with a ragtag collection of farmers and tradesmen, he expressed concern for his reputation should he fail.

His experience while serving with the British army had taught him their weaknesses. Yet, he endured humiliating defeats and was nearly relieved of his command in the fall of 1777. He won only three of the nine battles he commanded—but he also won the war. Still, he always wanted to command a proper European fighting force, with colorful uniforms and orderly battle lines. Perhaps his greatest accomplishment was keeping an ill-equipped and unpaid army of conscripts together through the dead of winter as many of their own families were abandoned to the dangers of the frontier. Washington's character likely contributed to their steadfastness. So did the gallows he erected for deserters in plain sight of camp.

In 1781 the British army surrendered and the colonies won their independence, although skirmishes and other hostile actions continued for two more years. In the winter of 1782–83, the Continental Army waited uneasily for its long overdue pay. This was the first test of the new republic. A victorious army stood poised to march on the capital, and if necessary, to take over. But Washington was not Caesar. He counseled patience and restraint, reminding his men that democracies sometimes work slowly. Finding his efforts ineffectual, he recalled he had a letter in his pocket from a congressman promising payment. He fumbled for his glasses and apologized for the interruption: "I have already grown gray in the service of my country. I am now going blind." His officers were moved to tears. What nearly became the second American Revolution dissolved.

Rarely since classical times had a victorious general relinquished his command to the civil government and sought no position or advantage for himself. To some, this was his most laudatory accomplishment. However, soon after the war ended, problems arose among the colonies. The new states considered themselves independent, and some came near warring with each other. In 1787 delegates from the states met together in Philadelphia to draw up plans for a centralized government. Washington was by then the very symbol of the nation—"The Indispensable Man" who bestowed full legitimacy to the Constitutional Convention. He was elected chairman, and the assembly produced a Constitution with a strong central government headed by a president. The sixty-nine electors of the ten states that had by then ratified the Constitution unanimously elected him to that office on April 30, 1789.

Almost at once, unplanned political parties arose on the national scene. Politically, Washington seemed more in sympathy with Hamilton's Federalists, who favored a strong central government run by rich and intelligent men. Republicans like Jefferson dreamed of independent farmers ruled by a minimum of government. With both bickering groups represented in his cabinet, Washington frequently acted as mediator.

He was reelected unanimously in 1792, this time by fifteen states. He showed an aversion for foreign alliances and, in the eyes of the French, reneged on a commitment of support as Napoléon went to war with most of Europe in 1796. By doing so, he kept the new nation out of a war it was ill prepared to fight. His refusal to seek a third term demonstrated that even Washington, Father of his Country, would not be "president for life."

He retired to the tranquility of Mount Vernon. On December 12, 1799, he was caught in a snowstorm while riding and got pneumonia; he died two days later. His reputation was now so great that even British ships fired salvos in his honor at news of his death, and Britain's King William IV pronounced him, "the greatest man who ever lived."

Personality

Ten raters evaluated Washington; they showed moderate agreement on his overall profile. He scored very high on Conscientiousness (98.6th percentile) and Character (85th); there was little range of opinion on these factors, and on Neuroticism, among raters. Washington scored low on Openness (14th) and Agreeableness (16th), and his score on Extraversion (28th) was quite a bit below most presidents.

On the NEO Facets, Washington received the following scores:

His very high score on Achievement Striving reflects his willingness to endure discomfort and setbacks to achieve his goals, as he did on many occasions during the Revolutionary War. His virtues were those of a soldier and reflect competence, control, and leadership. Consistent with his role as father of his country, he scored first among presidents in measures of respect, esteem, and at least one

CHART 13.1
Washington's Scores on Character and the Big Five Traits

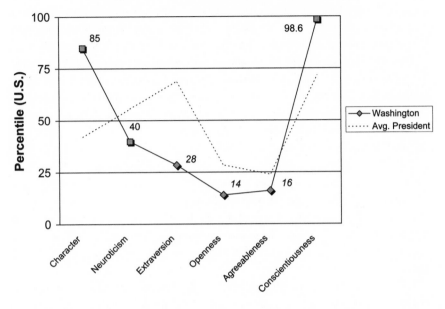

High	Percentile	Low	Percentile
Achievement Striving (C)	98	*Vulnerability* (N, -Ch)	5
Competence (C, Ch)	97	*Openness to Values*	5
Self-Discipline (C, Ch)	95	*Warmth* (E)	8
Deliberation (C, Ch)	94	*Tender-Mindedness* (A)	10
Assertiveness (E)	92		

index of Character and Conscientiousness. He scored lowest on Negative Valence (evil, sick, etc.).

On items, Washington's most outstanding quality was his particularly good sense of direction, perhaps developed by and undoubtedly an asset for his experience as a surveyor and soldier. He was also a good dancer, which reflected his longtime obsession with social graces and rituals.

He was not "talkative, verbose, wordy" and did not do most of the talking. He was not "casual, easygoing, informal, natural, relaxed" and did not brag. He would have rather been known as "just" than as "merciful" and was quite conscious of the impression he made on others. He rarely used superlatives, was not high-spirited or overtly happy, and had a reputation for being distant and cold. Once Pennsylvania's Gouverneur Morris shook hands with him and gently slapped him on the shoulder as they greeted. Washington "withdrew his hand, stepped suddenly back, fixed his eye on Morris for several minutes with an angry frown, until the latter retreated, abashed, and sought refuge in the crowd."[2]

Despite his personal reserve, people looked to him for advice and reassurance; they also looked to him for leadership. Unusual among introverted presidents, he was greatly admired and held in awe. Our raters perceived him to be "special," "impressive, remarkable," and "not an ordinary, everyday person." He was "high-ranking, powerful," worthy of admiration, and "excellent, first-rate." He was charismatic, forceful, and dominant.

He rarely acted before thinking and rarely indulged his impulses. He was cautious and planned carefully when he went on a trip. A French officer assigned to him admired the thoroughness with which he planned the route of his army and carefully listened to the locals regarding the terrain. But on one occasion, after an especially labored review, the officer exclaimed in frustration, "Oh, it is plain enough!" Washington scowled, went back to his analysis for a time, and then agreed.

He also was orderly in other ways; he kept his belongings neat and clean. When a task got difficult or work piled up, he did not look for something else to do; he got the job done. He was not "erratic, inconsistent, unpredictable"—he did not tolerate unethical behavior in others. He *was* reliable and dependable, efficient and effective, and very competent. He was known for his good sense and judgment and was "wise."

According to biographer G. W. Nordham, a paradox of Washington's personality was that he was mentally very cautious but physically adventurous. He was "brave, courageous, and daring," able to make good decisions under adversity, and capable in a crisis. He had fewer fears than most people, did not experience feelings of worthlessness, and did not act in ways that undermined or frustrated his own goals and desires. He was not hypocritical.

Miscellaneous Observations

Despite his social reserve, Washington was "good company." He had "innumerable friends" but few if any close ones. He had hardly any enemies. Throughout his life, he had an eye for attractive women, liked to flirt, and kept notes in his diary regarding the number and comeliness of women at his parties. He strongly believed in the principle of fairness in every human relationship,[3] teamwork, unity, self-discipline, and the subordination of personal interests to the public good. He believed that America should always be a haven for the poor and oppressed.

Several of our raters commented on his conviction of his worth, or even superiority, combined with his "successful profession of humility." He rarely undertook a public responsibility without voicing doubts about his worthiness and concern about his reputation should he fail. He liked uniforms and indications of rank (an obvious source of pride and esteem) but was uncomfortable when he received effusive praise. On some such occasions, he actually fled in embarrassment.

Though his score was not high enough to be listed in our table, Washington did score high on the NEO Self-Consciousness scale. He felt inferior to college-educated leaders such as John Adams, Jefferson, and Madison. Explaining why he did not complete an autobiography and discouraged others to write of his life, he wrote: (1) "a consciousness of a defective education;" (2) "Any memoirs of my life . . . would hurt my feelings rather than tickle my pride while I lived."

Some perceived him as "remarkably sensitive to hostile criticism" as president. "I think he feels those things more than any person I have ever met," Jefferson observed. One item from our questionnaire asks about one's adequacy as a person—whether conscious or not. Seven of the ten raters indicated that Washington had such doubts, at a level greater than two-thirds of other presidents. Two raters strongly rejected this judgment. Taken together, we believe the data suggest Washington had a precarious sense of self-esteem (less extreme than Wilson) that was heavily dependent on his success and reputation.[4] In fact, biographer George Washington Nordham indicated he was prone to melancholy and self-deprecation.

Washington's anger was also frequently noted. "[His] temper was naturally irritable and high-toned, and when it broke its bounds, he was most tremendous in his wrath," noted Jefferson. When Gen. Charles Lee disobeyed orders to attack, explaining American irregulars would not stand the British bayonets, Washington exploded, "You damned poltroon—you have never tried them!" Another display occurred when he was told that Gen. Arthur Sinclair had disregarded warnings about an Indian ambush and was massacred with his troops. Washington paced and cursed Sinclair's incompetence in private, then, regaining his composure, said, "General Sinclair will have full justice," and instructed his aide that his statements should not leave the room. These explosions were the exception. By nearly all accounts, he typically kept his anger in "wonderful control."

Despite Washington's devotion to his persona, several factors distorted his image for posterity. The first of these was his appearance. Though most know he had false teeth, he did not go from a full set of healthy teeth to dentures overnight. He likely had unattractive teeth for a considerable time and, for fear of exposing them, avoided smiling. His early dentures did not fit well and probably produced discomfort and some distortion of his mouth. Gilbert Stuart's pique over a misunderstanding may have led the artist to deliberately depict his mouth in an unflattering manner in his famous portrait. A life mask, designed to capture his features more objectively, was compromised when Washington laughed during the molding process. Lastly, the famous painting of him surrendering his army to the civilian government portrays him in a peculiar, ungainly pose.

Washington's views on religion are open to interpretation. DeGregorio wrote that religion played little role in his life: "He fashioned a moral code based on his own code of right and wrong and adhered to it rigidly. He referred rarely to God or Jesus in his writings, but rather to Providence, a rather amorphous supernatural substance that controlled men's lives. He strongly believed in fate."[5] Charles Meister reported that he turned to prayer to cope with stress, prayed often, credited God for his successes, and said that without religion, America would be lost.

As a young man, Washington's "ambition for wealth made him acquisitive and sometimes contentious." Even when financially secure in later life, "he would insist on payment of every farthing due him" and was determined "to get everything that he honestly could."

Washington Described

"[He is] polite with dignity, affable without familiarity, distant without haughtiness, grave without austerity, modest, wise, and good."—Abigail Adams

"He excites . . . respect which seems to spring from the sole idea that the safety of each individual is attached to his person. . . . The goodness and benevolence are evident in all that surrounds him, but the confidence that he calls forth never occasions improper familiarity."—Francois Jean De Chastellux (author, philosopher, soldier)

"[He] overcame ugly youthful ambition and greed to become what the people wanted from him."—biographer Lance Banning

"His mind was great and powerful, without being of the very first order; his penetration strong . . . and, as far as he saw, no judgment was ever sounder. It was slow in operation, being little aided by invention or imagination, but sure in conclusion. . . . Perhaps the strongest feature in his character was prudence, never acting until every circumstance, every consideration was maturely weighed

. . . but once decided, going through with his purpose, whatever obstacles opposed. His integrity was most pure, his justice the most inflexible I have ever known. . . . He was, indeed, in every sense of the words, a wise, a good, and a great man."—Thomas Jefferson

"[He] has so happy a faculty of appearing to accommodate and yet carrying his point that if he were not one of the best intentioned men in the world, he might be a very dangerous one."—Abigail Adams

"A conscientious and determined individual whose sound judgment won the highest respect because he sought out, listened to, and respected various viewpoints."—biographer G. W. Nordham

President Washington

Ridings and McIver found Washington to be the third highest rated president, just behind FDR and ahead of Jefferson. He was ranked first in Appointments, second on Character and Integrity, but seventh in Political Skill—his lowest rating.

He made peace with the Indians as well as with Britain and Spain. He put down the Whiskey Rebellion of 1794, a revolt by Pennsylvania farmers over government taxation of alcohol distilled from their grain. Perhaps his greatest accomplishments were the precedents he set. Ever mindful that he was the first and the model for presidents that followed, he held himself to the highest standards of integrity and fairness. Some of his positions, based solely on the politics of his day, remained in force into the twentieth century sustained by the weight of his precedent.

He was not an activist president—he "kept prima donnas together, otherwise did little," noted a respondent in the Ridings and McIver study. Yet, given his stature and the untested liberties of the new republic, Washington's restraint was reassuring. "His 'great looming presence' . . . allowed the roots of government to take to the soil of nationhood."

Washington's personality has two or three clear strengths for the presidency (see Chart 13.2). He was highly Competent (capable, prudent), even compared to other presidents, and he was goal oriented and persistent in meeting his aims (high Achievement Striving). He was self-sufficient and capable of handling his problems (low Vulnerability). However, he was relatively lacking in Positive Emotions and Tender-Mindedness. Our analyses indicate that Washington, based solely on his personality traits, would be expected both to be a slightly above average president and to show solid Ethics on the Job.

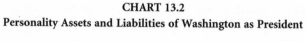

CHART 13.2
Personality Assets and Liabilities of Washington as President

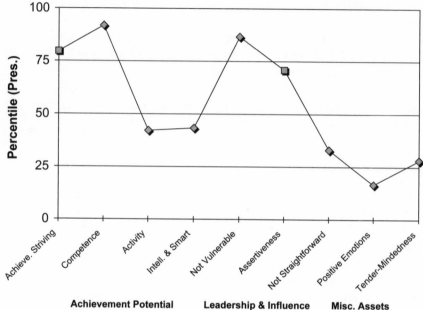

Behavior as President (our data)

Washington scored second highest among presidents on Interpersonal and Deliberative leadership styles. Consistent with historian polls, he got high ratings for his job performance, particularly for the quality of his work. He carefully considered opinions before making them public, was charismatic, and was recognized as a world figure. He did not place political success over effective policy, and his personality matched the needs of the nation during his presidency. He relied on his staff, deciding among options formulated by talented advisers who included Jefferson and Alexander Hamilton.

Washington in Perspective

Parson Weems, Washington's first biographer, called him a demigod and claimed he possessed all of the classic virtues: "It is hardly an exaggeration to say that Washington was as pious as Numa; just as Aristides; temperate as Epictetus; patriotic as Regulus; in giving public trusts, impartial as Severus . . ." and so on for modesty, prudence, courage, and devotion to law and liberty. Many anecdotes told by Weems, such as the famous cherry tree incident, now are regarded as fanciful. Washington was easily the most admired man in America for its first one hundred years and has more U.S. cities and streets named after him than any other man. When a character based on Washington appeared in a popular play *(The Virginians)*, there was a public outcry at portrayal of him as an ordinary human being. Then as now, there was a strong perception that he was not like other men.

To understand Washington requires an appreciation of the eighteenth-century emphasis on "reputation." A man's reputation was his most valuable possession. Like his carriage, it required care and occasional polishing. "Character" was a role one played until the actor became the role. But, character was also how others judged one's role—it was both the performance and the reviews. Washington, judged by his reviews, performed masterfully. He scrupulously edited his correspondence with an eye to how history would judge him, and his obsession with his reputation was obvious enough to be used tactically by those wishing to influence him.

George Washington was the most important man in the United States for nearly twenty-five years in the era of Benjamin Franklin, Alexander Hamilton, and Thomas Jefferson. When our raters describe him repeatedly by "impressive, remarkable" and other such terms, are they referring to his personality or his achievements? Are their perceptions skewed by the adoration his compatriots bestowed upon him?

Normally, willingness to rate someone in superlative terms is related to other positive personality traits, particularly Competence, Achievement Striving, Assertiveness, Openness to Ideas, and Activity, and the Big Five factors of Conscientiousness, Openness, and Extraversion. Washington was not outstanding on many of these qualities; he scored high on some but low on others. He certainly showed fewer of these virtues than TR, Thomas Jefferson, or even Jimmy Carter, none of whom receive the same level of admiration. But Washington's accomplishments were monumental: defeat of the world's only superpower (Great Britain) against all odds; the first victorious general since Cincinnatus to renounce political power; and the first and unanimously elected leader of the world's first democracy in eighteen hundred years. On his deathbed and grasping his own legacy, Napoléon lamented, "They wanted me to be another Washington."

These findings suggest several possibilities:

✔ That his exceptional accomplishments are more important than his personality traits in creating the perception of greatness,

✔ That his personality *was* unique, perhaps by his continued self-improvement,

✔ That his devotion to his reputation was highly successful, creating an unmatched public image that was at some variance with the actual man,

✔ That those around him were so moved by admiration that the perception of greatness is inextricably interwoven with Washington's memory,

✔ A combination of the above.

The Washington Monument, so bold and stark, seems a symbolic representation of his character, and contrasts dramatically with the benevolence and the cultural grandness of the Lincoln and Jefferson Memorials, respectively. Washington most resembles Eisenhower (r = .42), Madison (r = .28), and Coolidge (r = .22). He is least like Clinton (r = −.41) and Harding (r = −.39).

WASHINGTON VS. EISENHOWER: COMPARING TWO GENERALS

To help put Washington in perspective, we compared him with the president he most resembled. Both Washington and Eisenhower rated very high on Conscientiousness and only a bit lower on Character (see Chart 13.3). Eisenhower scored considerably higher on Extraversion and a bit higher on both Openness and Agreeableness.

On the NEO Facet Scales, Washington and Eisenhower scored generally high on all of the Conscientiousness facets and Assertiveness and low on Vulnerability, Openness to Values, and Tender-Mindedness (see Table 13.1). As presidents, both carefully considered opinions before making them public and were seen as world figures. Both saw difficult jobs through, were capable in a crisis, and had fewer fears than most people. Both were known for their good sense and judgment.

Eisenhower was rated considerably higher on Warmth and Positive Emotions, and moderately higher on Modesty, Openness to Feelings, and Openness to Ideas. Washington was rated higher on Self-Consciousness. Eisenhower was high-spirited and happy, cheerful, and optimistic; Washington was not. Eisenhower enjoyed talking to people more than Washington did and was average among presidents in his interest in abstract ideas and theories. Washington was more interested in women. Eisenhower was more stubborn and hardheaded and an "average, ordinary person"; he put greater effort into doing his work carefully and felt more able to handle most of his problems.

CHART 13.3
Washington and Eisenhower Compared

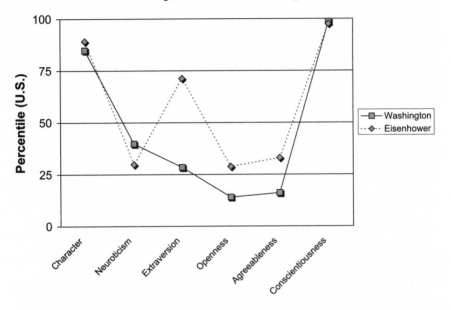

TABLE 13.1
Washington and Eisenhower Compared

	Eisenhower High	Eisenhower Low
Washington High	Achievement Striving, Self-Discipline, Competence, Deliberation, Assertiveness	NONE
Washington Low	NONE	Vulnerability, Openness to Values, Tender-Mindedness

BILL CLINTON

Bill Clinton was named William Jefferson Blythe at birth, but changed his name to Clinton as a gesture to his stepfather, Roger Clinton. Bill Blythe, his biological father, was a classic traveling salesman and lady-killer. Married four times before thirty, he was so charming that he managed to avoid animosity among his wives and past loves. He was killed in a freak accident at age twenty-nine, when he was thrown from his car, knocked unconscious, and drowned in a few inches of water. Bill Clinton never knew his father but was haunted by a sense of urgency—a vague feeling that life is unpredictable and sometimes unexpectedly short.

After Blythe's death, Bill's free-spirited mother, Virginia, met and married Roger Clinton, an alcoholic car dealer. Roger relied on his brother for help in his career and never really achieved success. He also became an abusive drunk, once firing a gun in the direction of his frightened wife. Virginia left Roger and filed charges after the incident, but eventually returned to him. There seems little other explanation than that she loved him. Bill did too—or at least he tried to.

Young Clinton was an exceptional child from an early age, showing a remarkable ability to reach out to others and solve interpersonal problems. When he was about eight, his mom sent him to the store on Thanksgiving Day to pick up extra food. Clinton returned without the food but with a new friend he found at the bus stop. Pointing to the bag the boy was holding, he asked, "Whoever heard of having a big bag of Fritos on Thanksgiving Day? Mother, we aren't going to stand for that." His mother nodded and reported later that "he was forever bringing people home to eat." There are many other anecdotes of Clinton's exceptional concern and charity toward others.

Billy Clinton was big for his age, but fat and clumsy. In one traumatic incident, he recalls being attacked repeatedly by a sheep and being too slow and awkward to escape. Living with his grandparents while his mother studied for her nursing degree, he learned to read by the age of three. His grandparents ran a grocery store in the black section of Hope, Arkansas, and there he learned his first lessons in racial tolerance. He was surrounded by a supportive network of aunts, uncles, and cousins—but his mother was gone much of the time. Hillary Rodham Clinton cited conflict between his mother and grandmother as an important trauma in his development.

As he grew older, Clinton's talents became obvious. He won first prize in the state saxophone competition and formed a three-piece jazz band. He was a National Merit Scholarship semifinalist and graduated fourth in his high school class of 323. But he was no bookworm. One classmate recalled him as the kind of person who "would come up to everyone new in high school and say: 'Hi, how are you? My name's Bill Clinton and I'm running for something.' We always thought, well, someday Bill will be president."

By his late teens, he was already a semiprofessional politician, greatly in demand for speeches at local meetings. In high school he was president of his junior class, and at Georgetown University he was elected class president in his freshman and sophomore years. While in college, he worked at the office of William Fulbright, Arkansas's junior senator and chair of the powerful Senate Foreign Relations Committee. Fulbright's criticism of the Vietnam War greatly influenced Clinton.

At Georgetown University Clinton took required courses in comparative religion and philosophy. His instructors were sometimes eccentric, often outstanding, with a gift for enlivening different perspectives. From them, Clinton learned to look at the world from more than one angle. In college he "exhibited all the signs of someone who was on the way somewhere else and in a hurry to get there. If he had not been so totally amiable, genuinely kind, open, and friendly, he would have been heartily disliked by one and all, but he had absolutely no pretence about him and that, of course, made him irresistible."[6] In addition to his studies, he helped a blind freshman learn his way around campus and worked as a counselor in a student clinic for alcoholics. He also did volunteer relief work in Washington after the riots following Martin Luther King's assassination. He graduated from Georgetown with a degree in International Affairs in 1968 at the height of the Vietnam War.

Clinton attended Oxford University for two years as a Rhodes scholar, studying politics, philosophy, and economics and focusing on the Communist Bloc in his second year. He helped organize peace demonstrations and smoked marijuana but was never a heavy drug user—perhaps because of his experiences with his stepfather. While at Oxford, "his circle marveled at how he juggled his love affairs without apparent collision," a statement highly reminiscent of his father's romantic style. "It seemed for a time there that he was going after and getting every woman who came within reach," including the girlfriends of friends.[7]

Clinton was classified 1-A for the draft while at Oxford, but his uncle helped him secure a slot with the Army Reserve Training Corps. Given a deferment, he later reneged on his Reserve enrollment after he drew a high number in the 1969 draft lottery. In 1992 he earnestly told the Los Angeles Times, "It was just a fluke" that he did not get drafted. "I certainly had no leverage to get special treatment from the draft board."[8]

He met Hillary Rodham, daughter of a staunch Republican family, at Yale Law School in 1970. They seemed an odd couple—the talkative and affable country boy and the intense, awkward city girl. Additionally, she was not his mother's type; Virginia thought he should date cheerleaders and beauty queens. Bill dated attractive girls, but he respected Hillary; they married in 1975. Though Virginia and Hillary did not hit it off and the marriage has been tumultuous, Clinton still holds his wife in awe.

Clinton ran for Congress in 1974 and lost but was elected Arkansas attorney general in 1976. He was a strong consumer advocate and a supporter of environmental causes. In 1978 he became the youngest governor in the country at thirty-two. His agenda was ambitious and progressive and his staff young, eager, and inexperienced. His transplanted wife refused to use her married name, irking many Arkansans. Clinton was turned out in the next election. He reflected painfully on his mistakes and practiced law for the next two years. The people of Arkansas returned him to the governor's mansion in the next four elections.[9] Education was a top priority, with Hillary helping him push through tougher standards for schools and a basic skills test for all teachers. In 1986 he was ranked the fifth most effective governor in the nation, and in 1991, the most effective. That year, he resigned as Arkansas governor and announced he would run for president, facing a then-formidable George H. W. Bush fresh off his Desert Storm victory over Iraq.

As graphic recordings substantiated rumors of an affair with Gennifer Flowers, a former nightclub singer, the 1992 Republican campaign refrain became "Bill Clinton doesn't have the character to be president."

Personality

Three experts rated Clinton. They showed very good agreement on his overall profile, on Character, and all the Big Five scales except Neuroticism (see Chart 13.4). He scored very high on Extraversion (99.9th percentile) and very low on Character (2nd) and Conscientiousness (5th). He also scored quite a bit above the average president on Openness (82nd), although generalists did not agree with this assessment. They also saw Clinton as higher in Conscientiousness but still quite low compared to most presidents.

On the NEO Facet Scales, he had many scores that were high or low compared to most Americans, as shown in the table on page 285.

He scored highest of all presidents on Impulsivity, Excitement Seeking, Tender-Mindedness, and Openness to Values. He scored lowest of all on Self-Discipline and Order, and second lowest on Conscientiousness, Dutifulness, and several measures of character.

Clinton most resembles Kennedy ($r = .57$), FDR ($r = .51$), LBJ ($r = .32$), and Harding ($r = .31$). He is least like Coolidge ($r = -.45$), Washington ($r = -.41$), and Hoover ($r = -.28$).

In this section, we describe how Clinton was like Kennedy, Harding, and LBJ and how he was different.[10] The men Clinton most resembled were all Extraverted, high on Impulsiveness, Gregariousness, Openness to Feelings, and Excitement Seeking, and all of them were reported to have had multiple affairs while in the White House. Nonetheless, only one item from our questionnaire meets

CHART 13.4

Clinton's Scores on Character and the Big Five Traits

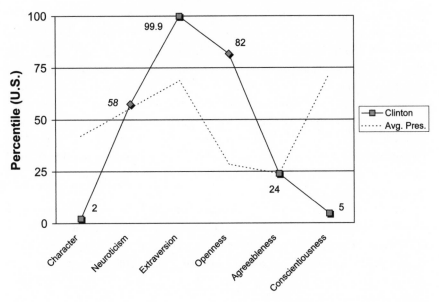

High	Percentile	Low	Percentile
Impulsiveness (N, -Ch)	99.8	Dutifulness (C, Ch)	0.4
Tender-Mindedness (A)	98.9	Straightforwardness (A, Ch)	1.4
Gregariousness (E)	98	Order (C)	4
Positive Emotions (E)	98	Self-Discipline (C, Ch)	5
Openness to Feelings	95	Modesty (A, Ch)	8
Excitement Seeking (E)	92	Deliberation (C, Ch)	9
Activity (E)	92		
Openness to Values	90		
Warmth (E)	90		

our criteria for all three men: "Has done things just for excitement." All three men were low on Deliberation, Dutifulness, and Straightforwardness.

We first show how Clinton compares to each of these men on the Big Five and Character, plotting scores of two presidents at a time. We then report personality and ability scales on which the two men being compared score alike and differently, then do the same for individual items on our questionnaire.

CLINTON VS. JFK

Clinton's identification with Kennedy is well known. It is not surprising that they are among the most similar of presidents and share many traits. On the Big Five factors and Character, the greatest difference between Clinton and Kennedy (and other Extraverted presidents) is on Neuroticism, where Kennedy scores low (26th percentile) and Clinton average (Chart 13.5). Both men were much more Open to Experience than the average Extraverted president, but Clinton outscored Kennedy on Agreeableness. Clinton was very talkative, wordy, and verbose, but Kennedy was no more so than other presidents. Both scored high on most of the Extraversion Facet Scales (Table 13.2). Each clearly had an appetite for thrills and excitement. They openly showed their feelings and were optimistic, cheerful, and outgoing and friendly.

Very Open to Feelings and to Values, neither man believed that controversial speakers mislead or confuse students. Clinton was particularly observant and took much greater pleasure in solving brain-teasing puzzles. Both were quick to grasp ideas and problems, but Kennedy scored much higher on the Openness to

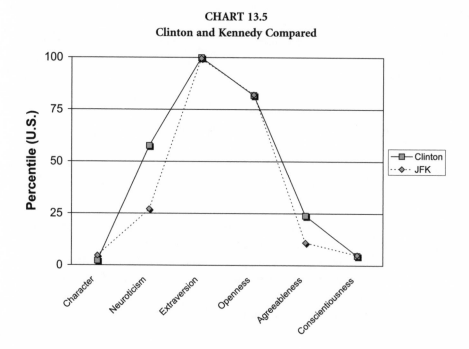

CHART 13.5
Clinton and Kennedy Compared

TABLE 13.2
Clinton and Kennedy Compared

	Kennedy High	Kennedy Low
Clinton High	Impulsive, Positive Emotions, Open to Feelings, Excitement Seeking, Tender-Minded, Gregarious, Active	NONE
Clinton Low	NONE	Dutiful, Straightforward, Deliberative

Fantasy scale, while Clinton was much more prone to value open-mindedness over devotion to principles and ideals.

Both scored low on Conscientiousness and most of its facets, but only one Conscientiousness item, which usually reflects high Conscientiousness, met our inclusion criterion for both men: Neither was aimless or unambitious. In fact, a related item provided one of the strongest contrasts between them. Clinton showed an exceptional tendency not to keep promises: "He talked a good game and he had big ideas, but he never followed through. . . . His word is no good," concluded Edwin Dunaway, a liberal Arkansas activist.

Very low scores on Straightforwardness combined with high scores on Tender-Mindedness characterized both men. So, while neither had a hard time deceiving people, they both felt that society can never do too much for the poor or elderly. But Clinton definitely *did not appear* straightforward and honest in dealing with others, hence, his "Slick Willie" reputation. Kennedy was average among presidents; though he also manipulated and dissembled, he was not perceived as doing so. Kennedy actually was a bit better at keeping his word than most presidents. Clinton was very prone to blame others for problems and was decidedly not hardheaded and tough-minded. Kennedy was average on both qualities.

Both men got high scores on Impulsivity, but no items met our inclusion criteria. Kennedy differed from Clinton by scoring low on Self-Consciousness and Vulnerability, while Clinton was a bit above average. Kennedy was below average on Angry Hostility; Clinton in the upper quarter. In contrast to Kennedy and most other presidents, Clinton was very unpredictable and changeable. A symptom of his Impulsivity: he would eat too much when having his favorite foods. But he did not suffer poor health during critical periods in office, while Kennedy showed a tendency to do so. As presidents, both men, and Harding as well, were charismatic, tended to their images, and were not shy or awkward in public.

CLINTON VS. HARDING

Widely regarded as the least intelligent and effective of all presidents, Harding's likeness to Clinton may surprise many readers. Yet, the similarities are clearly present. Chart 13.6 displays their personality scores, showing high concordance on Extraversion, Neuroticism, and Conscientiousness but a large difference on Openness and a moderate one on Agreeableness. Compared to the other Actors Clinton scores much higher on Openness and lower on Character.

Harding and Clinton scored high on many facets of Extraversion (Table 13.3). Both were warm and self-disclosing, outgoing, friendly to those they just met, and not detached, secretive, or reserved. Each enjoyed being part of a crowd and showed his emotions in his facial and body language. Neither had a reputation for being distant or cold, nor was "bashful, shy, timid." They preferred to do things with others rather than alone and made friends easily. But Clinton scored high on Assertiveness and Activity, did most of the talking, and was very Active. Harding was average in those qualities.

The two differed most on Openness to Experience. Both scored high on Openness to Feelings and empathized easily with others, but Clinton *definitely* valued open-mindedness and tolerance over adherence to principles and ideals; Harding's preference was moderately the other way. He clearly *did not* believe policies should change with the times, while Clinton did. Harding was conventional and traditional; Clinton plainly was not. Clinton was *not* conservative in values and did not believe that controversial speakers confuse or delude students. Clinton also scored much higher on one of our measures of general intellectual ability; Harding scored higher on Spatial and Musical Abilities. Lastly, Clinton was rated as "impressive, remarkable," while Harding most definitely was not.

Turning to Agreeableness, both men scored low on Straightforwardness, but Harding scored quite high on Trust, Altruism, and Compliance, but low on Tender-Mindedness. Clinton's scores were generally low in the areas in which

TABLE 13.3
Clinton and Harding Compared

	Harding High	Harding Low
Clinton High	*Optimism*, Gregariousness, Positive Emotions, Excitement Seeking, Warmth, Impulsivity, Openness to Feelings	Openness to Values, Openness to Ideas
Clinton Low	**NONE**	Dutifulness, Deliberation, Straightforwardness

CHART 13.6
Clinton and Harding Compared

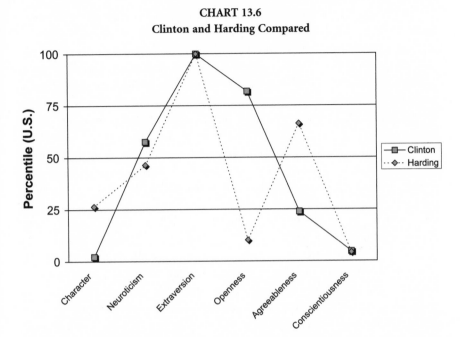

Harding was high, and of course, he scored very high on Tender-Mindedness. Unlike Harding, he definitely sympathized with panhandlers and believed political leaders should focus more on human problems.

Though both men scored low on Conscientiousness, Clinton scored high on Achievement Striving, where Harding was one of the lowest of all presidents (at about the U.S. average). Despite low scores on Conscientious and Dutifulness, he was somewhat more punctual than most presidents. Clinton was *not at all* prompt and punctual. Both had few traits related to Neuroticism except for high Impulsivity. Both undeniably had difficulty resisting temptation; Clinton was especially prone to indulge his impulses. Neither often felt self-conscious. As presidents, Clinton and Harding shared the features given under the section for Kennedy. But Harding was suspicious of reformers, while Clinton definitely was not.

CLINTON VS. LYNDON JOHNSON

LBJ and Clinton received similar scores on Extraversion and Character. However, Clinton was much more Open to Experience and considerably lower on

Conscientiousness than LBJ and the Dominators as a group. LBJ was a close match to the typical Dominator, though a bit more Extraverted and more Neurotic, differing significantly from Clinton.

Clinton and LBJ both were low on Character and some aspects of Conscientiousness. To an exceptional degree, both were willing to compromise on principles and clearly did *not* behave consistent with their own values. They also *weren't* moralistic. Neither was lazy or slothful. But there were also huge differences between the two: Clinton was exceedingly "indecisive, wishy-washy" and had great difficulty making up his mind.

The Arkansas legislature passed a bill making donations to colleges and universities 100 percent tax-deductible. Clinton vetoed it on the advice of his financial advisers, fearing the loss of tax revenue would bankrupt the government. He was reminded that he had not only supported the bill but also promised a group of college presidents to sign it. He hastily retrieved the vetoed document in the middle of the night before it could be recorded to smudge out his veto stamp. When the Department of Finance revolted, Clinton was forced to call a special session of the legislature to repeal the act. Since this fiasco, Clinton "will not make a decision until he's studied it from every angle known to man."[11] Johnson, on the other hand, was decisive to a fault and had less trouble making up his mind than most presidents.

Clinton was also extraordinarily unable to get organized, or at least to create the appearance of order, whereas Johnson was more organized than most.

Both men scored high on Impulsivity, were highly prone to indulge their cravings, and were self-indulgent. They also had a taste for excitement, and neither was even-tempered or emotionally unexpressive. However, LBJ scored high on the NEO Anxiety, Depression, and Self-Consciousness Facet Scales, while Clinton was average.

Neither had a hard time misleading others and both were willing to trick people to get their way. Both felt that society should do as much as it can to help the less fortunate and believed political leaders should attend more to the human dimension of issues. Both believed social policies should change with the times, and as presidents, were not suspicious of reformers. However, LBJ scored low on the NEO Trust scale and was distrustful of people, whereas Clinton scored above average and trusted even his political foes.[12] He was flexible and optimistic, whereas Johnson was average in those qualities. Clinton was not known as cold or distant while LBJ tended in that direction.

Though both men scored high on Extraversion, they shared only a few characteristics from this factor. Both did most of the talking in conversations and rarely let others speak more than them.

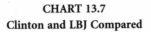

CHART 13.7
Clinton and LBJ Compared

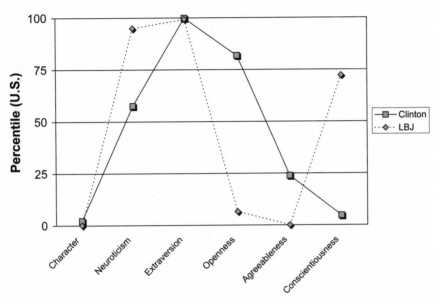

TABLE 13.4
Clinton and LBJ Compared

	LBJ High	LBJ Low
Clinton High	Impulsivity, Gregariousness, Activity, Openness to Feelings, Excitement Seeking, Tender-Mindedness, Achievement Striving	Openness to Ideas, Openness to Values
Clinton Low	NONE	Straightforwardness, Dutifulness, Modesty, Deliberation

CLINTON ALONE

Clinton had some notable qualities unrelated to how he was like or unlike Harding, Kennedy, or LBJ. He was given extraordinarily low (0.1 percentile)[13] ratings on the following items: "has self-discipline," "dependable, reliable, responsible," and "paces himself to get things done on time." He was *clearly not* "orderly, organized, systematic" and, *much* more than most presidents, was often late, delayed committing himself and taking action, and liked to keep his options open. He had an exceptional lack of self-control and expressed his emotions impulsively. During a campaign stop, he was aghast to learn a campaign worker had told local officials that townspeople weren't welcome. He ordered the worker found: "I want him dead, dead! I want him horsewhipped!" Later he softened a bit, ordering that the culprit be fired when found. When it turned out to be a lower level campaign worker Clinton knew personally, he said, "Damn it. I hope he gets a real talking to."[14] He was very likely to act before thinking, and often regretted it later; he *did not* plan carefully when taking a trip.

Clinton definitely attributed failures to temporary problems or circumstances, but he was also highly inclined to seek reassurance from others. He *did not* behave the same way with everyone. He was not bigoted or prejudiced; *not* miserly or stingy, *nor* "cold, impersonal, insensitive." He much preferred to be known as merciful than just. He would rather spend time at a crowded beach than at an isolated cabin in the woods, and as we all know, he was interested in women.[15] He had personal magnetism and was known as warm and friendly. He enjoyed talking to people a great deal, did not avoid crowds, and could speak well in public without preparation.

Clinton learned many different things quickly and was good at visualizing situations and recognizing faces. He liked pondering ideas and theories, and he did not judge people in conventional terms. As president, he was willing to make compromises and did not base decisions on willfulness, nervousness, or egotism.

Miscellaneous Observations

Clinton has sometimes been called a man without any defining beliefs or values, but his dedication to racial equality contradicts this assessment. A complex person, he seemed prone to contradiction:

- ✔ A Rhodes scholar with down-to-earth tastes, who once identified himself as "Bubba" on a radio program.
- ✔ A champion of sexual equality, who sexually used women and let his staff discredit them if they did not keep quiet.
- ✔ A man whose avowed goal was "to do good in the world," who lied to even those closest to him.
- ✔ A man of quick and penetrating insight who seemed to lose perspective when observing himself.
- ✔ A broad-minded cosmopolitan, who turned to religious counselors, rather than therapists, to address his personal weaknesses.

✔ A commander in chief who evaded military service.
✔ A man with a questionable capacity for real intimacy, who hugged almost everybody.

Several factors probably contribute to Clinton's seeming lack of a defining core. Despite a genuine devotion to the Baptist faith, his family, hometown, and role models provided endless exceptions, interpretations, or outright contradictions to Baptist teachings. Additionally, he grew up in the 1960s, with that decade's emphasis on tolerance and questioning of traditional authority and morals. His gregarious nature and personal travels exposed him to many different people and cultures. Finally, he showed above-average capacity for not acknowledging or resolving intellectual or personal contradictions. Yet, he had moments of self-awareness—in *Monica's Story*, he told Lewinski, as he broke up with her, of his struggle to be a good person and a better husband. His approach to politics, and to life in general, may have been to find and accept achievable compromises.

CLINTON DESCRIBED

"He has an unlimited, unbridled confidence in his ability, a vast compassion that is genuine, a thirst for success that causes him to compromise or change when he ought to stand firm."—Ernest Dumas, author of *The Clintons of Arkansas*

"He crawls into your soul for a minute or two, and then he looks over your shoulder for the next guy in the room he's going to do the same thing to."—Max Brantley, editor, *Arkansas Times*

"Bill Clinton is the larger than life embodiment of the American dream. A small town boy made good, he overcame the absence of his deceased father and the abuses of an alcoholic stepfather to excel as a model student. Through the force of his intellect, personality and dogged hard work, he rose to the presidency."—Barbara Perry, Sweet Briar College

"He needs to get a hard slap of reality in the face every once in a while. He has an arrogant side."—Robert Savage, University of Arkansas

PRESIDENT CLINTON

Though it's too early to assess Clinton's standing with history, the Ridings and McIver poll rated him as the twenty-third best president. His ranking was just below G. W. H. Bush and ahead of Hoover. His highest score was in Political Skill (twentieth), his lowest in Character and Integrity (thirty-eighth).

Our analyses indicate that Clinton, based on his personality assets alone, should have made a better-than-average president, perhaps in the upper quarter of the ranks. His strengths (see Chart 13.8) included Tender-Mindedness, enthusiasm and optimism (Positive Emotions), high energy level (Activity), low Straightforwardness, and intellectual ability.

Despite a generally positive profile for presidential success, his personality scores also predicted problems with ethical and moral behavior on the job. Our specialists rated Clinton before Paula Jones and Monica Lewinski began talking to the press. His ratings might be different if collected later. But his personality ratings still predicted ethical problems, even before they became public. Even then he showed poor judgment (low Competence) and high Vulnerability (reversed in chart).

Smart Man, Foolish Choices

One of the mysteries of Clinton's personality has been his continued penchant for getting into trouble, often through sexual escapades. Few people doubt that

CHART 13.8
Personality Assets and Liabilities of Clinton as President

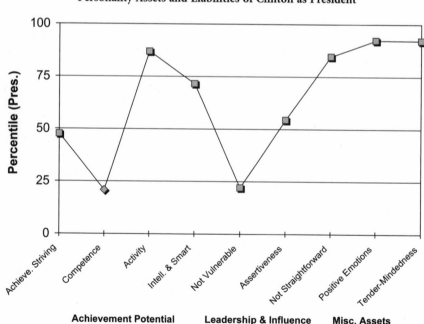

he is a very bright man, yet he behaves much like someone who does not think ahead or appreciate the consequences of his actions. Some psychologists have argued that the primary cause of many social ills are attributable to the low IQs of those involved. We believe a number of factors contribute to Clinton's misbehavior—none of which involve IQ.

Genetics: As we discussed in the first chapter, there is considerable evidence that about 50 percent of the personality differences among people are inherited. This holds true for the Big Five factors and their facets and presumably would be true for broader constructs such as character. Infidelity is more common among people low in Conscientiousness.

Another approach is to examine Clinton's parents for evidence of their sexual behavior and tendencies. Bill Blythe, his father, was an epic ladies' man. His mother has been described as a "party girl," and at least some neighbors suspected that she bore Clinton from an illicit relationship. When character issues surfaced about her son, she responded that she thought he was doing pretty well compared to her. Thus, though there is little direct evidence of infidelity, there is substantial evidence for both parents (see below) of a personality style that is decidedly not bound by rules, tradition, self-restraint, or principle.

Environment: In Clinton's family and his hometown, there was very little moral bedrock on the issue of fidelity. Successful men often had a woman on the side, and Roger Clinton, Bill's stepfather, was no model of restraint. Before they married, Virginia Kelly was tipped off that Roger was entertaining a stewardess in his apartment. She did not catch them, but the evidence was clear and convincing. She married him anyway over the strong objections of her family, who even threatened to take custody of Billy.

Characterized as "a notorious womanizer" himself, Roger often drunkenly accused his wife of infidelity. On one occasion, he beat a man "to a bloody pulp" in a public dance hall out of jealousy. A *New York Times* article summarized Virginia Kelly's perspective on morality: "The right people—herself, her family and friends—couldn't really do wrong."[16] This was largely the ethos of Hot Springs at the time that Clinton was developing his values.

"For nearly a century the little city in the gorge was a fount of vice and official venality, gambling and prostitution, protection rackets, and other graft that constituted a backroom criminal economy far larger than even the bustling open commerce along the Row." "A place where gangsters were cool, rules were meant to be bent, and money and power—however you got them—were the total measure of a man," according to Clinton's mother.[17]

Attitudes toward women and fidelity were also clear; drinking and wife abuse seemed to be a part of the culture of Hot Springs in those days. "The men got away with anything they wanted to. They had no respect for women. They all had mistresses. They all beat their wives. . . . The men had a way of compartmentalizing their lives. Honesty was never a trait with them."[18]

Lastly, Clinton's well-publicized identification with Kennedy bears comment. At the time Clinton came to Georgetown, Kennedy was being lionized in the school paper as "the ideal embodiment of manhood of our time." It was about this time that Clinton chose politics as his life's work. Given the close resemblance of their personalities, and the exalted reputation Kennedy had after his assassination, it's hardly surprising that Clinton looked to him as a role model. Like his protégé, Kennedy hung around with stars and lived the fast life, including illicit women. And for the most part, he got away with it.

A Caution: Though the environmental factors described above sound compelling, it is possible that they are superfluous. People of a particular genetic disposition, say Excitement Seeking and low Conscientiousness, are drawn to a town like Hot Springs. This appears to be the case for Bill Blythe, Roger Clinton, and Virginia Kelly. The children of these people would have similar genetic tendencies. They would probably, on the average, grow up to show similar traits regardless of where they were raised. However, growing up in a culture that views these traits as the norm, where your mother and your loved ones see the world in the same way, would make it even more difficult to understand Ken Starr's moral viewpoint.

BILL CLINTON VS. GEORGE WASHINGTON

Our special cases are nearly opposite in their reputations and their personalities. They also appeal to very different groups. Washington is probably the most admired president of conservatives; liberals favor Lincoln and FDR. Washington is admired for his character and courage, Lincoln and FDR for their compassion and warmth. Clinton clearly falls more in the latter group.

Chart 13.9 shows how Washington and Clinton compare on the Big Five dimensions and Character. The profiles are almost mirror images of each other—where one is high, the other is low. One departure from this pattern is for Agreeableness, where both score rather low. Clinton also scores much higher on Extraversion and Openness.

Do these two very different men share any qualities? They do, mostly on traits

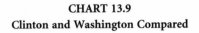

CHART 13.9
Clinton and Washington Compared

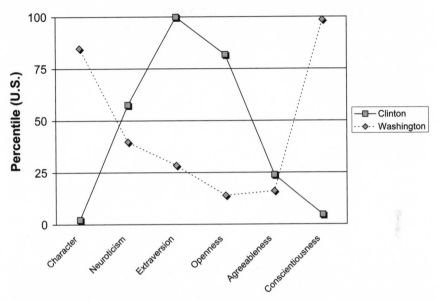

that are common to most presidents. Both were high on Dominance and Achievement Striving, and low on Modesty. Only six items out of nearly six hundred were judged as true of both, and these overlap considerably. Both appeared aware of the impressions they made on people and were seen as "impressive, remarkable"—not ordinary, everyday persons. Both had charisma and personal magnetism.

Clinton in Perspective

Clinton may represent a watershed in the perception of what is required in a president. As we have shown, he fits quite well in the pattern of recent, successful Democratic presidents, FDR being the prototype. Yet, Roosevelt lived a charmed life as president, at least in terms of the press. The nation was in crisis, with the Great Depression and World War II. To report that the president was really crippled, or was having an affair, would have seemed downright unpatriotic during such times. But the world has changed. Franklin Roosevelt proclaimed: "The Presidency is not merely an administrative office. That's the least of it. It is more than an engineering job, efficient or inefficient. It is preeminently a place of moral leadership."

In 1992 Republicans cried, in vain, that a president's character matters, and that Bill Clinton did not have enough of it. Our data support their claim about his character but suggest a more complex answer on whether it matters.

CHAPTER 14

George Walker Bush

Brief Biography (See also George H. W. Bush's biography)

ONLY THE SECOND CHILD of a president to achieve the White House (J. Q. Adams was the first), "Dubya" Bush was born on July 6, 1946, in New Haven, Connecticut, where his father was a student at Yale. In 1948 the family moved to Odessa, Texas, where George H. W. was a trainee at Dresser Industries, selling oil-field equipment. It was the oil under that dusty terrain that drew the Bushes, like other scions of elite Northeastern families, to the Permian Basin. Odessa was the "hardscrabble, hard-drinking, honky-tonk underbelly" of treeless, windswept West Texas. The Bushes had the only refrigerator on the block and briefly shared a bathroom with a mother and daughter team of prostitutes. In 1949, the family moved to California with Dresser before returning to settle in Midland.

Pauline Robinson "Robin" Bush was born in California but died of leukemia in 1953. George W. didn't know she was dying and was badly thrown by the loss, as well as by the death of a friend's six-month-old brother a short time later. He reportedly asked lots of questions, wondering, for example, if she could view baseball games from heaven. Psychologically, there were three outcomes of Robin's death: (1) His mother reportedly dealt with her grief by smothering him with love. Already close due to his father's heavy travel schedule, the two are reportedly much alike and often bristled with each other. (2) He now was at least seven years older than any of his siblings (Jeb, Neil, Marvin, and Dorothy). (3) He took responsibility for cheering up his bereaved parents by becoming the family clown; later he would continue this protective role as the family "enforcer."

George W. grew up seeking the approval of his frequently absent father above all else—many of his life decisions seem like dutiful emulations of him. He decided, for example, to become engaged at age twenty-five because that was the age at which his father became engaged to his mother, and a friend recalls hearing him say, "I want to be a fighter pilot because my father was."

The Bushes relocated to Houston in 1959, when George H. W. became increasingly involved in offshore drilling in the Gulf of Mexico. George W. was enrolled in the prestigious Kincaid School, which emphasized developing one's personal "style." He spent summers at the equally prestigious Longhorn Camp near Austin. There, with other wealthy Texas scions, he developed the "style, verve, and fierce competitiveness of a Teddy Roosevelt (or of his grandmother, Dorothy Walker Bush)." One of his camp mates was Kay Bailey Hutchison, whose Senate campaign allowed him to first demonstrate his political drawing power.

By his early teens, he was emulating his father by "working the room," joining, and leading groups. All of this seems to have come more naturally to him than to his father, though he reportedly is hard to get to know well. In 1961 following family tradition, he enrolled at Phillips Academy in Andover, Massachusetts. The oldest incorporated boarding school in the country, Phillips aimed at inculcating attention to the values and the expectations of others. More interested in socializing and cheerleading, George W. announced his goal was "to instill a sense of frivolity" in others. He excelled at this at Phillips as well as later at Yale.

He was president of the DKE fraternity in the last all-male class at Yale, a fraternity house known for its jocks and partying. Two of his Yale fraternity brothers agreed that John Belushi's character Bluto in the movie *Animal House* was the George W. Bush they knew in college.[1] Others describe him as a gentleman jock who defended the fraternity during the changing times and values of the late '60s. He also was "tapped" into the exclusive and secretive Skull & Bones Society, perhaps by his own father. There, and later at Harvard Business School, he sought solace in his family and hometown friends. He reportedly came away with a deep dislike for the "intellectual arrogance" he found there among people such as William Sloan Coffin Jr.

Shortly before graduating from Yale, he enlisted in the Texas Air National Guard, where he was assigned as a fighter pilot from 1968 to 1974. He worked at various jobs and helped his father campaign before deciding to pursue an MBA at Harvard in 1973. Then he used a small trust fund and his family's connections to get into the oil business in Midland. He met Laura Welch there and married her in 1977 after a brief courtship. He lost a 1978 congressional race to Kent Hance, who kept using his Yankee heritage against him. Shortly after his father's vice presidential inauguration in 1981, he and Laura became parents to twin girls.

Long prone to heavy drinking and carousing with people "below" him socially, he realized in 1986 that he risked alienating those closest to him and suddenly quit drinking. Some say that Laura forced him to choose between her and Jim Beam. Others say that it occurred to him that he might someday embarrass his father with his outrageous behavior. Whatever the reason, he reportedly never again took a drink of alcohol and pursued a healthier lifestyle. He also quit smoking and is known for his almost compulsive exercise regimen.

Described repeatedly as a very funny man and as having a competitive, even combative side to him, he increasingly became protective of his family in the years that followed. Known as the family's "enforcer," he controlled press access in his father's White House and is rumored to have been the one to tell John Sununu that he was no longer needed as his father's chief of staff.

In 1988 he spearheaded a buyout of the Texas Rangers baseball team. The later sale of his interest in the team and his oil business left him saying that he never again need worry about money. In 1994 he won the Texas governorship from the very popular Ann Richards, who had taunted his father at the 1992 Democratic Convention. Known as a "Giant Killer," he ran a close contest against Al Gore for the presidency in 2000. Voting irregularities in Florida clouded the 2000 election and the U.S. Supreme Court eventually decided the contest in Bush's favor.

The leveling of the World Trade Center and the smashing of the Pentagon by al Qaeda terrorists on September 11, 2001, greatly enhanced his popularity. Grabbing a bullhorn at the New York City crash site, the former cheerleader united the country behind him in a war on terror. He ordered invasions of Afghanistan and Iraq and reorganized the federal government to make apprehension of terrorists easier. His administration was faulted for limiting civil rights in the process.

Personality

We depart here from our usual method; rather than having biographers rate the president, the authors read biographies and then rated him. This was done for one simple reason: None of the few biographers available returned our questionnaires. Though Simonton and psychologist Aubrey Immelman used similar methods in earlier presidential research, this approach is a major departure from the method used elsewhere in this book. Dr. Immelman graciously agreed to provide his ratings on our questionnaire, and his data are incorporated in this chapter. His data was obtained right before the deadline for submitting our manuscript for printing, and time did not permit a full reworking of all the charts and tables that would be affected. Such changes should be minimal since Dr. Immelman's ratings were quite similar to ours. Although we did eventually obtain three raters, greater caution is called for here in reading our results for several reasons. None of us have a deep knowledge of Mr. Bush comparable to the presidential experts that provided the other ratings: We all relied on the respected biographies such as *First Son* by Bill Minutaglio as well as other published sources. Three nonexpert raters are best suited for discerning broad patterns of personality on the Big Five traits and making rough estimates of specific traits. Lastly, no data is available from Simonton or our generalists to corroborate our ratings. Therefore, the findings reported below should be viewed as tentative. Because of this, we give descriptions of Facet scores (low, average, high): We do not believe the data we have for Bush warrant more precise interpretation.

Chart 14.1 shows Bush compared to other presidents on the NEO scales. Bush's profile is remarkable for very high Extraversion, very low Openness, and for low scores on Character, Agreeableness, and Conscientiousness. Although the ratings from the three raters are highly similar, this should not be taken as strong evidence that they are accurate.

Bush's low rating on Character requires some explanation, since it seems contrary to his popular image. Character consists of many scales, including Dutifulness and Competence, and other scales that count against it (Impulsivity and Angry Hostility). Bush scored low on the former two and high on the latter two. This is similar to John Adams, who had a sterling reputation for integrity but scored low on personality scales associated with Character.

CHART 14.1

George W. Bush's Scores on Character and the Big Five Traits

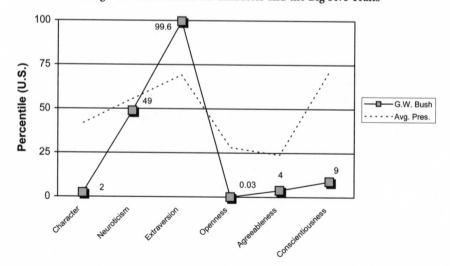

Table 14.1 shows Bush's highest and lowest NEO Facet Scores compared to average Americans. The remarkable thing is how big a role emotion (Openness to Feelings) seems to play in Bush's psychic life—an area where his father scored low. George W. scored low on the other Facet Scales comprising Openness (Openness to Fantasy, Aesthetics, Actions, [Liberal] Values, and Ideas). This pattern of scores suggests that his well-documented lack of doubt might be due to lack of introspection or inability to perceive things from a different perspective, as well as the Bush family ethic of avoiding self-analysis (at least publicly). He also scored low on Agreeableness Facets (Tender-Mindedness, Compliance, Straightforwardness) and three components of Conscientiousness (Deliberation, Dutifulness, Competence). He scored high on Positive Emotions, Angry Hostility, and Assertiveness, in addition to Openness to Feelings.

Table 14.2 shows Bush's scores compared to the averages for the eight presidential personality types. (Bush was not included in the analyses that yielded the typology.) Bush shows many similarities with the Extraverts, including high Extraversion, low Agreeableness and Conscientiousness, and average Neuroticism. The Extraverts tend to make successful presidents, as we presented in Chapter 4. However, Bush also resembles the Innocents by virtue of many of the same scores, plus very low Openness to Experience. This group contains two presidential failures (Grant and Harding) and one middling chief executive (Taft).

We also can compare Bush to other presidents. Bush most resembles Jackson

TABLE 14.1
G. W. Bush's Highest & Lowest NEO Facet Scores

High Scores	Low Scores
Openness to Feelings (O)	Openness to Ideas (O)
Positive Emotions (E)	Openness to Values (O)
Angry Hostility (N)	Deliberation (C, Ch)
Assertiveness (E)	Dutifulness (C, Ch)
	Competence (C, Ch)
	Openness to Actions (O)
	Tender-Mindedness (A)
	Openness to Aesthetics (O)
	Openness to Fantasy (O)
	Compliance (A, Ch)
	Straightforwardness (A, Ch)
	Anxiety (N)

NB: Italicized scale names indicate disagreement between the raters.

TABLE 14.2

Bush Compared to the Eight Presidential Types (Scores similar to Bush shown in bold)

| Type | Average Percentile Scores on the Big Five Factors (U.S. Norms) | | | | |
	Neuroticism	Extraversion	Openness	Agreeableness	Conscientiousness
Extraverts	**40**	**99**	27	**9**	**24**
Innocents	**44**	**93**	3	58	**17**
Maintainers	**50**	**83**	5	44	70
Dominators	84	**85**	13	**0.7**	74
Actors	**39**	**98**	31	40	**16**
Introverts	87	7	39	**12**	96
Philosophes	**50**	46	87	70	86
Good Guys	22	63	31	53	86

($r = .53$), Reagan ($r = .41$), and Harding ($r = .39$). He is least similar to Philosophes like Madison ($r = -.57$), Jefferson ($r = -.40$), and Carter ($r = -.30$). Bush does not closely resemble his father ($r = .02$), whose scores are shown in the bottom row in Table 14.3.

Republicans reportedly courted G. W. Bush as a conservative alternative to Bill Clinton—a young candidate with strong vote-getting ability. As the third row in Table 14.3 shows, they found a pretty good fit—Clinton's personality with conservative values and somewhat more Conscientiousness and Character, but without Clinton's impressive intellect and Openness to Experience.

Table 14.4 reports Bush's standing on the nine traits related to presidential success. His primary strength appears to be high levels of enthusiasm (Positive Emotions), somewhat above average Assertiveness, and low Straightforwardness. He is frequently described as vivacious, charming, and very funny—all aspects of Positive Emotions. And there is little doubt that he has a dominant personality

TABLE 14.3

Bush Compared to Similar Presidents and George H. W. Bush

(Scores similar to Bush shown in bold)

| President | Average Percentile Scores on the Big Five Factors (U.S. Norms) | | | | |
	Neuroticism	Extraversion	Openness	Agreeableness	Conscientiousness
Jackson	**56**	**99.0**	**0.5**	**0.1**	31
Reagan	4	**98**	**10**	**26**	9
Clinton	**58**	**99.9**	82	**24**	5
G. H. W. Bush	**58**	55	18	29	**23**

TABLE 14.4
G. W. Bush's Predictors of Presidential Success (Presidential Norms)

Success Factor	Score Range
Achievement Striving	Low
Competence	Low
Activity	Average
Intelligent & Smart	Low
Not Vulnerable	Average
Assertiveness	High Average
Not Straightforward	High Average
Positive Emotions	High
Tender-Mindedness	Low

and is described as bombastic, cocky, and swaggering. He was a boy who, when other kids chose teams for football, stepped out to be captain without being nominated. Though some dislike such qualities, high Assertiveness is a clear asset in a president. Low Straightforwardness is also an asset but not one that most presidents are quick to claim. As explained below, there is reason to be cautious in assigning this trait as an asset for Bush.

Bush's apparent weaknesses are low Competence, Achievement Striving, Tender-Mindedness, and rated intelligence (Intelligent and Smart). Bush has recently been portrayed as uninformed and uninterested in policy decisions,[2] and he has said things that have caused some to question his judgment ("Bring it on."). Items on the NEO Competence scale ask about such issues. The title of one Bush biography is *Ambling into History*, which does not connote the kind of drive, ambition, and focus that mark most successful presidents. Regarding rated intelligence, Bush does not enjoy a reputation as one of the brighter presidents, and his very low score on Openness to Experience (which correlates strongly with rated intelligence among presidents) also suggests a modest rating in this area.

There was little relevant information regarding Tender-Mindedness in the Bush biographies we read. There is one anecdote about him collecting signatures on a condolence card for a classmate whose mother died but no indication of concern for those outside his own social class. Biographies of Clinton and Kerry, in contrast, have numerous such anecdotes. One cannot be sure that the relative paucity in Bush's biographies reflects lack of the trait or that the biographers did not emphasize such occurrences. To some extent, this could be said of all the traits we examined. Again, the reader is urged to take our findings with a grain of salt.

Taken as a whole, Bush appears to have fewer qualities related to success than most presidents. His profile on these traits is quite similar to Jackson's and Reagan's. Jackson appears to be higher on Activity and Achievement Striving but lower on Positive Emotions. Bush appears somewhat higher than Reagan on Assertiveness and Not Straightforward, both of which are positive indications of presidential success.

Some low scores we observed may be due to factors other than Bush's standing on these traits. There is some evidence that raters have more difficulty accurately rating traits related to Conscientiousness than the other Big Five traits. Often biographies do not contain much detailed information to judge how consistently one worked at projects or the quality of his or her judgment. Generally, we assigned moderate ratings (Neutral) on items where the information did not allow us to answer otherwise with certainty. Unfortunately, for many items on the Conscientiousness scale, such a rating is not an average score—it is below average. Most adults are described as competent, capable, and as usually making good decisions. If we demurred on these items and assigned a "neutral" rating, these answers would contribute to a low score when the item scores were added up. It is possible that the scores reported above on Competence, Dutifulness, Straightforwardness, Tender-Mindedness, and Achievement Striving are partly due to this factor rather than to Bush's personal qualities. On the other hand, there was little clear evidence of this effect in the other persons we rated (Cleveland, Tyler, and Kerry). Only one rater out of three showed a tendency to use the neutral option frequently, and the scores he produced did not differ significantly from the other two raters.

Lastly, it is possible that Bush's ratings reflect a carryover from his "young and irresponsible" days before he quit drinking. Although we attempted to rate Bush in the five years before he assumed office, many colorful anecdotes about him stem from earlier periods in his life and may have colored our ratings. He reportedly became more responsible and focused on achievement after giving up drinking and possibly since assuming the presidency itself. Following the events of 9/11, he may have undergone further maturation and growth that is not reflected in our ratings. If true, Bush's current standing on Conscientiousness scales (Competence, Deliberation, Dutifulness) may have increased.

Another Psychologist's Analysis

Psychologist Aubrey Immelman profiled Bush in 1999–2000 using techniques similar to those used in this chapter.[3] The major differences are that Immelman relied on an inventory derived from the theoretical work of Theodore Millon and that he was the sole judge of whether the criteria for each item were met. His inventory was based on a personality theory that is well respected in clinical psychology and measures twelve traits. Another difference is that Immelman discussed Bush only in terms of personality patterns, as defined by elevations on one or more of the twelve scales. Rather than describing Bush directly, he described the typical characteristics of a person with the set of scores he assigned to Bush.

Immelman concluded that Bush shows prominent Outgoing and Dominant qualities, with moderate elevations on Dauntless, Accommodating, Ambitious, and Erratic scales. The Outgoing scale contains aspects of low Openness and Conscientiousness in addition to high Extraversion. Pertaining to Openness, Immelman says,

> The core diagnostic feature of the cognitive style of Outgoing individuals is unreflectiveness; they avoid introspective thought and focus on practical, concrete matters. . . . They tend to focus on external matters and the here-and-now, being neither introspective nor dwelling excessively on the past.[4]

Immelman also noted "Bush's less studied, more spontaneous, free-wheeling—and possibly impatient or impulsive leadership style."[5] Immelman did seem to portray Bush as more accommodating and agreeable than suggested by our ratings. For example, in presenting the description of Outgoing individuals, Immelman cited adjectives such as "amiable," "charming," and "engaging." However, with charm sometimes comes manipulation (low Straightforwardness): "Outgoing people may be highly skilled at manipulating people to meet their needs."[6] Further, Bush's elevation on Dominance suggested a tendency to be tough and unsentimental,[7] which are aspects of low Agreeableness. Lastly, Immelman noted that Bush's scores indicate high Extraversion. In sum, despite differences in measures and procedures, the two analyses come to very similar conclusions. This is true whether or not Dr. Immelman's ratings on our questionnaire are included in our analysis.

Bush Described

"A man chafing against and throwing off the formal constraints of the part he had signed up for, an irreverent rapscallion on intermittently good behavior, Jim Carrey trying to incorporate . . . Jimmy Stewart."—Frank Bruni, biographer (based on his presidential campaign)

"He was an easterner, really. He was, you know, a preppy. He was smart enough to not be a snob."—Peter Neumann, roommate at the XX Ranch in 1963

"Bush is still a boy. He is still convincing himself that the attitudes and mannerisms he once decided were ideal [Texas manliness] are actually his own. . . . He became tough and confrontational—but without risk. So he could never more than half believe it was really him."—Thomas de Zengotita, "The Romance of Empire," *Harper's*, July 2003

"He's a much better retail politician than a wholesale politician."—Ed Gillespie, Republican political consultant

"When Saddam ordered the assassination of George H. W. Bush, . . . Clinton responded by ordering a few cruise missiles fired at Baghdad. Shortly after 9/11, when President George W. Bush was asked what he would do, he retorted, 'I'm not going to fire a $2 million missile at a $10 empty tent and hit a camel in the butt.' (Later he noted) 'Let's not forget this man tried to kill my father.'"—Doug Wead, Bush adviser on the Christian right

George W. Bush Quoted

"People at Yale felt so intellectually superior and so righteous. They thought they had all the answers."

"I believe our nation ought to usher in what I call the responsibility era, an era that will stand in stark contrast to the last few decades."

"What I'm not willing to do is sell my soul to become the president."

"It's hard to describe the honor I feel every morning, walking into the Oval Office. I'm confident that my last day in office will be like my first. That Oval Office just inspires, I think, an awesome sense of responsibility."

"People are going to resist the flows of capital the likes of which we've never seen before, which is going to create tension—will create a sense of uncertainty on the one hand, but uncertainty on the other."

Conclusions Regarding George W. Bush

George W. Bush seems to combine characteristics of the Extravert and the Innocent types of presidents and bears strong similarities to Andrew Jackson, Ronald Reagan, and to a lesser extent, Bill Clinton. Though tentative, our data seem consistent with de Zengotita's contention that Bush is posing as an invulnerable leader while tending to overlook facts not consistent with his worldview. On the other hand, many other formulations would be consistent with our data. An interesting follow-up to our project would be to pose such formulations to our specialists and ask how true they ring to their expert ears. The step from data to formulations is just as big as from observations to assigning a score on a trait.

Epilogue

I N THIS BOOK, we have explored the utility of personality traits and tests in examining the presidents. We have shown that personality traits can help predict who will be a good president and that there are different personality types among the group. We hope the reader shares our opinion that we learned a lot. Where do we go from here?

There was a time when history was more a collection of stories about heroes than an objective discipline. Writers once believed that great men and women, like Napoléon and Catherine the Great, made history. In the last century, the focus has turned more to large and impersonal social and economic forces, such as capitalism and communism. In this view, individual people merely fill the role that the drama of history has provided for them.

We do not really have a position on this issue, being psychologists, not historians. However, we cannot help but notice that people differ enormously from one another. After World War I, Germany was primed for trouble. But can anyone doubt that Adolf Hitler was an especially unfortunate leader for this troubled country, with tragic consequences for the world? We believe that the ability to describe people objectively and compare them to each other may open a new vista on a subject that has not seen much light in nearly a century.

In the future, we hope to examine people like Julius Caesar, Cleopatra, Jesus, Joan of Arc, Napoléon, Hitler, Churchill, Stalin, and Einstein as we did in the current work. With sufficient resources, we would like to examine sports and religious figures, world leaders and generals, artists and writers, and celebrities. Although we did not rely on any outside funding in the current project, we would greatly appreciate the financial support of any person or corporation interested in furthering our work.

If you would like to know how you, or somebody you know, scores on the NEO and compares to the presidents, visit our website at www.Personalityin History.com. Personality portraits of private persons, as we presented on the presidents, may be obtained by special arrangement with the first author (www .SteveRubenzerPhD.com).

APPENDIX A

Rationale of the Study, Advantages of the Approach, and Technical Issues

BIOGRAPHERS HAVE long speculated about the motives and inner workings of the famous. With the advent of psychoanalysis, psychiatrists tried to probe even deeper in "psychohistories" or "psychobiographies." For example, Sigmund Freud and Eric Erickson applied the concepts of psychoanalysis to the lives of Leonardo DaVinci and Martin Luther. These early, provocative works differed from traditional biography more in degree than in kind. They also have been criticized for authoritatively stating interpretations without considering alternatives and for labeling everyday adult behavior as "infantile" and "neurotic."

Psychoanalysis is an established, and at times dogmatic, theory. While biographers are free to choose among competing explanations, analysts often remain true to the tenets of their school. This means an emphasis on unconscious motivations at the expense of other influences on behavior such as heredity, socioeconomic class, prestige, life goals, the environment, other people, habits, and other factors.

In this book we take a very different approach. Friendliness, energy level, and perseverance are the sort of everyday concepts we are interested in and can measure. By studying various presidents in depth, biographers did most of the hard work. We tried to mine their knowledge, focus their judgments, and provide a shared language and format. In this way, we hoped to measure the presidents on many different aspects of personality and ability and predict how well a president would do in office. This approach also allowed us to compare one chief executive to another, simultaneously taking into account many more aspects of personality than human memory can juggle. By quantifying and statistically analyzing a large number of personality judgments, we can improve thoroughness and objectivity, while testing for relationships among presidential personality, performance, and greatness.

Thoroughness

There are many theories that focus on only a few traits of personality. Though no complete listing of personality characteristics is possible, ratings on nearly six hundred items, drawn from three instruments designed to broadly cover the range of personal differences, would seem to be an improvement over two or three traits chosen and assessed subjectively.

Objectivity

To be objective means more than to be fair—it means to reach a finding that is not dependent on the judgment or perception of any one person. This is why any scientific discipline expects other researchers to reproduce the results of a study before they are fully accepted.

The main barrier to objectivity in the study of personality is that different observers, asked to evaluate the same person, often disagree. Consider, for example, biographers collecting and reporting on a person. Their experiences and personalities inevitably influence who they study, their sources and types of information, their initial impressions, their reactions to contradictory data, the conclusions they draw, and the words they use to report those conclusions. Some attempt to integrate seemingly disparate facts, others cite them as contradictions, and still others simply pass over or fail to notice them. Biographers who are cynical may provide cynical portraits of their subjects. Those who are creative may seek out evidence of this quality in their subjects, they may be more critical when they discover their subject does not share their gift, or they may unwittingly see drama or import simply out of boredom. One biographer may be overly cautious in making personality judgments—another may just shoot from the hip. The process of biography is necessarily personal and subjective, which by definition precludes objective, scientific analysis. Our study incorporates two strategies to improve this situation: multiple raters and the use of objective personality tests to reduce idiosyncratic judgments and bias.

Hot-rodders have a saying: "There's no substitute for cubic inches." In personality assessment, there is no substitute for a significant number of informed, reasonably unbiased judges. The number does not have to be large—the authors of the NEO report that more than four raters produce diminishing returns of accuracy. In our study, we had three or more raters for about 80 percent of presidents—FDR had thirteen, Jefferson, eleven, and Washington, ten. All of the presidents we profiled had at least three, with the exception of G. H. W. Bush with two.

Personality tests cannot eliminate rater bias, but they can reduce and expose it. The scales on the test we used, the Revised NEO-Personality Inventory, are relatively value neutral; most of the traits measured are not inherently good or bad. Research has shown that the NEO scales are relatively unaffected by the response style of the rater, such as a tendency to rate a person generally positively or negatively. The issue of potential bias in our data is further examined later in this section.

Just as important as reducing bias, personality scales help define a trait in a way that is consistent across raters. For example, suppose we assess Lyndon Johnson. Was he sensitive? Definitely yes, if "sensitive" means insecure and prone to emotional distress. If it means attuned to aesthetics and refined, definitely not. If it means attuned to the feelings of others in a caring way, sometimes yes and sometimes no. If raters understand "sensitive" differently, how can they agree?

Modern personality tests avoid ambiguous words, like "sensitive." In the early stages of their development, such items are identified and removed. What remains are a number of statements on each scale that share a common theme. *Together*, these items operationally define what is meant when we say Extraversion or Agreeableness. Since each rater responds to the same set of items, there is less room for idiosyncratic interpretations.

Lastly, when personality ratings are used, the opinion of one expert can be directly compared to other ratings of the same president. When each of a group of four experts rate the group's subject in the upper third of presidents on a particular item, an objectivity is achieved that is not possible in biography. With a large number of items, we can specifically state where the raters agree and where they disagree the most.

Ease of Making Comparisons (Norms)

What does it mean when a biographer or writer describes Nixon as duplicitous, or Reagan as optimistic? Compared to whom—people in general or other presidents? And how different do they have to be—more optimistic than three out of four people, or more so than ninety-nine out of a hundred? Given that each modern president is selected from more than 250 million people, it's quite plausible that they may have extreme scores on some personality traits.

Because each president is rated on the same items on the same rating scales, a questionnaire provides a standard frame of reference. Rather than relying on each biographer's habits of expression, presidents can be directly compared to each other. Moreover, because we used a test with norms for present-day Americans, for the first time presidents can be objectively compared to those they represent.

Exploration and Validation

If personality judgments are translated into numbers on a rating scale, then all the power of spreadsheets and statistical analyses can be harnessed to test the relationship between presidential greatness and six hundred personality and ability items. We can examine whether presidents who are more dishonest are also more likely to be unfaithful to their wives. And the analysis is completely objective, in the sense that anyone else using our data could replicate our conclusions using standard statistical tools. This is the essence of science.

RATING PROCEDURES

Specialist Raters

For our specialist raters, we sought experts who had written book-length biographies. In a few cases, we included those with protracted contact, whether professional or personal, with a president. Opportunity to observe and familiarity through intensive long-term study are likely to improve the reliabilities of ratings.[1] Using the various directories on the World Wide Web, national telephone directories on CD-ROM, and various *Who's Who*-type books, we identified approximately twelve hundred presidential experts of differing backgrounds. We limited our search to authors of biographies written after 1960 to increase the chances that they would still be living and up to the task of providing ratings on more than six hundred items.

Locating these experts proved difficult, since biographies seem to be written late in one's academic career or earlier in life as a function of one's celebrity. Celebrities, understandably, take pains to conceal their whereabouts and academics seem to retire with no forwarding addresses. Approximately one hundred fifty to two hundred potential raters had died, and another 175 declined to participate for various reasons. These included difficulty handling or completing materials (a few), poor health (a few), wanting to be paid (two), and lack of time (most). One hundred fifteen presidential specialists (plus the two authors) provided 176 completed questionnaires (some had written books on more than one president). The number of raters per president ranged from 1 to 13, with an average of 4.1 (SD = 2.9).

Generalist Raters

"Generalists," experts on the presidents as a group, were drawn from two sources: authors of reference books on the presidents and board members of the Center for the Study of the Presidency. Seven such experts rated all the presidents on a briefer personality questionnaire. Ten such experts completed a presidential job-performance questionnaire.

QUESTIONNAIRES

Specialists' Questionnaire

The questionnaire completed by specialists for the main part of the study contained 620 individual items. Twenty-eight items asked about the rater, and 592 items asked about the abilities, personality traits, and behavior in office of the president(s) rated. The Revised NEO Personality Inventory (described in Chapter 1) formed the heart of the questionnaire. It was administered according to standard instructions, with one exception. The NEO PI Conscientious scale is vulnerable to a response-style issue. If a rater is reluctant to give extreme ratings (i.e., "1" or "5" on the 5-point response scale), the person rated cannot obtain a high score on Conscientiousness. To overcome this, we instructed raters to feel free to use the extreme categories if this represented their best judgment. A pilot study indicated that these instructions had minimal influences on scale scores or standard deviations. Only one scale (Activity) showed a significant effect, a two-point difference, between raters who used the new instructions and those who used the standard ones. Although this difference might be attributed to chance and safely ignored, we adjusted the scores obtained on this scale to account for the differences we observed.

Two other widely used and respected techniques, both designed to cover the full range of normal personality, also were part of our questionnaire. The *California Q-sort* is a collection of one hundred personality descriptions that were carefully assembled by a team of researchers and therapists with the aim of creating a reasonably complete catalog of personality descriptions. Unlike the NEO, there are no scales—items are taken at face value. Paul Kowert used the Q-sort in a previous study of a half-dozen presidents. Unlike most personality questionnaires, the Q-sort does not yield data based on norms. Those completing the rating form indicate their level of agreement with each item (e.g., "makes friends easily") on a 1 to 9 scale, from *Very Uncharacteristic* to *Very Characteristic*, for each person being rated.

A third set of items was taken from research on the Five Factor Model. Lewis Goldberg conducted extensive studies on adjectives of the English language that are used as personality descriptions. We included his set of the one hundred *adjective synonym clusters* most commonly used to describe people. These include items like "bigoted, prejudiced" and "crafty, cunning, devious, sly." When you see strings of adjectives in our interpretations, they are most likely coming from one of Goldberg's items—whether or not they are enclosed in quotation marks. Like the Q-sort, adjective clusters were rated on a 9-point scale.

Of course, no instrument or set of questions can cover every possible aspect of personality. If someone is talkative, are they talkative with strangers or just with friends? Just when in a good mood, when anxious, or all the time? Any trait can be broken down into smaller pieces, but the pieces become increasingly trivial. Our instruments cover the domain of personality from the very broad to the moderately detailed level.

As mentioned in Chapter 1, we included items to measure various mental abilities or capacities. We began with a very broad list of possible items, using the broadest definitions of intelligence we could find. Howard Gardner argued for seven such abilities in *Frames of Mind*, based on his study of both geniuses and brain-damaged patients. Gardner believed that single measures of intelligence did not account for the Bachs and Picassos of the world, not to mention the Michael Jordans and Robin Williamses.

We conducted a pilot study looking for evidence for the separate factors that Gardner proposed. We found specific factors of Spatial Ability, Science and Math Ability, and Music and Kinesthetic Ability. (Dance was a blend.) We also found, as have most students of intellectual ability, a general factor equivalent to IQ. However, this included a number of items regarding social influence, such as "is able to persuade others" and "is able to control social situations." That FDR scored highest on this scale, above child prodigy J. Q. Adams and Thomas Jefferson, is a red flag that we are not dealing with the same thing as IQ measured by traditional intelligence tests.

Since we are relying primarily on the opinions of other people for our data, it was necessary to assess their answers for accuracy and bias. We included items that asked about the raters' level of and bases of knowledge for the people that they rated. We asked how much they respect the person and assessed how much the rater and subject were alike in terms of basic values. Some of the scales, particularly Positive Valence ("special") and Negative Valence ("evil") give a picture of a rater's general impression, good or bad, about the person being rated. Lastly, we calculated indexes to assess how consistently raters answered. If a rater becomes confused and answers in the wrong spot on the data form, obviously his data is spoiled. We were concerned about this, since many of our raters were elderly and not used to filling out computerized answer sheets. Fortunately, this was not a problem.

Generalists' Questionnaire

The sixty-item generalists' questionnaire contained mostly adjectives selected by Drs. Rubenzer and Ones to represent the Big Five personality traits, along with individual items to measure character and intellectual ability. Personality and ability items were rated on a scale from 1 (*Extremely Inaccurate*) to 9 (*Extremely Accurate*). The job-performance items (see Chapter 3) also were rated on a 1 to 9 point scale, with the labels *Very Poor* and *Outstanding* at each end.

TECHNICAL ISSUES

Use of Modern Norms

It's possible that the average American, as well as the average president, scored lower on Extraversion in the past. How can we justify using norms from the 1990s to assess George Washington or Thomas Jefferson? Actually, the prime purpose of the scores we report is communication. Living in the twenty-first century, we are familiar with only one historical group of people—those around us. Very few of our readers are likely to be knowledgeable about enough people from the eighteenth century to be able to use them as a norm group.

If we were somehow able to meet George Washington, either by going back to his time or bringing him to ours, we would still judge him in modern terms. The scores we report are expected to be the most meaningful available to our anticipated readers. Besides, the choice of norm groups does not make a difference if the purpose is to compare people within the group. If we use other presidents to generate the norms, the rank order of presidents will be exactly the same on every trait.

Scores on personality tests are typically the simple sum of scores on items. They are then converted to a standard score. But we should not forget where they come from. A high score on Angry Hostility means that a number of items, such as "has a reputation as temperamental" and "is quick-tempered." were endorsed. These items and what they ask probably were as valid and appropriate for the eighteenth century as now. Certainly, people have had such traits throughout history. However, we cannot fully answer some questions in this area until data is collected on a representative people from the same time and place, if this ever becomes possible to do.

Measurement Error

Although personality and IQ tests increase our ability to measure with accuracy, they are far from perfect. People who take a test one day may score better or worse if they test again a week later. They may score better on one brand of IQ test than another—maybe one test has a lot of vocabulary items and they always do "Word Power" in *Reader's Digest*. Any factor like these that diminishes our ability to measure something well is considered error.

Personality tests have another major source of error in addition to those listed above. The scores a person receives on a test depend almost as much on who does the rating as on who is being rated. Typically, if two people make ratings of a third, the two sets of ratings will correlate about .50. If a group of men take a self-report personality test and their wives fill out the test about them, the correlation may be as high as .60; but that is the upper limit. This means that if we want to measure someone's personality accurately, we should have more than one rater.

We can get a rough estimate of the accuracy of a rating based on the correlation among different raters. The following table shows the approximate range of error for somebody rated at the 90th percentile by different numbers of raters. All numbers are percentiles.

Number of Raters	1	3	5	10
Lowest likely true score	45.0	61.5	68.0	75.0
Highest likely true score	99.5	99.0	98.0	97.0

NB: Figures are based on an inter-rater reliability of .50, a 90 percent confidence interval, and an SD of 12 in T-scores, which was typical of NEO scales in our study.

Thus, for a woman who receives a rating at the 90th percentile but is rated by only one rater, her actual score (if it could be measured without error) may be as low as 45th(!). If she receives the same overall score, but this score is based on ten raters, it is quite likely that her "true" score is above the 75th percentile.

Statistically, there is a 90 percent chance that the "true" score from these same raters would be somewhere between the low and high score. With one rater, even a score at the 90th percentile is not reliably above average—the lowest likely score is below the 50th percentile. With three raters, we can have reasonable assurance that the high score reflects a true reading that is reliably above average.

However, the approach described above is not the only way that the error is estimated. Another approach does *not* assume that the raters are kept constant. If a different set of raters is used, this is another major source of variation in the scores we obtain. When this approach is used, the confidence interval is actually smaller, but the observed score is corrected and made less extreme—high scores are adjusted downward and low scores upward. This approach can yield even more conservative results than given above.

Another approach is to graphically display how the range of scores looks for a given president. Thirteen experts, the most of any president, rated FDR. The scores of each of the raters are plotted in Chart 1, along with the adjusted average. There are high levels of agreement on Extraversion,[2] but a considerable range of opinion on the other factors. Applying the formal index of agreement that we used throughout the chapters, only the range of scores for Agreeableness meets the criterion—and just barely. Raters were said to show reasonable agreement if the amount of variance in their scores was less than half the variance in the U.S. population or if all raters assigned a score in the upper or lower third of the U.S. population.

Inter-rater reliability is always a major constraint on measurement of personality. Political figures often are the subject of highly critical or, conversely, idealized analysis. Can biographers agree at all on the personalities they are portraying? Our data indicate they can. Though there is no generally recognized index of profile agreement across raters, there are a number of indexes to assess similarity of profiles of different individuals.[3] Of these, Cattell's (1949) r_p, bettered other indexes of agreement in an empirical comparison.[4] McCrae (1993) advocated use of an index (r_{pa}) to assess the degree of similarity between profiles on the NEO-PI-R, which he found outperformed Cattell's r_p. McCrae reported that the average level of agreement between self-ratings and those of spouses rating the same subject in the NEO-PI-R norm sample was .51 (SD = .26), and the respective figures for self/peer ratings was .41 (SD = .32). In our data, we found that randomly paired raters assessing the same president attained a mean value of .42, with an SD of .46. Though the average was approximately equal to the agreement among acquaintances in the NEO sample, there was a wider range of opinion (SD = .46 versus .32).

It should be noted that these approaches assess the overall agreement of raters across the Big Five dimensions. While this provides useful information, it may be more important to identify the particular scales and items on which the raters agreed and disagreed. We have favored this latter approach.

CHART A.1

Average Personality Scores of FDR with Scores Assigned by Different Raters

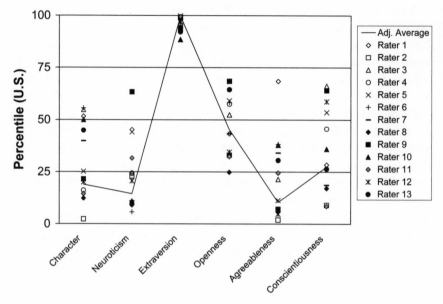

Assessing Personality Objectively

How can we know that our results are objective and unbiased? We were not able to randomly sample from all possible persons who could have provided ratings of each president—we had to rely on those identified experts who volunteered to participate. Certainly, such persons may differ from others who do not. The problem becomes especially acute if only a few raters are available, if there are large differences of opinion on a particular president, and if those who volunteer are motivated to praise or vilify their subject.

The questionnaires we use help to lessen the impact of rater bias and other idiosyncrasies, but they cannot eliminate them. A rater who has a very positive or negative opinion about a president will clearly be able to convey that on the questionnaire, and it will affect the scores that are obtained.

Extensive research on self-report tests of personality (where one answers questions about himself) has been conducted for many years. It is well known that some people portray themselves in an overly positive light, such as when applying for a job or in a custody battle, or in an overly negative light, as when attempting to fake an insanity defense. Though many tests have indexes or scales to detect these biases, attempts to statistically adjust for them generally have not been successful. In fact, the authors of the NEO felt so strongly about this issue that they did not include any such indexes in their test.

There are several ways we can address this concern. Two of the scales on the questionnaire (Positive Valence, Negative Valence) directly measure the tendency to describe the subject as exceptional and extraordinary (versus ordinary) or as evil, wicked, and sick. But some people *are* extraordinary and some *are* wicked and psychopathic. So these sorts of items can raise red flags, but they cannot distinguish a truly nefarious person from one who has been portrayed as one.

What we can do is compare our ratings with those from three other sources that are, potentially, less prone to bias and sampling error: the ratings we collected from experts on the presidents as a group (generalists), Simonton's data, and ratings of presidential job performance from previous polls of historians. Generalists were authors of general reference books on the presidents. Seven generalists participated and each rated most or all of the presidents on sixty personality and ability items. These items were chosen to parallel items and scales from our main questionnaire. Most pertinent to assessing bias, both questionnaires allowed us to assess Positive and Negative Valence and the raters' assessment of the presidents' performance on the job. The generalists have two potential advantages over specialists: They are not self-selected (volunteers) as experts on any particular president, and since they rated multiple presidents, any general rating bias (being overly critical, for example) is spread around to other presidents as well. Because they rated all presidents rather than just one or two, they provide a sort of constancy of perspective compared to individual experts each assessing his or her own subject. Conversely, generalists cannot be expected to have the same level of detailed knowledge of any given president as the specialists, and their questionnaire was necessarily much briefer. Still, the generalists provide a separate group of experts to gauge the ratings from our biographers. So do polls of presidential job performance. Here, we combined the results of two large and recent polls of presidential greatness (Murray and Blessing, Ridings and McIver) with the ratings from our generalists. This provides a robust and seemingly objective standard to compare the job-performance ratings obtained from specialists.

Positive Valence, Negative Valence, and ratings of job performance should speak a great deal about the raters' objectivity when compared to other sources. If there is a large difference in the ratings between our raters and the comparison group, the risk of bias is present. As it turns out, relatively few large differences are observed. These are indicated by pairs of scores in bold and italic in the table below. The scores shown are z-scores, which have a mean of 0 and a standard deviation of 1.0. A score of 1.0 is high and equivalent to about the 84th percentile; −1.0 is low and equivalent to about the 16th percentile.

As Table A.1 shows, there are pairs of scores, comparing specialists and generalists, that are significantly different (difference in scores greater than 1.0). However, it is also apparent that one pair of discrepant scores, say on Positive Valence, does not necessarily lead to disagreement on the other two comparisons (Negative Valence and Job Performance). Even when making ratings on highly evaluative qualities, raters clearly did make distinctions based on the content of the items.

Finally, it is not clear that a difference between generalists and specialists indicates bias on the part of the latter. Specialists may just plain know better—unlike generalists, they have studied the man in depth. Also, there are differences in the way Positive and Negative Valence were defined: Specialists answered multiple items for each scale, generalists but one.

We can also directly compare scores obtained from specialists and generalists on the Big Five traits as well as estimates of intelligence. These analyses were done. But there is still the question of what to do with such differences when they occur. For example, we could average the scores. However, in the absence of compelling evidence of bias, we believe the most justified approach is to accept the specialists' assessment but caution the reader that generalists did not see it the same.

Lastly, Simonton's data provides yet another check on our conclusions. Simonton assembled descriptions of presidents from respectable sources, presumably by journalists and other observers of the political scene. These descriptions were assembled into dossiers, all identification was removed, and groups of students translated the descriptions (e.g., "can't chew gum and walk at the same time") into a common language using checklists of adjectives ("clumsy," "preoccupied"). These adjectives were then sorted and combined into scales. Because a number of people who did not know the person they were rating (they just saw the descriptions) made the final ratings, Simonton's data may be more objective than ours. However, his ratings are clearly less direct, are probably more reliant on public behavior, and cannot reflect the sort of nuances available from expert raters. Although Simonton did not have any scales comparable to Positive Valence and Negative Valence in his study, several of his scales are conceptually similar to scales in our study and show sizable correlations with our data. These are shown in Table A.2.

As indicated, some variables that were expected to correlate substantially, such as Physical Attractiveness, did not. Although Simonton's data does not address the overall tendency to rate positive or negative, we can compare scores on the

TABLE A.1
Three Indices of Possible Bias

	Positive Valence		Negative Valence		Job Performance	
	Specialists	Generalists	Specialists	Generalists	Specialists	Historians
Washington	1.53	1.88	−.71	−1.25	1.55	1.61
Adams	.52	1.16	−.24	−.91	−.98	.54
Jefferson	1.18	1.55	−.40	−1.13	1.14	1.36
Madison	.96	.89	−.61	−1.06	.68	.30
Monroe	−1.63	.28	1.25	−.70		.27
Adams, J.Q.	1.49	.51	.41	−.63	−1.15	.12
Jackson	.03	.43	2.02	.31	.06	.72
Van Buren	.83	.11	−.62	−.19	−.36	−.38
Harrison, W	−1.57	−.59	−.45	−.61	−1.29	
Tyler	−.23	−.44	−.03	−.09	.46	−.88
Polk	−1.29	.16	1.87	−.56	1.03	.40
Taylor	.56	−.90	−.63	.00	.84	−1.11
Fillmore	.02	−1.04	−.70	−.39	1.25	−1.12
Pierce	−.73	−1.65	−.70	.36	−.13	−1.48
Buchanan	−.78	−.98	−.51	.18	−1.00	−1.46
Lincoln	.57	.97	−.44	−.96	1.23	1.72
Johnson, A.	−.60	−.83	1.53	.31	−1.65	−1.12
Grant	−.90	−1.61	−.74	1.44	−1.73	−1.56
Hayes	1.23	−.95	−.63	.02	.84	−.57
Garfield	.12	−.30	−.41	−.49	−1.18	
Arthur	−.11	−.99	−.63	.21	−.76	−.65
Cleveland	.32	.12	−.54	−.20	.31	.15
Harrison	−.61	−.69	−.62	−.07	.02	−.41
McKinley	−1.21	−.81	−.26	−.65	.31	.08
Roosevelt, T.	1.12	1.34	−.52	−.54	1.49	1.25
Taft	−.48	.29	−.03	−.61	−.73	.04
Wilson	.94	1.35	−.32	−.19	.96	1.21
Harding	−2.47	−2.29	.45	1.77	−1.00	−1.90
Coolidge	−.25	−1.18	.31	.50	−.36	−.93
Hoover	−.36	−.23	.36	−.14	−1.41	−.46
Roosevelt, F.	.95	1.63	−.28	−.58	1.62	1.77
Truman	−1.02	.55	−.54	−.44	.11	1.08
Eisenhower	.74	.63	−.74	−.47	1.18	.71
Kennedy	.93	.91	.27	.21	−.43	.60
Johnson, L.	.31	.36	2.39	1.45	.52	.63
Nixon	.13	−.67	3.14	3.26	.34	−.87
Ford	−.31	−.98	−.78	−.22	.02	−.25
Carter	.54	−.48	−.80	−.10	.30	−.16
Reagan	−.06	−.09	−.19	.66	−.20	.13
Bush, G. H. W.	.17	−.34	−.35	.58	−.58	.55
Clinton	.66	−.47	.72	.56	−.27	.23

TABLE A.2
Similar Scales from Our Study and Simonton's

Scale from Our Study	Simonton's Scale	Correlation
Straightforwardness	Machiavellianism	−.74
Warmth	Friendliness	.72
Intellectual Brilliance	Intellectual Brilliance	.67
Assertiveness	Forcefulness	.65
Order	Tidiness	.61
Achievement Striving	Achievement Striving	.50
Attractive	Attractive	.33
Openness to Values	Conservatism	−.18
Compliance	Flexibility	.11

scales that are similar and where the correlations are substantial (.60 and above). Comparing all possible scores (five variables times forty-one presidents, we found relatively few scores that differed by more than one standard score ($z = 1$), and the great majority of these were for presidents with only one rater.

Taking these observations together, we believe that little systematic bias exists in our data, and where it does it is primarily the result of having only one rater for a particular president. This source of error affects the accuracy with which we can assign a president to a type (and the validity of the typology itself) and lowers our ability to accurately assess their leadership potential. We believe the personality portraits are relatively unaffected.

Nonetheless, it must be said that all three sources rely on the ratings of people, by people, and that there is a common body of anecdotes and observations about each president. Some of these may be myths, such as Washington chopping down the cherry tree. All raters, whether our two groups or Simonton's, rely on such sources, whether directly or indirectly. To the extent that there are misrepresentations that are accepted by our raters, or that there exist personality-relevant facts that are not known about the man, there will be limitations in the ability to measure personality traits accurately. Ironically, this brings the process full circle. Although we relied on historians for the ratings reported here, future historians may find cause to challenge the perceptions of the raters who participated in our study.

Treatment of the Data

Different fields of study in psychology have different conventions when it comes to handling data. For the most part, we have followed tradition in the various areas of our project (calculating test scores, prediction, typology, and description), though this creates some inconsistencies from one chapter to another.

Personality test items are summed into scales, so the total score of a scale is the simple sum of the scores on its items. These *raw scores* may then be converted into standardized scores. Standardized scores are like IQs—a certain value, like 100, represents the average. Standard scores are necessary to compare scores from two different scales, such as Extraversion and Agreeableness.

The scoring for the NEO follows this general template, with a few refinements. Because we have multiple raters who do not agree perfectly, the mathematics of probability predict that it will be less likely for a person to be rated at the 99th percentile by each of ten raters than by a single rater. Therefore, the average score of the raters is adjusted by a formula that corrects for the number of raters.[5] For subjects rated by two or more raters, high scores will be adjusted upward, and low scores downward. In practice, the magnitude of the adjustment is modest, even with ten raters. This correction is not widely used in psychology, probably because, until recently, few instruments relied on multiple raters. The procedure is incorporated in the official scoring software of the NEO PI-R.

The NEO software also provides another refinement that is limited to the Big Five factor scales. Though each can be conceived as the sum of the six Facets we described in Chapter 1, a more complicated scoring procedure provides results that are more desirable in some technical ways. In this procedure, every single NEO Facet Scale contributes to each of the five factors, though most will contribute very little. Some scales, however, such as Angry Hostility and Warmth, clearly contribute to two of the factors. Warmth is a blend of Extraversion and Agreeableness, Angry Hostility a mix of Neuroticism and low Agreeableness.

The NEO software uses these secondary scales to help refine and complete the scoring of the factors. We used this procedure as well. Our scoring is equivalent to the official scoring routines of the NEO.

The treatment of data not from the NEO is slightly different. Here, we did not have norms from the general population. We had only the population of presidents. The typical president was rated by four experts, not by one rater, as in the case of the NEO norms. Regardless of the number of raters, McCrae's correction was applied to all scores.

The methodology in typology work is quite different than in prediction. As part of the preparation for this procedure, we first examined each rater's item level ratings. We calculated the average (mean) and standard deviation for each rater's ratings. Then new, "ipsatized" scores were calculated based on the mean and standard deviation for each rater. (These are comparable to standardized score, but for a single president/rater pair.) This aims to eliminate idiosyncrasies in a rater's style of responding. Some raters may be very reluctant to give extreme answers (i.e., 1 or 9). Others may give answers that average around 7 on a 9-point scale, rather than 5. Five-point (NEO PI-R), and 9-point (all other measures) item responses were analyzed separately to determine their respective means and SDs, then these figures were used to compute ipsatized scores for each item. This put everyone's ratings, for both questionnaires, on the same (ipsatized) scale.

Next, the ipsatized scores from different raters for the same president were averaged. Lastly, the means and standard deviations for these (average ipsatized) scores were calculated, and standard scores created from these figures. After carrying out these steps, each president could be directly compared to all other presidents on each of the 592 items in our questionnaire. Each item is now like a personality scale.

On the personality portraits, we used a combination of the approaches cited above. We scored the NEO according to the official software program, and adjusted the scores to reflect the number of raters. On the items, we used the same item scores that were used for the typology analysis. That is, we first standardized the item scores for each individual rater, then averaged across raters *for that president*. We then compared these average scores to the respective scores for other presidents. This allowed us to find the descriptions most distinctive for each president.

Other issues related to the personality portraits are discussed in Appendix B.

Methodology for Predicting Job Performance

In studying factors related to job success in other occupations, industrial–organizational psychologists typically measure various personal characteristics (e.g., cognitive ability, skills, personality) hypothesized to relate to superior job performance. This is commonly referred to as predictor measurement. Then supervisory ratings of job performance and other criteria of on the job success are obtained. This is referred to as criterion measurement. These two sets of data, predictor and criteria, then are correlated to examine which of the personal characteristics actually relate to job performance. In short, using the jargon of industrial psychology, this portion of our project may be described as a criterion-related validity study for the U.S. presidency.

We first computed bivariate correlations of personality predictors with two measures of greatness/job performance (the Murray and Blessing, 1980, historians' ratings, and our own generalists' ratings). Rather than relying on statistical significance tests, we focused on the magnitudes of the correlations obtained. Multiple regression analysis was used to derive equations for predicting the criteria of interest. Magnitudes of the bivariate correlations, were used in deciding whether or not a variable should be included in the regression equation being derived. We also sought to identify which variables would enhance the overall prediction based on the general job performance literature. Increments to multiple R's were used to judge whether a variable substantially improved prediction.

Methodology of the Typology Analysis

In creating the typology, we performed a Q-analysis, rather than the more commonly reported R-analysis. That is, rather than seeking clusters of items (or factors) to explain responses across a large group of people, we sought to find clusters of people across a large set of items. In order to successfully implement our analyses, we had to be careful to broadly cover all areas of personality at the risk of redundancy. The use of three measures, each designed to encompass the full range of normal personality, made this likely.

Cluster analysis, unlike most multivariate techniques, is a heuristic rather than a mathematically exact technique. It developed in many different fields with very different needs. For example, biologists seek to *cluster apart* animals with small differences, while astronomers seek to *cluster together* objects at vast distances. Computerized statistical programs implicitly consider these very different objectives but may not advise users of the effects they may have on the resultant clusters. Different objectives can distort cluster space by the rules used for including an item in a cluster, rules about how many clusters are desirable, and rules about outlying items. There is the very real danger of different clustering procedures yielding very different arrangements of the same data for reasons obscure to the user.[6]

We had no *a priori* assumptions about the cluster space of the American presidents, so an inclusion rule based on the average degree of relatedness seemed appropriate. We also sought a technique that could easily be communicated in words to those not familiar with statistics. Ideally, the technique could provide easily understood graphic representations of discrete presidential clusters, should these be needed. Finally, we sought a technique that included clear, reproducible, and explainable rules for including presidents in one cluster or another as well as for breaking a cluster into two or more clusters. None of the currently available software programs offered all of these options.

Fruchter offered a manual technique that meets all of these requirements.[7] Developed within psychology and based on correlations (familiar to most social scientists), it includes persons in clusters based on the ratio of their average overall relationship with those already in the cluster to their average relationship with those not in the cluster. A coefficient of belonging (*b*) allows the user to clearly explain why one president was included and another excluded from a particular cluster. Since we wished our results to be useful to historians and biographers, this was felt to be an especially important feature.

Both Q-factor analysis and the average distance method of cluster analysis develop clusters of people based on the average relationship standard, but neither provides discrete clusters with clear-cut rules of interpretation. An advantage is that there are statistical software packages (e.g., JMP, SAS Institute, 1995) that can instantly compute these analyses. We decided to use the readily available software packages as guides, but manually developed the actual typology using Fruchter's *b*-coefficient.

APPENDIX B

Producing Objective Personality Portraits

ITEM LEVEL INTERPRETATION

THIS MAY BE the most controversial part of our study from the standpoint of academic psychology. The conventional wisdom is that responses to individual items are too unreliable to warrant interpretation. There are several reasons, and some solid research, to question this conclusion. Before computer scoring was widely available, many personality tests used a *true-false* format to make scoring easier, despite findings that more options provided more reliable data.

There are several technical ways the term *reliable* is used in the measurement of psychological phenomena. Recently, it has been shown that one source of error typically overshadows all others in the measurement of personality—inter-rater reliability. Different raters typically agree about .50—far below the figures typically found for other types of reliability. Two meta-analytic studies have shown that scales fare virtually no better than individual items in terms of agreement among raters.[1]

In our study we had multiple raters for all of the presidents we profile. With several experts answering items on a 1–5 or 1–9 rating scale, the reliability of these averages are far better than when a single respondent answers a true-false question. This is particularly true when we add criteria for agreement at the level of each item. If all three experts for a given president rate their subject in the upper 33 percent of presidents, and the average of their scores is in the upper 16 percent (one standard deviation above the mean) of chief executives (with no one score buoying the others), we believe that this is solid evidence. A direct parallel exists in journalism—the three-source rule. Mainstream news media consider a story corroborated by two additional sources to be reliable enough for distribution, though not infallible. Collection of additional data in the future may result in some descriptions being dropped and others being added.

Although there have been only forty-two presidents to date (Cleveland only counts once), we can express scores among them as percentiles or standard scores. These scores contain more information than rankings, because rankings do not communicate how much one person differs from another—especially for adjacent rankings (e.g., first and second). Like scores on the SAT, we can think in terms of a potentially very large pool of presidents and estimate how many hypothetical presidents out of, say, ten thousand would score as high as TR did on Extraversion.

SELECTING ITEMS FOR USE IN PORTRAITS

For presidents rated by four or more raters, an item was included in the personality narrative for a president (as opposed to a presidential type) if, and only if, (1) the score on that item, averaged across all raters for that president, was in the upper or lower 16 percent of all presidents, AND (2) the variance among raters for that president was half or less the variance among all presidents rated, OR all raters agreed that the president scored in the upper or lower 33 percent of presidents consistent with the direction (high or low) of the average score.

If three raters rated a president, the second criterion was made more stringent: The variance among raters for that president must be half of or less than the variance among all presidents rated, AND all raters must agree that that president scores in the upper or lower 33 percent of presidents. However, if all three raters produced scores that were above or below 15 percent of all presidents, the requirement for limited variance was dropped.

Items that met these criteria were considered for our profiles. All items that received a total rating above the 95th or below the 5th percentile were presented unless clearly redundant with another, more highly rated, item. Those items with less extreme ratings were dropped if judged superfluous.

ORGANIZATION OF PERSONALITY PORTRAITS

Once we identified items that described a president, we decided how to organize and present them. Common sense suggests that the items with the highest or lowest score, relative to other presidents, should go first. The next highest item on the same general theme was presented next. An item did not necessarily form its own sentence; items of a similar theme might form a compound sentence. Paragraphs were sometimes based on one of the Big Five factors or Character, other times on one or more Facet Scales. We generally grouped items together based on research findings. Hence, items pertaining to Openness and abilities sometimes appeared together, even though they may seem to have little in common. Although the descriptions were designed to be as objective as possible, there are a few points where our judgment influenced what was portrayed:

- ✔ Judgment of what statements are redundant.
- ✔ Choice of a particular modifier (e.g., "clearly" vs. "definitely" talkative).
- ✔ Paraphrasing of the statements to preserve test security.
- ✔ Choice of the statistical cutoff points for including items and modifiers.

We view all of these as relatively minor judgments compared to those made by biographers and historians.

Though the paraphrased descriptions from our data are highly objective, the totality of our portraits are necessarily less so. Quotations and anecdotes are cited in the descriptions that seemed to us to support the traits being ascribed. Since we are not historians, other factors may have been at work, though, that make them not particularly good evidence of the trait we sought to illustrate. Still, our data and conclusions do not rest on this connection, and we enlisted our raters as reviewers of each chapter to ensure that biographical and historical data were correct and that the quotes and anecdotes were not misrepresented. For almost every president profiled, we were able to obtain two such reviews. However, this was always fewer than the number of raters who contributed formal data to the profile. Those who served as both raters and reviewers thus had a disproportionate influence relative to other experts to the extent their corrections and explanations were incorporated into the final portrayal.

APPENDIX C

Composition of Supplementary Scales

CHARACTER SCALES

WE CREATED a number of preliminary scales to assess character and integrity. These were based on items from the questionnaire or scales from the NEO that were deemed, in the judgment of Dr. Rubenzer or Dr. Ones, to relate to character/integrity.

Character Scale 1—Consists of the types of behaviors that make the news as indications of character or the lack of it (all are answered on a nine-point scale): Does not keep promises; Abuses power of positions held; Bullies others; Gambles; Disregards rights and feelings of others if not on their side; Steals; Frequently tardy; Endangers others (drives drunk, does not abide by or enforce safety precautions); Is frequently absent from work or duties; Is a good family man (husband and father) (+); Drinks alcohol; Knowingly distorts and misrepresents facts, lies; Cheats on taxes, at sports, or business; Had extramarital affairs; Had many sexual encounters; Swears frequently; Shows moral courage. (+); Plays on others' fears, insecurities; Hypocritical; Greedy.

Character Scale 2—Adjectives and descriptions that are obviously related to character: Ethical, honest, moral, principled, sincere, truthful; Abusive, disrespectful, impolite, impudent, rude, scornful (−); Cruel, ruthless, vindictive (−); Greedy, selfish, self-indulgent (−); Deceitful, dishonest, underhanded, unscrupulous (−); Dependable, reliable, responsible; Careless, negligent, undependable, unconscientious, unreliable (−); Lazy, slothful (−); Gives up and withdraws where possible in the face of frustration and adversity (−); Is subtly

TABLE C.1
Simonton's Personality Scales

Scales	Positive Items	Negative Items
Moderate	Moderate, modest, gentle, mild, considerate, meek, peaceable, relaxed, tactful, silent, cautious, cool, mannerly, conventional, pleasant, good-natured, easygoing, unassuming, shy, polished, poised	Temperamental, hasty, excitable, blustery, high-strung, outspoken, impulsive, argumentative, impatient, quarrelsome, defensive, headstrong, assertive, hardheaded, aggressive, intolerant, spontaneous, rude, dominant, tough, restless, bossy, stubborn, dissatisfied, demanding, coarse, anxious, tactless, rigid, self-pitying, suspicious, determined, active, courageous, energetic, persistent, self-confident
Friendliness	Friendly, outgoing, sociable, cheerful, affectionate, good-natured, charming, pleasant, natural, easygoing, attractive, considerate, jolly, handsome, good-looking, informal, healthy, witty, spontaneous, relaxed, humorous	Unfriendly, cold, stern, withdrawn, severe, rigid, shy, intolerant, silent, distrustful, formal, suspicious, stubborn, rude, hardheaded, persistent, complicated
Intellectual Brilliance	Interests wide, artistic, inventive, intelligent, sophisticated, complicated, insightful, wise, idealistic	Dull, commonplace
Machiavellianism	Sly, deceitful, unscrupulous, evasive, shrewd, greedy	Sincere, honest
Poise and Polish	Poised, polished, sophisticated, formal, mannerly, tactful	Simple, informal, unassuming, coarse, loyal
Achievement Drive	Industrious, persistent	Quitting, effeminate, confused
Forcefulness	Energetic, active, determined, demanding, restless	*None*
Wit	Humorous, witty, self-confident, cautious	*None*
Physical Attractiveness	Handsome, good-looking, attractive	*None*
Pettiness	Greedy, self-pitying	*None*
Tidiness	Methodical, organized, thrifty	Courageous

TABLE C.1 (continued)

Scales	Positive Items	Negative Items
Conservatism	Conservative, conventional	*None*
Inflexibility	Stubborn, persistent, hardheaded, rigid	*None*
Pacifism	Peaceable	Courageous

negativistic; tends to undermine and obstruct or sabotage (is more of a problem than a help when things need to be done). (−); Is guileful and deceitful, manipulative, opportunistic. (−); Has hostility toward others. (−); Creates and exploits dependency in people. (−); Is self-indulgent. (−); *Behaves* in an ethically consistent manner; is consistent with own personal standards.

Character Scale 3—More subtle adjectives and descriptions related to character: Direct, frank, straightforward; Benevolent, charitable, generous; Antagonistic, argumentative, combative, quarrelsome (−); Faultfinding, harsh, unforgiving, unsympathetic (−); Bossy, demanding, domineering, manipulative (−); Condescending, pompous, smug, snobbish (−); Cynical, distrustful, skeptical, suspicious (−); Caustic, curt, flippant, gruff, surly (−); Crafty, cunning, devious, sly (−); Bigoted, prejudiced (−); Inconsiderate, tactless, thoughtless (−); Industrious, persistent, tenacious, thorough; Disorganized, haphazard, inefficient, scatterbrained, sloppy, unsystematic (−); Erratic, inconsistent, unpredictable (−); Forgetful, absentminded (−); Foolhardy, rash, reckless (−); Indecisive, wishy-washy (−); Extravagant, frivolous, impractical (−); Nonconforming, rebellious, unconventional (−); Defensive, fretful, insecure, negativistic, self-critical, self-pitying (−); Temperamental, touchy, unstable (−); Envious, jealous (−); Intrusive, meddlesome, nosy (−); Foresighted, insightful, perceptive; Is a genuinely dependable and responsible person; Behaves in a giving way toward others; Is protective of those close to him; Tends to be self-defensive (quick to defend self from or deny criticism, humorless about own shortcomings) (−); Is thin-skinned, sensitive to anything that can be construed as an interpersonal slight (−); Behaves in a sympathetic or considerate manner; Overreactive to minor frustrations; irritable (−); Has a brittle ego-defensive system; Has a small reserve of integration; Would be disorganized and maladaptive when under stress or trauma (does not cope well under stress or strain) (−); Has a readiness to feel guilty; Is basically distrustful of people in general; questions their motivations (−); Is unpredictable and changeable in behavior and attitudes

TABLE C.2
Simonton's Presidential Style/Behavior Scales

Scales	Items
Charismatic	Characterized by others as a world figure. (Low score = he is seen as courthouse politician type).
	Tends to force decisions to be made prematurely.
	Dynamo of energy and determination.
	Skilled and self-confident as a negotiator.
	Finds dealing with the press challenging and enjoyable.
	Views the presidency as a vehicle for self-expression.
	Keeps in contact with the American public and its moods.
	Exhibits artistry in manipulation.
	Has ability to maintain popularity.
	Has a flair for the dramatic.
	Is charismatic.
	Consciously refines his own public image.
	Uses rhetoric effectively.
	Conveys clear-cut, highly visible personality.
	Is shy, awkward in public. (−)
	Enjoys the ceremonial aspects of the office.
Creative	Is a middle-of-the-roader. (−)
	Is innovative in his role as an executive.
	Initiates new legislation and programs.
Deliberative	Cautious, conservative in action.
	Able to visualize alternatives and weigh long-term consequences.
	Understands implications of his decisions; exhibits depth of comprehension.
	Keeps himself thoroughly informed; reads briefings, background reports.
	Impatient, abrupt in conference. (−)
	Indulges in emotional outbursts. (−)
Interpersonal	Supports constitutional government (low score = personal power orientation).
	Rarely permits himself to be outflanked. (−)
	Accepts recommendations of others only under protest. (−)
	Suspicious of reformers. (−)
	Bases decisions on willfulness, nervousness, and egotism. (−)
	Willing to make compromises.
	Is emphatic in asserting his judgments (low score implies he is deferential, modest, about the validity of his own views. (−)
	Is flexible.
	Endears himself to staff through his courtesy and consideration.
	Keeps members of his staff informed on matters concerning other departments.
	Emphasizes teamwork.
	Gives credit to others for work done.

TABLE C.2 (continued)

Scales	Items
	Allows cabinet members considerable independence. (Low score = staff used as merely subordinate consultants).
	Is frequently in contact with his advisers and cabinet.
	Believes he knows what is best for the people. (Low score = he considers himself a servant of the public). (−)
	Maintains close relationships with a wide circle of associates.
	Knows his limitations.
	Relies on a staff system, deciding among options formulated by his advisers.
	Encourages the exercise of independent judgment by aides.
Neurotic	Has direct, uncomplicated approach. (−)
	Places political success over effective policy.
	Suffers health problems that tend to parallel difficult and critical periods in office.
Unclassified	Carefully considers opinions before making them public.

(−); Is self-defeating (acts in ways which undermine, sabotage, or frustrate his own goals and desires) (−); Tends to be rebellious and nonconforming (−); Characteristically pushes and tries to stretch limits; Sees what he can get away with (−); Concerned with own adequacy as a person, either at conscious or unconscious level (−); Tends to perceive many different contexts in sexual terms; Eroticizes situations (−); Is subjectively unaware of self-concern; Feels satisfied with self; Has a clear-cut, internally consistent personality; Tends to project his/her own feelings and motivations onto others (tends to see feelings and motives in others which he prefers not to recognize in self) (−); Appears straightforward, forthright, and candid in dealing with others; Feels cheated and victimized by life; Self-pitying (−); Tends to ruminate and have persistent and preoccupying thoughts (−); Compares self to others. Is alert to real or fancied differences between self and other people (−); Is power-oriented; Values power in self and others (−); Is self-dramatizing; histrionic (−); Religious, spiritual; committed to a personal faith irrespective of church attendance; Idealistic; Confused (−).

Character Scale 4—This index consisted of the single item: "Has good moral character."

Character Index 5—Consisted of the NEO Facet Scales of: Angry Hostility (−), Impulsiveness (−), Altruism, Modesty, Tender-Mindedness, Self-Discipline, and Deliberation

Character Index 6—Consisted of Character Index 5 plus the additional NEO Facet Scales of Vulnerability (−), Excitement Seeking (−), Straightforwardness, Compliance, Competence, Dutifulness, and Achievement Striving.

Integrity Index 1—Conscientiousness + Agreeableness − Neuroticism

Integrity Index 2—Consisted of NEO Facet Scales including Angry Hostility (−), Impulsiveness (−), Excitement Seeking (−), Trust, Straightforwardness, Compliance, Competence, Dutifulness, Achievement Striving, Self-Discipline, Deliberation

TABLE C.3
Intellectual Ability Scales

Abilities	Positive Items	Negative Items
General Ability	Learns many different things quickly; Sees beyond facts to implications; Expresses ideas fluently/masterfully; Can speak publicly without preparation; Has an exceptional vocabulary; Analyzes his mistakes to profit from them; Forms friendships easily; Is able to persuade others; Can do several things at once efficiently.	Has difficulty grasping new ideas and problems
Science & Math	Prefers to solve problems in a quantitative, scientific manner; Understands advanced mathematics (for his time); Excelled in science in school or elsewhere; Interested in science.	Is not good with numbers
Musical Ability	Has a "good ear" for musical tone; Has a good sense of rhythm; Is a good dancer; Appreciates real talent (apart from popularity) in musicians Has a good memory for melodies; Sings well.	Uses gestures awkwardly
Visual Spatial Ability	Has a vivid imagination; Good at visualizing situations, faces, etc; Appreciates visual art (paintings, sculpture); Is good at recognizing faces; Has a good sense of direction.	*None*

Table C.1 lists Simonton's personality scales and the adjectives that compose them. Table C.2 lists the descriptions that compose the presidential style/behavior scales that he created. Table C.3 lists our intellectual ability scales and the items that make them up.

APPENDIX D

Correlations of Personality Measures to Measures of Success and Ethics on the Job as President

TABLE D.1

Correlations of Character and the Big Five to Measures of Success and Ethics on the Job as President

| | Presidential Success | | |
| | Historian Ratings | Overall Job | Ethics on |
Trait	of Greatness	Performance	the Job
Character	−.01	−.05	**.41**
Neuroticism	−.02	.07	.05
Extraversion	.20	.15	−.18
Openness to Experience	.32	.21	.31
Agreeableness	−.12	−.16	.18
Conscientiousness	.06	.11	.38

TABLE D.2

Correlations of the NEO Facets and Measures of Ability with Measures of Presidential Success and Ethics on the Job

Scale	Presidential Success		Ethics on the Job
	Historian Ratings of Greatness	Overall Job Performance	
Neuroticism			
Anxiety	.02	.07	.02
Angry Hostility	.11	.11	− .04
Depression	− .08	− .03	− .06
Self-Consciousness	− .05	.07	.07
Impulsiveness	.05	.07	− .20
Vulnerability	− .26	− .18	− .25
Extraversion			
Warmth	.07	.00	− .08
Gregariousness	.01	− .08	− .26
Assertiveness	**.44**	.37	.05
Activity	.30	.30	.04
Excitement Seeking	.24	.19	− .20
Positive Emotions	.30	.26	.05
Openness			
Fantasy	.24	.10	− .11
Aesthetics	.24	.21	**.40**
Feelings	.38	.19	− .01
Actions	.27	.13	.11
Ideas	.15	.10	.29
Values	.30	.19	.13
Agreeableness			
Trust	.10	.03	.14
Straightforwardness	− .29	− .33	.16
Altruism	− .08	− .11	.12
Compliance	− .18	− .23	− .02
Modesty	− .14	− .08	.19
Tender-Mindedness	.34	.30	.34
Conscientiousness			
Competence	.30	.31	**.48**
Order	− .23	− .13	.05
Dutifulness	− .08	− .09	.32
Achievement Striving	.32	**.42**	**.44**
Self-Discipline	.17	.13	.31
Deliberation	− .09	− .09	.26
Ability Ratings			
General Intelligence	.29	.18	.07
Science & Math Ability	.15	.16	**.44**
Spatial Ability	.29	.13	.01
Music & Kinesthetic Ability	.08	.11	.17
Total IQ score	.30	.21	.25
Smart	.23	.20	.24
Intellectually Brilliant	.31	.26	.33

APPENDIX E

Participants in the Study—Specialists

Names	Affiliations/Credentials*	Presidents
RATED		
C. Knight Aldrich	U. Virginia/Pres. biog., Charlottesville, VA	Coolidge
W. B. Allen	Michigan State U./Pres. biog., East Lansing, MI	Washington, Adams, Jefferson, Madison, Reagan
Harry Ammon	Southern Illinois U./Pres. biog., Carbondale, IL	Monroe
Donald F. Anderson	U. Michigan–Dearborn/Pres. biog.	Taft
Judith I. Anderson	California Polytechnic U./Pres. biog., Pomona, CA	Taft
Lance Banning	U. Kentucky/Pres. biog., Lexington, KY	Washington, Adams, Jefferson, Madison
James G. Barber	National Portrait Gallery/Pres. biog., Washington, DC	Jackson, Grant
Ryan J. Barilleaux	Miami U./Pres. author, Oxford OH	Bush

Paul H. Bergeron	U. Tennessee/Pres. biog., Knoxville, TN	Polk
Wallace H. Best	International Lincoln Assoc., Boulder City, NV	Washington, Jefferson, Lincoln, T. Roosevelt
Frederick Binder	Juniata College/Pres. biog., Huntingdon, PA	Buchanan
Hendrik Booraem IV	Pres. biog., Newtown, PA	Jackson, W. Harrison, Garfield, Coolidge
Peter G. Bourne	Carter Biography Project/Pres. biog., Washington, DC	Carter
James E. Brazier	U. North Carolina–Pembroke/ Pres. author	F. Roosevelt, Truman
Jeff Broadwater	Texas Woman's U./Pres. biog., Denton, TX	Truman
Jennifer Capps	Benjamin Harrison Home, Indianapolis, IN	B. Harrison
Jean Choate	Northern Michigan University– Presque Isle	F. Roosevelt
Kendrick A. Clements	U. South Carolina/Pres. biog., Columbia, SC	Wilson
James Codling	Mary Holmes College, West Point, MS	F. Roosevelt
Donald B. Cole	Exeter Academy (Emeritus)/Pres. biog., Exeter, NH	Jackson, Van Buren
Paolo E. Coletta	USNA (Emeritus), Annapolis, MD	Taft
Michael L. Collins	Midwestern State U./Pres. biog., Wichita Falls, TX	T. Roosevelt
David E. Conrad	Southern Illinois U./Pres. biog., Carbondale, IL.	L. Johnson
Jim Cooke	Actor (Coolidge portrayer), Dorchester, MA	Coolidge
Dale E. Cottrill	Presidential biographer, Clinton Township, MI	Harding, Coolidge

Wayne Cutler	Papers of James Polk, U. Tennessee/ Pres. biog., Knoxville, TN	Polk
James C. Davies	U. Oregon/Pres. biog., Eugene, OR	Jackson, Wilson, Carter
Ernest Dumas	U. Arkansas/Pres. biog., Fayetteville, AR	Clinton
Wilbur Edel	City U. of New York (Emeritus)/ Pres. biog., Mifflinburg, PA	Reagan
John D. Ehrlichman	former Nixon aide/Pres. biog., (deceased)	Nixon
Lucille Falkoff	Children's presidential biographer, Highland Park, IL	Tyler
Robert H. Ferrell	Indiana U./Pres. biog., Bloomington, IN	Coolidge
Mary V. Fox	Writer/Presidential biographer, Middleton, WI	Reagan
Rachel Francis	Presidential biographer, East Aurora, NY	Fillmore
John Gable	Theodore Roosevelt Assoc./ Pres. biog., Long Island, NY	T. Roosevelt
Robert E. Gilbert	Northeastern U./Pres. biog., Boston, MA	Coolidge
Stanley Godbold	Mississippi State U., Mississippi State, MS	Carter
Richard Goldhurst	Writer/Pres. biographer, Westport, CT	Grant
R. G. Gunderson	Indiana U., Bloomington, IN	Jackson, W. H. Harrison
Lawrence W. Haapanen	Lewis & Clarke State College, Lewiston, ID	Eisenhower
Mary W. Hargreaves	Historian/Pres. biographer, Lexington, KY	J. Q. Adams
Marie B. Hecht	Presidential biographer, Great Neck, NY	J. Q. Adams

Kenneth E. Hendrickson Jr.	Midwest. St. U., Wichita Falls, TX	F. Roosevelt, L. Johnson
Calvin W. Hines	Stephen F. Austin State U., Nacogdoches, TX	L. Johnson
Joan Hoff	Indiana U./Pres. biog., Bloomington, IN	Hoover, Nixon
Samuel B. Hoff	Delaware State U./Pres. author, Dover, DE	Bush
J. Michael Hogan	Indiana U./Pres. biog., Bloomington, IN	T. Roosevelt
Florence Holden	Pierce Brigade, Concord, NH	Pierce
Kenneth M. Holland	U. Memphis, Memphis, TN	Ford
Harold Holzer	Metropolitan Museum of Art/ Pres. biog., New York, NY	Lincoln
Ari A. Hoogenboom	Brooklyn College/Pres. biog., Brooklyn, NY	Hayes
Arthur R. Jarvis Jr.	Penn. State U./Pres. author, University Park, PA	F. Roosevelt
Polly Johnson	Pierce Brigade/Pres. author, Concord, NH	Pierce
John P. Kaminski	U. Wisconsin/Pres. biog, Madison, WI	Washington, Jefferson
Ralph L. Ketcham	Syracuse U. (Emeritus)/ Pres. biog, Syracuse, NY	Madison
David E. Kucharsky	Writer/Pres. biographer, White Plains, NY	Carter
Rebecca Larsen	*Marin Independent Journal*/ Pres. biog., Novato, CA	Nixon
J. Edward Lee	Winthrop U./Pres. author, Rock Hill, SC	Polk
Craig Lloyd	Columbus College/Pres. biog., Columbus, GA	Hoover
David E. Long	East Carolina U. /Pres. biog., Greenville, NC	Lincoln

Clifford R. Lovin	Western Carolina U./ Pres. author, Cullowhee, NC	Hoover
Alf J. Mapp Jr.	Old Dominion U./ Pres. biog., Norfolk, VA	Jefferson
Elizabeth W. Matthews	Librarian/Pres. bibliog., Naples, FL, & Carbondale, IL	Lincoln
Donald R. McCoy	U. Kansas/Pres. biog., Lawrence, KS	Harding
Richard L. McElroy	Historian/Pres. biog., Canton, OH	Garfield, McKinley
Barbara McEwan	Horticulturalist/Pres. biog., Forest, VA	Jefferson
Keith D. McFarland	Texas A&M U./Pres. author, Commerce, TX	Wilson, F. Roosevelt, Truman
Charles W. Meister	Writer/Pres. biographer, Pine, AZ	Washington, Madison
David M. Merrill	Benjamin Harrison Home, Indianapolis, IN	B. Harrison
Frank C. Mevers	State Archives, Concord, NH	Pierce
Richard L. Miller	Private Scholar/Pres. biographer, Kansas City, MO	Truman
Edmund Morris	Pulitzer-winning pres. biog., Washington, DC	T. Roosevelt, Reagan
Jerome Mushkat	Syracuse U. (Emeritus)/ Pres. biog., Akron, OH	Van Buren
Paul C. Nagel	U. Minnesota/Pres. biog., Minneapolis, MN	Adams, J. Q. Adams
W. John Niven	Claremont Grad. School/ Pres. biog., Claremont, CA	Van Buren
George W. Nordham	Presidential biographer, Waldwick, NJ	Washington
William D. Pederson	Louisiana State U.–Shreveport/ Pres. biog.	Lincoln, T. Roosevelt, Ford, Carter

William E. Pemberton	U. Wisconsin–La Crosse/ Pres. biog.	Truman, Reagan
Barbara A. Perry	Sweet Briar College/Pres. biog. Sweet Briar, VA	Clinton
Merrill D. Peterson	U. Virginia/Pres. biog., Charlottesville, VA	Jefferson
Joe Phipps	former LBJ aide/Pres. biographer, Longview, TX	L. Johnson
Wesley Pippert	Grad. Journalism Prog., U. Missouri/Pres. biog., Washington, DC	Carter
Robert M. Quackenbush	Children's writer/Pres. biog., New York, NY	Jefferson, Madison, Jackson, T. Roosevelt
Thomas C. Reeves	U. Wisconsin–Parkside/ Pres. biog.	Arthur
Michael P. Riccards	Fitchburg State Coll./ Pres. biog., Fitchburg, MA	Washington
William J. Ridings	Presidential rankings author, Pompano Beach, FL	Buchanan
Norman K. Risjord	Pres. biographer, Annapolis, MD	Washington, Adams, Jefferson
Michael P. Rogin	U. California–Berkeley/ Pres. biog.	Jackson
Douglas D. Rose	Tulane U., New Orleans, LA	F. Roosevelt
Herbert D. Rosenbaum	Hofstra U./Pres. biog., Hempstead, NY	Carter
Philip R. Rulon	N. Arizona U. /Pres. biog., Flagstaff, AZ	F. Roosevelt, Eisenhower, L. Johnson
Raymond J. Saulnier	Ike's Council of Econ. Advisors, Chestertown, MD	Eisenhower
Sean J. Savage	St. Mary's College/Pres. biog., Notre Dame, IN	F. Roosevelt, Truman

Robert J. Scarry	Presidential biographer, Moravia, NY	Fillmore
Jerome L. Shneidman	Adelphi U./Pres. biog., Garden City, NY	Kennedy
Thomas Silver	Claremont Institute/ Pres. biog. (deceased)	Coolidge
Henry B. Sirgo	McNeese State U./ Pres. author, Lake Charles, LA	Taft, Kennedy
David C. Skaggs	Bowling Green St. U./Pres. biog., Bowling Green, OH	Washington
Elbert B. Smith	U. Maryland/Pres. biog., College Park, MD	Taylor, Fillmore, Buchanan
Gene A. Smith	Texas Christian U./Pres. author, Fort Worth, TX	Jefferson
James M. Smith	Winterthur Museum/Pres. biog., Winterthur, DE	Washington, Adams, Jefferson, Madison
Allan B. Spetter	Wright St. U./Pres. biog., Dayton, OH	B. Harrison
William C. Spragens	Bowling Green St. U./Pres. biog., Bowling Green, OH	Hoover, Kennedy, L. Johnson, Ford, Clinton
Robert A. Strong	Washington & Lee U./Pres. author, Lexington, VA	Carter
Martha H. Swain	Mississippi St. U./Pres. author, Mississippi State, MS	F. Roosevelt
Dwight L. Tays	David Lipscomb U., Nashville, TN	Kennedy, L. Johnson
Naomi Topalian	Presidential biographer, Lexington, MA	Cleveland
Lyon Tyler Jr.	Historian/Family member/ Pres. author, Charleston, SC	Tyler

Frank Van Der Linden	Columnist/Pres. biog., Bethesda, MD	Reagan
William T. Walker	Chestnut Hill Coll. /Pres. author, Philadelphia, PA	F. Roosevelt
Robert Whelan	Shodokan Dojo, Salem, MA	A. Johnson
Lawrence E. Wikander	Northamp. Library/Pres. author, Northampton, MA	Coolidge
Arthur R. Williams	U. Missouri–Kansas City/Pres. author	Lincoln, Truman
Frank J. Williams	Abraham Lincoln Assoc./Pres. biog., Providence, RI	Lincoln
David L. Wilson	Southern Illinois U.–Carbondale/ Pres. biog.	Grant, Harding
Thomas P. Wolf	Indiana U.–Southeast/Pres. author, New Albany, IN	F. Roosevelt, Kennedy, Nixon

* See also References and Bibliography for relevant publications.

APPENDIX F

Specialist Raters for Each President

Washington	W. Allen, L. Banning, W. Best, J. Kaminski, C. Meister,* G. Nordham, M. Riccards,* D. N. Risjord, D. Skaggs, J. Smith
Adams	W. Allen,* L. Banning, P. Nagel,* D.N. Risjord, J. Smith,
Jefferson	W. Allen,* L. Banning, W. Best, J. Kaminski, A. Mapp, B. McEwan,* M. Peterson, R. Quackenbush, N. Risjord, G. Smith, J. Smith, (D. Rose)
Madison	W. Allen, L. Banning, R. Ketcham, C. Meister, R. Quackenbush, J. Smith
Monroe	H. Ammon
J. Q. Adams	M. Hargreave, M. Hecht, P. Nagel
Jackson	J. Barber, H. Booraem,* D. Cole,* J. Davies, R. Gunderson, R. Quackenbush, M. Rogin, (T. Wolf)
Van Buren	D. Cole, H. Booraem, W. Niven
W. Harrison	H. Booraem, R. Gunderson
Tyler	L. Falkof, L. Tyler
Polk	P. Bergeron, W. Cutler, J. Lee
Taylor	E. Smith
Fillmore	R. Francis, R. Scarry, E. Smith
Pierce	F. Holden, P. Johnson, F. Meyers
Buchanan	E. Smith
Lincoln	W. Best, H. Holzer, D. Long, E. Matthews,* W. Pederson, A. Williams, F. Williams, R. Whelan, (D. Rose)
A. Johnson	R. Whelan
Grant	J. Barber,* R. Goldhurst, D. Wilson*
Hayes	A. Hoogenboom

Garfield	H. Booraem, R. McElroy
Arthur	T. Reeves
Cleveland	N. Topalian
B. Harrison	J. Capps, D. Merrill, A. Spetter
McKinley	R. McElroy
T. Roosevelt	W. Best, M. Collins,* J. Gable,* J. Hogan, E. Morris, W. Pederson, R Quackensbush
Taft	D. Anderson, J. Anderson, P. Coletta, H. Sirgo
Wilson	K. Clements,* J. Davies, K. McFarland
Harding	D. McCoy, D. Cottrill, D. Wilson*
Coolidge	K. Aldrich, H. Booraem, J. Cooke, D. Cottrill, R. Ferrell, R. Gilbert, T. Silver, L. Wiklander
Hoover	J. Hoff, C. Lloyd, C. Lovin, W. Spragens
F. Roosevelt	J. Brazier, J. Choate, J. Codling, K. Hendricks, C. Hines, A. Jarvis, J. McFarland, D. Rose,* P. Rulon, S. Savage,* M. Swain, W. Walker, T. Wolf
Truman	J. Brazier, J. Broadwater, K. McFarland, R. Miller, W. Pemberton, S. Savage,* A. Williams
Eisenhower	L. Haapanen,* P. Rulon,* R. Saulnier
Kennedy	J. Shneidman,* H. Sirgo,* W. Spragens,* D. Tays,* T. Wolf*
L. Johnson	D. Conrad,* K. Hendricks, J. Phipps, P. Rulon, W. Spragens,* D. Tays* (H. Booraem)
Nixon	J. Ehrlichman, J. Hoff, R. Larsen, T. Wolf,* (H. Booraem)
Ford	K. Holland,* W. Pederson, W. Spragens*
Carter	P. Bourne, J. Davies, S. Godbold,* D. Kucharski,* W. Pederson, W. Pippert,* H. Rosenbaum, R. Strong, (D. Rose)
Reagan	W. Allen,* W. Edel, M. Fox, E. Morris,* W. Pemberton,* F. Van der Linden
Bush	R. Barilleaux,* S. Hoff
Clinton	E. Dumas,* B. Perry, W. Spragens*

NB: An asterisk denotes those experts who also reviewed our profile (including the biography and summary of administration) on that president. Those in parentheses did not serve as expert raters but merely reviewed the chapter. Though we generally incorporated their suggestions, we do not intend to indicate they endorsed our portraits or agreed with every point contained therein.

APPENDIX G

Generalist Raters

Generalists are experts on the presidents as a group. To enlist them, we followed two routes. We invited all board members of the Center for the Study of the Presidency to participate; only a few did. We also compiled a list of general reference books on the presidents published in the last thirty years and attempted to locate the authors through various directories and their publishers. Generalists were asked to volunteer for one or both of two tasks: rating the personalities and/ or the job performances of all forty-two presidents up until the time of the survey (1995–1996). (Cleveland served nonconsecutive terms, and they were assessed separately.) A few respondents for the personality portion returned questionnaires that were so incomplete or improperly completed that they were discarded. A few others skipped some presidents or indicated that they had insufficient knowledge to rate them—mainly nineteenth-century presidents on either side of Lincoln.

TABLE G.1
Generalist Raters and Data Provided

Participant	Affiliation/Credentials	Data Provided
James C. Clark	Columnist/Historian/Pres. biographer, Orlando, FL	JP
Homer F. Cunningham	Presidential biographer, Spokane, WA	P, JP
Byron W. Daynes	Brigham Young University, Provo, UT	JP
Daniel F. Hahn	Presidential scholar, Fort Myers, FL	P, JP
Louis W. Koenig	Presidential scholar, Garden City, NY	P, JP
Perri Lampe	Maple Woods Community College, Kansas City, MO	JP
Richard L. McElroy	Presidential biographer, Canton, OH	P, JP
Martin S. Nowak	Presidential scholar, Lancaster, NY	P
Henry B. Sirgo	McNeese State U., Lake Charles, LA	P, JP
Lloyd Ultan	Historian, Bronx, NY	P, JP
Melvin I. Urofsky	Virginia Commonwealth U., Richmond, VA	JP

NB: P-Personality ratings; JP-Job Performance ratings. Two generalists, Henry Sirgo and Richard McElroy, also provided specialist ratings on two individual presidents each.

Notes

CHAPTER 1

1. J. M. Digman. (1990). "Personality structure: Emergence of the Five-Factor model." *Annual Review of Psychology* 41: 417–440.

2. P. T. Costa Jr. and R. R. McCrae (1992). *Revised NEO Personality Inventory (NEO-PI-R). and NEO Five Factor Inventory (NEO-FFI): Professional Manual*, Odessa, FL: Psychological Assessment Resources.

3. D. S. Ones. (1993). *The Construct Validity Evidence for Integrity Tests*. Doctoral Dissertation, University of Iowa, Iowa City, IA. And D. S. Ones and C. Viswesvaran (1998). Integrity Testing in Organizations. In *Dysfunctional Behavior in Organizations: Vol. 23, Nonviolent Behaviors in Organizations*. Edited by R. W. Griffin, A. O'Leary-Kelly and J. M. Collins. Greenwich, CT: JAI Press.

CHAPTER 2

1. This is a dramatization of a real Johnson behavior.

2. D. K. Simonton. (1985). "Intelligence and personal influence in groups: Four non-linear models." *Psychological Review*, 92, No. 4, 532–547.

3. C. Cox. (1926). *The Early Mental Traits of Three Hundred Geniuses*, Stanford, CA: Stanford University Press.

4. Presidents differed more than the NEO norm group, consisting mostly of professionals (not the full range of the population). However, social class has little influence on NEO scores and the presidents are professionals.

5. We did not do significance tests because there is little chance that a statistical test could detect even a large true difference between such small groups. It also can be argued that there is no need for inferential statistics, since no inferences are being made. We are not dealing with samples, but with a population (all presidents).

6. This statement, like others in this section, is paraphrased to assure questionnaire item security.

7. It is possible that "Average Americans" in 1789 differed in personality from those today. Hence, it is possible (though not probable) that early presidents, called introverts today, were seen as extraverts in 1789.

8. D. G. Winter. (1987). "Leader Appeal, Leader Performance and the Motive Profiles of Leaders and Followers: A Study of American Presidents and Elections." *Journal of Personality and Social Psychology* 52: 196–202.

9. The three measures are Winter's motive scores coded from inaugural addresses, scales created by Dr. Rubenzer to measure these constructs as defined by McClelland on the specialists' questionnaires, and a single item measure on the generalists' questionnaires ("High in Need for Power [desires to have influence, impact on others; status]"; "High in Need for Affiliation [desires company and affection of others, values warm and close friendships]"). See Winter (1987), McClelland, (1961), and McClelland & Boyalzis (1982).

10. Our other three measures of Extraversion show a similar increase in variability into the twentieth century, but the more specific scales (Positive Emotions, Need for Power, etc.) do not.

CHAPTER 3

1. This paragraph is for introductory purposes only. See the rest of the chapter for actual qualities related to presidential success.

2. The word "integrity" is a specific and technical term in the field of personnel selection. The word "character" is not used. Dr. Ones, therefore, is reluctant to use the two as synonyms, though we do associate the two for continuity with the rest of the book. Although we created a number of scales to assess character and integrity, we did not use any of the published integrity scales.

3. A complete table, with separate correlations for historical greatness and overall job performance, is given in Appendix D.

4. For these analyses, we used an index of character that is an average of five other character indexes. None of the measures of character we used in our study was clearly related to Presidential Success.

5. This sort of study takes data from previous studies and examines them statistically. It is a way of quantitatively reviewing the existing research on a subject.

6. Scores must be expressed in standard scores, not percentiles, to use this index.

7. From a technical standpoint, researchers should use different data to demonstrate the value of their work than the data that led to their conclusions.

8. This analysis is based on the average total score of the index. Individual "good presidents" may score higher or lower. In order to calculate these estimates, we needed to estimate the score of presidents relative to others on IQ ratings, which we did based on a pilot study. Lastly, we needed to know the correlations among the scales on the index and apply a correction factor to account for this factor.

9. This formula actually applies to Overall Job Performance. A similar equation for historians' ratings of greatness can also be generated.

10. It should be pointed out that the item in the questionnaire includes the modifier. Low placement indicates personal power orientation.

CHAPTER 4

1. Technically, we first standardized scores for each rater, then averaged across raters. This reduced any differences due to extreme ratings.

2. According to testimony of Billie Sol Estes before a Robertson County, Texas, grand jury in 1984, as reported by E. Moore in 1996 ("Last one standing." *Texas Magazine of the Houston Chronicle*, June 23, 8–13), Malcolm Everett "Mac" Wallace was convicted in 1952 of an Austin, Texas, murder. Wallace was represented by an attorney with ties to LBJ and was given a five year suspended sentence. Thereafter he always worked directly for LBJ or in jobs secured by LBJ. Estes testified that he was present when LBJ directed Wallace to murder Henry Marshall, a U.S. Department of Agriculture official from Bryan, Texas. That was in 1961, when Johnson was vice president. Other murders possibly connected with LBJ and Wallace were those of George Krutilek, an El Paso accountant, Harold Orr, president of Superior Manufacturing, and Howard Pratt, a Commercial Solvents supplier from Chicago. Apparently, Estes knew of these murders because they were all related to illegal activities for which he subsequently was sent to prison. "Before I was convicted, Bobby Kennedy offered me a deal," says Estes. "He wanted me to turn evidence against Lyndon and they'd let me go free. I didn't take that deal. I'd have been free for 30 minutes. Then I'd have been dead. There were already some others who had gone that route."

3. Charts in this chapter indicate a wide range of opinion among raters with a diamond and a value shown in italics; scores where higher levels of agreement were present are denoted with a square and a data label in normal font.

4. The descriptions reported here are generally true of all Dominators. As a group, Dominators scored in the above 85th percentile (or below the 15th percentile) of non-Dominator presidents on all items listed. In addition, every Dominator scored above (or below) the average. However, for some Dominators, this might mean they were only slightly different from the average of all presidents.

5. We do not reference most of the quotations and anecdotes because, not being expert historians, we relied on quality secondary sources such as Boller (1996) and DeGregorio (1993) for most of them.

6. Unlike other descriptions of types, this one has been edited and shortened to remove redundancy.

CHAPTER 5

1. In Table 5.1, and in similar tables following, all scales in italics are based on presidential norms, some of which are from Simonton's work, not ours.

2. H. Booraem, 1995, personal communication.

3. Only the two authors and Dr. Immelman rated G. W. Bush, and only one expert rated Andrew Johnson.

4. R. Kessler. (1996). *Inside the White House.* New York: Pocket Books, 33.

5. R. Kessler, 1996, 21–22.

6. R. Kessler, 1996, 21–22.

7. R. Kessler, 1996, 1.

8. R. Kessler, 1996, 25.

9. R. Caro. (1982). *The Years of Lyndon Johnson: The Path to Power.* New York: Knopf.

10. R. Caro, 1982, 34.

11. Only one expert rated Andrew Johnson and Rutherford Hayes.

12. S. J. McCann and L. L. Stewin (1990). "Good and bad years: An index of American social, economic, and political threat (1920–1986)." *Journal of Psychology* 124(6): 601–617.

13. Remember that these statements reflect the responses of the raters, judged against the responses of other raters assessing other presidents. On the item "evil," Nixon was given an average rating of 5 on a 1 to 9 scale, which is an extreme rating compared to other presidents. If rated in the company of other historical figures, such as Napoléon or Hitler, Nixon's score might have been much more moderate.

14. "Nixon Tells Life Stories in Newly Released Tapes." (2000). *Houston Chronicle/AP*, July 8, A12.

15. J. Hoff, 1995, personal communication.

16. O. Friedrich. (1994). "I Have Never Been a Quitter." *Time*, May 2, 44.

17. O. Friedrich, 1994, 44.

18. S. McGuire and D. Ansen (1995). "Hollywood's Most Controversial Director Oliver Stone Takes On Our Most Controversial President Richard Nixon." *Newsweek*, 126, 24, December 11, 68.

19. Most of the quotations in this book were found in Boller (1996) and DeGregorio (1993), but we found this quotation by Nixon in E. Thomas and L. Shackelford (1997). "Nixon Off the Record." *Newsweek*, November 3, 53.

20. E. Thomas and L. Shackelford, 1997, 54.

21. G. Lardner Jr. (1997a). "Going After All the President's Enemies." *Washington Post/Houston Chronicle*, Jan 3.

22. G. Lardner Jr., 1997a.

23. G. Lardner Jr., (1997b). "Nixon, Aides Studied 'Blackmailing' LBJ Over War in Vietnam." *Washington Post/Houston Chronicle*, Jan. 25, 21A.

24. W. A. DeGregorio. (1993). *The Complete Book of U.S. Presidents*. 4th ed. New York: Barricade Books, 592.

25. Only one expert rated Hayes.

CHAPTER 6

1. A single rater rated Hayes.

2. We interpret this item in the broadest sense, not limiting it to racial prejudice. Wilson believed in white supremacy (W. A. DeGregorio (1993). *The Complete Book of U.S. Presidents*. 4th ed. New York: Barricade Books, 413).

3. In this particular instance, Wilson had good reason to be suspicious. The senator was a bitter political enemy, according to Kendrick Clements, and was trying to penetrate the cover-up surrounding the stroke.

4. This quotation departs from our usual rule of citing opinions that are consistent with our data. Not only was Roosevelt Wilson's political opponent, but Wilson denied TR's petition to fight in World War I. If sour grapes are not reason enough to doubt Roosevelt's perspective, one might add that most of his observations of other presidents also tended to be caustic. However, the genial Taft can also be quoted saying much the same. Even so, this does not mean it is true or accurate. It could be that these political opponents both found it good politics to attack his reputation for integrity.

5. Though our raters endorsed this generalization, one (KC) later wrote us that Wil-

son was quite inconsistent in this regard. He was said to be very flexible in negotiations with Congress in 1913 and 1914. On the other hand, "if matters were presented to him in a certain way, he could become stubborn and intransigent."

CHAPTER 7

1. W. A. DeGregorio. (1993). *The Complete Book of U.S. Presidents.* 4th ed. New York: Barricade Books, 527.

2. This appears to contradict Stephen Ambrose's descriptions of Eisenhower during several of his commands, notably Operation Torch, which we reported. It may be that our raters regarded the stress of these assignments as extraordinary, and thus did not count them against Eisenhower's resilience.

3. A single expert also rated A. Johnson.

4. We attempted to contact the raters to verify their opinions and distinguish this from the other items endorsed but were unable to reach them. Though numerous other items, as well as Ford's low score on the NEO Angry Hostility scale contradict this description, we include it out of compunction to report all items that met our criteria but question its accuracy.

5. R. Kessler. (1996). *Inside the White House.* New York: Pocket Books, 69.

6. Only two experts rated G. H. W. Bush, and only one expert rated Hayes.

CHAPTER 8

1. Though raters were asked to rate Grant in the five-year period before becoming president, one, who reviewed this chapter for us, thought this description was valid only after he became president.

2. Though all three of our raters endorsed this item, two of them objected to it after seeing it in text. Both suggested that Grant had a very low tolerance to alcohol, that the amount he actually drank was very modest, and that he was hardly ever drunk—and never as president.

3. This description is an item from our questionaire. It fit better in this section than elsewhere.

4. Only two experts rated G. H. W. Bush.

CHAPTER 9

1. Only two experts rated William Henry Harrison, and only the two authors and Dr. Immelman rated G. W. Bush.

2. W. A. DeGregorio. (1993). *The Complete Book of U.S. Presidents.* 4th ed. New York: Barricade Books, 634.

3. J. P. Pfiffner. (2004) *The Character Factor: How We Judge America's Presidents.* College Station: Texas A&M University Press

4. One rater, WA, wrote on a related issue, "To the contrary, when I have written

personally to him to criticize a reported remark, he has replied in his own hand with a substantive, theoretical defense of his position."

5. Wilbur Edel, on the data sheet complete for our study.

6. According to WA, it wasn't that Reagan did not know the words, but that he worked "exceedingly hard to convey important truths with unexceptional vocabularies."

7. This is an accurate paraphrase of the actual item, and Reagan rated quite low on it. However, a reviewer indicated that Reagan would strongly distinguish society's role from government's in charity.

8. It should be remembered, however, that our personality and ability scores account for only about 25 percent of historian's ratings of greatness.

9. Ronald Reagan, *The American Experience*, The Presidents Series.

10. Ibid.

11. Only the two authors and Dr. Immelman rated G. W. Bush.

CHAPTER 10

1. Only two experts rated Garfield.

2. The overall score for an item had to be in the top or bottom 10 percent of presidents, AND both raters must have assigned a score in upper or lower 15 percent.

CHAPTER 11

1. A. J. Mapp Jr. (1987). *Thomas Jefferson: A Strange Case of Mistaken Identity*. Lanham, MD: Madison Books, 111–112.

2. Only one expert rated Andrew Johnson.

3. Douglas Rose, personal communication.

4. D. Wilson. (2000). "Keeping Lincoln's Secrets." *Atlantic Monthly*, May, 78–87.

5. "[He] distinguished between equality as human beings and social and political equality; he attributed natural rights to the former and contingent, man-created rights to the latter." Douglas Rose, personal communication.

6. Only two experts rated Garfield, and only one expert rated Andrew Johnson.

7. Only the two authors and Dr. Immelman rated G. W. Bush.

CHAPTER 12

1. Though all raters gave this item a high rating, reviewer JG asserted this was not true after his asthma ceased.

2. However, JG responded: "Myth—he just thought fast."

3. A. M. Schlesinger Jr. (1965). *A Thousand Days: John F. Kennedy in the White House.* Boston: Houghton Mifflin, 95.

4. *Dangerous World: The Kennedy Years*, American Broadcasting Corporation.

CHAPTER 13

1. R. Brookhiser. (1996). *Founding Father: Rediscovering George Washington.* New York: Free Press, 163.

2. P. F. Boller Jr. (1996). *Presidential Anecdotes: Revised Edition.* New York: Oxford University Press, 4.

3. This is the judgment of one source. We acknowledge that it seems incongruent with the fact that he was a slaveholder.

4. Self-worth has at least two major determinants: a sense of capability and of being lovable. Washington's troubled relationship with his mother, as well as the frequent absence of his father, might have influenced the second component, despite his accomplishments. Additionally, by not differentiating between whether or not he was conscious of deficiencies in self-worth, others' judgments are necessarily subjective and confounded.

5. W. A. DeGregorio. (1993). *The Complete Book of U.S. Presidents.* 4th ed. New York: Barricade Books, 3.

6. P. F. Boller Jr., 1996, 378.

7. R. Morris. (1996). *Partners in Power: The Clintons and Their America.* New York: Holt, 86.

8. R. Morris, 1996, 79.

9. Beginning in 1987 the Arkansas governor's term in office increased from two years to four years. Clinton was elected governor of Arkansas in 1982, 1984, 1986, and 1990.

10. We use the past tense to refer to Clinton both for ease of expression and because he was rated in 1995. As for the other presidents, raters were to have assessed him for the five-year period before he became president.

11. P. F. Boller Jr., 1996, 386–387.

12. E. Dumas, 1995, personal communication.

13. Of course, this refers to the observed score and is subject to measurement error. Still there is little doubt that it represents an extreme score.

14. P. F. Boller Jr., 1996, 389.

15. The only mystery here is why this item was not deemed true for the other three, especially Kennedy. Four out of five of JFK's raters did endorse this item as highly true, but one gave a very low rating. Perhaps he interpreted it differently or mismarked it.

16. M. Kelly. (1994). "The president's past." *The New York Times,* July 31.

17. R. Morris, 1996, 38.

18. D. Maraniss. (1995). *First in his Class: A Biography of Bill Clinton.* New York: Simon & Schuster, 35.

CHAPTER 14

1. B. Minutaglio. (1999). *First Son: George W. Bush and the Bush Family Dynasty.* New York: Random House, 95.

2. R. Suskind (2004). *The Price of Loyalty: George W. Bush, the White House, and the Education of Paul O'Neill.* New York: Simon & Schuster.

3. A. Immelman. (2002). The Political Personality of U.S. President George W. Bush.

In *Political Leadership for the New Century: Personality and Behavior Among American Leaders.* Edited by L. O. Valenty and O. Feldman. Westport, CT: Praeger, 81–103.

4. A. Immelman, 2002, 94, 99.

5. A. Immelman, 2002, 95–96, 99.

6. A. Immelman, 2002, 92.

7. A. Immelman, 2002, 96.

APPENDIX A

1. C. Viswesvaran, D. S. Ones, and F. L. Schmidt (1996). "Comparative Analysis of the Reliability of Job Performance Ratings." *Journal of Applied Psychology* 81: 557–560; Viswesvaran and Ones, in press.

2. In actuality there was a fair range of opinion for Extraversion as well, but this is not apparent when scores are charted as percentiles rather than as standard scores. The standard deviation for Openness to Experience ratings was actually considerably smaller than for Extraversion.

3. R. R. McCrae (1993). "Agreement of personality profiles across observers." *Multivariate Behavioral Research* 28: 25–40.

4. R. M. Carroll and J. Field (1974). "A Comparison of the Classification Accuracy of Profile Similarity Measures." *Multivariate Behavioral Research* 9 (3): 373–380.

5. SDp = SQRT(1 + (k-1)r/k, where SDp = the adjusted SD, k = number of raters, and r = correlation among raters; Robert McCrae, personal communication, May 1997.

6. M. S. Aldenderfer and R. K. Blashfield. (1984). *Cluster Analysis.* Newbury Park, CA: Sage.

7. B. Fruchter. (1954). *Introduction to Factor Analysis.* Princeton, NJ: Van Nostrand.

APPENDIX B

1. J. M. Conway and A. L. Huffcutt (1997). "Psychometric Properties of Multisource Performance Ratings: A Meta-analysis of Subordinate, Supervisor, Peer, and Self-ratings." *Journal of Human Performance* 10, 331–360. And C. Viswesvaran, D. S. Ones, and F. L. Schmidt (1996). "Comparative Analysis of the Reliability of Job Performance Ratings." *Journal of Applied Psychology* 81: 557–560.

REFERENCES AND BIBLIOGRAPHY

Agnew, S. P. (1980). *Go Quietly . . . or Else.* New York: Morrow.

Aitkin, J. (1994). *Nixon: A Life.* Washington, DC: Regnery.

Aldenderfer, M. S., and R. K. Blashfield. (1984). *Cluster Analysis.* Newbury Park, CA: Sage.

Aldrich, C. K. (1992). *The President's Grief: An Exercise in Psychohistory.* Charlottesville: University of Virginia Claude Moore Health Sciences Library (audio).

Allen, W.B. (1988). *George Washington: A Collection.* Indianapolis, IN: Liberty Fund.

Allen, W.B. (1993). *Let the Advice Be Good: A Defense of Madison's Democratic Nationalism.* Lanham, MD: University Press of America.

Ambrose, S. E. (1983). *Eisenhower: Soldier, General of the Army, President-Elect, 1890–1952.* New York: Simon & Schuster.

Ambrose, S. E. (1989). *Nixon: The Triumph of a Politician, 1962–1972.* New York: Simon & Schuster.

Ambrose, S. E. (1991). *Nixon: Ruin and Recovery, 1973–1990.* New York: Simon & Schuster.

Ambrose, S. E. (1991). *Eisenhower: Soldier and President.* New York: Simon & Schuster.

American Experience (undated). "The Presidents." Arlington, VA: PBS Home Video. Videocassette.

Ammon, H. (1990). *James Monroe: The Quest for National Identity.* Charlottesville: University Press of Virginia.

Anderson, D. F. (1973). *William Howard Taft: A Conservative's Conception of the Presidency.* Ithaca, NY: Cornell University Press.

Anderson, J. I. (1981). *William Howard Taft: An Intimate History.* New York: Norton.

Banning, L. G. (1978). *The Jeffersonian Persuasion: Evolution of a Party Ideology.* Ithaca, NY: Cornell University Press.

Banning, L. G. (1989). *After the Constitution: Party Conflict in the New Republic.* Belmont, CA: Wadsworth.

Banning, L. G. (1995). *Jefferson and Madison: Three Conversations from the Founding.* Madison, WI: Madison House.

Banning, L. G. (1995). *The Sacred Fire of Liberty: James Madison and the Founding of the Federal Republic.* Ithaca, NY: Cornell University Press.

Barber, J. D. (1992). *The Presidential Character.* 4th ed. Englewood Cliffs, NJ: Prentice-Hall.

Barber, J. G. (1985). *U.S. Grant: The Man and the Image*. Washington, DC: National Portrait Gallery.

Barber, J. G. (1991a). *Old Hickory: A Life Sketch of Andrew Jackson*. Seattle: University of Washington Press.

Barber, J. G. (1991b). *Andrew Jackson: A Portrait Study*. Washington, DC: National Portrait Gallery.

Barber, J. G. (2000). *Eyewitness: Presidents*. Smithsonian Juvenile. New York: Dorling Kindersley.

Barber, J. G., A. Fern, and The National Portrait Gallery, Smithsonian (eds.). (1994). *To the President: Folk Portraits by the People*. Lanham, MD: Madison Books.

Barilleaux, R. J., and M. E. Stuckey, eds. (1992). *Leadership of the Bush Presidency: Prudence or Drift in an Era of Change?* Westport, CT: Greenwood.

Bauer, K. J. (1985/1994). *Zachary Taylor: Soldier, Planter, Statesman of the Old Southwest*. Baton Rouge: Louisiana State University Press.

Bell, C. I. (1980). *They Knew Franklin Pierce (And Others Thought They Did)*. Springfield, VT: April Hill.

Bergeron, P. H. (1987). *The Presidency of James K. Polk*. Lawrence: University Press of Kansas.

Bergeron, P. H., ed. (1994–1997). *The Papers of Andrew Johnson* (multiple vols.). Knoxville: University of Tennessee Press.

Beschloss, M. R. ed. (1998). *Taking Charge: The Johnson White House Tapes, 1963–1964*. New York: Simon & Schuster.

Beschloss, M. R. ed. (2001). *Reaching for Glory: Lyndon Johnson's Secret White House Tapes, 1964–1965*. New York: Simon & Schuster.

Binder, F. M. (1994). *James Buchanan and the American Empire*. Cranbury, NJ: Susquehanna University Press.

Blinder, M. (1999). *Fluke*. Sag Harbor, NY: The Permanent Press (Harding).

Boller, P. F. Jr. (1984). *Presidential Campaigns*. New York: Oxford University Press.

Boller, P. F. Jr. (1996). *Presidential Anecdotes: Revised Edition*. New York: Oxford University Press.

Booraem, H. IV (1988). *The Road to Respectability: James A. Garfield and His World, 1844–1852*. Cranbury, NJ: Associated University Presses.

Booraem, H. IV (1995). *The Provincial: Calvin Coolidge and His World, 1885–1895*. Lewisberg, PA: Bucknell University Press.

Booraem, H., IV (2001). *Young Hickory: The Making of Andrew Jackson*. Dallas, TX: Taylor Trade Pub.

Bourne, P. G. (1997). *Jimmy Carter: A Comprehensive Biography from Plains to Postpresidency*. New York: Scribner's.

Brands, H. W. (1997). *T. R.: The Last Romantic*. New York: Basic Books.

Brazier, J. E. (1993). Who Controls the Administrative State?: Congress and the President Adopt the Administrative Procedures Act of 1946. Doctoral Dissertation, Michigan State University.

Broadwater, J. (1992). *Eisenhower and the Anti-Communist Crusade.* Chapel Hill: University of North Carolina Press.

Broadwater, J. (1994). *Adlai Stevenson and American Politics: The Odyssey of a Cold War Liberal.* Old Tappan, NJ: Scribner's Reference.

Brookhiser, R. (1996). *Founding Father: Rediscovering George Washington.* New York: Free Press.

Bruni, F. (2002). *Ambling into History: The Unlikely Odyssey of George W. Bush.* New York: HarperCollins.

Bruning, J. L., and B. L. Kintz (1968). *Computational Handbook of Statistics.* Glenview, IL: Scott, Foresman.

Burns, J. M. (1970). *Roosevelt: The Soldier of Freedom.* New York: Harcourt.

Burns, K. (Director). (1990). *The Civil War.* Arlington, VA: PBS Home Video.

Cannon, L. S. (1982). *Reagan. New York:* Putnam.

Cannon, L. S. (1992). *President Reagan: The Role of a Lifetime.* New York: Simon & Schuster.

Caro, R. (1982). *The Years of Lyndon Johnson: The Path to Power.* New York: Knopf.

Caro, R. (1991). *The Years of Lyndon Johnson: Means of Ascent.* Vol. 2. New York: Knopf.

Caro, R. (2002). *The Years of Lyndon Johnson: Master of the Senate.* New York: Knopf.

Carroll, R. M., and J. Field (1974). "A Comparison of the Classification Accuracy of Profile Similarity Measures." *Multivariate Behavioral Research* 9(3): 373–380.

Carter, J. E. (1996). *Living Faith.* New York: Times Books.

Cattell, R. B., E. F. Maxwell, B. H. Light, and M. P. Unger (1949). "The Objective Measurement of Attitudes." *British Journal of Psychology* 40: 81–90.

Choiniere, R., and D. Keirsey (1992). *Presidential Temperament.* Del Mar, CA: Prometheus Nemesis Book Co.

Clark, J. C. (1985). *Faded Glory.* New York: Praeger.

Clark, J. C. (1994). *The Murder of James A. Garfield: The President's Last Days and the Trial and Execution of His Assassin.* Jefferson, NC: McFarland

Clements, K. A. (1987). *Woodrow Wilson: World Statesman.* New York: Macmillan.

Clements, K. A. (1992). *The Presidency of Woodrow Wilson.* Lawrence: University Press of Kansas.

Cole, D. B. (1984). *Martin Van Buren and the American Political System.* Princeton, NJ: Princeton University Press.

Cole, D. B. (1993). *The Presidency of Andrew Jackson.* Lawrence: University Press of Kansas.

Coletta, P. E. (1973). *The Presidency of William Howard Taft.* Lawrence: University Press of Kansas.

Coletta, P. E. (1989). *William Howard Taft: A Bibliography.* Westport, CT: Greenwood.

Collier, P., and D. Horowitz (1994). *The Roosevelts: An American Saga.* New York: Simon & Schuster.

Collins, M. L. (1989). *That Damned Cowboy: Theodore Roosevelt and the American West, 1883–1898.* New York: Peter Lang.

Comrey, A. L. (1973). *A First Course in Factor Analysis*. New York: Academic Press.

Conkin, P. K. (1986). *Big Daddy from the Pedernales: Lyndon Baines Johnson*. Boston: Twayne.

Conway, J. M., and A. L. Huffcutt (1997). "Psychometric Properties of Multisource Performance Ratings: A Meta-analysis of Subordinate, Supervisor, Peer, and Self-ratings." *Journal of Human Performance* 10, 331–360.

Cooke, J. (Reader). (1992). *Selections from the Autobiography of Calvin Coolidge*. Boston: I Do Not Choose to Run Productions (audiocassette).

Corwin, E. S., and L. W. Koenig (1956). *The Presidency Today*. New York: New York University Press.

Costa, P. T. Jr., and R. R. McCrae (1992). *Revised NEO Personality Inventory (NEO-PI-R). and NEO Five Factor Inventory (NEO-FFI): Professional Manual*. Odessa, FL: Psychological Assessment Resources.

Cottrill, D. E. (1969). *The Conciliator*. Philadelphia: Dorrance.

Cox, C. (1926). *The Early Mental Traits of Three Hundred Geniuses*. Stanford, CA: Stanford University Press.

Cunningham, H.F. (1989). *The Presidents' Last Years: George Washington to Lyndon B. Johnson*. Jefferson, NC: McFarland.

Curtis, J. C. (1970). *Fox at Bay: Martin Van Buren and the Presidency, 1837–1841*. Lexington: University Press of Kentucky.

Curtis, J. C. (1976). *Andrew Jackson and the Search for Vindication*. Boston: Little, Brown.

Cutler, W. (1986). *North for Union: John Appleton's Journal of a Tour to New England Made by President Polk in June and July 1847*. Nashville, TN: Vanderbilt University Press.

Cutler, W. (multiple vols., some with Hall, R. G., and Defiore, J. C.). eds. (1993–). *Correspondence of James K. Polk*. Knoxville: University of Tennessee Press.

Dallek, R. (1991). *Lone Star Rising: Lyndon Johnson and His Times, 1908–1960*. New York: Oxford University Press.

Dallek, R. (1998). *Flawed Giant: Lyndon Johnson and His Times, 1961–1973*. New York: Oxford University Press.

Dangerous World: The Kennedy Years, American Broadcast Corporation.

Davies, J. C. (1978). *Human Nature in Politics: The Dynamics of Political Behavior*. Westport, CT: Greenwood.

Davies, J. C. (1987). "Lincoln: The Saint and the Man." *Presidential Studies Quarterly* 19, Winter: 71–94.

Davis, P. (1995). *Angels Don't Die: My Father's Gift of Faith*. New York: Harper.

Daynes, B. W., W. D. Pederson, and M. P. Riccards (1997). *The New Deal and Public Policy*. New York: Palgrave.

DeGregorio, W. A. (1993). *The Complete Book of U.S. Presidents*. 4th ed. New York: Barricade Books.

De Zangotita, T. (2003). "The Romance of Empire and the Politics of Self-Love." *Harper's Magazine* 306, July: 31–39.

Digman, J. M. (1990). "Personality structure: Emergence of the Five-Factor model." *Annual Review of Psychology* 41: 417–440.

Donald, D. H. (1995). *Lincoln*. London: Jonathan Cape.

Dumas, E. (1993). *The Clintons of Arkansas: An Introduction by Those Who Know Them Best*. Fayetteville: University of Arkansas Press.

Edel, W. (1992). *The Reagan Presidency: An Actor's Finest Performance*. New York: Hippocrene.

Ehrlichman, J. D. (1982). *Witness to Power: The Nixon Years*. New York: Simon & Schuster.

Eisenhower, D. D. (1976). *The Eisenhower Diaries*. Edited by R. H. Ferrell. New York: Norton.

Ellis, J. J. (1997). *American Sphinx: The Character of Thomas Jefferson. New York*: Knopf.

Falkoff, L. (1988a). *John F. Kennedy, 35th President of the United States*. Ada, OK: Garrett.

Falkoff, L. (1988b). *Ulysses S. Grant, 18th President of the United States*. Ada, OK: Garrett.

Falkoff, L. (1989a). *George Washington, First President of the United States*. Ada, OK: Garrett.

Falkoff, L. (1989b). *Lyndon Johnson, 36th President of the United States*. Ada, OK: Garrett.

Falkoff, L. (1990a). *William H. Taft, 27th President of the United States*. Ada, OK: Garrett.

Falkoff, L. (1990b). *John Tyler, 10th President of the United States*. Ada, OK: Garrett.

Faschingbauer, T. R., S. J. Rubenzer, and D. S. Ones (1996). *Personality and the Presidency, Technical Report # 1*. Houston, TX: Honeycomb Publishing Co.

Ferling, J. E. (1992). *John Adams: A Life*. Knoxville: University of Tennessee Press.

Ferrell, R. H. (1983). *Woodrow Wilson and World War I, 1917–1921*. New York: Harper.

Ferrell, R. H. (1991). *Harry S. Truman: His Life on the Family Farms*. Worland, WY: High Plains.

Ferrell, R. H. (1994). *Choosing Truman: The Democratic Convention of 1944*. Columbia: University of Missouri Press.

Ferrell, R. H. (1996a). *Harry S. Truman: A Life*. Columbia: University of Missouri Press.

Ferrell, R. H., ed. (1996b). *Harry S. Truman and the Bomb: A Documentary History*. Worland, WY: High Plains.

Ferrell, R. H., ed. (1997). *Off the Record, The Private Papers of Harry S. Truman*. Columbia: University of Missouri Press.

Ferrell, R. H. (1998a). *The Strange Death of President Harding*. Columbia: University of Missouri Press.

Ferrell, R. H., ed. (1998b). *Dear Bess: The Letters from Harry to Bess Truman*. New York: Norton.

Ferrell, R. H. (1998c). *The Dying President: Franklin D. Roosevelt, 1944–1945*. Columbia: University of Missouri Press.

Ferrell, R. H. (1998d). *The Presidency of Calvin Coolidge*. Lawrence: University Press of Kansas.

Ferrell, R. H. (1999). *Truman and Pendergast*. Columbia: University of Missouri Press.

Ferrell, R. H., and E. A. Ayers, eds. (1991). *Truman in the White House: The Diary of Eban A. Ayers*. Columbia: University of Missouri Press.

Ferrell, R. H., and J. C. Hagerty, eds. (1983). *The Diary of J. C. Hagerty: Eisenhower in Mid-Course, 1954–1955*. Bloomington: Indiana University Press.

Fischer, D. H. (1989). *Albion's Seed: Four British Folkways in America*. New York: Oxford University Press.

Fishman, E. M., W. D. Pederson, and M. J. Rozell, eds. (2001). *George Washington: Foundation of Presidential Leadership and Character*. New York: Praeger.

Fox, M. V. (1982). *Mr. President: The Story of Ronald Reagan*. Hillside, NJ: Enslow.

Friedrich, O. (1994). "I Have Never Been a Quitter." *Time*, May 2.

Fruchter, B. (1954). *Introduction to Factor Analysis*. Princeton, NJ: Van Nostrand.

Frum, D. (2003). *The Right Man*. New York: Random House.

Gable, J. A. (1978). *The Bull Moose Years: Theodore Roosevelt and the Progressive Party*. Port Washington, NY: Kennicat Press.

Gable, J. A. (1986). *The Many-Sided Theodore Roosevelt: American Renaissance Man*. Washington, DC: Roosevelt Center for American Policy.

Gable, J. A. (1989). *Theodore Roosevelt Cyclopedia*. Westport, CT: Greenwood.

Gardner, H. (1983). *Frames of Mind: The Theory of Multiple Intelligences*. New York: Basic Books.

George, A. L., and J. L. George. (1998). *Presidential Personality and Performance*. Boulder, CO: Westview Press.

George Bush: A Sense of Duty, an A&E Biography production.

Gilbert, R. E. (1988a). "Psychological Pain in the Presidency: The Case of Calvin Coolidge." *Political Psychology* Mar. 9(1): 75–100.

Gilbert, R. E. (1988b). Franklin Delano Roosevelt. In *Popular Images of American Presidents*, edited by William C. Spragens. Westport, CT: Greenwood.

Gilbert, R. E. (1992). *The Mortal Presidency: Illness and Anguish in the White House*. New York: Basic Books.

Gilbert, R. E., ed. (2000). *Managing Crisis: Presidential Disability and the Twenty-Fifth Amendment*. New York: Fordham University Press.

Goldberg, L. R. (1990). "An Alternative 'Description of Personality': The Big Five Factor Structure." *Journal of Personality and Social Psychology* 59: 1215–1229.

Goldhurst, R. (1975). *Many Are the Hearts: The Agony and the Triumph of Ulysses S. Grant*. Pleasantville, NY: Readers Digest Press.

Gorsuch, R. L. (1983). *Factor Analysis*. Hillsdale, NJ: Erlbaum.

Gould, L. L. (1980). *The Presidency of William McKinley*. Lawrence: University Press of Kansas.

Grant, U.S. (1885/1993). *Personal Memoirs of Ulysses S. Grant*. New York: Konecky and Konecky.

Greenstein, F. I. (2000) *The Presidential Difference: Leadership Style from FDR to Clinton*. Princeton: Princeton University Press.

Griffith, D. W., (1915). *Birth of a Nation*. Chatsworth, CA: Image Entertainment (video).

Grubin, D. (Prod), (2001). *The American Experience: Abraham and Mary Lincoln: A House Divided*. Arlington, VA: PBS Home Video.

Hamilton, N. (1996). *JFK: Reckless Youth*. New York: Random House.

Hargreaves, M. W. (1985). *The Presidency of John Quincy Adams*. Lawrence: University Press of Kansas.

Hatfield, J. H. (2002). *Fortunate Son: George Bush and the Making of an American President*. Brooklyn: Soft Skull Press.

Haynes, S. W., and O. Handling, ed. (1956/1997). *James K. Polk and the Expansionist Impulse*. New York: Addison-Wesley.

Hays, W. L. (1963). *Statistics*. New York: Holt, Rinehart and Winston.

Hecht, M. B., and K. E. Speirs, eds. (1977/1995). *John Quincy Adams: A Personal History of an Independent Man*. Newtown, CT: American Political Biography Press.

Heckler, K., and R. H. Ferrell, eds. *Working with Truman: A Personal Memoir of the White House Years*. New York: Putnam.

Heckscher, A. (1991). *Woodrow Wilson: A Biography*. New York: Scribner's.

Hoff, J. (1994). *Nixon Reconsidered*. New York: Basic Books.

Hoff, S. B. (1999). National Party Committees 2nd Presidential Campaigns. In *"We Get What We Vote For . . . Or Do We?": The Impact of Elections on Governing*. Edited by P. E. Scheele. Westport, CT: Greenwood.

Hoff–Wilson, J. (1975). *Herbert Hoover: Forgotten Progressive*. Boston: Little, Brown.

Hoff–Wilson, J., and M. Lightman, eds. (1984). *Without Precedent: The Life and Career of Eleanor Roosevelt*. Bloomington: Indiana University Press.

Hogan, J. M., and J. R. Andrews (1995). Woodrow Wilson. In *U.S. Presidents as Orators: A Biocritical Source Book*. Edited by Ryan Halford Ross.Westport, CT: Greenwood.

Hogan, R., G. J. Curphy, and J. Hogan (1994). "What we know about leadership: Effectiveness and personality." *American Psychologist* 49, No. 6: 493–504.

Holland, K. M., and T. Fulwiler (1990). *Political Science*. Boston: Houghton Mifflin.

Holzer, H., ed. (1993a). *Dear Mr. Lincoln: Letters to the President*. Reading, MA : Addison-Wesley.

Holzer, H., ed. (1993b). *The Lincoln–Douglas Debates: The First Unexpurgated Text*. New York: Harper.

Holzer, H. (1993c). *Washington and Lincoln Portrayed: National Icons in Popular Prints*. Jefferson, NC: McFarland.

Holzer, H., ed (1998). *The Lincoln Mailbag: America Writes to the President, 1861–1865*. Carbondale: Southern Illinois University Press.

Holzer, H., ed. (1999). *Lincoln as I Knew Him: Gossip, Tributes and Revelations from His Best Friends and Worst Enemies*. New York: Workman Pub.

Holzer, H., ed. (2000a). *Abraham Lincoln the Writer: A Treasury of His Greatest Speeches and Letters*. Honesdale, PA: Boyds Mills Press.

Holzer, H., ed. (2000b). *Lincoln Seen and Heard*. Lawrence: University Press of Kansas.

Holzer, H., G. S. Boritt, and M. E. Neely Jr. (2001). *The Lincoln Image: Abraham Lincoln and the Popular Press*. Urbana and Chicago: University of Illinois Press.

Holzer, H., and M. Cuomo, eds. (1990). *Lincoln on Democracy*. New York: Harper.

Holzer, H., and M. E. Neely (1990). *The Lincoln Family Portrait*. New York: Doubleday.

Hoogenboom, A. A. (1988). *The Presidency of Rutherford B. Hayes*. Lawrence: University Press of Kansas.

Hoogenboom, A. A. (1995). *Rutherford B. Hayes: Warrior and President*. Lawrence: University Press of Kansas.

Hoogenboom, A. A. (1999). *Rutherford B. Hayes: One of the 'Good' Colonels*. Abilene, TX: McWhiney Foundation Press.

Hudson Parsons, L., and N. K. Risjord, eds. (1999). *John Quincy Adams*. Madison, WI: Madison House.

Immelman, A. (2002). The Political Personality of U.S. President George W. Bush. In *Political Leadership for the New Century: Personality and Behavior Among American Leaders*. Edited by L. O. Valenty and O. Feldman.Westport, CT: Praeger.

Jang, K. L., W. J. Lively, and P. A. Vernon (1996). "Heritability of the Big Five Personality Dimensions and Their Facets." *Journal of Personality* 64 (3): 577–591.

Jarvis, A. R. Jr. (2001). The WPA's Forgotten Muse. In. *Franklin D. Roosevelt and the Shaping of American Political Culture*. Vol 1. Edited by N. B. Young, W. D. Pederson, and B. W. Daynes. Armonk, NY: Sharpe.

John, O. P. (1990). The 'Big Five' Factor Taxonomy: Dimensions of Personality in the Natural Language and in Questionnaires." In *Handbook of Personality Theory and Research*. Edited by L. Pervin. New York: Guilford.

Kaminsky, J. P., ed. (1994). *Citizen Jefferson: The Wit and Wisdom of an American Sage*. Madison, WI: Madison House.

Kaminsky, J. P., ed. (1999). *Jefferson in Love: The Love Letters Between Thomas Jefferson and Maria Cosway*. Madison, WI: Madison House.

Kaminsky, J. P., and R., L. Leffler. eds. (1989). *Federalists and Antifederalists: The Debate over the Ratification of the Constitution*. Madison, WI: Madison House.

Kaminsky, J. P., and J. A. McCaughan, eds. (1998). *A Great and Good Man: George Washington in the Eyes of His Contemporaries*. Madison, WI: Madison House.

Kelly, M. (1994). "The president's past." *The New York Times*, July 31.

Kengor, P. (1998). "Comparing presidents Reagan and Eisenhower." *Presidential Studies Quarterly* 28, No. 2: 366–393.

Kennedy, J. F. (1940). *Why England Slept*. New York: Funk.

Kennedy, J. F., (1956). *Profiles in Courage*. New York: Harper.

Kerner, F., and H. Holzer, eds. (1965/1997). *A Treasury of Lincoln: Quotations*. Chicago: Abraham Lincoln Bookshop.

Kessler, R. (1996). *Inside the White House*. New York: Pocket Books.

Ketcham, R.L. (1971). *James Madison*. New York: Macmillan.

Ketcham, R. L. (1987). *Presidents above Party: The First American Presidency, 1789–1829*. Chapel Hill: University of North Carolina Press.

Ketcham, R.L. (1990). *James Madison: a Biography*. Charlottesville: University Press of Virginia.

Koenig, L. W. (1986). *The Chief Executive*. New York: Harcourt Brace Jovanovich.

Koenig, L. W. (1991a). Presidency of the United States. In *Grolier Multimedia Encyclopedia*. Danbury, CT: Grolier.

Koenig, L. W. (1991b). The Modern Presidency and the Constitution: Foreign Policy. In *The Constitution and the American Presidency*. Edited by M. L. Fausold and A. Shank. Albany: State University of New York Press.

Koenig, L. W., J. C. Hsiung, and K. Y. Chang, eds. (1985). *Congress, the Presidency and the Taiwan Relations Act.* Westport, CT: Greenwood.

Kowert, P. A. (1996). "Where does the buck stop: Assessing the impact of presidential personality." *Political Psychology* 17: 421–452.

Kucharsky, D. E. (1979). *The Man from Plains: The Mind and Spirit of Jimmy Carter.* New York: Harper.

Kutler, S. I., ed. (1997). *Abuse of Power: The New Nixon Tapes.* New York: Free Press.

Landes, W. A., ed. (1996). *Cato by Joseph Addison.* Studio City, CA: Players Press.

Lardner, G. Jr. (1997a). "Going After All the President's Enemies." *Washington Post/Houston Chronicle,* Jan 3.

Lardner, G. Jr., (1997b). "Nixon, Aides Studied 'Blackmailing' LBJ Over War in Vietnam." *Washington Post/Houston Chronicle,* Jan. 25.

Larsen, R. (1991a). *Franklin D. Roosevelt: Man of Destiny.* New York: Watts/Grolier.

Larsen, R. (1991b). *Richard Nixon: Rise and Fall of a President.* New York: Watts/Grolier.

Larsen, R. (1994). *Ronald Reagan.* New York: Watts/Grolier.

Lee, J. E., and H. C. Haynesworth (2002). *Nixon, Ford and the Abandonment of South Vietnam.* Jefferson, NC: McFarland.

Lloyd, C. (1973). *Aggressive Introvert: A Study of Herbert Hoover and Public Relations.* Columbus: Ohio State University Press.

Long, D. E. (1997). *The Jewel of Liberty: Abraham Lincoln's Re-election and the End of Slavery.* Mechanicsburg, PA: Stackpole.

Long, D. E. (2001). *Lincoln and Liberty: The Emergence of a President.* Mechanicsburg, PA: Stackpole.

Lovin, C. R. (1997). *A School for Diplomats: The Paris Peace Conference of 1919.* Lanham, MD: University Press of America.

Mapp, A. J. Jr. (1987). *Thomas Jefferson: A Strange Case of Mistaken Identity.* Lanham, MD: Madison Books.

Mapp, A. J. Jr. (1991). *Thomas Jefferson: Passionate Pilgrim: The Presidency, the Founding of the University, and the Private Battle.* Lanham, MD: Madison Books.

Maraniss, D. (1995). *First in His Class: A Biography of Bill Clinton.* New York: Simon & Schuster.

Matthews, E. W. (1991). *Lincoln as a Lawyer: An Annotated Bibliography.* Carbondale: Southern Illinois State University Press.

McCann, S. J. H. (1992). "Alternative formulas to predict the greatness of U.S. presidents: Personological, situational, and zeitgeist factors." *Journal of Personality and Social Psychology* 62: 469–479.

McCann, S. J., and L. L. Stewin (1990). "Good and bad years: An index of American social, economic, and political threat (1920–1986)." *Journal of Psychology* 124(6): 601–617.

McClelland, D. C. (1961). *The Achieving Society.* Princeton, NJ: Van Nostrand.

McClelland, D. C., and R. E. Boyalzis (1982). "Leadership motive patterns and long term success in management." *Journal of Applied Psychology* 67: 737–743.

McCoy, D. R. (1973). *Quest and Response: Minority Rights and the Truman Administration.* Lawrence: University Press of Kansas.

McCoy, D. R. (1977). *Coming of Age: The United States During the 1920's and 1930's.* Harmondsworth, UK: Penguin Books, Ltd.

McCoy, D. R. (1988). *Calvin Coolidge: The Quiet President.* Lawrence: University Press of Kansas.

McCrae, R. R. (1993). "Agreement of personality profiles across observers." *Multivariate Behavioral Research* 28 25–40.

McCrae, R. R., and P. T. Costa Jr. (1989). "Different points of view: Self-reports and ratings in the assessment of personality." In *Recent Advances in Social Psychology: An International Perspective,* Edited by J. P. Forgas and M. J. Innes. Amsterdam: Elsevier Science.

McCrae, R. R., and P. T. Costa Jr. (1989). *Personality in Adulthood.* New York: Oxford Press.

McCullough, D. G. (1992). *Truman.* New York: Simon & Schuster.

McElroy, R. L. (1984). *American Presidents: Fascinating Facts, Stories and Questions of Our Chief Executives and Their Families.* Canton, OH: Daring Books.

McElroy, R. L. (1986). *James A. Garfield: His Life and Times: A Pictorial History.* Canton, OH: Daring Books

McElroy, R. L. (1996). *William McKinley and Our America: A Pictorial History.* Canton, OH: Stark County Historical Society.

McEwan, B. (1991). *Thomas Jefferson: Farmer.* Jefferson, NC: McFarland.

McEwan, B. (1992). *White House Landscapes: Horticultural Achievements of American Presidents.* New York: Walker and Co.

McFarland, K. D. (1975). *Harry H. Woodring: A Political Biography of FDR's Controversial Secretary of War.* Lawrence: University Press of Kansas.

McFeely, W. S. (1982). *Grant: A Biography.* New York: Norton.

McGuire, S., and D. Ansen (1995). "Hollywood's Most Controversial Director Oliver Stone Takes On Our Most Controversial President Richard Nixon." *Newsweek,* 126, 24, December 11.

Means, G. B., and M. D. Thacker (1930). *The Strange Death of President Harding.* New York: Gold Label.

Meister, C. W. (1987). *The Founding Fathers.* Jefferson, NC: McFarland.

Mevers, F. C. (1993). *Composite Index to Volumes XIV–XVII (Revolutionary War Rolls of the New Hampshire State Papers).* Bowie, MD: Heritage Books.

Miller, R. L. (1985). *Truman: The Rise to Power.* New York: McGraw-Hill.

Minutaglio, B. (1999). *First Son: George W. Bush and the Bush Family Dynasty.* New York: Random House, 95.

Moore, E. (1996). "Last one standing." *Texas Magazine of the Houston Chronicle,* June 23.

Morison, E. E., ed. (1954). *The Letters of Theodore Roosevelt.* Vol. VII. Cambridge, MA: Harvard University Press.

Morris, E. (1980). *The Rise of Theodore Roosevelt.* New York: Coward, McCann and Geoghan.

Morris, E. (1999). *Dutch: A Memoir of Ronald Reagan.* New York: Random House.

Morris, E. (2001). *Theodore Rex.* New York: Random House.

Morris, K. E. (1996). *Jimmy Carter: American Moralist.* Athens: University of Georgia Press.

Morris, R. (1996). *Partners in Power: The Clintons and Their America.* New York: Holt.

Murray, R. K., and T. H. Blessing (1980). *Greatness in the White House: Rating the Presidents, Washington Through Carter.* University Park: Pennsylvania State University Press.

Mushkat, J., and J. G. Rayback (1997). *Martin Van Buren: Law, Politics, and the Shaping of the Republican Ideology.* Dekalb: University of Illinois Press.

Nagel, P. C. (1982). *Descent from Glory: Four Generations of the John Adams Family.* New York: Oxford University Press.

Nagel, P. C. (1987). *The Adams Women: Abigail and Louisa Adams, Their Sisters and Daughters.* New York: Oxford University Press.

Nagel, P. C. (1997). *John Quincy Adams: A Public Life, A Private Life.* New York: Knopf.

Nagel, P. C., and J. Riggenbach, (Reader). (2000). *John Quincy Adams.* Ashland, OR: Blackstone Audio Books.

Nash, B. D., M. S. Eisenhower, R. G. Hoxie, and W. C. Spragens (1980). *Organizing and Staffing the Presidency: Proceedings.* Vol. III, No. I. New York: Center for the Study of the Presidency.

Neustadt, R. E. (1990). *Presidential Power and the Modern Presidents: The Politics of Leadership from Roosevelt to Reagan.* New York: Free Press.

Nichols, R. F. (1931/1993). *Franklin Pierce: Young Hickory from the Granite Hills.* Newtown, CT: American Political Biography Press.

Niven, W. J. (1983). *Martin Van Buren: The Romantic Age of American Politics.* New York: Oxford University Press.

"Nixon Tells Life Stories in Newly Released Tapes." (2000). *Houston Chronicle/AP*, July 8, A12.

Nordham, G. W. (1977a). *George Washington, Vignettes and Memorabilia.* Pittsburgh, PA: Dorrance.

Nordham, G. W. (1977b). *George Washington's Women.* Pittsburgh, PA: Dorrance.

Nordham, G. W. (1982). *George Washington and Money.* Lanham, MD: University Press of America.

Nordham, G. W. (1986). *George Washington's Religious Faith.* Waldwick, NJ: Nordham.

Nordham, G. W. (1989). *The Age of Washington: George Washington's Presidency.* Boston: Adams Pub. Group, Ltd.

Ones, D. S. (1993). *The Construct Validity Evidence for Integrity Tests.* Doctoral Dissertation, University of Iowa, Iowa City, IA.

Ones, D. S., L. M. Hough, and C. Viswesvaran (2000). "Personality Predictors of Performance for Managers and Executives." American Psychological Association. Washington, DC, August.

Ones, D. S., and C. Viswesvaran (1998). Integrity Testing in Organizations. In *Dysfunctional Behavior in Organizations: Vol. 23, Nonviolent Behaviors in Organizations.* Edited by R. W. Griffin, A. O'Leary-Kelly and J. M. Collins. Greenwich, CT: JAI Press.

Ones, D. S., and C. Viswesvaran, (2001). Personality at Work: Criterion-focused Occupational Personality Scales (COPS). Used in Personnel Selection. In *Applied Personality Psychology*. Edited by B. Roberts and R. T. Hogan. Washington, DC: American Psychological Association.

Owsley, F. L. Jr., and Smith, G. A. (1997). *Filibusters and Expansionists: Jeffersonian Manifest Destiny in the Spanish Gulf South, 1800–1821*. Tuscaloosa: University of Alabama Press.

Parmet, H. S. (1997). *George Bush: The Life of a Lone Star Yankee*. New York: Simon & Schuster.

Pemberton, W. E. (1988). *Harry S. Truman: Fair Dealer and Cold Warrior*. Boston: Twayne.

Pemberton, W. E. (1993). *George Bush*. Vero Beach, FL: Rourke (Juv.).

Pemberton, W. E. (1997). *Exit with Honor: The Life and Presidency of Ronald Reagan*. Armonk, NY: Sharpe.

Perry, B. A. (1989). *Unfounded Fears: Myths and Realities of a Constitutional Convention*. Westport, CT: Greenwood.

Perry, B. A. (1998). John F. Kennedy. In *The American Presidents*. Edited by Melvin Urofsky. New York: Garland.

Peskin, A. (1978). *Garfield: A Biography*. Kent, OH: Kent State University Press

Peterson, M. D. (1960). *The Jefferson Image in the American Mind*. New York: Oxford University Press.

Peterson, M. D., ed. (1977). *The Portable Thomas Jefferson*. New York: Viking.

Peterson, M. D. (1978). *Adams and Jefferson: A Revolutionary Dialogue*. New York: Oxford University Press

Peterson, M. D., ed. (1984). *Thomas Jefferson: Writings*. New York: Library of America.

Peterson, M. D. (1986). *Thomas Jefferson and the New Nation: A Biography*. New York: Oxford University Press.

Peterson, M. D. (1987). *Jefferson and Madison and the Making of Constitutions*. Charlottesville: University Press of Virginia.

Peterson, M. D., ed. (1989). *Visitors to Monticello*. Charlottesville: University Press of Virginia.

Peterson, M. D., ed. (1993). *The Political Writings of Thomas Jefferson*. Charlottesville, VA: Thomas Jefferson Memorial Foundation.

Peterson, M. D. (1994). *Lincoln in American Memory*. New York: Oxford University Press.

Pfiffner, J. P. (2004) *The Character Factor: How We Judge America's Presidents*. College Station: Texas A&M University Press

Phipps, J. (1992). *Summer Stock: Behind the Scenes with LBJ in '48: Recollections of a Political Drama*. Fort Worth: Texas Christian University Press.

Pippert, W. G. (1978). *The Spiritual Journey of Jimmy Carter: In His Own Words*. New York: Macmillan.

Pool, W. C., E. Craddock, and D. E. Conrad (1965). *LBJ: The Formative Years*. San Marcos: Southwest Texas State College Press.

Q-Sort (1978). Palo Alto, CA: Consulting Psychologists Press.

Quackenbush, R. M. (1984). *Don't You Dare Shoot That Bear!: A Story of Theodore Roosevelt*. Englewood Cliffs, NJ: Prentice-Hall (Juv.).

Quackenbush, R. M. (1986). *Who Let Muddy Boots into the White House?: A Story of Andrew Jackson*. New York: Simon & Schuster (Juv.).

Quackenbush, R. M. (1989). *I Did It with My Hatchet!: A Story of George Washington*. New York: Pippin (Juv.).

Quackenbush, R. M. (1992). *James Madison and Dolly Madison and Their Times*. New York: Pippin (Juv.).

Quackenbush, R. M. (1994). *John Adams, Abigail Adams and Their Times*. New York: Pippin (Juv.).

Reagan, R. (1990). *Ronald Reagan: An American Life*. New York: Simon & Schuster.

Reeves, T. C. (1975). *Gentleman Boss: The Life of Chester Alan Arthur*. New York: Random House.

Reeves, T. C. (1990). *John F. Kennedy: The Man, the Politician, the President*. Melbourne, FL: Krieger.

Reeves, T. C. (1998). *A Question of Character: A Life of John F. Kennedy*. New York: Prima.

Remini, R. V. (1977/1998). *Andrew Jackson*. Vol 1: *The Course of American Empire, 1767–1821*. New York: History Book Club.

Remini, R. V. (1981/1998). *Andrew Jackson*. Vol 2: *The Course of American Freedom, 1822–1832*. New York: History Book Club.

Remini, R. V. (1984/1998). *Andrew Jackson*. Vol 3: *The Course of American Democracy, 1833–1845*. New York: History Book Club.

Remini, R. V. (2001). *The Life of Andrew Jackson*. New York: Harper.

Renshon, S. A. (1996). *The Psychological Assessment of Presidential Candidates*. New York: New York University Press.

Riccards, M. P. (1987). *A Republic, If You Can Keep It: The Foundation of the American Presidency: 1700–1800*. Westport, CT: Greenwood.

Riccards, M. P. (1995). *The Ferocious Engine of Democracy: The American Presidency from 1789 to 1989, Vol. 1: From the Origins through McKinley*. Lanham, MD: Madison Books.

Riccards, M. P. (1995). *The Ferocious Engine of Democracy: The American Presidency from 1789 to 1989. Vol 2: Theodore Roosevelt through George Bush*. Lanham, MD: Madison Books.

Riccards, M. P. (2001). *The Presidency and the Middle Kingdom*. Lanham, MD: Lexington Books.

Ridings, W. J. Jr., and S. B. McIver (1997). *Rating the Presidents*. Secaucus, NJ: Carol Publishing Group.

Risjord, N. K. (1978). *Chesapeake Politics, 1781 to 1800*. Falls Church, VA: College and University Press.

Risjord, N. K. (1981). *The Colonists*. Boston: Houghton Mifflin.

Risjord, N. K. (1991). *Jefferson's America: 1760–1815*. Madison, WI: Madison House.

Risjord, N. K. (1994). *Thomas Jefferson*. Madison, WI: Madison House.

Rogin, M. P. (1975). *Fathers and Children: Andrew Jackson and Subjugation of the American Indian.* New York: Knopf.

Rogin, M. P (1987). *Ronald Reagan, the Movie and Other Episodes in Political Demonology.* Berkeley: University of California Press.

Rogin, M. P (1992). " 'JFK': The Movie." *American Historical Review* 97 No.2, April: 500–506.

Roosevelt, T. R. (1995) *Winning of the West.* Vol. 1: *From the Alleghenies to the Mississippi 1769–1776.* Introduction by J. M. Cooper Jr. Lincoln: University of Nebraska Press.

Roosevelt, T. R. (1999). *The Naval War of 1812.* Introduction by H. W. Brands. New York: Da Capo.

Rose, D. D., ed. (1992). *The Emergence of David Duke and the Politics of Race.* Chapel Hill: University of North Carolina Press.

Rosenbaum, H. D., ed. (1994). *Jimmy Carter: Foreign Policy and Post-presidential Years.* Westport, CT: Greenwood.

Rosenbaum, H. D., and E. Bartelme, (1987). *Franklin Delano Roosevelt: the Man, the Myth, the Era, 1882–1945.* Westport, CT: Greenwood.

Rosenbaum, H. D., and A. Ugrinsky eds. (1994). *The Presidency and Domestic Policies of Jimmy Carter.* Westport, CT: Greenwood.

Rozell, M. J., and W. D. Pederson eds. (1997). *FDR and the Modern Presidency.* New York: Praeger.

Rozell, M. J., W. D. Pederson, and F. J. Williams, eds. (2001). *George Washington and the Origins of the American Presidency.* New York: Praeger.

Rubenzer, S. J., T. J. Faschingbauer, and D. S. Ones (2000). "Assessing the U.S. Presidents Using the NEO PI-R." *Assessment* 7: 403–419.

Rubenzer, S. J., T. J. Faschingbauer, and D. S. Ones (2002). Assessment of America's Chief Executives: Insights from Biographers and Objective Personality Measures. In *Political Leadership for the New Century: Personality and Behavior Among American Leaders.* Edited by L. O. Valenty and O. Feldman. Westport, CT: Praeger.

Rulon, P. R. (1981). *The Compassionate Samaritan: The Life of Lyndon Baines Johnson.* Acton, MA: Burnham.

St. George, J., and D. Small. (2000). *So You Want to Be President?* New York: Philomel Books (Juv.).

Saulnier, R. J. (1991). *Constructive Years: The U.S. Economy Under Eisenhower.* Lanham, MD: University Press of America.

Savage, S. J. (1991). *Roosevelt: The Party Leader, 1932–1945.* Lawrence: University Press of Kansas.

Savage, S. J. (1997). *Truman and the Democratic Party, 1932–1945.* Lawrence: University Press of Kansas.

Scarry, R. J. (1982). *Millard Fillmore, Thirteenth President of the United States.* Moravia, NY: Scarry.

Schapsmeier, E. L., and F. H. Schapsmeier (1989). *Gerald R. Ford's Date with Destiny.* New York: Peter Lang.

Schlesinger, A. M. Jr. (1965). *A Thousand Days: John F. Kennedy in the White House.* Boston: Houghton Mifflin.

Schulte Nordholt, J. W. (1991). *Woodrow Wilson: A Life for World Peace.* Transl. H. H. Rowen. Berkeley: University of California Press.

Seager, R. II (1963). *And Tyler too: A Biography of John and Julia Gardiner Tyler.* New York: McGraw-Hill.

Seligman, M. E. P. (1990). *Learned Optimism: How to Change Your Mind and Your Life.* New York: Pocket Books.

Shneidman, J. L., and P. Schwab. (1974). *John F. Kennedy.* Boston: Twayne.

Sidney, H. (2004). *Hugh Sidney's Portraits of the President: Power and Personality in the Oval Office.* New York: Time Books, Inc.

Silver, T. B. (1982). *Calvin Coolidge and the Rhetoric of the Declaration of Independence.* Claremont, CA: Claremont Institute.

Silver, T. B. (1986). *Coolidge and the Historians.* Durham, NC: Carolina Academic Press.

Silver, T. B. (1994). The Reagan Legacy and Liberal Opportunities. In *Consequences of the Clinton Victory: Essays on the First Year.* Edited by P. W. Schramm. Ashland, OH: Ashbrook Press.

Simon, J. Y., H. Holzer, and W. D. Pederson, eds. (1999). *The Lincoln Forum: Abraham Lincoln, Gettysburg, and the Civil War.* New York: Da Capo.

Simon, J. Y., and D. L. Wilson, eds. (1988). *The Papers of Ulysses S. Grant: May 1–December 31, 1865.* Carbondale: Southern Illinois University Press.

Simonton, D. K. (1985). "Intelligence and personal influence in groups: Four nonlinear models." *Psychological Review, 92,* No. 4, 532–547.

Simonton, D. K. (1986). "Presidential personality: Biographical use of the Gough Adjective Check List." *Journal of Personality and Social Psychology* 51, No.1: 149–160.

Simonton, D. K. (1987). *Why Presidents Succeed: A Political Psychology of Leadership.* New Haven, CT: Yale University Press.

Simonton, D. K. (1988). "Presidential style: Personality, Biography and Performance." *Journal of Personality and Social Psychology* 55 (6): 928–936.

Sirgo, H. B. (1995). "John F. Kennedy and the Nationalization of Presidential Elections." Louisiana Political Science Association, Louisiana State University—Shreveport, Mar. 3–4.

Sirgo, H. B. (1995). "FDR and Conservation." FDR After Fifty Years Conference, Louisiana State University-Shreveport, September 14–16.

Sirgo, H. B. (1999). George Washington as the Natural President. In *George Washington in and as Culture: Bicentenary Explorations.* Edited by K.L. Cope. New York: AMS Press.

Skaggs, D. C. (1973). *Roots of Maryland Democracy, 1753–1776.* Westport, CT: Greenwood.

Skaggs, D. C. (1988). George Washington. In *Popular Images of American Presidents.* Edited by William C. Spragens. Westport, CT: Greenwood.

Smith, E. B. (1988). *The Presidency of James Buchanan.* Lawrence: University Press of Kansas.

Smith, E. B. (1988). *The Presidencies of Zachary Taylor and Millard Fillmore.* Lawrence: University Press of Kansas.

Smith, G. A. (1995). *"For the Purpose of Defense": The Politics of the Jeffersonian Gunboat Program*. Newark: University of Delaware Press.

Smith, J. M., ed. (1969). *George Washington, a Profile*. New York: Hill and Wang.

Smith, J. M. (1966). *Freedom's Fetters: The Alien and Sedition Laws and American Civil Liberties*. Ithaca, NY: Cornell University Press

Smith, J. M., ed. (1995). *The Republic of Letters: The Correspondence Between Thomas Jefferson and James Madison 1776–1826*. Vol. 1–3. New York: Norton.

Smith, R. N. (1993). *Patriarch: George Washington and the New American Nation*. Boston: Houghton Mifflin.

Smith, R. N. (1984). *An Uncommon Man: The Triumph of Herbert Hoover*. Worland, WY: High Plains.

Sobel, R. (1998). *Coolidge: An American Enigma*. Washington, DC: Regnery.

Spetter, A. B., and H. E. Socolofsky (1987). *The Presidency of Benjamin Harrison*. Lawrence: University Press of Kansas.

Spielman, W. C. (1954). *William McKinley: Republican Stalwart*. New York: Exposition.

Spragens, W. C., ed. (1988). *Popular Images of American Presidents*. Westport, CT: Greenwood.

Stein, S. R., P. J. Hatch, L. C. Stanton, and M. D. Peterson (1997). *Monticello: A Guide Book*. Charlottesville, VA: Thomas Jefferson Memorial Foundation.

Steinberg, A. (1967). *The First Ten: The Founding Presidents and Their Administrations*. New York: Doubleday.

Strong, R. A. (1986). *Bureaucracy and Statesmanship: Henry Kissinger and the Making of American Foreign Policy*. Lanham, MD: University Press of America.

Strong, R. A. (1986). "Recapturing Leadership: The Carter Administration and the Crisis of Confidence." *Presidential Studies Quarterly* (Fall).

Strong, R. A. (1987). Eisenhower and Arms Control. In *Reevaluating Eisenhower: American Foreign Policy in the Fifties*. Edited by R. Melanson and D. Mayer. Champaign: University of Illinois Press.

Strong, R. A. (1988a). "Richard Nixon Revisited." *The Virginia Quarterly Review* (Summer).

Strong, R. A., and M. Zeringue (1988b). "The Carter Administration and the Neutron Bomb." *Southeastern Political Science Review* (Spring).

Strong, R. A. (1991). "Jimmy Carter and the Panama Canal Treaties." *Presidential Studies Quarterly* (Spring).

Strong, R. A. (1994). "Anecdote and Evidence: Jimmy Carter's Annapolis Address on U.S.–Soviet Relations." *Miller Center Journal* (Spring).

Strong, R. A. (1996). "Clinton's Complexities." *Miller Center Journal* (Spring).

Strong, R. A. (1998a). Jimmy Carter and the Neutron Bomb: The Making of an Indecision. In *The President, The Bureaucracy, and World Regions in Arms Control*. Edited by K. W. Thompson. Lanham, MD: University Press of America.

Strong, R. A. (1998b). *Decisions and Dilemmas: Case Studies in Presidential Foreign Policy Making*. Englewood Cliffs, NJ: Prentice-Hall

Strong, R. A. (2000). *Working in the World: Jimmy Carter and the Making of American Foreign Policy*. Baton Rouge: Louisiana State University Press.

Suskind, R. (2004). *The Price of Loyalty: George W. Bush, the White House, and the Education of Paul O'Neill*. New York: Simon & Schuster.

Swain, M. H. (1978). *Pat Harrison: The New Deal Years*. Jackson: University Press of Mississippi.

Swain, M. H. (1995). *Ellen S. Woodward: New Deal Advocate for Women*. Jackson: University Press of Mississippi.

Thomas, E., and L. Shackelford (1997). "Nixon Off the Record." *Newsweek*, November 3.

Topalian, N. G., and P. Topalian (1995). *Legacy of Honor: President Grover Cleveland and Son Francis*. Lexington, MA: Topalian.

Trani, E. P., and D. L.Wilson (1977). *The Presidency of Warren G. Harding*. Lawrence: Regents Press of Kansas.

Trefousse, H. L. (1989). *Andrew Johnson: a Biography*. New York: Norton.

Tregaskis, R. (1962). *John F. Kennedy and PT-109*. New York: Harper.

Truman, H. S., and R. H. Ferrell (1980). *The Autobiography of Harry S. Truman*. Lawrence: University Press of Kansas.

Truman, H. S., and L. W. Koenig (1979). *Truman Administration, Its Principles and Practice*. Westport, CT: Greenwood.

Tyler, L. G. Jr. (1970). *Letters and Times of the Tylers (3 Vols.)*. New York: Da Capo.

Urofsky, M. I., ed. (2000). *The American Presidents: Critical Essays*. New York: Garland.

Valenty, L. O., and O. Feldman, eds. (2002). *Political Leadership for the New Century: Personality and Behavior Among American Leaders*. Westport, CT: Praeger

Van Der Linden, F. (1972). *Nixon's Quest for Peace*. New York: McKay.

Van Der Linden, F. (1998). *Lincoln: The Road to War*. Golden, CO: Fulcrum.

Van Der Linden, F. (2000). *The Turning Point: Jefferson's Battle for the Presidency*. Golden, CO: Fulcrum.

Van Der Linden, F. (1981). *The Real Reagan: What He Believes, What He Has Accomplished, What We Can Expect of Him*. New York: Morrow.

Viswesvaran, C., D. S. Ones, and F. L. Schmidt (1996). "Comparative Analysis of the Reliability of Job Performance Ratings." *Journal of Applied Psychology* 81: 557–560.

Viswesvaran, C., and D. S. Ones (2000). "Measurement Error in 'Big Five Factors' of Personality Assessment: Reliability Generalization Across Studies and Measures." *Educational and Psychological Measurement* 60: 224–235.

Walker, W. T. (1996). *Encyclopedia of Revolutions and Civil Wars in the Twentieth Century*. Santa Barbara, CA: ABC-CLIO.

Washington, G., and G. Hovland (2001). *Georgisms: The 110 Rules George Washington Wrote Down when He Was Fourteen—and Lived by All His Life*. New York: Simon & Schuster Children's.

Weaver, H., and W. Cutler, eds. (1972). *Correspondence of James K. Polk*. Vol. 1. Knoxville: University Tennessee Press.

Westfeldt, W., and D. S. Wilson, Producers (1998). "George Bush: A President's Story." *One on One with David Frost*. New York: A&E Television Network (video).

Wicker, T. (1991). *One of Us: Richard Nixon and the American Dream*. New York: Random House.

Wikander, L. E., and R. H. Ferrell, eds. (1993). *The Autobiography of Grace Coolidge*. Woodstock, VT: Countryman Press.

Williams. A. R., K. F. Johnson, and M. P. Barrett (2001). Cutting the Deck: New Deal, Fair Deal, and the Employment Act of 1946: Problems of Study and Interpretation. In *Franklin D. Roosevelt and Congress: The New Deal and Its Aftermath*. Edited by T. P. Wolf, B. W. Dayne and W.D. Pederson. Armonk, NY: Sharpe.

Williams, F. J., and W. D. Pederson, eds. (1996). *Abraham Lincoln: Contemporary: An American Legacy*. New York: Da Capo.

Williams, F. J., W. D. Pederson, and V. J. Marsala, eds. (1994). *Abraham Lincoln: Sources and Style of Leadership*. Westport, CT: Greenwood.

Wilson, D. (2000). "Keeping Lincoln's Secrets." *Atlantic Monthly*, May, 78–87.

Wilson, D. L., and J. Y. Simon, eds. (1981). *Ulysses S. Grant: Essays and Documents*. Carbondale: Southern Illinois University Press.

Wilson, W. T. (1902). *A History of the American People*. Multiple vols. New York: Harper.

Winter, D. G. (1987). "Leader Appeal, Leader Performance and the Motive Profiles of Leaders and Followers: A Study of American Presidents and Elections." *Journal of Personality and Social Psychology* 52: 196–202.

Woodward, B. (1996). *The Choice*. New York: Simon & Schuster.

Wolf, T. P., B. W. Dayne, and W. D. Pederson, eds. (2001). *Franklin D. Roosevelt and Congress: The New Deal and Its Aftermath*. Armonk, NY: Sharpe.

Young, N. B., W. D. Pederson, and D. W. Daynes, eds. (2001). *Franklin D. Roosevelt and the Shaping of American Political Culture*. Vol. 1. Armonk, NY: Sharpe.

INDEX

ABOUT THE AUTHORS

Steve Rubenzer, Ph.D., is a forensic psychologist in Houston, Texas. He has served as adjunct faculty member of Sam Houston State University and as a reviewer for Division 5 (Evaluation, Measurement and Statistics) for the American Psychological Association (APA). For four years, he performed psychological evaluations for a metropolitan community mental system and subsequently has conducted over eight thousand psycholegal evaluations for criminal courts in the Houston area involving competency to stand trial, insanity, and risk assessment. He founded the Houston Psychological Assessment Association and chaired possibly the largest symposium ever on personality assessment at the centennial meeting of the APA. He has published on these topics in peer-reviewed scientific journals. His research on the personality of U.S. presidents has garnered national and international interest from both the public and the research communities and led to appearances on CNN, *NBC Nightly News*, C-SPAN, Fox, the BBC and coverage in *Newsweek, George, Self*, and *Entrepreneur*. He has published in peer-reviewed journals on this topic as well as on computerized psychological assessment. He is listed in the 2004 Marquis' *Who's Who in America*.

Dr. Thomas R. Faschingbauer has over thirty years experience in psychology. He obtained a B.A. (*summa cum laude*) from the University of Minnesota and a Ph.D. from the University of North Carolina (both in psychology), and has held professorships at Duke University Medical School and the University of Texas Medical School at Houston. He was chief psychologist at the Fort Bend County (Texas) Juvenile Probation Department and was elected to The New York Academy of Sciences. He created the first short form of the Minnesota Multiphasic Personality Inventory (MMPI) and the first test to measure grief (The Texas Revised Inventory of Grief, TRIG).